Pursuing Happiness

A BEDFORD SPOTLIGHT READER

Pursuing Happiness

A BEDFORD SPOTLIGHT READER

Matthew Parfitt
Boston University

Dawn Skorczewski
Brandeis University

Bedford/St. Martin's
A Macmillan Education Imprint

Boston • New York

For Bedford/St. Martin's
Vice President, Editorial, Macmillan Higher Education Humanities: Edwin Hill
Editorial Director, English and Music: Karen S. Henry
Senior Publisher for Composition, Business and Technical Writing, Developmental Writing: Leasa Burton
Executive Editor: John E. Sullivan III
Developmental Editor: Rachel Childs
Publishing Services Manager: Andrea Cava
Production Supervisor: Carolyn Quimby
Marketing Manager: Joy Fisher Williams
Project Management: Books By Design, Inc.
Director of Rights and Permissions: Hilary Newman
Senior Art Director: Anna Palchik
Text Design: Castle Design; Janis Owens, Books By Design, Inc.
Cover Design: William Boardman
Cover Art: © Jean Louis Aubert/Getty Images
Composition: Achorn International, Inc.
Printing and Binding: RR Donnelley and Sons

Manufactured in the United States of America.

0 9 8 7 6
f e d c b

For information, write: Bedford/St. Martin's, 75 Arlington Street, Boston, MA 02116 (617-399-4000)

ISBN 978-1-4576-8377-0

Acknowledgments
Text acknowledgments and copyrights appear at the back of the book on pages 341–42, which constitute an extension of the copyright page. Art acknowledgments and copyrights appear on the same page as the art selections they cover. It is a violation of the law to reproduce these selections by any means whatsoever without the written permission of the copyright holder.

About the Bedford Spotlight Reader Series

The Bedford Spotlight Reader Series is a line of single-theme readers, each featuring Bedford's trademark care and quality. The readers in the series collect thoughtfully chosen readings sufficient for an entire writing course—about thirty selections—to allow instructors to provide carefully developed, high-quality instruction at an affordable price. Bedford Spotlight Readers are designed to help students make inquiries from multiple perspectives, opening up topics such as borders, monsters, happiness, money, food, sustainability, and gender to critical analysis. An editorial board of more than a dozen compositionists whose programs focus on specific themes have assisted in the development of the series.

Spotlight Readers offer plenty of material for a composition course while keeping the price low. Each volume in the series includes multiple perspectives on the topic and its effects on individuals and society. Chapters are built around central questions such as "What Makes People Happy?" and "What Is the Attraction of Monsters?" and so offer numerous entry points for inquiry and discussion. High-interest readings, chosen for their suitability in the classroom, represent a mix of genres, disciplines, and accessible and challenging selections to allow instructors to tailor their approach to each classroom. Each chapter thus brings to light related—even surprising—questions and ideas.

A rich editorial apparatus provides a sound pedagogical foundation. A general introduction, chapter introductions, and headnotes supply context. Following each selection, writing prompts provide avenues of inquiry tuned to different levels of engagement, from reading comprehension ("Understanding the Text"), to critical analysis ("Reflection and Response"), to the kind of integrative analysis appropriate to the research paper ("Making Connections"). A Web site for the series offers support for teaching, with sample syllabi, additional assignments, Web links, and more: **macmillanhighered.com/spotlight**.

Preface for Instructors

What does it mean to be happy? How do I attain happiness? We all ask ourselves these questions, and we know that each of us must find answers for ourselves—answers that suit our particular personalities, gifts, and circumstances. Happiness can mean anything from pure pleasure to material wealth to athletic achievement to spiritual fulfillment. But these questions are perhaps most relevant to the college student who encounters them while becoming an adult in a culture that does not offer easy answers. In fact, no culture has offered easy answers to these questions. But in today's climate of ever-proliferating studies and news and manifestos about the happy life, sorting through the various theories of what makes us happy can become confusing. For this reason, in recent years, we have found them ideal questions to focus a writing course.

In the last two decades, the pursuit of happiness has become a matter of great interest, among both academic researchers and the general public, perhaps because the views of prior generations no longer seem quite right for today's rapidly changing realities. Indeed, "happiness studies" has become an interdisciplinary field in its own right, and new areas of happiness research have opened up in psychology, economics, sociology, neuroscience, and other disciplines.

Our writing courses focused on happiness have addressed new studies of happiness in the twenty-first century. We have learned from positive psychologists about what happy people do. But we have also returned with our students to ancient wisdom, including Western philosophy and Eastern spiritual traditions, in order to discover perspectives on happiness that may not have figured into their educations or upbringing. To take one example, the spiritual leader of Tibet, the Dalai Lama, has become a best-selling author in the United States by explaining how Buddhist practices can be adapted to ordinary lives in the modern world.

This collection includes selections that represent the new sciences of happiness as well as ancient traditions. Entering these conversations—scientific, philosophical, and spiritual—necessarily invites students to be critical thinkers, to make sense of different perspectives, approaches, assumptions, and core beliefs in relation to our own. Some of the conclusions that researchers and philosophers have reached may surprise you. And many of their ideas are not just theoretical: they are eminently practical. The readings in this book—including the scholarly articles—are ones that can change what our students do, how they think, and what choices they make.

We wanted selections that represented a wide range of genres, including scholarly articles, poems, classic essays, self-improvement literature, scientific studies, and journalistic pieces. Selections offer different levels and types of challenge for student readers. Some (Nussbaum, Mill, Keats) are difficult and will introduce students to and give them practice in reading and rereading the type of texts that they will encounter in upper-level college courses. Others are more accessible (Gilbert, Haybron, Rubin) and will more readily spark lively discussion. This book also includes a number of images that ask students to analyze visual evidence for their arguments.

We wanted selections that could be used in a variety of ways: as provocative discussion starters or as rich, complex texts that can focus extended essays or launch a major research project. And we wanted selections that represented the very different ways that happiness can be thought about—different approaches that do not necessarily conflict with each other but complement and enrich each other.

This book does not simply ask students to think about happiness. We trust that the titles that frame each chapter, along with the headnotes that introduce the readings and the questions that follow them, will spark productive discussion and critical engagement. The chapter titles are in the form of questions: they suggest general directions for discussion and writing and help students to orient themselves to the various lenses through which experts view "happiness." We hope they will help your students to read carefully, consider all aspects of the evidence, and challenge their own values and beliefs as they construct their own arguments. The end-of-selection questions are much more specific, geared to particular texts, specific concerns, and well-defined problems. These questions fall into three categories—Understanding the Text, Reflection and Response, and Making Connections—and offer students opportunities to think critically about what they've read, synthesize texts, form reasoned arguments, and use evidence to support their assertions. They can be used to launch or guide a class discussion, or they can be used as prompts for writing. A major research paper might focus on the chapter-title questions, for example, or a mini-essay could address just one of the questions. Working through these guiding questions as they think about the topic of happiness and react to the text can lead students to discoveries they had not anticipated and challenges to already formed ideas that no longer seem useful to them—much as they will be doing throughout their college careers.

Acknowledgments

We would like to thank the many people who inspired and assisted us in the creation of this book. Most of all, we thank our students, who have read and written about these texts and imagined new possibilities for thinking about happiness. Special thanks go to Carli Schmidt, who helped research materials for the instructor Web site. We thank our editors at Bedford/St. Martin's, Kylie Paul and Rachel Childs, for helping us manage the shape and scope of the book. Much gratitude goes to John Sullivan for his usual editorial wisdom and encouragement. Thanks go to Leasa Burton for her ongoing support and insight. We were fortunate to have very supportive reviewers who we would like to thank: Robert Cummings, University of Mississippi; Lynée Gaillet, Georgia State University; Karen Gardiner, University of Alabama; Deborah Gussman, Richard Stockton College of New Jersey; Christine Howell, Metropolitan Community College, Penn Valley; and Ann Rea, University of Pittsburgh at Johnstown. We thank Ellen and David Rome for offering useful sources and excellent food for thought. Finally, we thank Jeff Welch and Lewis Kirshner for leading us toward ever-happier versions of ourselves and each other.

Matt Parfitt
Dawn Skorczewski

Get the Most Out of Your Course with *Pursuing Happiness*

Bedford/St. Martin's offers resources and format choices that help you and your students get even more out of your book and course. To learn more about or to order any of the following products, contact your Bedford/St. Martin's sales representative, e-mail sales support (**sales_support@bfwpub.com**), or visit the Web site at **macmillanhighered.com/spotlight**.

Select Value Packages

Add value to your text by packaging one of the following resources with *Pursuing Happiness: A Bedford Spotlight Reader.* To learn more about package options for any of the following products, contact your Bedford/St. Martin's sales representative or visit **macmillanhighered.com/spotlight**.

Writer's Help 2.0 is a powerful online writing resource that helps students find answers whether they are searching for writing advice on their own or as part of an assignment.

- **Smart search**
  Built on research with more than 1,600 student writers, the smart search in *Writer's Help 2.0* provides reliable results even when students use novice terms, such as *flow* and *unstuck*.
- **Trusted content from our best-selling handbooks**
  Choose *Writer's Help 2.0 for Hacker Handbooks* or *Writer's Help 2.0 for Lunsford Handbooks* and ensure that students have clear advice and examples for all of their writing questions.
- **Adaptive exercises that engage students**
  Writer's Help 2.0 includes LearningCurve, game-like online quizzing that adapts to what students already know and helps them focus on what they need to learn.

Student access is packaged with *Pursuing Happiness* at a significant discount. Contact your sales representative for *Writer's Help 2.0 for Hacker Handbooks* or *Writer's Help 2.0 for Lunsford Handbooks* package ISBNs to ensure your students have easy access to online writing support. Students who rent a book or buy a used book can purchase access to *Writer's Help 2.0* at **macmillanhighered.com/writershelp2**.

Instructors may request free access by registering as an instructor at **macmillanhighered.com/writershelp2**. For technical support, visit **macmillanhighered.com/getsupport**.

LaunchPad Solo for Readers and Writers allows students to work on whatever they need help with the most. At home or in class, students learn at their own pace, with instruction tailored to each student's unique needs. *LaunchPad Solo for Readers and Writers* features:

- **Pre-built units that support a learning arc**
  Each easy-to-assign unit includes a pre-test check, multimedia instruction and assessment, and a post-test that assesses what students have learned about critical reading, the writing process, using sources, grammar, style, mechanics, and help for multilingual writers.
- **A video introduction to many topics**
  Introductions offer an overview of the unit's topic, and many include a brief, accessible video to illustrate the concepts at hand.
- **Adaptive quizzing for targeted learning**
  Most units include LearningCurve, game-like adaptive quizzing that focuses on the areas in which each student needs the most help.
- **The ability to monitor student progress**
  Use our Gradebook to see which students are on track and which need additional help with specific topics.

LaunchPad Solo for Readers and Writers can be **packaged at a significant discount**. Contact your local Bedford/St. Martin's sales representative for a package ISBN to ensure that your students can take full advantage. Visit **macmillanhighered.com/catalog/readwrite** for more information.

***Critical Reading and Writing: A Bedford Spotlight Rhetoric*, by Jeff Ousborne**, is a brief supplement that provides coverage of critical reading, thinking, writing, and research. It is designed to work with any of the books in the Bedford Spotlight Reader Series. *Critical Reading and Writing: A Bedford Spotlight Rhetoric* (a $10 value!) can be packaged for **free** with your book. Contact your sales representative for a package ISBN.

***Portfolio Keeping*, Third Edition, by Nedra Reynolds and Elizabeth Davis**, provides all the information students need to use the portfolio method successfully in a writing course. *Portfolio Teaching*, a companion guide for instructors, provides the practical information instructors and writing program administrators need to use the portfolio method successfully in a writing course. To order *Portfolio Keeping* packaged with this text, contact your sales representative for a package ISBN.

Make Learning Fun with *Re:Writing 3*

Bedford's free and open online resource includes videos and interactive elements to engage students in new ways of writing. You'll find tutorials about using common digital writing tools, an interactive peer review game, Extreme Paragraph Makeover, and more. Visit **macmillanhighered.com/rewriting**.

Instructor Resources

You have a lot to do in your course. Bedford/St. Martin's wants to make it easy for you to find the support you need—and to get it quickly.

You can find teaching resources, including classroom activities and sample syllabi for *Pursuing Happiness*, on our online catalog at **macmillanhighered.com/spotlight**.

Teaching Central offers the entire list of Bedford/St. Martin's print and online professional resources in one place. You'll find landmark reference works, sourcebooks on pedagogical issues, award-winning collections, and practical advice for the classroom—all free for instructors. Visit **macmillanhighered.com/teachingcentral**.

Bedford *Bits* collects creative ideas for teaching a range of composition topics in a frequently updated blog. A community of teachers—leading scholars, authors, and editors such as Andrea Lunsford, Elizabeth Losh, Jack Solomon, and Elizabeth Wardle—discuss assignments, activities, revision, research, grammar and style, multimodal composition, technology, peer review, and much more. Take, use, adapt, and pass the ideas around. Then, come back to the site to comment or share your own suggestions. Visit **community.macmillan.com**.

Contents

Contents by Discipline

Art and Literature

Journalism

Neuroscience

Philosophy

Psychology

Religion

Sociology

Contents by Theme

Materialism

Mindfulness

Mortality and the Afterlife

Morality and Virtue

Pain and Pleasure

Society and Culture

Introduction for Students

Am I happy? How can I become happier? How do ideas of happiness differ among different cultures, age groups, and social groups? Can I ever be perfectly happy, or must I settle for something less? Does everyone seek happiness as the ultimate goal? Should they? Fundamental but complex questions like these stand at the center of this book. Happiness is a matter that concerns us all because, although most of us, perhaps all of us, seek to be happy, few of us know exactly how to achieve happiness.

Questions about happiness interest us especially in America, where "life, liberty, and the pursuit of happiness" stand as "unalienable rights." (What do those words mean, exactly?) Yet many of us have never thought about happiness as such — "Happiness" as opposed to "my own happiness" — in any systematic or informed way. Happiness Studies are not (yet) a standard part of the curriculum in American high schools and colleges, and to many the fact that academic areas such as "positive psychology" and "happiness studies" even exist comes as a surprise. In fact, they are flourishing, and changing our understanding of what this thing called happiness really means and how it may be achieved. As a college student, choosing a major, preparing for a career, meeting new people, and facing new possibilities, you may find that questions about happiness have a special urgency and resonance. At no other point in your life, perhaps, will it be so important to ask these questions and to think seriously about the answers.

This book is designed for a writing course that takes questions about happiness as its subject. It will ask you to contemplate happiness from many perspectives. You will consider readings from the natural sciences, the social sciences, and the humanities, as well as from nonacademic sources, such as opinion columns, memoirs, and self-help books. Each reading has something to contribute to our understanding of happiness. And you will bring your own experience, values, and ideas to bear on the questions that are raised. You will produce writing of your own, informed by the readings and by your own views. In our experience, happiness is a topic that inspires good writing, in part because it arouses strong interest and raises good questions. We hope this is your experience, too.

At first glance, happiness may seem like a simple matter, perhaps not one that needs to be studied by researchers and college students, but as soon as you scratch the surface it becomes complicated — and fascinating. The word "happiness" names something more than a good feeling: it names a condition and a goal. Perhaps happiness is the fulfillment of our desires — but which of our desires? And when (if) all our desires are satisfied, will we then be truly happy? Or does true and lasting happiness actually come from some other direction?

In many of our earliest spiritual and philosophical texts, ideas about happiness — at least in the sense of ideas about how best to live one's life — play a central role. And even though human experience has changed enormously over the centuries, many of these ancient ideas still speak to us. Most of us learn early in our lives that happiness doesn't come simply from indulging our every impulse. Happiness must come somehow from living "right" and from knowing that we are living right, even if that involves hardship and sacrifice. This might be the beginning of all wisdom: the renunciation of a good feeling right now for some more enduring and "higher" good feeling later on. So we can agree that the pursuit of happiness involves making choices. And to make good choices, we need good information.

Over the last thirty years or so, scholars in disciplines like economics and psychology have become newly interested in questions relating to happiness. They have brought the empirical and quantitative methods of their disciplines to bear on some age-old questions. Much of what they have learned is counterintuitive: for example, the fact that people tend to report greater life-satisfaction after middle age, and the highest levels in old age, and that wealthy people are only slightly happier on average than middle-income people. Yet in another sense, the old saying "money can't buy happiness" turns out to be false: people with adequate means *do* seem to be happier than the very poor. Research on such matters is still at an early stage: "happiness studies" is in its infancy, and a great many questions remain unanswered.

Some readings in this book are quite difficult, but we've included them because they repay the time and effort they demand. Read such texts at least twice; mark them up and take careful notes. Bring your questions about them to class and participate in the discussion. In our experience, difficult readings are often the starting point for rich, insightful writing.

As a topic for academic writing, "happiness" allows for different kinds of approaches: it may well give you the opportunity to learn about the conventions of academic writing in a field you might want to pursue or to learn about the conventions in fields you have never explored before. As a writer, you may be able to draw on your own experience as well as on research. It may even be possible for you to conduct your own research and produce your own data by administering surveys or polls. As you read the selections, look for the unresolved issues, the open questions, the still unknown. Look for the remaining gaps in our understanding of happiness. Think big: consider the problem of happiness not only as it relates to you personally but also as it relates to others — members of other societies, other generations, other cultures. This is the surest way to expand your horizons and see the question in completely fresh ways. Our hope is that learning and writing about happiness will itself prove to be a happy experience — and one that leads to greater happiness.

Organization of the Book

This book is organized around five key questions for you to explore, each of which starts with an introduction summarizing the central themes at play in the readings that follow. Each reading is contextualized by a headnote, providing the background and expertise of the author. Three sets of questions follow, testing your comprehension, asking you to reflect on what you've read given your own experience, and challenging you to make connections across readings in the book.

Chapter 1, "Does Spiritual Practice Lead to Happiness?," offers texts that express the ancient wisdom about happiness as found in Taoism,

Buddhism, Hinduism, Christianity, Judaism, and Islam. These selections are not intended to be representative of all major religious traditions, but they offer a sense of the variety of ways that ancient religions continue to shape modern thinking about the nature of happiness and the paths to its achievement.

Chapter 2, "What Are the Ethics of Happiness?," offers readings that represent or draw on the Western philosophical tradition, starting from Aristotle's famous chapters from the *Nicomachean Ethics*. Selections from the *Enchiridion* of the Stoic philosopher Epictetus (55–135 CE) provide a sense of how Greek philosophy became a pragmatic code in the age of the Roman Empire. A selection from John Stuart Mill's *Utilitarianism* shows how a "felicific calculus" — roughly, the greatest good for the greatest number — could be used to determine a course of action. Martha Nussbaum's "Who Is the Happy Warrior?" demonstrates how a contemporary philosopher can draw on ancient thinking to critique, and potentially strengthen, recent psychological studies on happiness.

Chapter 3, "What Makes People Happy?," provides selections that represent recent work in "positive psychology," "happiness studies," and neuroscience, work that uses the tools of empirical science to help us understand the sources and nature of happiness. This chapter includes writing by some of the pioneers in these fields, including Martin Seligman, Ed Diener, Mihaly Csikszentmihalyi, and Sonja Lyubomirsky. These research fields are still in their infancy, and a great deal of interesting work remains to be done, but the research in these fields is already having an impact on policy decisions and individual choices through reporting in the media and the popular press.

Chapter 4, "Do We Deserve to Be Happy?," raises questions from several perspectives about the adequacy of our notions of happiness. Is it narcissistic or even futile to pursue a life based on pleasure — even the highest sort of pleasure? Are human beings "meant" to be happy, after all? The selections here do not attempt to debunk the views and findings expressed in the other chapters, but they complicate the questions in ways that students will find challenging and pertinent.

Finally, Chapter 5, "Can We Create Our Own Happiness?," draws on the rich body of recent writing that addresses the practical matters of how to become a happier person. Gretchen Rubin's engaging and enormously popular book *The Happiness Project* is represented, as well as articles by Noelle Oxenhandler and Graham Hill that suggest concrete strategies for achieving greater happiness.

Happiness itself is a subject that's surprisingly controversial (see Chapter 4, "Do We Deserve to Be Happy?"). *Should* our individual happiness be our ultimate goal? Indeed, should even the happiness of *others* be our ultimate goal — or is there some higher value or higher good? Is "happiness" as we normally conceive it really an adequate goal to fulfill our human potential and satisfy our highest aspirations and deepest yearnings? These are some of the questions we hope you can answer yourself as you chart your own journey through the issues raised in this book.

© Jean Louis Aubert/Getty Images

1 Does Spiritual Practice Lead to Happiness?

Religions are belief systems concerned with the most basic questions we face: What does it mean to be human? What is our purpose? How should we act and to what end? Consequently, most religions are deeply concerned about happiness — in this life or a future life or both. But happiness is imagined very differently from one religion to the next, sometimes even within the same religion. Some imagine it as a reward bestowed by a deity, a place, or a condition sometimes called "heaven." Others imagine it as the goal or outcome of spiritual practices, a state of nonbeing sometimes called "nirvana." Still others imagine it as prosperity in the here and now: physical and mental health, a large family, material wealth, and the like.

We begin this book with ancient wisdom about happiness. Although in most cases, each reading was composed by a single author, they all reflect traditions that developed over hundreds or thousands of years. The major world religions today divide into two families: Eastern and Western. The major Western religions, Judaism, Christianity, and Islam, all have their roots in the Fertile Crescent (roughly, the eastern Mediterranean coast to the Persian Gulf), where the first cities were established about 10,000 years ago and where, not very much later, writing was first invented. The major Eastern religions have their origins in India and China. Buddhism has its roots in the world's oldest living religion, Hinduism, and soon spread from India to China and beyond. Taoism derives from ancient Chinese beliefs that long predate the arrival of Buddhism.

Since the 1960s, many Americans have turned to Eastern spiritual practices, such as meditation, yoga, chanting, or tea ceremony, in order to improve their well-being, without necessarily adopting the tradition's other practices and beliefs. Certainly a great many in the West continue to draw inspiration from sources such as the Dalai Lama of Tibet, the thirteenth-century Islamic Sufi poet Rumi, or Hindu scriptures such as the *Bhagavad*

Gita. Indeed, for many, spiritual practice is more closely concerned with the quest for happiness than with devotion to any particular God or gods.

This chapter does not aim to give a representative overview of ideas about happiness in the world's major religions. Instead, it offers readings that deeply challenge some prevailing contemporary assumptions about happiness. How do these writers reason about happiness? How do they offer ways of looking at happiness that differ from popular, or mainstream, ways today?

From The Tao Te Ching

Laozi*

The *Tao Te Ching* (pronounced "Dow Day Jhing," and meaning *The Book of the Way*), by Laozi (or Lao Tzu), was written around the sixth century BCE and is one of the classic texts of China. Little is known about Laozi (the name simply means "Old Master"), but he was believed to be a near contemporary of Confucius (551–479 BCE) and a court philosopher and poet of the Zhou Dynasty (1046–256 BCE). He sought to express principles for living well that had been developed over several centuries. The *Tao Te Ching* is the fundamental text of "Taoism," a tradition that stresses the importance of living in harmony — with others, with nature, and with ourselves. "The Tao" means "the Way," both "the way things are" and "the path." Other schools of Chinese thought, such as Chinese Buddhism and Confucianism, drew on Taoism in forming their own approaches to happiness and peace. Ideas about the afterlife, sin, and even good and evil, are absent from the *Tao*. Rather, it emphasizes a way of arranging one's mind and one's conduct to eliminate conflict and distress.

6

The Tao° is called the Great Mother:
empty yet inexhaustible,
it gives birth to infinite worlds.

It is always present within you.
You can use it any way you want. 5

8

The supreme good is like water,
which nourishes all things without trying to.
It is content with the low places that people disdain.
Thus it is like the Tao.

*Translator: Stephen Mitchell.

Tao (pronounced "dou," rhymes with "ow") is a Chinese word meaning "way." While the meaning is too rich to be precisely defined, it refers to the order or principle that underlies the universe.

In dwelling, live close to the ground. 10
In thinking, keep to the simple.
In conflict, be fair and generous.
In governing, don't try to control.
In work, do what you enjoy.
In family life, be completely present. 15

When you are content to be simply yourself
and don't compare or compete,
everybody will respect you.

9

Fill your bowl to the brim
and it will spill. 20
Keep sharpening your knife
and it will blunt.
Chase after money and security
and your heart will never unclench.
Care about people's approval 25
and you will be their prisoner.

Do your work, then step back.
The only path to serenity.

13

Success is as dangerous as failure.
Hope is as hollow as fear. 30

What does it mean that success is as dangerous as failure?
Whether you go up the ladder or down it,
your position is shaky.
When you stand with your two feet on the ground,
you will always keep your balance. 35

What does it mean that hope is as hollow as fear?
Hope and fear are both phantoms
that arise from thinking of the self.
When we don't see the self as self,
what do we have to fear? 40

See the world as your self.
Have faith in the way things are.
Love the world as your self;
then you can care for all things.

20

Stop thinking, and end your problems. 45
What difference between yes and no?
What difference between success and failure?
Must you value what others value,
avoid what others avoid?
How ridiculous! 50

Other people are excited,
as though they were at a parade.
I alone don't care,
I alone am expressionless,
like an infant before it can smile. 55

Other people have what they need;
I alone possess nothing.
I alone drift about,
like someone without a home.
I am like an idiot, my mind is so empty. 60

Other people are bright;
I alone am dark.
Other people are sharp;
I alone am dull.

Other people have a purpose; 65
I alone don't know.
I drift like a wave on the ocean,
I blow as aimless as the wind.

I am different from ordinary people.
I drink from the Great Mother's breasts. 70

Children playing with kites, a popular diversion in China since the age of Laozi.

Children playing with kites (gouache on paper), Chinese School (eighteenth century)/ Bibliothèque des Arts Décoratifs, Paris, France/Archives Charmet/Bridgeman Images

33

Knowing others is intelligence;
knowing yourself is true wisdom.
Mastering others is strength;
mastering yourself is true power.

If you realize that you have enough, 75
you are truly rich.
If you stay in the center
and embrace death with your whole heart,
you will endure forever.

44

Fame or integrity: which is more important? 80
Money or happiness: which is more valuable?
Success or failure: which is more destructive?

If you look to others for fulfillment,
you will never truly be fulfilled.
If your happiness depends on money, 85
you will never be happy with yourself.

Be content with what you have;
rejoice in the way things are.
When you realize there is nothing lacking,
the whole world belongs to you. 90

67

Some say that my teaching is nonsense.
Others call it lofty but impractical.
But to those who have looked inside themselves,
this nonsense makes perfect sense.
And to those who put it into practice, 95
this loftiness has roots that go deep.

I have just three things to teach:
simplicity, patience, compassion.
These three are your greatest treasures.

Simple in actions and in thoughts, 100
you return to the source of being.
Patient with both friends and enemies,
you accord with the way things are.
Compassionate toward yourself,
you reconcile all beings in the world. 105

Understanding the Text

1. All the verses shed some light on the nature of the *Tao*, but you may have found some particularly illuminating. Choose two or three verses that helped you understand what is meant by "the Tao." What do these verses tell us about its meaning?
2. The *Tao Te Ching* often uses paradox — statements that at first seem absurd or self-contradictory. For example, verse 19 states, "Throw away morality and justice / And people will do the right thing." Choose two or three such paradoxical statements. In the light of the text as a whole, what sense can you make of those statements? How might you explain them, within the context of the whole selection?

Reflection and Response

3. Analyze the role of opposites in three of the verses. Does the *Tao* use the play of opposites to make arguments? For what? Against what?
4. What is the work of the reader of the *Tao*? As an intelligent person of the world, what does it call you to do?

Making Connections

5. Consider the theory of happiness expressed in this selection compared to the theory of happiness offered by the Dalai Lama in "The Sources of Happiness" (p. 21), from *The Art of Happiness*. Do they agree? Explain.
6. In question 4, we asked you to consider the work of the reader of the *Tao*. Now compare the way this text invents its reader to the way Eric G. Wilson addresses his reader in "Terrible Beauty" (p. 247), from his book *Against Happiness*. What do these texts call you, the reader, to do? Write an essay in which you analyze the "human subject" Laozi is speaking to versus the "human subject" being addressed by Wilson in *Against Happiness*. How would you account for the differences that you notice?

From The Dhammapada

Acharya Buddharakkhita*

The *Dhammapada* is a collection of 423 sayings of "the Buddha," Siddhartha Gautama (d. circa 400 BCE), the founder of Buddhism, now the world's fourth largest religion. These teachings were passed on orally for several centuries before being written down and compiled as the text we have today. *Dhamma* is Pali for "doctrine" or "teaching," and *pada* for "path." So while the name has several meanings and connotations, it could be translated as the "path of the Buddha's external truth," a guide for those who wish to follow the Buddha's teaching.

Tradition holds that the Buddha, a prince born into great luxury, was until age 29 shielded from any hint of the great misery and suffering beyond the walls of his father's estate. When at last he discovered that world of suffering, he left the estate and became an ascetic, depriving himself of all material goods and food except the utmost essentials. Eventually, he abandoned extreme asceticism and adopted a "middle way." At age 35 he attained enlightenment, or "awakening," while meditating under a bodhi tree. He spoke the words of the *Dhammapada* on many different occasions to a variety of communities to teach the path of awakening to his followers. Today, the *Dhammapada* is considered the central text of Theravada literature, a collection of texts from the oldest surviving school of Buddhism.

3. Cittavagga: The Mind

33. Just as a fletcher° straightens an arrow shaft, even so the discerning man straightens his mind—so fickle and unsteady, so difficult to guard.

34. As a fish when pulled out of water and cast on land throbs and quivers, even so is this mind agitated. Hence should one abandon the realm of Mara.°

35. Wonderful, indeed, it is to subdue the mind, so difficult to subdue, ever swift, and seizing whatever it desires. A tamed mind brings happiness.

*Translator.

fletcher: a person who makes arrows.
Mara: a demon who tempts human beings with delusive attractions and concerns.

36. Let the discerning man guard the mind, so difficult to detect and extremely subtle, seizing whatever it desires. A guarded mind brings happiness.

37. Dwelling in the cave (of the heart), the mind, without form, wanders far and alone. Those who subdue this mind are liberated from the bonds of Mara.

38. Wisdom never becomes perfect in one whose mind is not steadfast, who knows not the Good Teaching and whose faith wavers.

39. There is no fear for an awakened one, whose mind is not sodden (by lust) nor afflicted (by hate), and who has gone beyond both merit and demerit.

40. Realizing that this body is as fragile as a clay pot, and fortifying this mind like a well-fortified city, fight out Mara with the sword of wisdom. Then, guarding the conquest, remain unattached.

41. Ere long, alas! this body will lie upon the earth, unheeded and lifeless, like a useless log.

42. Whatever harm an enemy may do to an enemy, or a hater to a hater, an ill-directed mind inflicts on oneself a greater harm.

43. Neither mother, father, nor any other relative can do one greater good than one's own well-directed mind.

15. Sukhavagga: Happiness

197. Happy indeed we live, friendly amidst the hostile. Amidst hostile men we dwell free from hatred.

198. Happy indeed we live, friendly amidst the afflicted (by craving). Amidst afflicted men we dwell free from affliction.

199. Happy indeed we live, free from avarice amidst the avaricious. Amidst the avaricious men we dwell free from avarice.

"Victory begets enmity; the defeated dwell in pain. Happily the peaceful live, discarding both victory and defeat."

200. Happy indeed we live, we who possess nothing. Feeders on joy we shall be, like the Radiant Gods.

201. Victory begets enmity; the defeated dwell in pain. Happily the peaceful live, discarding both victory and defeat.

202. There is no fire like lust and no crime like hatred. There is no ill like the aggregates (of existence) and no bliss higher than the peace (of Nibbāna).°

203. Hunger is the worst disease, conditioned things the worst suffering. Knowing this as it really is, the wise realize Nibbāna, the highest bliss.

204. Health is the most precious gain and contentment the greatest wealth. A trustworthy person is the best kinsman, Nibbāna the highest bliss.

205. Having savored the taste of solitude and peace (of Nibbāna), pain-free and stainless he becomes, drinking deep the taste of the bliss of the Truth. 20

206. Good is it to see the Noble Ones; to live with them is ever blissful. One will always be happy by not encountering fools.

207. Indeed, he who moves in the company of fools grieves for longing. Association with fools is ever painful, like partnership with an enemy.

But association with the wise is happy, like meeting one's own kinsmen.

208. Therefore, follow the Noble One, who is steadfast, wise, learned, dutiful and devout. One should follow only such a man, who is truly good and discerning, even as the moon follows the path of the stars.

20. Maggavagga: The Path

273. Of all the paths the Eightfold Path is the best; of all the truths the Four Noble Truths° are the best; of all things passionlessness is the best: of men the Seeing One (the Buddha) is the best. 25

274. This is the only path; there is none other for the purification of insight. Tread this path, and you will bewilder Mara.

275. Walking upon this path you will make an end of suffering. Having discovered how to pull out the thorn of lust, I make known the path.

276. You yourselves must strive; the Buddhas only point the way. Those meditative ones who tread the path are released from the bonds of Mara.

Nibbāna: Nirvana.
Eightfold Path, Four Noble Truths: the essential teachings of the Buddha. On the Four Noble Truths, see Matthieu Ricard, "The Alchemy of Suffering" (p. 34).

277. "All conditioned things are impermanent"—when one sees this with wisdom, one turns away from suffering. This is the path to purification.

278. "All conditioned things are unsatisfactory"—when one sees this with wisdom, one turns away from suffering. This is the path to purification. 30

279. "All things are not-self"—when one sees this with wisdom, one turns away from suffering. This is the path to purification.

280. The idler who does not exert himself when he should, who though young and strong is full of sloth, with a mind full of vain thoughts—such an indolent man does not find the path to wisdom.

281. Let a man be watchful of speech, well controlled in mind, and not commit evil in bodily action. Let him purify these three courses of action, and win the path made known by the Great Sage.

282. Wisdom springs from meditation; without meditation wisdom wanes. Having known these two paths of progress and decline, let a man so conduct himself that his wisdom may increase.

283. Cut down the forest (lust), but not the tree; from the forest springs fear. Having cut down the forest and the underbrush (desire), be passionless, O monks! 35

284. For so long as the underbrush of desire, even the most subtle, of a man towards a woman is not cut down, his mind is in bondage, like the sucking calf to its mother.

285. Cut off your affection in the manner of a man [who] plucks with his hand an autumn lotus. Cultivate only the path to peace, Nibbāna, as made known by the Exalted One.

286. "Here shall I live during the rains, here in winter and summer"—thus thinks the fool. He does not realize the danger (that death might intervene).

287. As a great flood carries away a sleeping village, so death seizes and carries away the man with a clinging mind, doting on his children and cattle.

288. For him who is assailed by death there is no protection by kinsmen. None there are to save him—no sons, nor father, nor relatives. 40

289. Realizing this fact, let the wise man, restrained by morality, hasten to clear the path leading to Nibbāna.

Understanding the Text

1. This reading is divided into three sections, "Cittavagga: The Mind," "Sukhavagga: Happiness," and "Maggavagga: The Path." What do these titles reveal about the text? What, in your opinion, is the connection among the three sections?
2. What lessons about the workings of the human mind can you derive from this reading?
3. One of the quotations under "Cittavagga: The Mind" reads, "Wonderful, indeed, it is to subdue the mind, so difficult to subdue, ever swift, and seizing whatever it desires. A tamed mind brings happiness" (par. 3). To what extent would you agree that a "tamed mind brings happiness"?

Reflection and Response

4. Imagine you are in charge of compiling modern quotations based on this text. Choose several quotations and rewrite them. Expand on this exercise as a process: Which quotations did you pick to change, and why? How are your words either different from or similar to the original text? Would an audience today be receptive to your quotations?
5. Single out one quotation from each section and connect them to each other. How can they be used together to highlight some Buddhist principles? What might this tell you about the meaning behind the larger connection between "the mind" and "the path"?
6. Choose your favorite quotation from any section. Using it as your title, write a post for a Happiness blog of your own design.

Making Connections

7. You might deduce from this reading that a calm mind is the way to achieve happiness. Does the Dalai Lama and Howard Cutler's "The Sources of Happiness" (p. 21) support this principle? What are the similarities (and perhaps differences) in how these two readings present the way to achieve and maintain happiness?
8. How would Martha Nussbaum's essay "Who Is the Happy Warrior?" (p. 106) work as a commentary on this text? Write an essay in which you detail the differences and similarities in the points of view of these essays.

The Sources of Happiness

His Holiness the Dalai Lama and Howard Cutler

Tenzin Gyatso (born 1935), known as "the Dalai Lama," is the fourteenth in the line of Tibetan Dalai Lamas. He was born Lhamo Dhondup to a family of farmers in northeastern Tibet, but at age two he was recognized as the reincarnation of the thirteenth Dalai Lama and an avatar of the Bodhisattva of Compassion. He was enthroned in 1950 and functioned as the political leader of Tibet until the Chinese invasion of 1954. Since 1959, the Dalai Lama has led a government-in-exile in Dharamsala in northern India.

As the spiritual leader of Tibet, the Dalai Lama serves his community as a Buddhist monk and promotes a life of simplicity and compassion through lectures, books, and (increasingly) social media.

The following selection is an excerpt from *The Art of Happiness* by Howard Cutler and the Dalai Lama. Cutler is an American writer and psychiatrist with a particular interest in bringing together Buddhist spiritual practice and Western psychology. The book is based on a series of interviews Cutler conducted with the Dalai Lama in 1993–1994.

Two years ago, a friend of mine had an unexpected windfall. Eighteen months before that time, she had quit her job as a nurse to go to work for two friends who were starting a small health-care company. The company enjoyed meteoric success, and within the eighteen months they were bought out by a large conglomerate for a huge sum. Having gotten in on the ground floor of the company, my friend emerged from the buyout dripping with stock options—enough to be able to retire at the age of thirty-two. I saw her not long ago and asked how she was enjoying her retirement. "Well," she said, "it's great being able to travel and do the things that I've always wanted to do. But," she added, "it's strange; after I got over all the excitement of making all that money, things kinda returned to normal. I mean things are different—I bought a new house and stuff—but overall I don't think I'm much happier than I was before."

Just around the time that my friend was cashing in on her windfall profits, I had another friend of the same age who found out he was HIV positive. We spoke about how he was dealing with his HIV status. "Of course, I was devastated at first," he said. "And it took me almost a year just to come to terms with the fact that I had the virus. But over the past year things have changed. I seem to get more out of each day than I ever did before, and on a moment-to-moment basis, I feel happier than I ever have. I just seem to appreciate everyday things more, and I'm grateful that so far I haven't developed any severe AIDS symptoms and I can really enjoy the things I have. And even though I'd rather not be HIV positive, I have to admit that in some ways it has transformed my life . . . in positive ways . . ."

"In what ways?" I asked.

"Well, for instance, you know that I've always tended to be a confirmed materialist. But over the past year coming to terms with my mortality has opened up a whole new world. I've started exploring spirituality for the first time in my life, reading a lot of books on the subject and talking to people . . . discovering so many things that I've never even thought about before. It makes me excited about just getting up in the morning, about seeing what the day will bring."

Both these people illustrate the essential point that *happiness is determined more by one's state of mind than by external events.*[5] Success may result in a temporary feeling of elation, or tragedy may send us into a period of depression, but sooner or later our overall level of happiness tends to migrate back to a certain baseline. Psychologists call this process *adaptation,* and we can see how this principle operates in our everyday life; a pay raise, a new car, or recognition from our peers may lift our mood for a while, but we soon return to our customary level of happiness. In the same way, an argument with a friend, a car in the repair shop, or a minor injury may put us in a foul mood, but within a matter of days our spirits rebound.

This tendency isn't limited to trivial, everyday events but persists even under more extreme conditions of triumph or disaster. Researchers surveying Illinois state lottery winners and British pool winners, for instance, found that the initial high eventually wore off and the winners returned to their usual range of moment-to-moment happiness. And other studies have demonstrated that even those who are struck by catastrophic events such as cancer, blindness, or paralysis typically recover their normal or near-normal level of day-to-day happiness after an appropriate adjustment period.

So, if we tend to return to our characteristic baseline level of happiness no matter what our external conditions are, what determines this baseline? And, more important, can it be modified, set at a higher level? Some researchers have recently argued that an individual's characteristic level of happiness or well-being is genetically determined, at least to some degree. Studies such as one that found that identical twins (sharing the same genetic constitution) tend to have very similar levels of well-being—regardless of whether they were raised together or apart—have led these investigators to postulate a biological set point for happiness, wired into the brain at birth.

But even if genetic makeup plays a role in happiness—and the verdict is still out on how large that role is—there is general agreement among psychologists that no matter what level of happiness we are endowed with by nature, there are steps we can take to work with the "mind factor," to enhance our feelings of happiness. This is because our moment-to-moment happiness is largely determined by our outlook. In fact, whether we are feeling happy or unhappy at any given moment often has very little to do with our absolute conditions but rather, it is a function of *how we perceive our situation, how satisfied we are with what we have.*

The Comparing Mind

What shapes our perception and level of satisfaction? *Our feelings of contentment are strongly influenced by our tendency to compare.* When we compare our current situation to our past and find that we're better off, we feel happy. This happens, for instance, when our income suddenly jumps from $20,000 to $30,000 a year, but it's not the *absolute* amount of income that makes us happy, as we soon find out when we get used to our new income and discover that we won't be happy again unless we're making $40,000 a year. We also look around and compare ourselves to others. No matter how much we make, we tend to be dissatisfied with our income if our neighbor is making more. Professional athletes complain bitterly about annual salaries of $1 million, $2 million, or $3 million, citing the higher salary of a teammate as justification for their unhappiness. This tendency seems to support H. L. Mencken's definition of a wealthy man: one whose income is $100 a year higher than his wife's sister's husband.

10

So we can see how our feeling of life satisfaction often depends on who we compare ourselves to. Of course, we compare other things besides income. Constant comparison with those who are smarter, more beautiful, or more successful than ourselves also tends to breed envy, frustration, and unhappiness. But we can use this same principle in a positive way; we can *increase* our feeling of life satisfaction by comparing ourselves to those who are less fortunate than us and by reflecting on all the things we have.

Researchers have conducted a number of experiments demonstrating that one's level of life satisfaction can be enhanced simply by shifting one's perspective and contemplating how things could be worse. In one study, women at the University of Wisconsin at Milwaukee were shown images of the extremely harsh living conditions in Milwaukee at the turn of the century or were asked to visualize and write about going through personal tragedies such as being burned or disfigured. After completing this exercise, the women were asked to rate the quality of their own lives. The exercise resulted in an increased sense of satisfaction with their lives. In another experiment at the State University of New York at Buffalo, subjects were asked to complete the sentence "I'm glad I'm not a . . ." After five repetitions of this exercise, the subjects experienced a distinct elevation in their feelings of life satisfaction. Another group of subjects was asked by the experimenters to complete the sentence "I wish I were a . . ." This time, the experiment left the subjects feeling more dissatisfied with their lives.

These experiments, which show that we can increase or decrease our sense of life satisfaction by changing our perspective, clearly point to the supremacy of one's mental outlook in living a happy life.

The Dalai Lama explains, "Although it is possible to achieve happiness, happiness is not a simple thing. There are many levels. In Buddhism, for instance, there is a reference to the four factors of fulfillment, or happiness: wealth, worldly satisfaction, spirituality, and enlightenment. Together they embrace the totality of an individual's quest for happiness.

"Let us leave aside for a moment ultimate religious or spiritual aspirations like perfection and enlightenment and deal with joy and happiness as we understand them in an everyday or worldly sense. Within this context, there are certain key elements that we conventionally acknowledge as contributing to joy and happiness. For example, good health is considered to be one of the necessary factors for a happy life. Another factor that we regard as a source of happiness is our material facilities, or the wealth that we accumulate. An additional factor is to have friendship, or companions. We all recognize that in order to enjoy a fulfilled life, we need a circle of friends with whom we can relate emotionally and trust.

"Now, all of these factors are, in fact, sources of happiness. But in order for an individual to be able to fully utilize them towards the goal of enjoying a happy and fulfilled life, *your state of mind is key.* It's crucial.

"If we utilize our favorable circumstances, such as our good health or wealth, in positive ways, in helping others, they can be contributory factors in achieving a happier life. And of course we enjoy these things—our material facilities, success, and so on. But without the right mental attitude, without attention to the mental factor, these things have very little impact on our long-term feelings of happiness. For example, if you harbor hateful thoughts or intense anger somewhere deep down within yourself, then it ruins your health; thus it destroys one of the factors.

Also, if you are mentally unhappy or frustrated, then physical comfort is not of much help. On the other hand, if you can maintain a calm, peaceful state of mind, then you can be a very happy person even if you have poor health. Or, even if you have wonderful possessions, when you are in an intense moment of anger or hatred, you feel like throwing them, breaking them. At that moment your possessions mean nothing. Today there are societies that are very developed materially, yet among them there are many people who are not very happy. Just underneath the beautiful surface of affluence there is a kind of mental unrest, leading to frustration, unnecessary quarrels, reliance on drugs or alcohol, and in the worst case, suicide. So there is no guarantee that wealth alone can give you the joy or fulfillment that you are seeking. The same can be said of your friends too. When you are in an intense state of anger or hatred, even a very close friend appears to you as somehow sort of frosty, or cold, distant, and quite annoying.

"All of this indicates the tremendous influence that the mental state, the mind factor, has on our experience of daily life. Naturally, then, we have to take that factor very seriously.

"So leaving aside the perspective of spiritual practice, even in worldly terms, in terms of our enjoying a happy day-to-day existence, the greater the level of calmness of our mind, the greater our peace of mind, the greater our ability to enjoy a happy and joyful life."

The Dalai Lama paused for a moment as if to let that idea settle, then added, "I should mention that when we speak of a calm state of mind or peace of mind, we shouldn't confuse that with a totally insensitive, apathetic state of mind. Having a calm or peaceful state of mind doesn't mean being totally spaced out or completely empty. Peace of mind or a calm state of mind is rooted in affection and compassion. There is a very high level of sensitivity and feeling there."

Summarizing, he said, "As long as there is a lack of the inner discipline that brings calmness of mind, no matter what external facilities or conditions you have, they will never give you the feeling of joy and happiness that you are seeking. On the other hand, if you possess this inner quality, a calmness of mind, a degree of stability within, then even if you lack various external facilities that you would normally consider necessary for happiness, it is still possible to live a happy and joyful life."

Inner Contentment

Crossing the hotel parking lot on my way to meet with the Dalai Lama one afternoon, I stopped to admire a brand-new Toyota Land Cruiser, the type of car I had been wanting for a long time. Still thinking of that car as I began my session, I asked, "Sometimes it seems that our whole culture, Western culture, is based on material acquisition; we're surrounded, bombarded, with ads for the latest things to buy, the latest car and so on. It's difficult not to be influenced by that. There are so many things we want, things we desire. It never seems to stop. Can you speak a bit about desire?"

"I think there are two kinds of desire," the Dalai Lama replied. "Certain desires are positive. A desire for happiness. It's absolutely right. The desire for peace. The desire for a more harmonious world, a friendlier world. Certain desires are very useful.

"But at some point, desires can become unreasonable. That usually leads to trouble. Now, for example, sometimes I visit supermarkets. I really love to see supermarkets, because I can see so many beautiful things. So, when I look at all these different articles, I develop a feeling of desire, and my initial impulse might be, 'Oh, I want this; I want that.' Then, the second thought that arises, I ask myself, 'Oh, do I really need this?' The answer is usually no. If you follow after that first desire, that initial impulse, then very soon your pockets will empty. However, the other level of desire, based on one's essential needs of food, clothing, and shelter, is something more reasonable.

"Sometimes, whether a desire is excessive or negative depends on the circumstances or society in which you live. For example, if you live in a prosperous society where a car is required to help you manage in your daily life, then of course there's nothing wrong in desiring a car. But if you live in a poor village in India where you can manage quite well without a car but you still desire one, even if you have the money to buy it, it can ultimately bring trouble. It can create an uncomfortable feeling among your neighbors and so on. Or, if you're living in a more prosperous society and have a car but keep wanting more expensive cars, that leads to the same kind of problems."

25

"But," I argued, "I can't see how wanting or buying a more expensive car leads to problems for an individual, as long as he or she can afford it. Having a more expensive car than your neighbors might be a problem for them—they might be jealous and so on—but having a new car would give you, yourself, a feeling of satisfaction and enjoyment."

The Dalai Lama shook his head and replied firmly, "No. . . . Self-satisfaction alone cannot determine if a desire or action is positive or negative. A murderer may have a feeling of satisfaction at the time he is committing the murder, but that doesn't justify the act. All the nonvirtuous actions—lying, stealing, sexual misconduct, and so on—are committed by people who may be feeling a sense of satisfaction at the time.

The demarcation between a positive and a negative desire or action is not whether it gives you an immediate feeling of satisfaction but whether it ultimately results in positive or negative consequences. For example, in the case of wanting more expensive possessions, if that is based on a mental attitude that just wants more and more, then eventually you'll reach a limit of what you can get; you'll come up against reality. And when you reach that limit, then you'll lose all hope, sink down into depression, and so on. That's one danger inherent in that type of desire.

"So I think that this kind of excessive desire leads to greed—an exaggerated form of desire, based on overexpectation. And when you reflect upon the excesses of greed, you'll find that it leads an individual to a feeling of frustration, disappointment, a lot of confusion, and a lot of problems. When it comes to dealing with greed, one thing that is quite characteristic is that although it arrives by the desire to obtain something, it is not satisfied by obtaining. Therefore, it becomes sort of limitless, sort of bottomless, and that leads to trouble. One interesting thing about greed is that although the underlying motive is to seek satisfaction, the irony is that even after obtaining the object of your desire, you are still not satisfied. *The true antidote of greed is contentment.* If you have a strong sense of contentment, it doesn't matter whether you obtain the object or not; either way, you are still content."

• • •

So, how can we achieve inner contentment? There are two methods. One method is to obtain everything that we want and desire—all the money, houses, and cars; the perfect mate; and the perfect body. The Dalai Lama has already pointed out the disadvantage of this approach; if our wants and desires remain unchecked, sooner or later we will run up against something that we want but can't have. The second, and more reliable, method is not to have what we want but rather to want and appreciate what we have.

The other night, I was watching a television interview with Christopher Reeve, the actor who was thrown from a horse in 1994 and suffered a spinal cord injury that left him completely paralyzed from the neck down, requiring a mechanical ventilator even to breathe. When questioned by the interviewer about how he dealt with the depression resulting from his disability, Reeve revealed that he had experienced a brief period of complete despair while in the intensive care unit of the hospital. He went on to say, however, that these feelings of despair passed relatively quickly, and he now sincerely considered himself to be a "lucky guy." He cited the blessings of a loving wife and children but also spoke gratefully about the rapid advances of modern medicine (which he estimates will find a cure for spinal cord injury within the next decade), stating that if he had been hurt just a few years earlier, he probably would have died from his injuries. While describing the process of adjusting to his paralysis, Reeve said that while his feelings of despair resolved rather quickly, at first he was still troubled by intermittent pangs of jealousy that could be triggered by another's innocent passing remark such as, "I'm just gonna run upstairs and get something." In learning to deal with these feelings, he said, "I realized that the only way to go through life is to look at your assets, to see what you can still do; in my case, fortunately I didn't have any brain injury, so I still have a mind I can use." Focusing on his resources in this manner, Reeve has elected to use his mind to increase awareness and educate the public about spinal cord injury, to help others, and has plans to continue speaking as well as to write and direct films.

Inner Worth

30

We've seen how working on our mental outlook is a more effective means of achieving happiness than seeking it through external sources such as wealth, position, or even physical health. Another internal source of happiness, closely linked with an inner feeling of contentment, is a sense of self-worth. In describing the most reliable basis for developing that sense of self-worth, the Dalai Lama explained:

"Now in my case, for instance, suppose I had no depth of human feeling, no capacity for easily creating good friends. Without that, when I lost my own country, when my political authority in Tibet came to an end, becoming a refugee would have been very difficult. While I was in Tibet, because of the way the political system was set up, there was a certain degree of respect given to the office of the Dalai Lama and people related to me accordingly, regardless of whether they had true affection towards me or not. But if that was the only basis of people's relation towards me, then when I lost my country, it would have been extremely difficult. But there is another source of worth and dignity from which you can relate to other fellow human beings. *You can relate to them because you are still a human being, within the human community. You share that bond. And that human bond is enough to give rise to a sense of worth and dignity. That bond can become a source of consolation in the event that you lose everything else.*"

The Dalai Lama stopped for a moment to take a sip of tea, then shaking his head he added, "Unfortunately, when you read history, you'll find cases of emperors or kings in the past who lost their status due to

Free yoga classes are offered each week in Manhattan's Bryant Park. Even today, yoga (with roots in ancient Hinduism and Buddhism) remains a popular form of personal reflection and spiritual meditation.
David Grossman/The Image Works

some political upheaval and were forced to leave the country, but the story afterwards wasn't that positive for them. I think without that feeling of affection and connection with other fellow human beings, life becomes very hard.

"Generally speaking, you can have two different types of individuals. On the one hand, you can have a wealthy, successful person, surrounded by relatives and so on. If that person's source of dignity and sense of worth is only material, then so long as his fortune remains, maybe that person can sustain a sense of security. But the moment the fortune wanes, the person will suffer because there is no other refuge. On the other hand, you can have another person enjoying similar economic status and financial success, but at the same time, that person is warm and affectionate and has a feeling of compassion. Because that person has another source of worth, another source that gives him or her a sense of dignity, another anchor, there is less chance of that person's becoming depressed if his or her fortune happens to disappear. Through this type of reasoning you can see the very practical value of human warmth and affection in developing an inner sense of worth."

Happiness Versus Pleasure

Several months after the Dalai Lama's talks in Arizona, I visited him at his home in Dharamsala. It was a particularly hot and humid July afternoon, and I arrived at his home drenched in sweat after only a short hike from the village. Coming from a dry climate, I found the humidity to be almost unbearable that day, and I wasn't in the best of moods as we sat down to begin our conversation. He, on the other hand, seemed to be in great spirits. Shortly into our conversation, we turned to the topic of pleasure. At one point in the discussion, he made a crucial observation:

"Now sometimes people confuse happiness with pleasure. For example, 35 not long ago I was speaking to an Indian audience at Rajpur. I mentioned that the purpose of life was happiness, so one member of the audience said that Rajneesh teaches that our happiest moment comes during sexual activity, so through sex one can become the happiest," the Dalai Lama laughed heartily. "He wanted to know what I thought of that idea. I answered that from my point of view, the highest happiness is when one reaches the stage of Liberation, at which there is no more suffering. That's genuine, lasting happiness. True happiness relates more to the mind and heart. Happiness that depends mainly on physical pleasure is unstable; one day it's there, the next day it may not be."

• • •

On the surface, it seemed like a fairly obvious observation; of course, happiness and pleasure were two different things. And yet, we human beings are often quite adept at confusing the two. Not long after I returned home, during a therapy session with a patient, I was to have a concrete demonstration of just how powerful that simple realization can be.

Heather was a young single professional working as a counselor in the Phoenix area. Although she enjoyed her job working with troubled youth, for some time she had become increasingly dissatisfied with living in that area. She often complained about the growing population, the traffic, and the oppressive heat in the summer. She had been offered a job in a beautiful small town in the mountains. In fact, she had visited that town many times and had always dreamed of moving there. It was perfect. The only problem was the fact that the job she was offered involved an adult clientele. For weeks, she had been struggling with the decision whether to accept the new job. She just couldn't make up her mind. She tried making up a list of pros and cons, but the list was annoyingly even.

She explained, "I know I wouldn't enjoy the work as much as my job here, but that would be more than compensated for by the pure pleasure of living in that town! I really love it there. Just being there makes me feel good. And I'm so sick of the heat here. I just don't know what to do."

Her mention of the term "pleasure" reminded me of the Dalai Lama's words, and, probing a bit, I asked, "Do you think that moving there would bring you greater happiness or greater pleasure?"

She paused for a moment, uncertain what to make of the question. 40 Finally she answered, "I don't know . . . You know, I think it would bring me more pleasure than happiness . . . Ultimately, I don't think I'd really be happy working with that clientele. I really *do* get a lot of satisfaction working with the kids at my job. . . ."

Simply reframing her dilemma in terms of "Will it bring me happiness?" seemed to provide a certain clarity. Suddenly it became much easier to make her decision. She decided to remain in Phoenix. Of course, she still complained about the summer heat. But, having made the conscious decision to remain there on the basis of what she felt would ultimately make her happier, somehow made the heat more bearable.

• • •

Every day we are faced with numerous decisions and choices. And try as we may, we often don't choose the thing that we know is "good for us." Part of this is related to the fact that the "right choice" is often the difficult one—the one that involves some sacrifice of our pleasure.

In every century, men and women have struggled with trying to define the proper role that pleasure should play in their lives—a legion of philosophers, theologists, and psychologists, all exploring our relationship with pleasure. In the third century BC, Epicurus based his system of ethics on the bold assertion that "pleasure is the beginning and end of the blessed life." But even Epicurus acknowledged the importance of common sense and moderation, recognizing that unbridled devotion to sensual pleasures could sometimes lead to pain instead. In the closing years of the nineteenth century, Sigmund Freud° was busy formulating his own theories about pleasure. According to Freud, the fundamental motivating force for the entire psychic apparatus

"The 'right choice' is often the difficult one — the one that involves some sacrifice of our pleasure."

Sigmund Freud (1856–1939): Austrian psychotherapist and the founder of psychoanalysis.

was the wish to relieve the tension caused by unfulfilled instinctual drives; in other words, our underlying motive is to seek pleasure. In the twentieth century, many researchers have chosen to sidestep more philosophical speculations, and, instead, a host of neuroanatomists have taken to poking around the brain's hypothalamus and limbic regions with electrodes, searching for the spot that produces pleasure when electrically stimulated.

None of us really need dead Greek philosophers, nineteenth-century psychoanalysts, or twentieth-century scientists to help us understand pleasure. We know it when we feel it. We know it in the touch or smile of a loved one, in the luxury of a hot bath on a cold rainy afternoon, in the beauty of a sunset. But many of us also know pleasure in the frenetic rhapsody of a cocaine rush, the ecstasy of a heroin high, the revelry of an alcohol buzz, the bliss of unrestrained sexual excess, the exhilaration of a winning streak in Las Vegas. These are also very real pleasures—pleasures that many in our society must come to terms with.

45

Although there are no easy solutions to avoiding these destructive pleasures, fortunately we have a place to begin: the simple reminder that what we are seeking in life is happiness. As the Dalai Lama points out, that is an unmistakable fact. If we approach our choices in life keeping that in mind, it is easier to give up the things that are ultimately harmful to us, even if those things bring us momentary pleasure. The reason why it is usually so difficult to "Just say no!" is found in the word "no"; that approach is associated with a sense of rejecting something, of giving something up, of denying ourselves.

But there is a better approach: framing any decision we face by asking ourselves, "Will it bring me happiness?" That simple question can be a powerful tool in helping us skillfully conduct all areas of our lives, not just in the decision whether to indulge in drugs or that third piece of banana cream pie. It puts a new slant on things. Approaching our daily decisions and choices with this question in mind shifts the focus from what we are denying ourselves to what we are seeking—ultimate happiness. A kind of happiness, as defined by the Dalai Lama, that is stable and persistent. A state of happiness that remains, despite life's ups and downs and normal fluctuations of mood, as part of the very matrix of our being. With this perspective, it's easier to make the "right decision" because we are acting to give ourselves something, not denying or withholding something from ourselves—an attitude of moving toward rather than moving away, an attitude of embracing life rather than rejecting it. This underlying sense of moving toward happiness can have a very profound effect; it makes us more receptive, more open, to the joy of living.

Understanding the Text

1. How does the Dalai Lama explain the relationship between greed and contentment? Does this offer any insight into the author's desire for a new car?
2. *Happiness* and *pleasure* seem to be key terms for the Dalai Lama. How does the author explain the difference between these two things?
3. What steps does the Dalai Lama say we must take if we want to be happy?

Reflection and Response

4. In this conversation between the Dalai Lama and a psychiatrist, the Dalai Lama sometimes distinguishes his work from that of psychology. Do you also see these two professions as having different goals and different means to achieve them?
5. The role of education in the pursuit of happiness is central to this text. What moments in your educational journey have contributed to your own journey toward happiness? Would you offer any criticism of the Dalai Lama's teachings about education and happiness?

Making Connections

6. According to the Dalai Lama, "bringing about discipline in our minds" is the key to opening the heart. Would you say that the Gospel of Matthew (p. 59) provides a path to such discipline? Compare the road to happiness in these two texts.
7. C. S. Lewis, in Chapter 4, claims that we have no right to happiness (p. 227). And yet the Dalai Lama does not seem to agree. Assess their theories and decide for yourself: Do we have a right to happiness?
8. Drawing from this essay and Matthieu Ricard's "The Alchemy of Suffering" (p. 34), discuss the relationships between happiness and suffering.

The Alchemy of Suffering

Matthieu Ricard

Matthieu Ricard (born 1946) is the son of French intellectuals (his mother was an artist and his father a well-known philosopher). Ricard earned a Ph.D. in biology and became a scientist specializing in genetic research, but he gave up his academic career to become a Buddhist monk in the Tibetan tradition. In 2012, neuroscientist Richard Davidson attached sensors to Ricard's brain and discovered that it had developed a greater capacity for happiness than any subject previously studied. Several newspapers called Ricard "the happiest man in the world."

Ricard lives as a Buddhist monk in the Himalayas. He has studied with some "great masters" of Tibetan Buddhism, including his beloved teacher Dilgo Khyentse Rinpoche, a Vajrayana master, poet, and teacher who headed the Nyingma school of Tibetan Buddhism. Ricard has written several books on meditation, spirituality, and compassion, and he has translated several Buddhist texts. In 2003, he published *Plaidoyer pour le bonheur*, translated into English and published as *Happiness: A Guide to Developing Life's Most Important Skills*. In this book, he explores how a person gains fulfillment from leading a compassionate life.

If there is a way to free ourselves from suffering
We must use every moment to find it.
Only a fool wants to go on suffering.
Isn't it sad to knowingly imbibe poison?

—SEVENTH DALAI LAMA

A long time ago, the son of a king of Persia was raised alongside the son of the grand vizier, and their friendship was legendary. When the prince ascended to the throne, he said to his friend: "While I attend to the affairs of the kingdom, will you please write me a history of men and the world, so that I can draw the necessary lessons from it and thus know the proper way to act."

The king's friend consulted with the most famous historians, the most learned scholars, and the most respected sages. Five years later he presented himself proudly at the palace.

"Sire," he said, "here are thirty-six volumes relating the entire history of the world from creation to your accession."

"Thirty-six volumes!" cried the king. "How will I ever have time to read them? I have so much work administering my kingdom and seeing to my two hundred queens. Please, friend, condense your history."

Two years later, the friend returned to the palace with ten volumes. But the king was at war against the neighboring monarch. He was found on a mountaintop in the desert, directing the battle.

"The fate of our kingdom is being played out as we speak. Where would I find the time to read ten volumes? Abridge your history even further."

The vizier's son left and worked three years on a single volume that gave an accurate picture of the essence. The king was now caught up in legislating.

"How lucky you are to have the time to write quietly. While you've been doing that, I've been debating taxes and their collection. Bring me tenfold fewer pages—I'll spend an evening mining them."

Two years later, it was done. But when the friend returned, he found the king bedridden, in dreadful pain. The friend himself was no longer young; his wrinkled face was haloed by a mane of white hair.

"Well?" whispered the king with his dying breath. "The history of men?"

His friend gazed steadily at him and, as the king was about to die, he said:

"They suffer, Majesty."

Yes, they suffer, at every moment and throughout the world. Some die when they've just been born; some when they've just given birth. Every second, people are murdered, tortured, beaten, maimed, separated from their loved ones. Others are abandoned, betrayed, expelled, rejected. Some are killed out of hatred, greed, ignorance, ambition, pride, or envy. Mothers lose their children, children lose their parents. The ill pass in never-ending procession through the hospitals. Some suffer with no hope of being treated, others are treated with no hope of being cured. The dying endure their pain, and the survivors their mourning. Some die of hunger, cold, exhaustion; others are charred by fire, crushed by rocks, or swept away by the waters.

This is true not only for human beings. Animals devour each other in the forests, the savannahs, the oceans, and the skies. At any given moment tens of thousands of them are being killed by humans, torn to pieces, and canned. Others suffer endless torments at the hands of their owners, bearing heavy burdens, in chains their entire lives; still others are hunted, fished, trapped between teeth of steel, strangled in snares, smothered under nets, tortured for their flesh, their musk, their ivory, their bones, their fur, their skin, thrown into boiling water or flayed alive.

These are not mere words but a reality that is an intrinsic part of our daily lives: death, the transitory nature of all things, and suffering. Though we may feel overwhelmed by it all, powerless before so much pain, turning away from it is only indifference or cowardice. We must be intimately concerned with it, and do everything we possibly can to relieve the suffering.

The Modalities of Suffering

Buddhism speaks of pervasive suffering, the suffering of change, and the multiplicity of suffering. Pervasive suffering is comparable to a green fruit on the verge of ripening; the suffering of change, to a delicious meal laced with poison; and the multiplicity of suffering, to the eruption of an abscess on a tumor. Pervasive suffering is not yet recognized as such. The suffering of change begins with a feeling of pleasure and turns to pain. The multiplicity of suffering is associated with an increase in pain.

These correspond to three modes of suffering: visible suffering, hidden suffering, and invisible suffering. Visible suffering is evident everywhere. Hidden suffering is concealed beneath the appearance of pleasure, freedom from care, fun. A gourmet eats a fine dish and moments later is gripped by the spasms of food poisoning. A family is happily gathered for a picnic in the country when a child is suddenly bitten by a snake. Partygoers are merrily dancing at the county fair when the tent abruptly catches fire. This type of suffering may potentially arise at any moment in life, but it remains hidden to those who are taken in by the illusion of appearances and cling to the belief that people and things last, untouched by the change that affects everything.

There is also the suffering that underlies the most ordinary activities. It is not easy to identify or so readily localized as a toothache. It sends out no signal and does not prevent us from functioning in the world, since, on the contrary, it is an integral part of the daily routine. What could be more innocuous than a boiled egg? Farm-raised hens may not have it so bad, but let's take a brief look into the world of battery farming. Male chicks are separated at birth from the females and sent straight to the grinder. The hens are fed day and night under artificial lighting to make them grow faster and lay more eggs. Overcrowding makes them aggressive, and they continually tear at each other's feathers. None of this history is apparent in your breakfast egg.

Invisible suffering is the hardest to distinguish because it stems from the blindness of our own minds, where it remains so long as we are in the grip of ignorance and selfishness. Our confusion, born of a lack of judgment and wisdom, blinds us to what we must do and avoid doing to ensure that our thoughts, our words, and our actions engender happiness and not suffering. This confusion and the tendencies associated with it drive us to reenact again and again the behavior that lies at the source of our pain. If we want to counteract this harmful misjudgment, we have to awaken from the dream of ignorance and learn to identify the very subtle ways in which happiness and suffering are generated.

Are we capable of identifying ego-clinging as the cause of that suffering? Generally speaking, no. That is why we call this third type of suffering invisible. Selfishness, or rather the feeling that one is the center of the world—hence "self-centeredness"—is the source of most of our disruptive thoughts. From obsessive desire to hatred, not to mention jealousy, it attracts pain the way a magnet attracts iron filings. 20

So it would seem that there is no way to escape the suffering that prevails everywhere. Prophets have followed upon wise men and saints upon potentates, and still the rivers of suffering flow. Mother Teresa° toiled for fifty years on behalf of the dying of Calcutta, but if the hospices she founded were to disappear, those patients would be back on the streets as if they'd never existed. In adjacent neighborhoods, they're still dying on the sidewalks. We gauge our impotence by the omnipresence, magnitude, and perpetuity of suffering. Buddhist texts say that in the cycle of death and rebirth, no place, not even one the size of a needle's point, is exempt from suffering.

Can we allow such a view to drive us to despair, discouragement, or worse yet, indifference? Unable to bear its intensity, must we be destroyed by it?

The Causes of Suffering

Is there any way to put an end to suffering? According to Buddhism, suffering will always exist as a *universal phenomenon*, but *every individual* has the potential for liberation from it.

As for human beings in general, we cannot expect suffering to simply vanish from the universe, because, in the Buddhist view, the universe is without beginning or end. There can be no real beginning because *nothing* cannot suddenly become *something*. *Nothingness* is a word that allows us to picture for ourselves the absence or even nonexistence of worldly phenomena, but a mere idea cannot give birth to anything at all.

Mother Teresa (1910–1997): Roman Catholic nun and founder of the Order of Missionaries of Charity, who worked among the poor and dying in Calcutta, India. She was awarded the Nobel Peace Prize in 1979.

As for a real end, in which *something* becomes *nothing*, it is equally impossible. As it happens, wherever life exists in the universe, so does suffering: disease, old age, death, separation from loved ones, forced coexistence with our oppressors, denial of basic necessities, confrontations with what we fear, and so on.

Despite all that, this vision does not lead Buddhism to the view held by certain Western philosophers for whom suffering is *inevitable* and happiness out of reach. The reason for that is simple: unhappiness has causes that can be identified and acted upon. It is only when we misidentify the nature of those causes that we come to doubt the possibility of healing.

The first mistake is believing that unhappiness is inevitable because it is the result of divine will or some other immutable principle and that it will therefore be forever out of our control. The second is the gratuitous idea that unhappiness has no identifiable cause, that it descends upon us randomly and has no relation to us personally. The third mistake draws on a confused fatalism that boils down to the idea that whatever the cause, the effect will always be the same.

If unhappiness had immutable causes, we would never be able to escape it. The laws of causality would have no meaning—anything could come from anything else, flowers could grow in the sky and light create darkness and, as the Dalai Lama says, it would be easier "not to go to all the trouble of constantly ruminating over our suffering. It would be better just to think about something else, go to the beach, and have a nice cold beer!" Because if there were no cure for suffering, it would be pointless to make it worse by stressing over it. It would be better to accept it fully and to distract oneself so as to feel it less harshly.

"Arising from impermanent causes, unhappiness is itself subject to change and can be transformed. There is neither primordial nor eternal suffering."

But everything that occurs *does* have a cause. What inferno does not start with a spark, what war without thoughts of hatred, fear, or greed? What inner pain has not grown from the fertile soil of envy, animosity, vanity, or, even more basically, ignorance? Any active cause must itself be a changing one; nothing can exist autonomously and unchanging. Arising from impermanent causes, unhappiness is itself subject to change and can be transformed. There is neither primordial nor eternal suffering.

We all have the ability to study the causes of suffering and gradually to free ourselves from them. We all have the potential to sweep away the veils of ignorance, to free ourselves of the selfishness and misplaced desires that trigger unhappiness, to work for the good of others and extract the essence from our human condition. It's not the magnitude of the task that matters, it's the magnitude of our courage.

The Four Truths of Suffering

Over 2,500 years ago, seven weeks after attaining enlightenment under the Bodhi tree, the Buddha gave his first teaching in the Deer Park outside Varanasi. There he taught the Four Noble Truths. The first is the truth of suffering—not only the kind of suffering that is obvious to the eye, but also the kind, as we have seen, that exists in subtler forms. The second is the truth of the causes of suffering—ignorance that engenders craving, malice, pride, and many other thoughts that poison our lives and those of others. Since these mental poisons can be eliminated, an end to suffering—the third truth—is therefore possible. The fourth truth is the path that turns that potential into reality. The path is the process of using all available means to eliminate the fundamental causes of suffering. In brief, we must:

> *Recognize suffering,*
> *Eliminate its source,*
> *End it*
> *By practicing the path.*

When Affliction Becomes Suffering

Just as we distinguished between happiness and pleasure, we also have to clarify the difference between unhappiness and ephemeral discomforts. The latter depend on external circumstances, while unhappiness is a profound state of dissatisfaction that endures even in favorable external conditions. Conversely, it's worth repeating that one can suffer physically or mentally—by feeling sad, for instance—without losing the sense of fulfillment that is founded on inner peace and selflessness. There are two levels of experience here, which can be compared respectively to the waves and the depths of the ocean. A storm may be raging at the surface, but the depths remain calm. The wise man always remains connected to the depths. On the other hand, he who knows only the surface and is unaware of the depths is lost when he is buffeted by the waves of suffering.

But how, you might ask, can I avoid being shattered when my child is sick and I know he's going to die? How can I not be torn up at the sight of thousands of civilian war victims being deported or mutilated? Am I supposed to stop feeling? What could ever make me accept something like that? Who wouldn't be affected by it, including the most serene of wise men? The difference between the sage and the ordinary person is that the former can feel unconditional love for those who suffer and do everything in his power to attenuate their pain without allowing his lucid vision of existence to be shaken. The essential thing is to be available to others without giving in to despair when the natural episodes of life and death follow their course.

For the past few years I've had a friend, a Sikh in his sixties with a fine white beard, who works at the Delhi airport. Every time I pass through, we have a cup of tea together and discuss philosophy and spirituality, taking up the conversation where we left off several months earlier. One day he told me: "My father died a few weeks ago. I'm devastated, because his death seems so unfair to me. I can't understand it and I can't accept it." And yet the world cannot in itself be called unfair; all it does is reflect the laws of cause and effect, and impermanence—the instability of all things—is a natural phenomenon.

35

As gently as possible, I told him the story of the woman who, overwhelmed by the death of her son, came to the Buddha and begged him to restore the boy to life. The Buddha told her that in order to do so, he needed a handful of earth from a house that had never experienced any death. Having visited every house in the village and come to see that none had escaped bereavement, the woman returned to the Buddha, who comforted her with words of love and wisdom.

I also told him the story of Dza Mura Tulku, a spiritual master who lived in the early twentieth century in eastern Tibet. He had a family, and throughout his life he felt a deep affection for his wife, which she reciprocated. He did nothing without her and always said that if anything should happen to her, he could not long outlive her. And then she died suddenly. The master's friends and disciples hurried to his side. Recalling what they had heard him say so often, none dared tell him the news. Finally, as tactfully as possible, one disciple told the master that his wife had died.

The tragic reaction they'd feared failed to occur. The master looked at them and said: "Why do you look so upset? How many times have I told you that phenomena and beings are impermanent? Even the Buddha had to leave the world." No matter how tenderly he'd felt for his wife, and despite the great sadness he most surely felt, allowing himself to be consumed by grief would have added nothing to his love for her. It was more important for him to pray serenely for the deceased and to make her an offering of that serenity.

Remaining painfully obsessed with a situation or the memory of a departed loved one, to the point of being paralyzed by grief for months or years on end, is evidence not of affection, but of an attachment that does no good to others or to oneself. If we can learn to acknowledge that death is a part of life, distress will gradually give way to understanding and peace. "Don't think you're paying me some kind of great tribute if you let my death become the great event of your life. The best tribute you can pay to me as a mother is to go on and have a good and fulfilling life." These words were spoken by a mother to her son only moments before her death.

So the way in which we experience these waves of suffering depends a great deal on our attitude. It is therefore always better to familiarize ourselves with and prepare ourselves for the kind of suffering we are likely to encounter, some of which will be unavoidable, such as illness, old age, and death, rather than to be caught off guard and sink into anguish. A physical or moral pain can be intense without destroying our positive outlook on life. Once we have acquired inner well-being, it is easier to maintain our fortitude or to recover it quickly, even when we are confronted externally by difficult circumstances.

Does such peace of mind come simply because we wish it to? Hardly. 40 We don't earn our living just by wishing to. Likewise, peace is a treasure of the mind that is not acquired without effort. If we let ourselves be overwhelmed by our personal problems, no matter how tragic, we only increase our difficulties and become a burden on those around us. If our mind becomes accustomed to dwelling solely on the pain that events or people inflict on it, one day the most trivial incident will cause it infinite sorrow. As the intensity of this feeling grows with practice, everything that happens to us will eventually come to distress us, and peace will find no place within us. All manifestations will assume a hostile character and we will rebel bitterly against our fate, to the point of doubting the very meaning of life. It is essential to acquire a certain inner sense of well-being so that without in any way blunting our sensitivities, our love, and our altruism, we are able to connect with the depths of our being.

Understanding the Text

1. Ricard states that the three modes of suffering are "visible suffering, hidden suffering, and invisible suffering" (par. 17). What are the differences among these three kinds of suffering? Which one, in your opinion, is the hardest to heal from?

2. According to Buddhism, "suffering will always exist as a *universal phenomenon* but *every individual* has the potential for liberation from it" (par. 23, emphasis in original). Explain this in your own words. What do you think Buddhism is trying to teach about the individual?
3. What strategies does the text offer for a person to overcome suffering and move toward a life of peace? What are some other strategies that are absent from the text?

Reflection and Response

4. This text uses several metaphors and stories to explain the intensity of suffering. Draw upon the one you find most compelling and discuss it at greater length. How might this metaphor or story apply to an experience in your own life?
5. Ricard opens the essay with a parable that leads to the conclusion that the history of humankind can be summed up in two words: "They suffer." Why do all human beings suffer? What is it about the human condition that makes suffering inevitable? What are the root causes of suffering in human lives?

Making Connections

6. In Chapters 2 and 3, several essays discuss similar perspectives on happiness. Daniel Gilbert ("Paradise Glossed," p. 96) discusses happiness in terms of "meaning making," while Stefan Klein ("Enjoyment," p. 198) establishes a correlation between pleasure and pain. How might you discuss this article on suffering in relation to these arguments?
7. In "What Suffering Does" (p. 284), David Brooks writes, "People shoot for happiness but feel formed through suffering" (par. 2). In the *Handbook* (p. 88), the Stoic philosopher Epictetus writes, "An uneducated person accuses others when he is doing badly; a partly educated person accuses himself, an educated person accuses neither someone else nor himself" (par. 7). Like Ricard, these writers believe that painful experiences often have value — perhaps greater value than those that we wished for. Drawing on Brooks, Epictetus, Ricard, and an experience of your own (for example, a disappointment or a loss), write an essay about the uses of suffering. What role does suffering play in a moral education?

From The Book of Psalms

Kaufmann Kohler*

The Book of Psalms, as it is known in the Christian Bible, is unnamed in the Hebrew Bible, but it has come to be known as the *Sefer Tehillim*, or the Book of Songs of Praise. Though traditionally attributed to David (about 1040–970 BCE), the second king of Israel and Judah, the Psalms are now believed to have been composed by many hands over the course of several centuries, between about 1000 and 500 BCE. The book contains 150 psalms in the Hebrew Bible (151 in some Christian Bibles), divided into five books. As a rule, each line of each psalm has two halves with some sort of parallelism between them, such as similar meaning or syntax or an equal number of accents, or a combination of these. Although the psalms served many purposes — some are songs of lament, some of thanksgiving, some of praise, and so on — as a group they convey movingly the Hebrews' sense of their relationship with their God. The translations here are from *The Holy Scriptures according to the Masoretic Text*, published by the Jewish Publication Society of America in 1917. The principal translator of the psalms was Kaufmann Kohler (1843–1926).

1

Happy is the man that hath not walked in the counsel of the wicked,
Nor stood in the way of sinners,
Nor sat in the seat of the scornful.
But his delight is in the law° of the LORD;
And in His law doth he meditate day and night, 5
And he shall be like a tree planted by streams of water,
That bringeth forth its fruit in its season,
And whose leaf doth not wither;
And in whatsoever he doeth he shall prosper.

Not so the wicked; 10
But they are like the chaff which the wind driveth away.
Therefore the wicked shall not stand in the judgment,

*Translator.

law: the precepts and commandments given in the Torah (the first five books of the Bible).

Nor sinners in the congregation of the righteous.
For the LORD regardeth the way of the righteous;
But the way of the wicked shall perish. . . . 15

23

The LORD is my shepherd; I shall not want.
He maketh me to lie down in green pastures;
He leadeth me beside the still waters.
He restoreth my soul;
He guideth me in straight paths for His name's sake. 20
Yea, though I walk through the valley of the shadow of death,
I will fear no evil,
For Thou art with me;
Thy rod and Thy staff,° they comfort me.
Thou preparest a table before me in the presence of mine enemies; 25
Thou hast anointed my head with oil; my cup runneth over.
Surely goodness and mercy shall follow me all the days of my life;
And I shall dwell in the house of the LORD for ever. . . .

32

Happy is he whose transgression is forgiven, whose sin is pardoned.
Happy is the man unto whom the LORD counteth not iniquity, 30
And in whose spirit there is no guile.

When I kept silence, my bones wore away
Through my groaning all the day long.
For day and night Thy hand was heavy upon me;
My sap was turned as in the droughts of summer. 35
I acknowledged my sin unto Thee and mine iniquity have I not hid;
I said: 'I will make confession concerning my transgressions unto the
LORD'—
And Thou, Thou forgavest the iniquity of my sin.

For this let every one that is godly pray unto Thee in a time when
Thou mayest be found;

Thy rod and Thy staff: The rod (a shorter stick like a club) and the staff (a longer stick like a pole) were instruments carried by shepherds to guide sheep and fight off predators.

Surely, when the great waters overflow, they will not reach unto him. 40
Thou art my hiding-place; Thou wilt preserve me from the
adversary;°
With songs of deliverance Thou wilt compass me about.
I will instruct thee and teach thee in the way which thou shalt go;
I will give counsel, Mine eye being upon thee.'
Be ye not as the horse, or as the mule, which have no understanding; 45
Whose mouth must be held in with bit and bridle,
That they come not near unto thee.

Many are the sorrows of the wicked;
But he that trusteth in the LORD, mercy compasseth him about.
Be glad in the LORD, and rejoice, ye righteous; 50
And shout for joy, all ye that are upright in heart.

33

Rejoice in the LORD, O ye righteous,
Praise is comely for the upright.
Give thanks unto the LORD with harp,
Sing praises unto Him with the psaltery° of ten strings. 55
Sing unto Him a new song;
Play skilfully amid shouts of joy.

For the word of the LORD is upright;
And all His work is done in faithfulness.
He loveth righteousness and justice; 60
The earth is full of the loving-kindness of the LORD.
By the word of the LORD were the heavens made;
And all the host of them by the breath of His mouth.
He gathereth the waters of the sea together as a heap;
He layeth up the deeps in store-houses. 65
Let all the earth fear the LORD;
Let all the inhabitants of the world stand in awe of Him.
For He spoke, and it was;
He commanded, and it stood.

adversary: the foe or enemy. It can refer to a political enemy or a spiritual one.
psaltery: a stringed musical instrument.

The LORD bringeth the counsel of the nations to nought;° 70
He maketh the thoughts of the peoples to be of no effect.
The counsel of the LORD standeth for ever,
The thoughts of His heart to all generations.

Happy is the nation whose God is the LORD;
The people whom He hath chosen for His own inheritance. 75
The LORD looketh from heaven;
He beholdeth all the sons of men;
From the place of His habitation He looketh intently
Upon all the inhabitants of the earth;
He that fashioneth the hearts of them all, 80
That considereth all their doings.
A king is not saved by the multitude of a host;°
A mighty man is not delivered by great strength.
A horse is a vain thing for safety;
Neither doth it afford escape by its great strength. 85
Behold, the eye of the LORD is toward them that fear Him,
Toward them that wait for His mercy;
To deliver their soul from death,
And to keep them alive in famine.

Our soul hath waited for the LORD; 90
He is our help and our shield.
For in Him doth our heart rejoice,
Because we have trusted in His holy name.
Let Thy mercy, O LORD, be upon us,
According as we have waited for Thee. . . . 95

84

For the Leader; upon the Gittith. A Psalm of the sons of Korah.

How lovely are Thy tabernacles° O LORD of hosts!
My soul yearneth, yea, even pineth for the courts of the LORD;
My heart and my flesh sing for joy unto the living God.

The Lord bringeth the counsel of the nations to nought: He nullifies the plans of foreign countries.
host: an army.
tabernacles: portable tents that functioned as sanctuaries or dwelling places of the divine.

Yea, the sparrow hath found a house, and the swallow a nest for herself, 100
Where she may lay her young;
Thine altars, O LORD of hosts,
My King, and my God—.
Happy are they that dwell in Thy house,
They are ever praising Thee. 105

Happy is the man whose strength is in Thee;
In whose heart are the highways.
Passing through the valley of Baca they make it a place of springs;
Yea, the early rain clotheth it with blessings.
They go from strength to strength, 110
Every one of them appeareth before God in Zion.

O LORD God of hosts, hear my prayer;
Give ear, O God of Jacob.
Behold, O God our shield,
And look upon the face of Thine anointed. 115
For a day in Thy courts is better than a thousand;
I had rather stand at the threshold of the house of my God,
Than to dwell in the tents of wickedness.
For the LORD God is a sun and a shield;
The LORD giveth grace and glory; 120
No good thing will He withhold from them that walk uprightly.
O LORD of hosts,
Happy is the man that trusteth in Thee. . . .

119

Aleph°

Happy are they that are upright in the way,
Who walk in the law of the LORD. 125
Happy are they that keep His testimonies,
That seek Him with the whole heart.
Yea, they do no unrighteousness;
They walk in His ways.

Aleph: Every eighth line of this psalm begins with a different letter of the Hebrew alphabet. This may have been a mnemonic device (an aid to memory).

Thou hast ordained Thy precepts, 130
That we should observe them diligently.
Oh that my ways were directed
To observe Thy statutes!
Then should I not be ashamed,
When I have regard unto all Thy commandments. 135
I will give thanks unto Thee with uprightness of heart,
When I learn Thy righteous ordinances.
I will observe Thy statutes;
O forsake me not utterly.

Beth

Wherewithal shall a young man keep his way pure? 140
By taking heed thereto according to Thy word.
With my whole heart have I sought Thee;
O let me not err from Thy commandments.
Thy word have I laid up in my heart
That I might not sin against Thee. 145
Blessed art Thou, O LORD;
Teach me Thy statutes.
With my lips have I told
All the ordinances of Thy mouth.
I have rejoiced in the way of Thy testimonies, 150
As much as in all riches.
I will meditate in Thy precepts,
And have respect unto Thy ways.
I will delight myself in Thy statutes.
I will not forget Thy word. 155

Gimel

Deal bountifully with Thy servant, that I may live,
And I will observe Thy word.
Open Thou mine eyes, that I may behold
Wondrous things out of Thy law.
I am a sojourner in the earth; 160
Hide not Thy commandments from me.
My soul breaketh for the longing
That it hath unto Thine ordinances at all times.
Thou hast rebuked the proud that are cursed,
That do err from Thy commandments. 165
Take away from me reproach and contempt;

For I have kept Thy testimonies.
Even though princes sit and talk against me,
Thy servant doth meditate in Thy statutes.
Yea, Thy testimonies are my delight, 170
They are my counsellors.

Daleth

My soul cleaveth° unto the dust;
Quicken Thou me according to Thy word.
I told of my ways, and Thou didst answer me;
Teach me Thy statutes. 175
Make me to understand the way of Thy precepts,
That I may talk of Thy wondrous works.
My soul melteth away for heaviness;
Sustain me according unto Thy word.
Remove from me the way of falsehood; 180
And grant me Thy law graciously.
I have chosen the way of faithfulness;
Thine ordinances have I set [before me].
I cleave unto Thy testimonies;
O LORD, put me not to shame. 185
I will run the way of Thy commandments,
For Thou dost enlarge my heart.

He

Teach me, O LORD, the way of Thy statutes;
And I will keep it at every step.
Give me understanding, that I keep Thy law 190
And observe it with my whole heart.
Make me to tread in the path of Thy commandments;
For therein do I delight.
Incline my heart unto Thy testimonies,
And not to covetousness. 195
Turn away mine eyes from beholding vanity,
And quicken me in Thy ways.
Confirm Thy word unto Thy servant,
Which pertaineth unto the fear of Thee.

cleaveth: adheres (the line might be paraphrased as "my soul has been laid low in the dust").

Turn away my reproach which I dread; 200
For Thine ordinances are good.
Behold, I have longed after Thy precepts;
Quicken me in Thy righteousness.

Vau

Let Thy mercies also come unto me, O LORD,
Even Thy salvation, according to Thy word; 205
That I may have an answer for him that taunteth me;
For I trust in Thy word.
And take not the word of truth utterly out of my mouth;
For I hope in Thine ordinances;
So shall I observe Thy law continually 210
For ever and ever;
And I will walk at ease,
For I have sought Thy precepts;
I will also speak of Thy testimonies before kings,
And will not be ashamed. 215
And I will delight myself in Thy commandments,
Which I have loved.
I will lift up my hands also unto Thy commandments, which I
have loved;
And I will meditate in Thy statutes.

Zain

Remember the word unto Thy servant, 220
Because Thou hast made me to hope.
This is my comfort in my affliction,
That Thy word hath quickened me.
The proud have had me greatly in derision;
Yet have I not turned aside from Thy law. 225
I have remembered Thine ordinances which are of old, O LORD,
And have comforted myself.
Burning indignation hath taken hold upon me, because of the wicked
That forsake Thy law.
Thy statutes have been my songs 230
In the house of my pilgrimage.
I have remembered Thy name, O LORD, in the night,
And have observed Thy law.
This I have had,
That I have kept Thy precepts. 235

Heth

My portion° is the LORD,
I have said that I would observe Thy words.
I have entreated Thy favour with my whole heart;
Be gracious unto me according to Thy word.
I considered my ways, 240
And turned my feet unto Thy testimonies.
I made haste, and delayed not,
To observe Thy commandments.
The bands of the wicked have enclosed me;
But I have not forgotten Thy law. 245
At midnight I will rise to give thanks unto Thee
Because of Thy righteous ordinances.
I am a companion of all them that fear Thee,
And of them that observe Thy precepts.
The earth, O LORD, is full of Thy mercy; 250
Teach me Thy statutes.

Teth

Thou hast dealt well with Thy servant,
O LORD, according unto Thy word.
Teach me good discernment and knowledge;
For I have believed in Thy commandments. 255
Before I was afflicted, I did err;
But now I observe Thy word.
Thou art good, and doest good;
Teach me Thy statutes.
The proud have forged a lie against me; 260
But I with my whole heart will keep Thy precepts.
Their heart is gross like fat;
But I delight in Thy law.
It is good for me that I have been afflicted,
In order that I might learn Thy statutes. 265
The law of Thy mouth is better unto me
Than thousands of gold and silver.

Iod

Thy hands have made me and fashioned me;
Give me understanding, that I may learn Thy commandments.

portion: the lot or inheritance that has been given.

They that fear Thee shall see me and be glad, 270
Because I have hope in Thy word.
I know, O LORD, that Thy judgments are righteous,
And that in faithfulness Thou hast afflicted me.
Let, I pray thee, Thy lovingkindness be ready to comfort me,
According to Thy promise unto Thy servant. 275
Let Thy tender mercies come unto me, that I may live;
For Thy law is my delight.
Let the proud be put to shame, for they have distorted my cause with falsehood;
But I will meditate in Thy precepts.
Let those that fear Thee return unto me, 280
And they that know Thy testimonies.
Let my heart be undivided in Thy statutes,
In order that I may not be put to shame.

Caph

My soul pineth for Thy salvation;
In Thy word do I hope. 285
Mine eyes fail for Thy word,
Saying: 'When wilt Thou comfort me?'
For I am become like a wine-skin in the smoke;°
Yet do I not forget Thy statutes.
How many are the days of Thy servant? 290
When wilt Thou execute judgment on them that persecute me?
The proud have digged pits for me,
Which is not according to Thy law.
All Thy commandments are faithful;
They persecute me for nought; help Thou me. 295
They had almost consumed me upon earth;
But as for me, I forsook not Thy precepts.
Quicken me after Thy lovingkindness,
And I will observe the testimony of Thy mouth.

Lamed

For ever, O LORD, 300
Thy word standeth fast in heaven.
Thy faithfulness is unto all generations;

like a wine-skin in the smoke: A flask made of skin, when hung in a smoky tent, becomes shriveled and dry (and thus susceptible to cracking).

Thou hast established the earth, and it standeth.
They stand this day according to Thine ordinances;
For all things are Thy servants. 305
Unless Thy law had been my delight,
I should then have perished in mine affliction.
I will never forget Thy precepts;
For with them Thou hast quickened me.
I am Thine, save me; 310
For I have sought Thy precepts.
The wicked have waited for me to destroy me;
But I will consider Thy testimonies.
I have seen an end to every purpose;
But Thy commandment is exceeding broad. 315

Mem

Oh how love I Thy law!
It is my meditation all the day.
Thy commandments make me wiser than mine enemies;
For they are ever with me.
I have more understanding than all my teachers; 320
For Thy testimonies are my meditation.
I understand more than mine elders,
Because I have kept Thy precepts.
I have refrained my feet from every evil way,
In order that I might observe Thy word. 325
I have not turned aside from Thine ordinances;
For Thou hast instructed me.
How sweet are Thy words unto my palate!
Yea, sweeter than honey to my mouth!
From Thy precepts I get understanding; 330
Therefore I hate every false way.

Nun

Thy word is a lamp unto my feet,
And a light unto my path.
I have sworn, and have confirmed it,
To observe Thy righteous ordinances. 335
I am afflicted very much;
Quicken me, O LORD, according unto Thy word.
Accept, I beseech Thee, the freewill-offerings of my mouth, O LORD,
And teach me Thine ordinances.

My soul is continually in my hand;° 340
Yet have I not forgotten Thy law.
The wicked have laid a snare for me;
Yet went I not astray from Thy precepts.
Thy testimonies have I taken as a heritage for ever;
For they are the rejoicing of [my] heart. 345
I have inclined my heart to [perform] Thy statutes,
For ever, at every step.

Samech

I hate them that are of a double mind;
But Thy law do I love.
Thou art my covert and my shield. 350
In Thy word do I hope.
Depart from me, ye evil-doers;
That I may keep the commandments of my God.
Uphold me according unto Thy word, that I may live;
And put me not to shame in my hope. 355
Support Thou me, and I shall be saved;
And I will occupy myself with Thy statutes continually.
Thou hast made light of all them that err from Thy statutes;
For their deceit is vain.
Thou puttest away all the wicked of the earth like dross; 360
Therefore I love Thy testimonies.
My flesh shuddereth for fear of Thee;
And I am afraid of Thy judgments.

Ain

I have done justice and righteousness;
Leave me not to mine oppressors. 365
Be surety for Thy servant for good;
Let not the proud oppress me.
Mine eyes fail for Thy salvation,
And for Thy righteous word.
Deal with Thy servant according unto Thy mercy, 370
And teach me Thy statutes.
I am Thy servant, give me understanding;
That I may know Thy testimonies.
It is time for the LORD to work;

My soul is continually in my hand: My life is at risk.

They have made void Thy law. 375
Therefore I love Thy commandments
Above gold, yea, above fine gold.
Therefore I esteem all [Thy] precepts concerning all things to be right;
Every false way I hate.

Pe

Thy testimonies are wonderful; 380
Therefore doth my soul keep them.
The opening of Thy words giveth light;
It giveth understanding unto the simple.
I opened wide my mouth, and panted;
For I longed for Thy commandments. 385
Turn Thee towards me, and be gracious unto me,
As is Thy wont to do unto those that love Thy name.
Order my footsteps by Thy word;
And let not any iniquity have dominion over me.
Redeem me from the oppression of man, 390
And I will observe Thy precepts.
Make Thy face to shine upon Thy servant;
And teach me Thy statutes.
Mine eyes run down with rivers of water,
Because they observe not Thy law. 395

Tzade

Righteous art Thou, O LORD,
And upright are Thy judgments.
Thou hast commanded Thy testimonies in righteousness
And exceeding faithfulness.
My zeal hath undone me, 400
Because mine adversaries have forgotten Thy words.
Thy word is tried to the uttermost,
And Thy servant loveth it.
I am small and despised;
Yet have I not forgotten Thy precepts. 405
Thy righteousness is an everlasting righteousness,
And Thy law is truth.
Trouble and anguish have overtaken me;
Yet Thy commandments are my delight.
Thy testimonies are righteous for ever; 410
Give me understanding, and I shall live.

Koph

I have called with my whole heart; answer me, O LORD;
I will keep Thy statutes.
I have called Thee, save me,
And I will observe Thy testimonies. 415
I rose early at dawn, and cried;
I hoped in Thy word.
Mine eyes forestalled the night-watches,
That I might meditate in Thy word.
Hear my voice according unto Thy lovingkindness; 420
Quicken me, O LORD, as Thou art wont.
They draw nigh that follow after wickedness;
They are far from Thy law.
Thou art nigh, O LORD;
And all Thy commandments are truth. 425
Of old have I known from Thy testimonies
That Thou hast founded them for ever.

Resh

O see mine affliction, and rescue me;
For I do not forget Thy law.
Plead Thou my cause, and redeem me; 430
Quicken me according to Thy word.
Salvation is far from the wicked;
For they seek not Thy statutes.
Great are Thy compassions, O LORD;
Quicken me as Thou art wont. 435
Many are my persecutors and mine adversaries;
Yet have I not turned aside from Thy testimonies.
I beheld them that were faithless, and strove with them;
Because they observed not Thy word.
O see how I love Thy precepts; 440
Quicken me, O LORD, according to Thy lovingkindness.
The beginning of Thy word is truth;
And all Thy righteous ordinance endureth for ever.

Shin

Princes have persecuted me without a cause;
But my heart standeth in awe of Thy words. 445
I rejoice at Thy word,

As one that findeth great spoil.
I hate and abhor falsehood;
Thy law do I love.
Seven times a day do I praise Thee, 450
Because of Thy righteous ordinances.
Great peace have they that love Thy law;
And there is no stumbling for them.
I have hoped for Thy salvation, O LORD,
And have done Thy commandments. 455
My soul hath observed Thy testimonies;
And I love them exceedingly.
I have observed Thy precepts and Thy testimonies;
For all my ways are before Thee.

Tau

Let my cry come near before Thee, O LORD; 460
Give me understanding according to Thy word.
Let my supplication come before Thee;
Deliver me according to Thy word.
Let my lips utter praise:
Because Thou teachest me Thy statutes. 465
Let my tongue sing of Thy word
For all Thy commandments are righteousness.
Let Thy hand be ready to help me;
For I have chosen Thy precepts.
I have longed for Thy salvation, O LORD; 470
And Thy law is my delight.
Let my soul live, and it shall praise Thee;
And let Thine ordinances help me.
I have gone astray like a lost sheep[;] seek Thy servant;
For I have not forgotten Thy commandments. 475

Understanding the Text

1. How is God conceived of and represented in these psalms? What are his powers, qualities, and characteristics? Write a list or brief description of them, citing specific lines that support each.
2. Choose ten lines of a psalm and type them out. Then write your own modern-day version of these lines. Substitute word for word and image for image. Finally, write a few sentences about what this exercise has taught you about the language of the psalm.

Reflection and Response

3. How would you describe the conception of happiness that we find in these psalms? How is this happiness achieved? What role does God — "the Lord" — play in granting that happiness?
4. What do these psalms tell us about the way of life of the people who wrote them and sang them? What evidence do they provide of the people's occupations, their principal concerns, their customs, their hardships, and their activities?

Making Connections

5. Several psalms begin with blessings or "beatitudes"; for example, "Happy whose way is blameless / who walk in the Lord's teaching." Compare these to the beatitudes in the Gospel of Matthew (p. 59). How is the path to happiness imagined or conceived in each text? In what ways are they similar and in what ways different?
6. Compare the conception of happiness in these psalms to the conception of happiness offered by Krishna in the *Bhagavad Gita* (p. 67).

Gospel of Matthew

The Bible*

The Gospel of Matthew, written between 70 and 110 CE, is one of four gospels that have been accepted into the New Testament of the Christian Bible. (The word "gospel" means "good news.") The first book in the New Testament tells the story of Jesus's birth, his work as a teacher, his death by crucifixion, and his resurrection. Like the other books of the New Testament, it was written in Greek, the language most widely used by educated people in the period of the Roman Empire. Scholars believe that its author drew from an earlier text, now lost, composed of Jesus's sayings. Although nothing is known about its author, scholars believe that the writer was Jewish; the Gospel aims to demonstrate continuity between the Jewish law and Jesus's teaching, and to establish Jesus as the Jewish Messiah (that is, deliverer). The selection that follows is from "the Sermon on the Mount," Jesus's first extended discourse in this Gospel. The nine verses that begin with the words "Blessed are . . ." are known collectively as "the Beatitudes." The term "blessed" translates the Greek word *makarios*, meaning "happy" or "fortunate," a term normally used to refer to the gods or the wealthy elite.

5

Seeing the crowds, he° went up on the mountain, and when he sat down his disciples came to him. [2]And he opened his mouth and taught them, saying:

3 "Blessed are the poor in spirit, for theirs is the kingdom of heaven.

4 "Blessed are those who mourn, for they shall be comforted.

5 "Blessed are the meek, for they shall inherit the earth.

6 "Blessed are those who hunger and thirst for righteousness, for they shall be satisfied. 5

7 "Blessed are the merciful, for they shall obtain mercy.

8 "Blessed are the pure in heart, for they shall see God.

9 "Blessed are the peacemakers, for they shall be called sons of God.

10 "Blessed are those who are persecuted for righteousness' sake, for theirs is the kingdom of heaven.

11 "Blessed are you when men revile you and persecute you and utter all kinds of evil against you falsely on my account. [12]Rejoice and be 10

*Translation: Revised Standard Version.
he: Jesus.

glad, for your reward is great in heaven, for so men persecuted the prophets who were before you.

13 "You are the salt of the earth; but if salt has lost its taste, how shall its saltness be restored? It is no longer good for anything except to be thrown out and trodden under foot by men.

14 "You are the light of the world. A city set on a hill cannot be hid. [15]Nor do men light a lamp and put it under a bushel, but on a stand, and it gives light to all in the house. [16]Let your light so shine before men, that they may see your good works and give glory to your Father who is in heaven. . . .

17 "Think not that I have come to abolish the law and the prophets;° I have come not to abolish them but to fulfil them. [18]For truly, I say to you, till heaven and earth pass away, not an iota,° not a dot, will pass from the law until all is accomplished. [19]Whoever then relaxes one of the least of these commandments and teaches men so, shall be called least in the kingdom of heaven; but he who does them and teaches them shall be called great in the kingdom of heaven. [20]For I tell you, unless your righteousness exceeds that of the scribes and Pharisees,° you will never enter the kingdom of heaven. . . .

21 "You have heard that it was said to the men of old, 'You shall not kill; and whoever kills shall be liable to judgment.' [22]But I say to you that every one who is angry with his brother shall be liable to judgment; whoever insults his brother shall be liable to the council,° and whoever says, 'You fool' shall be liable to the hell of fire. [23]So if you are offering your gift at the altar, and there remember that your brother has something against you, [24]leave your gift there before the altar and go; first be reconciled to your brother, and then come and offer your gift. [25]Make friends quickly with your accuser, while you are going with him to court, lest your accuser hand you over to the judge, and the judge to the guard, and you be put in prison; [26]truly, I say to you, you will never get out till you have paid the last penny. . . .

27 "You have heard that it was said, 'You shall not commit adultery.' 15 [28]But I say to you that every one who looks at a woman lustfully has already committed adultery with her in his heart. [29]If your right eye causes you to sin, pluck it out and throw it away; it is better that you lose one of

the law and the prophets: This phrase is usually taken to refer to the Torah (the Law) and the prophetic books of Jewish scripture. These form the basis of the Old Testament of the Christian Bible.
iota: the name for the Greek letter *i*.
Pharisees: members of a sect who were known for their strict observance of Jewish law.
the council: the high court in ancient Jerusalem, known as the Sanhedrin.

your members than that your whole body be thrown into hell. [30]And if your right hand causes you to sin, cut it off and throw it away; it is better that you lose one of your members than that your whole body go into hell. . . .

31 "It was also said, 'Whoever divorces his wife, let him give her a certificate of divorce.' [32]But I say to you that every one who divorces his wife, except on the ground of unchastity, makes her an adulteress; and whoever marries a divorced woman commits adultery. . . .

33 "Again you have heard that it was said to the men of old, 'You shall not swear falsely, but shall perform to the Lord what you have sworn.' [34]But I say to you, Do not swear at all, either by heaven, for it is the throne of God, [35]or by the earth, for it is his footstool, or by Jerusalem, for it is the city of the great King. [36]And do not swear by your head, for you cannot make one hair white or black. [37]Let what you say be simply 'Yes' or 'No'; anything more than this comes from evil. . . .

38 "You have heard that it was said, 'An eye for an eye and a tooth for a tooth.' [39]But I say to you, Do not resist one who is evil. But if any one strikes you on the right cheek, turn to him the other also; [40]and if any one would sue you and take your coat, let him have your cloak as well; [41]and if any one forces you to go one mile, go with him two miles. [42]Give to him who begs from you, and do not refuse him who would borrow from you. . . .

43 "You have heard that it was said, 'You shall love your neighbor and hate your enemy.' [44]But I say to you, Love your enemies and pray for those who persecute you, [45]so that you may be sons of your Father who is in heaven; for he makes his sun rise on the evil and on the good, and sends rain on the just and on the unjust. [46]For if you love those who love you, what reward have you? Do not even the tax collectors do the same? [47]And if you salute only your brethren, what more are you doing than others? Do not even the Gentiles° do the same? [48]You, therefore, must be perfect, as your heavenly Father is perfect. . . .

7

"Judge not, that you be not judged. [2]For with the judgment you pronounce you will be judged, and the measure you give will be the measure you get. [3]Why do you see the speck that is in your brother's eye, but do not notice the log that is in your own eye? [4]Or how can you say to your brother, 'Let me take the speck out of your eye,' when there is the log in

20

Gentiles: those who are not Jewish.

your own eye? [5]You hypocrite, first take the log out of your own eye, and then you will see clearly to take the speck out of your brother's eye.

6 "Do not give dogs what is holy; and do not throw your pearls before swine, lest they trample them under foot and turn to attack you.

7 "Ask, and it will be given you; seek, and you will find; knock, and it will be opened to you. [8]For every one who asks receives, and he who seeks finds, and to him who knocks it will be opened. [9]Or what man of you, if his son asks him for bread, will give him a stone? [10]Or if he asks for a fish, will give him a serpent? [11]If you then, who are evil, know how to give good gifts to your children, how much more will your Father who is in heaven give good things to those who ask him! [12]So whatever you wish that men would do to you, do so to them; for this is the law and the prophets. . . .

"How can you say to your brother, 'Let me take the speck out of your eye,' when there is the log in your own eye?"

13 "Enter by the narrow gate; for the gate is wide and the way is easy, that leads to destruction, and those who enter by it are many. [14]For the gate is narrow and the way is hard, that leads to life, and those who find it are few. . . .

15 "Beware of false prophets, who come to you in sheep's clothing but inwardly are ravenous wolves. [16]You will know them by their fruits. Are grapes gathered from thorns, or figs from thistles? [17]So, every sound tree bears good fruit, but the bad tree bears evil fruit. [18]A sound tree cannot bear evil fruit, nor can a bad tree bear good fruit. [19]Every tree that does not bear good fruit is cut down and thrown into the fire. [20]Thus you will know them by their fruits. . . .

21 "Not every one who says to me, 'Lord, Lord,' shall enter the kingdom of heaven, but he who does the will of my Father who is in heaven. [22]On that day many will say to me, 'Lord, Lord, did we not prophesy in your name, and cast out demons in your name, and do many mighty works in your name?' [23]And then will I declare to them, 'I never knew you; depart from me, you evildoers.' . . .

24 "Every one then who hears these words of mine and does them will be like a wise man who built his house upon the rock; [25]and the rain fell, and the floods came, and the winds blew and beat upon that house, but it did not fall, because it had been founded on the rock. [26]And every one who hears these words of mine and does not do them will be like a foolish man who built his house upon the sand; [27]and the rain fell, and the floods came, and the winds blew and beat against that house, and it fell; and great was the fall of it." . . .

28 And when Jesus finished these sayings, the crowds were astonished at his teaching, [29]for he taught them as one who had authority, and not as their scribes.

Understanding the Text

1. Matthew 5:1–10 are blessings over various types of people: the poor, the meek, the merciful, the pure in heart, the peacemakers, and so on. Matthew 5:11 closes the "blessings" by blessing those who are affected by persecution in the name of God. What purpose do you think these blessings serve when reading the text as a whole? How does blessing 5:11 capture the meaning of the preceding blessings?
2. Several verses appear to challenge one another in what message they aim to convey. Highlight an example of the verses in which this appears. Do you think these verses are more powerful when read together or apart? Make an argument for your opinion.

Reflection and Response

3. Choose the verse with which you had the most challenges when reading. First, use your own words to rewrite this verse. Next, construct an argument in which you discuss the importance of this verse versus the text as a whole. What does this verse suggest about happiness and leading a meaningful and an important life of happiness and peace?
4. Biblical scholars and theologians spend their careers interpreting the Bible. Imagine that it is your responsibility to interpret this section of the Gospel of Matthew for an audience who has never read it. How would you describe it to them? What would you highlight from the text, and what would you ignore? Which sections, if any, would you expand upon in your own words (and how might you do that)?
5. It has been suggested by biblical scholars that the Bible was composed by various sources at different times throughout history. From reading this text, what might you infer about the historical period in which it was written? What principles do you think were valued at this time? Would you argue that the society in which you live today values the same principles?

Making Connections

6. How does this reading, specifically as a religious text, compare to the other texts in this chapter? To what extent does this text discuss happiness differently from the other texts in the chapter?
7. Write one or two of your own beatitudes based on the work of one of your favorite singers or writers. Use the style of this text as your guide.

How Should the Soul

Rumi

Jalāl ad-Dīn Muhammad Rūmī (1207–1273), known in the English-speaking world simply as Rumi, was a Persian Sufi mystic who was born and lived in the province of Balkh in what is now Tajikistan.

Sufism is a mystical branch of Islam that seeks a direct personal experience of God through spiritual discipline. Sufis live in fraternal orders gathered around the teachings of a spiritual leader. In Sufi poetry, the soul is frequently depicted as a loving wife and God the beloved husband for whom she yearns. The sect seems to be almost as old as Islam itself, but it flourished in the thirteenth century. Rumi's long poem *Mašnavī-yi Ma'navī* has become, for Persian mystics, the most important religious text save for the Qur'ān. It inspired the most famous order of Sufis, the dervishes, known for their practice of "whirling" in order to achieve a state of spiritual ecstasy.

In the United States, interest in Rumi's poems has surged since translations began appearing in the 1970s, and he is now one of the most widely read poets in English. The following poem is from *Look! This Is Love: Poems of Rumi*, a selection of Rumi's verses translated by Annemarie Schimmel (1922–2003), an influential scholar of Sufism and professor of Indo-Muslim Languages and Culture at Harvard University from 1970 through 1992.

How should the soul not take wings
  when from the Glory of God
It hears a sweet, kindly call:
  "Why are you here, soul? Arise!"
How should a fish not leap fast   5
  into the sea from dry land
When from the ocean so cool
  the sound of the waves reached its ear?
How should the falcon not fly
  back to his king from the hunt   10
When from the falconer's drum
  it hears the call: "Oh, come back!"?
Why should not every Sufi
  begin to dance atom-like
Around the Sun of duration   15
  that saves from impermanence?
What graciousness and what beauty!
  What life-bestowing! What grace!

If anyone does without that, woe—
  what error, what suffering! 20
Oh fly, oh fly, O my soul-bird,
  fly to your primordial home!
You have escaped from the cage now—
  your wings are spread in the air.
Oh travel from brackish water 25
  now to the fountain of life!
Return from the place of the sandals
  now to the high seat of souls!
Go on! Go on! we are going,
  and we are coming, O soul, 30
From this world of separation
  to union, a world beyond worlds!
How long shall we here in the dust-world
  like children fill our skirts
With earth and with stones without value, 35
  with broken shards without worth?
Let's take our hand from the dust grove,
  let's fly to the heavens high,
Let's fly from our childish behavior
  and join the banquet of men!
Call out, O soul, to proclaim now
  that you are ruler and king!
You have the grace of the answer,
  you know the question as well!

Understanding the Text

1. Write one stanza of this poem at the top of your page. Then rewrite it in your own words. In two pages, discuss what you learned from completing this act of translation.
2. Who do you imagine to be the audience of this poem? Which lines tell you that?

Reflection and Response

3. Rumi's speaker identifies two very different worlds in this poem: the one we live in and the one we are heading toward. What are the attributes of each world in this poem? How would you respond to this assessment of our present space and our future possibilities?
4. This poem begins with a series of questions involving the word "not." But it ends very differently, with lines that begin with "let's" and "you." What is the relationship between these early and later lines? Does the speaker

make a kind of argument here? Restate the poem's many-stepped argument in your own words.

Making Connections

5. Compare the concept of happiness (the experience of "flow") presented by Mihaly Csikszentmihalyi in "If We Are So Rich, Why Aren't We Happy?" (p. 140) with the notion of happiness that is embedded in Rumi's lines. Using textual evidence to support your argument, how would you explain the similarities and differences between their views?
6. Rumi is one of the most popular poets in America today. Find another Rumi poem that speaks to you. Construct a letter to a friend who is struggling with something important and include Rumi's poem as an example of something you are trying to convey to your friend.

A selfie at Europe's prehistoric Stonehenge blends the old with the new, much like the continued relevance of Rumi's words on love dating back to the thirteenth century.
Holly Zappola

Freedom through Renunciation

The Bhagavad Gita*

The *Bhagavad Gita* (or "Song of Bhagavan"), composed in India around the fourth century BCE, is a sacred Hindu text. It forms part of a much longer epic, the *Mahabharata*, that depicts a war between two branches of the Kuru clan for the throne of Hastinapura. The *Bhagavad Gita* relates a dialogue before a major battle, in which Prince Arjuna expresses to his charioteer his reluctance to go to war against members of his own clan. His charioteer is the "Blessed Lord" Krishna, an incarnation of the Hindu god Vishnu. Krishna advises Arjuna to do his god-given duty (*dharma*) without clinging to any personal interest in the results of his actions. The selection that follows is from the conclusion of the *Gita*; here, Arjuna distinguishes among *tamasic*, *rajasic*, and *sattvic* states of mind or principles of conduct (*guna*). In the end, it is the state of mind that matters.

ARJUNA SAID:
Teach me this lesson, Krishna:
what it means to renounce,
what it means to relinquish,
and the difference between the two.

THE BLESSED LORD SAID:
To give up desire-bound actions 5
is what is meant by *renouncing*;
to give up the results of all actions
is what the wise call to *relinquish*.

Some sages say that all action
is tainted and should be relinquished; 10
others permit only acts
of worship, control, and charity.

Here is the truth: these acts
of worship, control, and charity
purify the heart and therefore 15
should not be relinquished but performed.

*Translator: Stephen Mitchell.

But even the most praiseworthy acts
should be done with complete nonattachment
and with no concern for results;
this is my final judgment. 20

Relinquishment is of three kinds:
When any obligatory action
is relinquished because of delusive
thinking—that is *tamasic*.

When a man relinquishes action 25
because it is hard or painful—
that relinquishment is *rajasic*,
and cannot guide him toward freedom.

But when, out of duty, a man
performs an obligatory action, 30
relinquishing all results—
that relinquishment is called *sattvic*.

The man who is able to relinquish,
beyond doubt, does not avoid
unpleasant actions, nor is he 35
attached to actions that are pleasant.

An embodied being can never
relinquish actions completely;
to relinquish the *results* of actions
is all that can be required. 40

For those who cling to it, action
has three results when they die—
desired, undesired, and mixed;
but for those who renounce, it has none.

Now I will teach you the five 45
elements that must be present
for an action to be accomplished,
as philosophers have declared:

the physical body, the agent,
the various organs of sense, 50

the various kinds of behavior,
and divine providence as fifth.

In whatever action a man takes
with his body, his speech, or his mind,
whether it is right or wrong, 55
these five things must be present.

Since this is so, when a man
of limited understanding
sees himself as sole agent,
he is not seeing the truth. 60

A man who is free from the I-sense
and is pure, even if he kills
these warriors, does not kill,
nor is he bound by his actions.

Knowledge, the known, and the knower 65
are the three things that motivate action;
instrument, action, and agent
are the three components of action.

Knowledge, action, and agent
are of three kinds, according to the *guna*° 70
that prevails in each one. Listen,
and I will explain these distinctions.

Knowledge that sees in all things
a single, imperishable being,
undivided among the divided— 75
this kind of knowledge is *sattvic*.

Rajasic knowledge perceives
a multiplicity of beings,
each one existing by itself,
separate from all the others. 80

guna: quality or tendency (*sattva*, or pure; *tamas*, or inert; and *raja*, or changeable).

Knowledge is called *tamasic*
when it clings to one thing as if it
were the whole, and has no concern
for the true cause and essence of things.

Obligatory action, performed 85
without any craving or aversion
by a man unattached to results—
this kind of action is *sattvic*.

Rajasic action is performed
with a wish to satisfy desires, 90
with the thought "I am doing this,"
and with an excessive effort.

Action is *tamasic* when
it begins in delusion, with no
concern that it may cause 95
harm to oneself or others.

An agent who is free from attachment
and the I-sense, courageous, steadfast,
unmoved by success or failure—
this kind of agent is *sattvic*. 100

A *rajasic* agent is impulsive,
seeks to obtain results,
is greedy, violent, impure,
and buffeted by joy and sorrow.

An agent is called *tamasic* 105
when he is undisciplined, stupid,
stubborn, mean, deceitful,
lazy, and easily depressed.

Listen as I describe
the three kinds of understanding 110
and the three kinds of will, according
to the *guna* that prevails in each.

The understanding that knows
what to do and what not to,

safety and danger, bondage 115
and liberation, is *sattvic.*

Rajasic understanding
fails to know right from wrong,
when from when not to act,
what should from what should not be done. 120

Understanding is *tamasic*
when, thickly covered in darkness,
it imagines that wrong is right
and sees the world upside down.

The unswerving will that controls 125
the functions of mind, breath, senses
by the practice of meditation—
this kind of will is *sattvic.*

Rajasic will is attached
to duty, sensual pleasures, 130
power, and wealth, with anxiety
and a constant desire for results.

That will is called *tamasic*
by which a stupid man keeps
clinging to grief and fear, 135
to torpor, depression, and conceit.

Now, Arjuna, I will tell you
about the three kinds of happiness.
The happiness which comes from long practice,
which leads to the end of suffering, 140

which at first is like poison, but at last
like nectar—this kind of happiness,
arising from the serenity
of one's own mind, is called *sattvic.*

Rajasic happiness comes 145
from contact between the senses
and their objects, and is at first
like nectar, but at last like poison.

Happiness is called *tamasic*
when it is self-deluding 150
from beginning to end, and arises
from sleep, indolence, and dullness.

No being on earth, Arjuna,
or among the blithe gods in heaven
is free from the conditioning 155
of these three Nature-born *gunas*.

The duties of priests, of warriors,
of laborers, and of servants
are apportioned according to the *gunas*
that arise from their inborn nature. 160

Serenity, control, austerity,
uprightness, purity, patience,
knowledge, piety, and judgment
are the natural duties of priests.

Boldness, the ability to lead, 165
largeheartedness, courage in battle,
energy, stamina, and strength
are the natural duties of warriors.

Farming, cowherding, and trade
are the natural duties of laborers; 170
serving the needs of others
is the natural duty of servants.

Content with his natural duty,
each one achieves success.
Listen now: I will tell you 175
how this success can be found.

A man finds success by worshiping
with his own right actions the One
from whom all actions arise
and by whom the world is pervaded. 180

It is better to do your own duty
badly than to perfectly do

another's; when you do your duty,
you are naturally free from sin.

No one should relinquish his duty, 185
even though it is flawed;
all actions are enveloped by flaws
as fire is enveloped by smoke.

Self-mastered, with mind unattached
at all times, beyond desire, 190
one attains through renunciation
the supreme freedom from action.

Learn from me briefly, Arjuna,
that when a man gains success
he also gains perfect freedom, 195
the ultimate state of knowledge.

With a purified understanding,
fully mastering himself,
relinquishing all sense-objects,
released from aversion and craving, 200

solitary, eating lightly,
controlling speech, mind, and body,
absorbed in deep meditation
at all times, calm, impartial,

free from the "I" and "mine," 205
from aggression, arrogance, greed,
desire, and anger, he is fit
for the state of absolute freedom.

Serene in this state of freedom,
beyond desire and sorrow, 210
seeing all beings as equal,
he attains true devotion to me.

By devotion he comes to realize
the meaning of my infinite vastness;
when he knows who I truly am, 215
he instantly enters my being.

Relying on me in his actions
and performing them for my sake,
he reaches, by my great kindness,
the eternal, unchanging place. 220

Give up all actions to me;
love me above all others;
steadfastly keep your mind
focused on me alone.

Focused on me at all times, 225
you will overcome all obstructions;
but if you persist in clinging
to the I-sense, then you are lost.

And even if, clinging to the I-sense,
you say that you will not fight, 230
your intention will be in vain:
Nature will compel you to act.

The thing that, in your delusion,
you wish not to do, you will do,
even against your will, 235
since your own karma binds you.

The Lord dwells deep in the heart
of all beings, by his wondrous power
making them all revolve
like puppets on a carousel. 240

Devoted to him, Arjuna,
take refuge in him alone;
by his kindness, you will attain
the state of imperishable peace.

Thus I have taught you the secret 245
of secrets, the utmost knowledge;
meditate deeply upon it,
then act as you think best.

Now listen to my final words, 250
the deepest secret of all;

I am speaking for your own welfare,
since you are precious to me.

If you focus your mind on me
and revere me with all your heart,
you will surely come to me; this 255
I promise, because I love you.

Relinquishing all your duties,
take refuge in me alone.
Do not fear: I will free you
from the evils of birth and death. 260

These teachings must not be spoken
to men without self-control
and piety, or to men
whose hearts are closed to my words.

He who teaches this primal 265
secret to those who love me
has acted with the greatest love
and will come to me, beyond doubt.

No one can do me a service
that is more devoted than this, 270
and no one on earth is more
precious to me than *he* is.

Whoever earnestly studies
this sacred discourse of ours—
I consider that he has worshiped 275
and loved me with the yoga of knowledge.

Even the man who hears it
with faith and an open mind—
he also, released, will go to
the joyous heavens of the pure. 280

Have you truly heard me, Arjuna?
Has my teaching entered your heart?
Have my words now driven away
your ignorance and delusion?

ARJUNA SAID:
Krishna, I see the truth now, 285
by your immeasurable kindness.
I have no more doubts; I will act
according to your command.

SANJAYA° SAID:
O King, as I heard this wondrous
discourse between Lord Krishna 290
and Arjuna, the man of great soul,
the hair stood up on my flesh.

By the poet Vyasa's kindness,
I heard this most secret doctrine
directly from the mighty Lord 295
of Yoga, Krishna himself.

O King, the more I remember
this wondrous and holy discourse
between the Lord and Arjuna,
the more I shudder with joy. 300

And as often as I remember
the Lord's vast, wondrous form,
each time I am astonished;
each time I shudder with joy.

Where Krishna is—Lord of Yoga— 305
and Arjuna the archer: there,
surely, I think, is splendor
and virtue and spiritual wealth.

Sanjaya: the narrator of the *Bhagavad Gita* and a character in the *Mahabharata,* the epic poem that includes it. Sanjaya is charioteer to the blind king Dhritarashtra. He describes to the king the events of the final battle between the Pandavas and the Kauravas.

Understanding the Text

1. Krishna distinguishes three *gunas*: *rajasic*, *tamasic*, and *sattvic*. What are the characteristics of *sattvic* relinquishment, knowledge, action, agency, understanding, will, and happiness?
2. Arjuna is about to go into battle and is reluctant to harm or kill his enemies. But Krishna declares that he must do his duty. Why? How does Krishna explain Arjuna's obligation to perform the actions of a warrior and a prince rather than to renounce them?
3. According to Krishna, what sort of mental and spiritual attitude is required of Arjuna as he goes into battle?

Reflection and Response

4. How might the sort of mental and spiritual attitude that Krishna requires of Arjuna bring Arjuna happiness?
5. How might a person in the modern world — say, a college student — enact Krishna's advice?

Making Connections

6. Write a one-page version of this text in the style of the Gospel of Matthew (p. 59) and then in the style of the *Tao* (p. 10). What did you learn from this exercise?
7. Chapter 2 contains a text from Aristotle ("Nicomachean Ethics," p. 82) with similar structure. Which text, in your opinion, provides a stronger argument for maintaining a life of happiness and peace? Cite specific quotations as examples for your argument to help explain what happiness entails and how it is achieved.
8. In this chapter, you read a variety of spiritual texts. Write an argument defending these texts as essential tools for happiness. How do they differ from each other? How might they teach you something different from the lessons derived from secular, nonspiritual texts on happiness?

2 What Are the Ethics of Happiness?

The Western philosophical tradition begins with the ancient Greeks, and it is from them that we get the word "philosophy" — the love of wisdom. Plato (428/427–348/347 BCE), the student of Socrates, was the first philosopher to leave a substantial body of writing. His student Aristotle (384–322 BCE) established a philosophical and scientific system for examining the fundamental questions of life in a rational and methodical way. Ethics is the branch of philosophy that deals with the question of morals — of what is right and wrong, and how we should live. In the *Nicomachean Ethics*, Aristotle argued that virtue is generally a "mean," or middle way, between two extremes. The happy life is shown to be the virtuous life.

Later, in ancient Rome, two dominant philosophical and ethical systems emerged, Stoicism and Epicureanism. Whereas Epicureanism emphasized the pursuit of pleasure (if in a refined sense), Stoics such as Epictetus (55–135 CE) and Marcus Aurelius (121–180 CE) believed that the best life could be achieved by cultivating equanimity, an attitude of imperturbability in the face of good fortune or bad.

In the medieval period, Christian philosophers strove to reconcile the teachings of the Bible with the preeminent Greek philosophers, especially Plato and Aristotle. But during the Enlightenment of the eighteenth century, philosophers began to develop systems that held religious belief at a distance. Utilitarianism, the philosophy of "the greatest good for the greatest number," contrived by Jeremy Bentham (1748–1832), was well suited to an industrial age when science and technology were transforming the old traditions and way of life.

Although Western philosophy has produced a wide array of ideas about the good life, we are not left with mere confusion. The careful reasoning of philosophers can be brought to bear on new ways of thinking about happiness, and the critique can bring greater depth and rigor to these conceptions, as philosopher Martha Nussbaum shows in her essay "Who Is the Happy Warrior?"

Nor can ethical thinking be easily separated from other branches of philosophy such as epistemology, the branch concerned with what it means to know. As psychologist Daniel Gilbert ("Paradise Glossed," p. 96) shows, the pursuit of happiness is intimately tied up with ways of knowing and points of view, and not simply circumstances or situation. And as philosopher Daniel M. Haybron ("Happiness and Its Discontents," p. 131) argues, language can lead us astray, and we must carefully examine the terms we use to define our ultimate goals.

From Nicomachean Ethics

Aristotle*

Aristotle (384–322 BCE) is one of the most influential thinkers in Western history. He was the first philosopher to separate human knowledge into distinct fields of inquiry and the first to develop a comprehensive way of organizing beings through a system of classification that became known as the *scala naturae*, or Great Chain of Being. The works of Aristotle that we possess today are chiefly lecture notes taken by students at the Lyceum, and for this reason can at times be puzzling. In the *Nicomachean Ethics* (named for his son, Nicomachus, who is believed to have been the editor of these notes), Aristotle aims to discover what is "the supreme good for man" — that is, what is the best way to lead our lives and to give them meaning. For Aristotle, a thing is best understood by looking at its end, purpose, or goal.

Aristotle was the son of a court physician who was educated in medicine. He studied philosophy at Plato's Academy for twenty years. When Plato died, and Aristotle was not appointed the head of the Academy, Aristotle left Greece to travel in Asia and study biology. When he returned to Greece, he became tutor to the Macedonian prince Alexander the Great. After Alexander conquered Athens, Aristotle returned to Athens and set up a school of his own, known as the Lyceum.

Let us again return to the good we are seeking, and ask what it can be. It seems different in different actions and arts; it is different in medicine, in strategy, and in the other arts likewise. What then is the good of each? Surely that for whose sake everything else is done. In medicine this is health, in strategy victory, in architecture a house, in any other sphere something else, and in every action and choice the end; for it is for the sake of this that all men do whatever else they do. Therefore, if there is an end for all that we do, this will be the good achievable by action, and if there are more than one, these will be the goods achievable by action.

So the argument has by a different course reached the same point; but we must try to state this even more clearly. Since there are evidently more than one end, and we choose some of these (e.g. wealth, flutes, and in general instruments) for the sake of something else, clearly not all ends are complete ends; but the chief good is evidently something complete. Therefore, if there is only one complete end, this will be what we are seeking,

*Translator: J. L. Ackrill.

and if there are more than one, the most complete of these will be what we are seeking. Now we call that which is in itself worthy of pursuit more complete than that which is worthy of pursuit for the sake of something else, and that which is never desirable for the sake of something else more complete than the things that are desirable both in themselves and for the sake of that other thing, and therefore we call complete without qualification that which is always desirable in itself and never for the sake of something else.

Now such a thing happiness, above all else, is held to be; for this we choose always for itself and never for the sake of something else, but honour, pleasure, reason, and every excellence we choose indeed for themselves (for if nothing resulted from them we should still choose each of them), but we choose them also for the sake of happiness, judging that through them we shall be happy. Happiness, on the other hand, no one chooses for the sake of these, nor, in general, for anything other than itself.

From the point of view of self-sufficiency the same result seems to follow; for the complete good is thought to be self-sufficient. Now by self-sufficient we do not mean that which is sufficient for a man by himself, for one who lives a solitary life, but also for parents, children, wife, and in general for his friends and fellow citizens, since man is sociable by nature. But some limit must be set to this; for if we extend our requirement to ancestors and descendants and friends' friends we are in for an infinite series. Let us examine this question, however, on another occasion; the self-sufficient we now define as that which when isolated makes life desirable and lacking in nothing; and such we think happiness to be; and further we think it most desirable of all things, without being counted as one good thing among others—if it were so counted it would clearly be made more desirable by the addition of even the least of goods; for that which is added becomes an excess of goods, and of goods the greater is always more desirable. Happiness, then, is something complete and self-sufficient, and is the end of action.

"Happiness, then, is something complete and self-sufficient, and is the end of action."

5 Presumably, however, to say that happiness is the chief good seems a platitude, and a clearer account of what it is is still desired. This might perhaps be given, if we could first ascertain the function of man. For just as for a flute-player, a sculptor, or any artist, and, in general, for all things that have a function or activity, the good and the "well" is thought to reside in the function, so would it seem to be for man, if he has a

function. Have the carpenter, then, and the tanner certain functions or activities, and has man none? Is he naturally functionless? Or as eye, hand, foot, and in general each of the parts evidently has a function, may one lay it down that man similarly has a function apart from all these? What then can this be? Life seems to be common even to plants, but we are seeking what is peculiar to man. Let us exclude, therefore, the life of nutrition and growth. Next there would be a life of perception, but it also seems to be common even to the horse, the ox, and every animal. There remains, then, an active life of the element that has a rational principle (of this, one part has such a principle in the sense of being obedient to one, the other in the sense of possessing one and exercising thought); and as this too can be taken in two ways, we must state that life in the sense of activity is what we mean; for this seems to be the more proper sense of the term. Now if the function of man is an activity of soul in accordance with, or not without, rational principle, and if we say a so-and-so and a good so-and-so have a function which is the same in kind, e.g. a lyre-player and a good lyre-player, and so without qualification in all cases, eminence in respect of excellence being added to the function (for the function of a lyre-player is to play the lyre, and that of a good lyre-player is to do so well): if this is the case, and we state the function of man to be a certain kind of life, and this to be an activity or actions of the soul implying a rational principle, and the function of a good man to be the good and noble performance of these, and if any action is well performed when it is performed in accordance with the appropriate excellence: if this is the case, human good turns out to be activity of soul in conformity with excellence, and if there are more than one excellence, in conformity with the best and most complete.

But we must add "in a complete life." For one swallow does not make a summer, nor does one day; and so too one day, or a short time, does not make a man blessed and happy.

Let this serve as an outline of the good; for we must presumably first sketch it roughly, and then later fill in the details. But it would seem that any one is capable of carrying on and articulating what has once been well outlined, and that time is a good discoverer or partner in such a work; to which facts the advances of the arts are due; for anyone can add what is lacking. And we must also remember what has been said before, and not look for precision in all things alike, but in each class of things such as accords with the subject-matter, and so much as is appropriate to the inquiry. For a carpenter and a geometer look for right angles in different ways; the former does so in so far as the right angle is useful for his work, while the latter inquires what it is or what sort of thing it is; for he is a spectator of the truth. We must act in the same way, then, in all other matters as well, that our main task may not be subordinated to minor questions. Nor must we demand the cause in all matters alike; it is enough in some cases that the fact be well established, as in the case of the first principles; the *fact* is a primary thing or first principle. Now of first principles we see some by induction, some by perception, some by a certain habituation, and others too in other ways. But each set of principles we must try to investigate in the natural way, and we must take pains to determine them correctly, since they have a great influence on what follows. For the beginning is thought to be more than half of the whole, and many of the questions we ask are cleared up by it.

• • •

We must consider it, however, in the light not only of our conclusion and our premisses, but also of what is commonly said about it; for with a true view all the facts harmonize, but with a false one they soon clash. Now goods have been divided into three classes, and some are described as external, others as relating to soul or to body; and we call those that relate to soul most properly and truly goods. But we are positing actions and activities relating to soul. Therefore our account must be sound, at least according to this view, which is an old one and agreed on by philosophers. It is correct also in that we identify the end with certain actions and activities; for thus it falls among goods of the soul and not among external goods. Another belief which harmonizes with our account is that the happy man lives well and fares well; for we have practically defined happiness as a sort of living and faring well. The characteristics that are looked for in happiness seem also, all of them, to belong to what we have defined happiness as being. For some identify happiness with excellence, some with practical wisdom, others with a kind of philosophic wisdom, others with these, or one of these, accompanied by pleasure or not without pleasure; while others include also external prosperity. Now some of these views have been held by many men and men of old, others by a few persons; and it is not probable that either of these should be entirely mistaken, but rather that they should be right in at least some one respect or even in most respects.

With those who identify happiness with excellence or some one excellence our account is in harmony; for to excellence belongs activity in accordance with excellence. But it makes, perhaps, no small difference whether we place the chief good in possession or in use, in state or in activity. For the state may exist without producing any good result, as in a man who is asleep or in some way quite inactive, but the activity cannot; for one who has the activity will of necessity be acting, and acting well. And as in the Olympic Games it is not the most beautiful and the strongest that are crowned but those who compete (for it is some of these that are victorious), so those who act rightly win the noble and good things in life.

Their life is also in itself pleasant. For pleasure is a state of soul, and to each man that which he is said to be a lover of is pleasant; e.g. not only is a horse pleasant to the lover of horses, and a spectacle to the lover of sights, but also in the same way just acts are pleasant to the lover of justice and in general excellent acts to the lover of excellence. Now for most men their pleasures are in conflict with one another because these are not by nature pleasant, but the lovers of what is noble find pleasant the things that are by nature pleasant; and excellent actions are such, so that these are pleasant for such men as well as in their own nature. Their life, therefore, has no further need of pleasure as a sort of adventitious charm, but has its pleasure in itself. For, besides what we have said, the man who does not rejoice in noble actions is not good at all; for no one would call a man just who did not enjoy acting justly, nor any man liberal who did not enjoy liberal actions; and similarly in all other cases. If this is so, excellent actions must be in themselves pleasant. But they are also *good* and *noble*, and have each of these attributes in the highest degree, since the good man judges well about these attributes and he judges in the way we have described. Happiness then is the best, noblest, and most pleasant thing, and these attributes are not severed as in the inscription at Delos— 10

> Most noble is that which is justest, and best is health;
> But pleasantest is it to win what we love.

For all these properties belong to the best activities; and these, or one—the best—of these, we identify with happiness.

Yet evidently, as we said, it needs the external goods as well; for it is impossible, or not easy, to do noble acts without the proper equipment. In many actions we use friends and riches and political power as instruments; and there are some things the lack of which takes the lustre from blessedness, as good birth, satisfactory children, beauty; for the man who is very ugly in appearance or ill-born or solitary and childless is hardly happy, and perhaps a man would be still less so if he had thoroughly bad children or friends or had lost good children or friends by death. As we said, then, happiness seems to need this sort of prosperity in addition; for which reason some identify happiness with good fortune, though others identify it with excellence.

Understanding the Text

1. The Greek word that Aristotle uses, *eudaemonia*, is translated as "happiness" here. But the concept of *eudaemonia* may have somewhat different connotations when we talk about "happiness" today — as, for example, when we wish someone a "happy birthday." Based on a careful reading of this selection, how is *eudaemonia* compared to the typical American notion of happiness? For example, does happiness seem to be something internal — a feeling — for Aristotle? Or something external? Something permanent or something temporary? Something objective or something subjective?
2. Why do you think Aristotle claims, "[W]e must add 'in a complete life'" (par. 6)? Why must a life, in his view, be "complete" before a person can be declared "blessed and happy"?
3. Aristotle reasons logically, starting from certain premises — statements that function as basic starting points — and he works out conclusions that follow from these premises. What are the premises of his argument? What basic assumptions about our human nature, our possibilities, our purposes, our aims, our situation, and so on, does he begin from?

Reflection and Response

4. Aristotle identifies three different ways of living a good and happy life: a life of pleasure, a life of politics, and a life of philosophy. What are the advantages and disadvantages of each, in Aristotle's view? How would you respond to this analysis?
5. According to Aristotle, what role do material wealth and temporary pleasure play in the achievement of true happiness? How does he explain and justify his view of the place of these good things in relation to other good things?

Making Connections

6. Consider the applicability of Aristotle's view of happiness to our current cultural situation. Using Gretchen Rubin's essay "July: Buy Some Happiness" (p. 291) as a source, discuss how Aristotle might complicate or confirm her understanding of happiness.
7. Rubin offers a weekly column for her readers on her blog. Write two entries for your own "column" in which you speak as if you are Aristotle offering advice to his readers. (Don't worry about sounding like Aristotle so much as using his ideas.)

From The Handbook of Epictetus

Epictetus*

The Stoic philosopher Epictetus (55–135 CE) was born a slave, but his wealthy master, himself a former slave, allowed Epictetus to study philosophy. In 93 CE, the emperor banished all philosophers from Rome, and Epictetus fled to Nicopolis in Greece, where he remained for the rest of his life. His teachings were written down by his pupil, Arrian.

Stoicism was a school of philosophy founded in Athens by Zeno of Citium in about 300 BCE. By the time of Epictetus's birth, it was already one of the most influential philosophies in the Roman world, and Epictetus became its most renowned teacher, by virtue of both his example and his words. Stoics believed that, because we cannot control what happens to us, the wise course is to control our thoughts and emotions and cultivate a steady and dispassionate mental attitude. Since riches only burden life with complications, Epictetus lived simply with few material goods. In old age, he married and then adopted a son. The following is a selection from the *Encheiridion*, or "Handbook," a brief compilation of practical advice.

1. Some things are up to us and some are not up to us. Our opinions are up to us, and our impulses, desires, aversions—in short, whatever is our own doing. Our bodies are not up to us, nor are our possessions, our reputations, or our public offices, or, that is, whatever is not our own doing. The things that are up to us are by nature free, unhindered, and unimpeded; the things that are not up to us are weak, enslaved, hindered, not our own. So remember, if you think that things naturally enslaved are free or that things not your own are your own, you will be thwarted, miserable, and upset, and will blame both gods and men. But if you think that only what is yours is yours, and that what is not your own is, just as it is, not your own, then no one will ever coerce you, no one will hinder you, you will blame no one, you will not accuse anyone, you will not do a single thing unwillingly, you will have no enemies, and no one will harm you, because you will not be harmed at all.

As you aim for such great goals, remember that you must not undertake them by acting moderately,[1] but must let some things go completely

*Translator: Nicholas P. White.

[1]This may mean simply that the proposed undertaking is difficult . . . , or it may mean (as I believe) that the aim cannot be achieved by the Aristotelian policy of pursuing a mean or middle course between extremes.

and postpone others for the time being. But if you want both those great goals and also to hold public office and to be rich, then you may perhaps not get even the latter just because you aim at the former too; and you certainly will fail to get the former, which are the only things that yield freedom and happiness.[2]

From the start, then, work on saying to each harsh appearance,[3] "You are an appearance, and not at all the thing that has the appearance." Then examine it and assess it by these yardsticks that you have, and first and foremost by whether it concerns the things that are up to us or the things that are not up to us. And if it is about one of the things that is not up to us, be ready to say, "You are nothing in relation to me."

2. Remember, what a desire proposes is that you gain what you desire, and what an aversion proposes is that you not fall into what you are averse to. Someone who fails to get what he desires is *un*fortunate, while someone who falls into what he is averse to has met *mis*fortune. So if you are averse only to what is against nature among the things that are up to you, then you will never fall into anything that you are averse to; but if you are averse to illness or death or poverty, you will meet misfortune. So detach your aversion from everything not up to us, and transfer it to what is against nature among the things that are up to us. And for the time being eliminate desire completely, since if you desire something that is not up to us, you are bound to be unfortunate, and at the same time none of the things that are up to us, which it would be good to desire, will be available to you. Make use only of impulse and its contrary, rejection,[4] though with reservation, lightly, and without straining.

3. In the case of everything attractive or useful or that you are fond of, remember to say just what sort of thing it is, beginning with the least little things. If you are fond of a jug, say "I am fond of a jug!" For then when it is broken you will not be upset. If you kiss your child or your 5

[2]Epictetus recommends aiming to have one's state of mind in accord with nature, in the sense explained in the previous paragraph. . . . His point here is that if you aim for that and also simultaneously for certain "externals" like wealth, you will probably have neither and clearly will not have the former.

[3]The word "appearance" translates *phantasia*, which some translators render by "impression" or "presentation." An appearance is roughly the immediate experience of sense or feeling, which may or may not represent an external state of affairs. (The Stoics held, against the Sceptics, that some appearances self-evidently do represent external states of affairs correctly.)

[4]Impulse and rejection (*hormē* and *aphormē*) are, in Stoic terms, natural and non-rational psychological movements, so to speak, that are respectively toward or away from external objects.

wife, say that you are kissing a human being; for when it dies you will not be upset.

4. When you are about to undertake some action, remind yourself what sort of action it is. If you are going out for a bath, put before your mind what happens at baths—there are people who splash, people who jostle, people who are insulting, people who steal. And you will undertake the action more securely if from the start you say of it, "I want to take a bath and to keep my choices in accord with nature"; and likewise for each action. For that way if something happens to interfere with your bathing you will be ready to say, "Oh, well, I wanted not only this but also to keep my choices in accord with nature, and I cannot do that if I am annoyed with things that happen."

5. What upsets people is not things themselves but their judgments about the things. For example, death is nothing dreadful (or else it would have appeared dreadful to Socrates),° but instead the judgment about death that it is dreadful—*that* is what is dreadful. So when we are thwarted or upset or distressed, let us never blame someone else but rather ourselves, that is, our own judgments. An uneducated person accuses others when he is doing badly; a partly educated person accuses himself, an educated person accuses neither someone else nor himself.

6. Do not be joyful about any superiority that is not your own. If the horse were to say joyfully, "I am beautiful," one could put up with it. But certainly you, when you say joyfully, "I have a beautiful horse," are joyful about the good of the horse. What, then, is your own? Your way of dealing with appearances. So whenever you are in accord with nature in your way of dealing with appearances, then be joyful, since then you are joyful about a good of your own. . . .

17. Remember that you are an actor in a play, which is as the playwright wants it to be: short if he wants it short, long if he wants it long. If he wants you to play a beggar, play even this part skillfully, or a cripple, or a public official, or a private citizen. What is yours is to play the assigned part well. But to choose it belongs to someone else. . . .

21. Let death and exile and everything that is terrible appear before your eyes every day, especially death; and you will never have anything contemptible in your thoughts or crave anything excessively. . . . 10

Socrates (470/469 BCE–399 BCE): Greek philosopher who was held in the highest esteem not only as a thinker but also as a model of conduct.

According to Socrates, "The unexamined life is not worth living."
ScienceCartoonsPlus.com

27. Just as a target is not set up to be missed, in the same way nothing bad by nature happens in the world.[5]

28. If someone turned your body over to just any person who happened to meet you, you would be angry. But are you not ashamed that you turn over your own faculty of judgment to whoever happens along, so that if he abuses you it is upset and confused?

29. For each action, consider what leads up to it and what follows it, and approach it in the light of that. Otherwise you will come to it enthusiastically at first, since you have not borne in mind any of what will happen next, but later when difficulties turn up you will give up disgracefully. You want to win an Olympic victory? I do too, by the gods, since that is a fine thing. But consider what leads up to it and what follows it, and undertake the action in the light of that. You must be disciplined, keep a strict diet, stay away from cakes, train according to strict routine at a fixed time in heat and in cold, not drink cold water, not drink wine when you feel like it, and in general you must have turned yourself over

[5]According to the Stoic view, the universe as a whole is perfect . . . , and everything in it has a place in its overall design, so that nothing can exist or occur that is bad in its relation to that overall design.

to your trainer as to a doctor, and then in the contest "dig in,"[6] sometimes dislocate your hand, twist your ankle, swallow a lot of sand, sometimes be whipped, and, after all that, lose. Think about that and then undertake training, if you want to. Otherwise you will be behaving the way children do, who play wrestlers one time, gladiators another time, blow trumpets another time, then act a play. In this way you too are now an athlete, now a gladiator, then an orator, then a philosopher, yet you are nothing wholeheartedly, but like a monkey you mimic each sight that you see, and one thing after another is to your taste, since you do not undertake a thing after considering it from every side, but only randomly and half-heartedly.

In the same way when some people watch a philosopher and hear one speaking like Euphrates[7] (though after all who can speak like him?), they want to be philosophers themselves. Just you consider, as a human being, what sort of thing it is; then inspect your own nature and whether you can bear it. You want to do the pentathlon,° or to wrestle? Look at your arms, your thighs, inspect your loins. Different people are naturally suited for different things. Do you think that if you do those things you can eat as you now do, drink as you now do, have the same likes and dislikes? You must go without sleep, put up with hardship, be away from your own people, be looked down on by a little slave boy, be laughed at by people who meet you, get the worse of it in everything, honor, public office, law course, every little thing. Think about whether you want to exchange these things for tranquillity, freedom, calm. If not, do not embrace philosophy, and do not like children be a philosopher at one time, later a tax-collector, then an orator, then a procurator° of the emperor. These things do not go together. You must be one person, either good or bad. You must either work on your ruling principle,[8] or work on

"Do not like children be a philosopher at one time, later a tax-collector, then an orator, then a procurator of the emperor. These things do not go together. You must be one person."

pentathlon: an athletic event comprising five contests: jumping, running, discus-throwing, spear-throwing, and wrestling.
procurator: a financial administrator or officer.

[6]Nobody knows just what this expression means in this context.
[7]Euphrates was a Stoic lecturer noted for his eloquence.
[8]The "ruling principle" (or "governing principle"), the *hēgemonikon*, in the rather complicated psychological theory adopted by the Stoics, is that central part of the soul that can understand what is good and decide to act on that understanding.

externals, practice the art either of what is inside or of what is outside, that is, play the role either of a philosopher or of a non-philosopher.

30. Appropriate actions[9] are in general measured by relationships. He is a father: that entails taking care of him, yielding to him in everything, putting up with him when he abuses you or strikes you. "But he is a bad father." Does nature then determine that you have a good father? No, only that you have a father.[10] "My brother has done me wrong." Then keep your place in relation to him; do not consider his action, but instead consider what you can do to bring your own faculty of choice into accord with nature. Another person will not do you harm unless you wish it; you will be harmed at just that time at which you take yourself to be harmed. In this way, then, you will discover the appropriate actions to expect from a neighbor, from a citizen, from a general, if you are in the habit of looking at relationships. . . . 15

46. Never call yourself a philosopher and do not talk a great deal among non-philosophers about philosophical propositions, but do what follows from them. For example, at a banquet do not say how a person ought to eat, but eat as a person ought to. Remember that Socrates had so completely put aside ostentation that people actually went to him when they wanted to be introduced to philosophers, and he took them.[11] He was that tolerant of being overlooked. And if talk about philosophical propositions arises among non-philosophers, for the most part be silent, since there is a great danger of your spewing out what you have not digested. And when someone says to you that you know nothing and you are not hurt by it, then you know that you are making a start at your task. Sheep do not show how much they have eaten by bringing the feed to the shepherds, but they digest the food inside themselves, and outside themselves they bear wool and milk. So in your case likewise do not display propositions to non-philosophers but instead the actions that come from the propositions when they are digested. . . .

48. The position and character of a non-philosopher: he never looks for benefit or harm to come from himself but from things outside. The

[9]"Appropriate actions" are *kathēkonta,* which Cicero called *officia,* and are in English translations often called "duties," though the notion is actually somewhat different from that of duty. They are the actions that are of a type generally in accord with nature, or with a particular sort of person's place in it.

[10]The idea here is, roughly, that there are certain relationships of affinity established by the natural order, and that having a father represents one of them, but that having a good father is not entailed by it.

[11]The allusion is perhaps to the events in the early part of Plato's *Protagoras.*

position and character of a philosopher: he looks for all benefit and harm to come from himself.

Signs of someone's making progress: he censures no one; he praises no one; he blames no one; he never talks about himself as a person who amounts to something or knows something. When he is thwarted or prevented in something, he accuses himself. And if someone praises him he laughs to himself at the person who has praised him; and if someone censures him he does not respond. He goes around like an invalid, careful not to move any of his parts that are healing before they have become firm. He has kept off all desire from himself, and he has transferred all aversion onto what is against nature among the things that are up to us. His impulses toward everything are diminished. If he seems foolish or ignorant, he does not care. In a single phrase, he is on guard against himself as an enemy lying in wait.

Understanding the Text

1. Epictetus makes clear but complicated distinctions between ownership and freedom. Cite and evaluate his claims about slavery, ownership, and freedom.
2. Read the last paragraph about how we might identify "signs of . . . progress." How does the last sentence relate to the rest of the paragraph? What is progress, really, for Epictetus?
3. Epictetus spends a good deal of time on what is up to us and what is not up to us. What are the things Epictetus believes are and are not up to us? Do you agree with him? Why or why not?

Reflection and Response

4. Although he advises us to pursue what we want "without straining" (par. 4), Epictetus also claims that we cannot be moderate as we pursue our goals. Is this a contradiction? How does his theory of the process of self-improvement correspond to his notion of what real progress is?
5. Epictetus holds strong views of how we should consider our relationships to others. Citing three examples of your own recent writing from a social media site of your choice, consider whether you follow his advice about relating to others.
6. Much of this selection urges us to make choices "in accord with nature" (par. 6). Citing examples from the text, explain what Epictetus means by this. Is his argument still relevant today?

Making Connections

7. Epictetus argues that we should eliminate desire completely if we are to be happy. How does his claim relate to the *Tao Te Ching* (p. 10) and the *Bhagavad Gita* (p. 67)?

8. Consider the applicability of Epictetus's view of happiness to our current cultural situation. Using Stefan Klein's "Enjoyment" (p. 198) as a source, discuss how Epictetus might complicate or confirm Klein's understanding of happiness.
9. Write a letter from C. S. Lewis ("We Have No Right to Happiness," p. 227) to Epictetus in which Lewis evaluates and responds to Epictetus's argument. Cite both essays as you construct the letter.

Paradise Glossed

Daniel Gilbert

Daniel Gilbert (born 1957) is Edgar Pierce Professor of Psychology at Harvard University, where he has taught since 1996. He has authored or coauthored more than 100 academic articles, but he is widely known as the author of the bestseller *Stumbling on Happiness* (2005) and as cowriter and host of the NOVA television series *This Emotional Life*, which aired on PBS in 2010. Much of Gilbert's research focuses on "affective forecasting" — that is, the way we predict or imagine the impact of events on our emotional state (for example, how much happier would I be if I won the lottery, or how much unhappier would I be if I lost my job?). Gilbert has taken a special interest in the role of cognitive bias in affective forecasting. The following selection from *Stumbling on Happiness* argues that the way we interpret reality, even the way we delude ourselves, plays an essential role in our sense of happiness.

> For there is nothing either good or bad, but thinking makes it so.
>
> —SHAKESPEARE, *HAMLET PRINCE OF DENMARK*

Forget yoga. Forget liposuction. And forget those herbal supplements that promise to improve your memory, enhance your mood, reduce your waistline, restore your hairline, prolong your lovemaking, and improve your memory. If you want to be happy and healthy, you should try a new technique that has the power to transform the grumpy, underpaid chump you are now into the deeply fulfilled, enlightened individual you've always hoped to be. If you don't believe me, then just consider the testimony of some folks who've tried it:

- "I am so much better off physically, financially, mentally, and in almost every other way." (*JW from Texas*)
- "It was a glorious experience." (*MB from Louisiana*)
- "I didn't appreciate others nearly as much as I do now." (*CR from California*)

Who are these satisfied customers, and what is the miraculous technique they're all talking about? Jim Wright, former Speaker of the United States House of Representatives, made his remark after committing sixty-nine ethics violations and being forced to resign in disgrace. Moreese Bickham, a former inmate, made his remark upon being released from the Louisiana State Penitentiary where he'd served thirty-seven years for defending himself against the Ku Klux Klansmen who'd shot him. And Christopher

Reeve, the dashing star of *Superman*, made his remark after an equestrian accident left him paralyzed from the neck down, unable to breathe without the help of a ventilator. The moral of the story? If you want to be happy, healthy, wealthy, and wise, then skip the vitamin pills and the plastic surgeries and try public humiliation, unjust incarceration, or quadriplegia instead.

Uh-huh. Right. Are we really supposed to believe that people who lose their jobs, their freedom, and their mobility are somehow *improved* by the tragedies that befall them? If that strikes you as a far-fetched possibility, then you are not alone. For at least a century, psychologists have assumed that terrible events—such as having a loved one die or becoming the victim of a violent crime—must have a powerful, devastating, and enduring impact on those who experience them. This assumption has been so deeply embedded in our conventional wisdom that people who *don't* have dire reactions to events such as these are sometimes diagnosed as having a pathological condition known as "absent grief." But recent research suggests that the conventional wisdom is wrong, that the absence of grief is quite normal, and that rather than being the fragile flowers that a century of psychologists have made us out to be, most people are surprisingly resilient in the face of trauma. The loss of a parent or spouse is usually sad and often tragic, and it would be perverse to suggest otherwise. But the fact is that while most bereaved people are quite sad for a while, very few become chronically depressed and most experience relatively low levels of relatively short-lived distress. Although more than half the people in the United States will experience a trauma such as rape, physical assault, or natural disaster in their lifetimes, only a small fraction will ever develop any post-traumatic pathology or require any professional assistance. As one group of researchers noted, "Resilience is often the most commonly observed outcome trajectory following exposure to a potentially traumatic event." Indeed, studies of those who survive major traumas suggest that the vast majority do quite well, and that a significant portion claim that their lives were *enhanced* by the experience. I know, I know. It sounds suspiciously like the title of a country song, but the fact is that most folks do pretty darn good when things go pretty darn bad.

> "Rather than being the fragile flowers that a century of psychologists have made us out to be, most people are surprisingly resilient in the face of trauma."

If resilience is all around us, then why are statistics such as these so surprising? Why do most of us find it difficult to believe that *we* could ever consider a lifetime behind bars to be "a glorious experience" or come to see paralysis as "a unique opportunity" that gave "a new direction" to our lives? Why do most of us shake our heads in disbelief when an athlete who has been through several grueling years of chemotherapy tells us that "I wouldn't change anything," or when a musician who has become permanently disabled says, "If I had it to do all over again, I would want it to happen the same way," or when quadriplegics and paraplegics tell us that they are pretty much as happy as everyone else? The claims made by people who have experienced events such as these seem frankly outlandish to those of us who are merely imagining those events—and yet, who are we to argue with the folks who've actually been there?

The fact is that negative events do affect us, but they generally don't affect us as much or for as long as we expect them to. When people are asked to predict how they'll feel if they lose a job or a romantic partner, if their candidate loses an important election or their team loses an important game, if they flub an interview, flunk an exam, or fail a contest, they consistently overestimate how awful they'll feel and how long they'll feel awful. Able-bodied people are willing to pay far more to avoid becoming disabled than disabled people are willing to pay to become able-bodied again because able-bodied people underestimate how happy disabled people are. As one group of researchers noted, "Chronically ill and disabled patients generally rate the value of their lives in a given health state more highly than do hypothetical patients [who are] imagining themselves to be in such states." Indeed, healthy people imagine that eighty-three states of illness would be "worse than death," and yet, people who are actually in those states rarely take their own lives. If negative events don't hit us as hard as we expect them to, then why do we expect them to? If heartbreaks and calamities can be blessings in disguise, then why are their disguises so convincing? The answer is that the human mind tends to *exploit ambiguity*—and if that phrase seems ambiguous to you, then just keep reading and let me exploit it.

Stop Annoying People

The only thing more difficult than finding a needle in a haystack is finding a needle in a needlestack. When an object is surrounded by similar objects it naturally blends in, and when it is surrounded by dissimilar objects it naturally stands out. Look at figure 2.1. If you had a stopwatch that counted milliseconds, you'd find that you can locate the letter *O* in the array on the top (where it is surrounded by numbers) a bit more quickly than you can locate it in the array on the bottom (where it is surrounded by other letters). And that makes sense, because it is harder to 5

1	5	9	3	1	5	4	4	2	9
6	8	4	2	1	6	2	2	3	3
9	2	7	6	9	7	5	5	1	1
5	3	7	2	7	6	2	7	8	9
3	7	5	9	6	8	8	2	9	8
4	8	3	1	2	1	6	8	1	8
4	3	4	2	3	9	1	7	O	9
6	2	4	1	8	6	7	5	2	3
7	6	4	2	9	6	5	4	4	5
9	5	2	3	6	7	8	4	5	3

L	G	V	C	L	G	E	E	P	V
I	T	E	P	L	I	P	P	C	C
V	Q	R	I	V	R	G	G	L	L
G	C	R	P	R	I	P	R	T	V
C	R	G	V	I	T	T	P	V	T
E	T	C	L	P	L	I	T	L	T
E	C	E	P	C	V	L	R	O	V
I	P	E	L	T	I	R	G	P	C
R	I	E	P	V	I	G	E	E	G
V	G	Q	C	I	R	T	E	G	C

Figure 2.1

find a letter among letters than a letter among numbers. And yet, had I asked you to look for "zero" instead of "the letter *O*," you would have been a bit faster to find it in the array at the bottom than in the array at the top. Now, most of us think that a basic sensory ability such as vision is pretty well explained by its wiring, and if you wanted to understand this ability, you would do well to learn about luminance, contrast, rods, cones, optic nerves, retinas, and the like. But once you knew everything there was to know about the physical properties of the arrays shown in figure 2.1 and everything there was to know about the anatomy of the human eye, you would still not be able to explain why a person can find the circle more quickly in one case than in the other unless you also knew what that person thought the circle *meant*.

Meanings matter for even the most basic psychological processes, and while this may seem perfectly obvious to reasonable folks like you and me, ignorance of this perfectly obvious fact sent psychologists on a wild-goose chase that lasted nearly thirty years and produced relatively few geese. For much of the last half of the twentieth century, experimental psychologists timed rats as they ran mazes and observed pigeons as they

THE
CAT

Figure 2.2 **The middle shape has different meanings in different contexts.**

pecked keys because they believed that the best way to understand behavior was to map the relation between a stimulus and an organism's response to that stimulus. By carefully measuring what an organism did when it was presented with a physical stimulus, such as a light, a sound, or a piece of food, psychologists hoped to develop a science that linked observable stimuli to observable behavior without using vague and squishy concepts such as *meaning* to connect them. Alas, this simpleminded project was doomed from the start, because while rats and pigeons may respond to stimuli as they are *presented* in the world, people respond to stimuli as they are *represented* in the mind. Objective stimuli in the world create subjective stimuli in the mind, and it is these subjective stimuli to which people react. For instance, the middle letters in the two words in figure 2.2 are physically identical stimuli (I promise—I cut and pasted them myself), and yet, most English speakers respond to them differently—see them differently, pronounce them differently, remember them differently—because one represents the letter *H* and the other represents the letter *A*. Indeed, it would be more appropriate to say that one *is* the letter *H* and the other *is* the letter *A* because the identity of an inky squiggle has less to do with how it is objectively constructed and more to do with *how we subjectively interpret it*. Two vertical lines with a crossbar *mean* one thing when flanked by *T* and *E* and they *mean* another thing when flanked by *C* and *T*, and one of the many things that distinguishes us from rats and pigeons is that we respond to the *meanings* of such stimuli and not to the stimuli themselves. That's why my father can get away with calling me "doodlebug" and you can't.

Disambiguating Objects

Most stimuli are ambiguous—that is, they can mean more than one thing—and the interesting question is how we *disambiguate* them—that is, how we know which of a stimulus's many meanings to infer on a particular occasion. Research shows that *context, frequency,* and *recency* are especially important in this regard.

- Consider *context*. The word *bank* has two meanings in English: "a place where money is kept" and "the land on either side of a river." Yet we never misunderstand sentences such as "The boat ran into the bank" or "The robber ran into the bank" because the words *boat* and *robber* provide a context that tells us which of the two meanings of *bank* we should infer in each case.
- Consider *frequency*. Our past encounters with a stimulus provide information about which of its meanings we should embrace. For example, a loan officer is likely to interpret the sentence "Don't run into the bank" as a warning about how to ambulate through his place of business and not as sound advice about the steering of boats because in the course of a typical day the loan officer hears the word *bank* used more frequently in its financial than in its maritime sense.
- Consider *recency*. Even a boater is likely to interpret the sentence "Don't run into the bank" as a reference to a financial institution rather than a river's edge if she recently saw an ad for safe-deposit boxes and thus has the financial meaning of *bank* still active in her mind. Indeed, because I've been talking about banks in this paragraph, I am willing to bet that the sentence "He put a check in the box" causes you to generate a mental image of someone placing a piece of paper in a receptacle and not a mental image of someone making a mark on a questionnaire. (I'm also willing to guess that your interpretation of the title of this section depends on whether you annoyed someone more or less recently than someone annoyed you.)

Unlike rats and pigeons, then, we respond to meanings—and context, frequency, and recency are three of the factors that determine which meaning we will infer when we encounter an ambiguous stimulus. But there is another factor of equal importance and greater interest. Like rats and pigeons, each of us has desires, wishes, and needs. We are not merely spectators of the world but investors in it, and we often *prefer* that an ambiguous stimulus mean one thing rather than another. Consider, for example, the drawing of a box in figure 2.3. This object (called the Necker cube after the Swiss crystallographer who discovered it in 1832) is inherently ambiguous, and you can prove this to yourself simply by staring at it for a few seconds. At first, the box appears to be sitting on its side

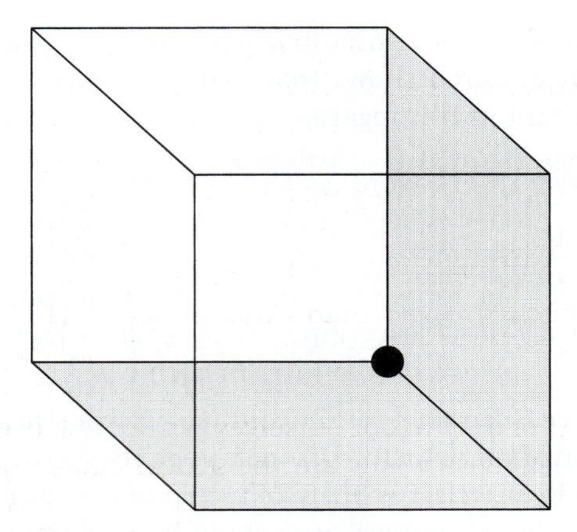

Figure 2.3 **If you stare at a Necker cube, it will appear to shift its orientation.**

and you have the sense that you're looking out at a box that is *across* from you. The dot is inside the box, at the place where the back panel and the bottom panel meet. But if you stare long enough, the drawing suddenly shifts, the box appears to be standing on its end, and you have the sense that you're looking down on a box that is *below* you. The dot is now perched on the upper right corner of the box. Because this drawing has two equally meaningful interpretations, your brain merrily switches back and forth between them, keeping you mildly entertained until you eventually get dizzy and fall down. But what if one of these meanings were better than the other? That is, what if you *preferred* one of the interpretations of this object? Experiments show that when subjects are rewarded for seeing the box across from them or below them, the orientation for which they were rewarded starts "popping out" more often and their brains "hold on" to that interpretation without switching. In other words, when your brain is at liberty to interpret a stimulus in more than one way, it tends to interpret it the way it *wants* to, which is to say that your preferences influence your interpretations of stimuli in just the same way that context, frequency, and recency do.

This phenomenon is not limited to the interpretation of weird drawings. For example, why is it that you think of yourself as a talented person? (C'mon, give it up. You know you do.) To answer this question, researchers asked some volunteers (definers) to write down their definition of *talented* and then to estimate their talent using that definition as a guide. Next, some other volunteers (nondefiners) were given the definitions that the first group had written down and were asked to estimate their own talent using those definitions as a guide. Interestingly, the definers rated themselves as more talented than the nondefiners did. Because definers were given the liberty to define the word *talented* any way they wished, they defined it *exactly* the way they wished—namely, in terms of some activity at which they just so happened to excel ("I think *talent* usually refers to *exceptional artistic achievement* like, for example, this painting I just finished," or "*Talent* means *an ability you're born with,* such as being much stronger than other people. Shall I put you down now?"). Definers were able to set the standards for talent, and not coincidentally, they were more likely to meet the standards they set. One of the reasons why most of us think of ourselves as talented, friendly, wise, and fair-minded is that these words are the lexical equivalents of a Necker cube, and the human mind naturally exploits each word's ambiguity for its own gratification.

Disambiguating Experience

10 Of course, the richest sources of exploitable ambiguity are not words, sentences, or shapes but the intricate, variegated, multi-dimensional *experiences* of which every human life is a collage. If a Necker cube has two possible interpretations and *talent* has fourteen possible interpretations, then *leaving home* or *falling ill* or *getting a job with the U.S. Postal Service* has hundreds or thousands of possible interpretations. The things that *happen* to us—getting married, raising a child, finding a job, resigning from Congress, going to prison, becoming paralyzed—are much more complex than an inky squiggle or a colored cube, and that complexity creates loads of ambiguity that just begs to be exploited. It doesn't have to beg hard. For example, volunteers in one study were told that they would be eating a delicious but unhealthy ice cream sundae (ice cream eaters), and others were told that they would be eating a bitter but healthful plate of fresh kale (kale eaters). Before actually eating these foods, the researchers asked the volunteers to rate the similarity of a number of foods, including ice cream sundaes, kale, and Spam (which everyone considered both unpalatable and unhealthful). The results showed that ice cream eaters thought that Spam was more like kale than it was like ice cream. Why? Because for some odd reason, ice cream eaters were thinking about food in terms of its *taste*—and unlike kale and Spam, ice cream tastes delicious. On the other hand, kale eaters thought that Spam was more like ice cream than it was like kale. Why? Because for some odd reason, kale eaters were thinking about food in terms of its *healthfulness*—and unlike kale, ice cream and Spam are unhealthful. The odd reason isn't really so odd. Just as a Necker cube is both across from you and below you, ice cream is both fattening and tasty, and kale is

both healthful and bitter. Your brain and my brain easily jump back and forth between these different ways of thinking about the foods because we are merely reading about them. But if we were preparing to *eat* one of them, our brains would automatically exploit the ambiguity of that food's identity and allow us to think of it in a way that pleased us (delicious dessert or nutritious veggie) rather than a way that did not (fattening dessert or bitter veggie). As soon as our *potential* experience becomes our *actual* experience—as soon as we have a stake in its goodness—our brains get busy looking for ways to think about the experience that will allow us to appreciate it.

Because experiences are inherently ambiguous, finding a "positive view" of an experience is often as simple as finding the "below-you view" of a Necker cube, and research shows that most people do this well and often. Consumers evaluate kitchen appliances more positively after they buy them, job seekers evaluate jobs more positively after they accept them, and high school students evaluate colleges more positively after they get into them. Racetrack gamblers evaluate their horses more positively when they are leaving the betting window than when they are approaching it, and voters evaluate their candidates more positively when they are exiting the voting booth than when they are entering it. A toaster, a firm, a university, a horse, and a senator are all just fine and dandy, but when they become *our* toaster, firm, university, horse, and senator they are instantly finer and dandier. Studies such as these suggest that people are quite adept at finding a positive way to view things once those things become their own.

Understanding the Text

1. What common understandings of human behavior does this essay seek to displace? What is the "real story," in Gilbert's opinion? Make a chart of the misunderstandings that Gilbert exposes and highlight the explanations of the facts as he understands them. In your view, how accurate is Gilbert's opinion?
2. Gilbert discusses meaning making from a variety of perspectives. Discuss in greater detail the similarities and differences among these perspectives. What kinds of variables might we consider as we think about several problems humans experience today? Which variables are the simplest, and which are more complex?

Reflection and Response

3. Gilbert inserts graphics to teach about human perception. First, look at these graphics. What is each meant to illuminate with regard to the main thesis of this selection? Then write an essay about perception in which you

include three graphics of your own to illustrate the truth about our ways of perceiving happiness. You may borrow a graphic from another text, but be sure to cite the source.

4. How does Gilbert differentiate between what is happening now and what might happen in the future? What would you do if you were to take his advice about the next ten years of your life? Use quotations from his essay as jumping-off points to considering your future happiness.

Making Connections

5. Write an essay about the relationships between ownership and meaning. In addition to your own opinion, use the arguments presented by Gilbert, Ed Diener and Martin Seligman ("Very Happy People," p. 210), and C. S. Lewis ("We Have No Right to Happiness," p. 227) as supporting evidence. Discuss the similarities and differences among these ways of approaching the discussion regarding ownership and meaning. To what extent do these arguments intersect with your own opinion?
6. Consider Noelle Oxenhandler's "Ah, But the Breezes . . ." (p. 314) as a dialogue with Gilbert's essay. How does her essay connect with Gilbert's concepts? In your view, would Oxenhandler challenge Gilbert? Or, similarly, would Gilbert challenge her in any way?
7. Gilbert opens with the example of people who should be less content than they are in reality. In doing so, he highlights several cultural conceptions of happiness. How might Gilbert's argument be considered in relation to Matthieu Ricard's in "The Alchemy of Suffering" (p. 34)? Write an essay in which you explore these authors' perspectives on the meanings of human suffering.

Who Is the Happy Warrior? Philosophy Poses Questions to Psychology

Martha C. Nussbaum

Martha Nussbaum (born 1947) is Ernst Freund Distinguished Service Professor of Law and Ethics in the Law School, Philosophy Department, and Divinity School at the University of Chicago. She earned her Ph.D. in philosophy from Harvard University in 1975. She holds more than fifty honorary degrees from universities around the world. She has published more than twenty-five books, including *The Fragility of Goodness: Luck and Ethics in Greek Tragedy and Philosophy* (2001) and *Not for Profit: Why Democracy Needs the Humanities* (2010). Her work addresses a wide range of philosophical and political questions, with an emphasis on the philosophy of ancient Greece and Rome, feminism, and ethics. The following essay, which takes its title from William Wordsworth's poem "Character of the Happy Warrior" (composed 1807), offers a philosophical critique of the concepts of happiness used by psychologists and social scientists.

> Who is the happy Warrior? Who is he
> That every man in arms should wish to be?
> [Wordsworth, "Character of the Happy Warrior," 1807]

> Man does not strive after happiness; only the Englishman does that. [Nietzsche, "Maxims and Arrows," 1889]

Psychology has recently focused attention on subjective states of pleasure, satisfaction, and what is called "happiness." The suggestion has been made in some quarters that a study of these subjective states has important implications for public policy. Sometimes, as in the case of Martin Seligman's "positive psychology" movement, attempts are made to link the empirical findings and the related normative judgments directly to the descriptive and normative insights of ancient Greek ethics and modern virtue ethics. At other times, as with Daniel Kahneman's work, the connection to Aristotle and other ancient Greek thinkers is only indirect, and the connection to British Utilitarianism is paramount; nonetheless, judgments are made that could be illuminated by an examination of the rich philosophical tradition that runs from Aristotle through to John Stuart Mill's criticisms of Bentham.°

The aim of my paper is to confront this increasingly influential movement within psychology with a range of questions from the side of philosophy. Often these questions have a very long history in the discipline, going back at least to Aristotle; the more thoughtful Utilitarians, above all Mill, also studied them in depth. Some of these questions are conceptual; others are normative. After going through quite a number of them, I will attempt to correct some misunderstandings, within this psychological literature, of my own "objective-list" conception and the role I think it ought to play in public policy. And I will say what I think some appropriate roles for subjective-state analysis in public policy might be.

Conceptual Issues

What Is Pleasure?

Psychologists often talk about pleasure, and also about subjects' hedonic state.° Too rarely, however, do they ask some very obvious questions about it that greatly affect any research program involving the concept. Two central questions are, is pleasure a single thing, varying only in intensity or duration, or is it plural, containing qualitative differences? And is it a sensation, or is it something more like a way of attending to the world, or even a way of being active?

Jeremy Bentham famously held that pleasure was a single sensation, varying only along the quantitative dimensions of intensity and duration (see my discussion in Nussbaum 2004). Modern psychology follows Bentham. Indeed, Kahneman explicitly traces his own conception of "hedonic flow" to Bentham (see, for example, Kahneman and Krueger 2006, p. 4). And yet, is Bentham correct? Does his account correctly capture the complexity of our experience of pleasures of many sorts? We speak of pleasure as a type of experience, but we also refer to activities as "my pleasures," saying things like, "My greatest pleasures are listening to Mahler° and eating steak." We also use verbal locutions, such as

Bentham: Jeremy Bentham (1748–1832), philosopher and founder of modern Utilitarianism, the view that the best course is the one that maximizes "utility," or the greatest benefit. John Stuart Mill (p. 123) accepted the Utilitarian view in general but was critical of some of Bentham's ideas.
hedonic state: the level of the subject's experience of pleasure.
Mahler: Gustav Mahler (1860–1911), Austrian composer, known especially for his ten symphonies.

"enjoying" and "taking delight in." (The ancient Greeks used such verbal locutions much more frequently than they used the noun.) Such ways of talking raise two questions: Is pleasure a sensation at all, if such very different experiences count as pleasures? And is it single? Could there be any one thing that both eating a steak and listening to Mahler's Tenth, that harrowing confrontation with grief and emptiness, have in common?

These questions were subtly discussed by Plato, Aristotle, and a whole line of subsequent philosophers.[1] Bentham simply ignores them. As Mill writes in his great essay "On Bentham," "Bentham failed in deriving light from other minds." For him, pleasure simply must be a single homogeneous sensation, containing no qualitative differences. The only variations in pleasure are quantitative. Pleasures can vary in intensity, duration, certainty or uncertainty, propinquicy or remoteness, and, finally, in causal properties (tendency to produce more pleasure, and so on). The apparent fact that pleasures differ in quality, that the pleasure of steak eating is quite different from the pleasure of listening to Mahler's Tenth, bothered Bentham not at all; he does not discuss such examples.

Perhaps the reason for this problem is that Bentham's deepest concern is with pain and suffering, and it is somewhat more plausible to think of pain as a unitary sensation varying only in intensity and duration. Even here, however, qualitative differences seem crucial: the pain of a headache is very different from the pain of losing a loved one to death. As Mill says, Bentham's view expresses "the empiricism of one who has had little experience"—either external, he adds, or internal, through the imagination.

Nor was Bentham worried about interpersonal comparisons, a problem on which economists in the Utilitarian tradition have spent great labor, and one that any program to use subjective satisfaction for public policy must face. For Bentham there was no such problem. When we move from one person to many people, we just add a new dimension of quantity. Right action is ultimately defined as that which produces the greatest pleasure for the greatest number. Moreover, Bentham sees no problem in extending the comparison class to the entire world of sentient animals. One of the most attractive aspects of his thought is its great compassion for the suffering of animals, which he took to be un-

[1] For one good philosophical overview, see Gosling and Taylor (1982); see also the excellent treatment in Taylor (1976). An admirable general philosophical discussion is Gosling (1969).

problematically comparable to human suffering.[2] This attractive aspect, however, is marred by his failure even to consider whether animal pains and pleasures are qualitatively different, in at least some respects, from human pains and pleasures.

What is appealing about Bentham's program is its focus on urgent needs of sentient beings for relief from suffering and its determination to take all suffering of all sentient beings into account. But Bentham cannot be said to have developed anything like a convincing account of pleasure and pain, far less of happiness. Because of his attachment to a strident simplicity, the view remains a sketch crying out for adequate philosophical development.

Modern philosophers starting off from the Greco-Roman tradition have noticed that already in that tradition there is a widespread sense that Bentham's sort of answer will not do. A proto-Benthamite answer is familiar, in views of hedonists such as Eudoxus[3] and the title character in Plato's *Philebus* who represented Eudoxus's position. But there is an equally widespread sense among the Greek thinkers that this view will not do. The young interlocutor Protarchus, in the *Philebus*, is quickly brought by Socrates to reject it: he sees that the sources of pleasure color the pleasure itself, and that the pleasure of philosophizing is just not the same qualitatively as the pleasure of eating and sex. (The name "Philebus" means "lover of young men," and the character is represented as using his unitary view of pleasure to seduce attractive youths.)[4]

Aristotle takes up where the *Philebus* left off. Throughout his work he insists on the tremendous importance of qualitative distinctions among the diverse constituent parts of human life; he later suggests that these distinctions affect the proper analysis of the concept of pleasure. Notoriously, however, he offers two very different conceptions of pleasure, one in book VII and one in book X of the *Nicomachean Ethics*. The first identifies pleasure with unimpeded activity (not so odd if we remember that we speak of "my pleasures" and "enjoyments"). The second, and probably better, account holds that pleasure is something that comes along with, supervenes on, activity, "like the bloom on the cheek of youth." In other words, it is so closely linked to the relevant activities that it cannot 10

[2]He denied that animals suffered at the very thought of death, and thus he argued that the painless killing of an animal is sometimes permitted.

[3]No writings of Eudoxus survive; we know his views through Aristotle's characterization of them in *Nicomachean Ethics* 1172b9 ff. and by reports of later doxographers; he is usually taken to be the inspiration for the title character in Plato's *Philebus*.

[4]In the Greek world, this would not mark him as depraved, only as greedy: he is the Greek equivalent of a womanizer.

be pursued on its own, any more than bloom can be adequately cultivated by cosmetics. To get that bloom you have to pursue health. Similarly, one gets the pleasure associated with an activity by doing that activity in a certain way, apparently a way that is not impeded or is complete. It would seem that what Aristotle has in mind is that pleasure is a kind of awareness of one's own activity, varying in quality with the activity to which it is so closely linked. In any case, pleasure is not a single thing, varying only in intensity and duration (the Eudoxan position). It contains qualitative differences, related to the differences of the activities to which it attaches.

J. S. Mill follows Aristotle. In a crucial discussion in *Utilitarianism*, he insists that "[n]either pains nor pleasures are homogenous." There are differences "*in kind*, apart from the question of intensity," that are evident to any competent judge. We cannot avoid recognizing qualitative differences, particularly between "higher" and "lower" pleasures. How, then, to judge between them? Like Plato in *Republic* book IX, Mill refers the choice to a competent judge who has experienced both alternatives.

This famous passage shows Mill thinking of pleasures as very like activities (with Aristotle in Book VII) or, with Aristotle in Book X, as experiences so closely linked to activities that they cannot be pursued apart from them. In a later text, he counts music, virtue, and health as major pleasures. Elsewhere he shows that he has not left sensation utterly out of account: he refers to "which of two modes of existence is the most grateful to the feelings." Clearly, however, the unity of the Benthamite calculus has been thrown out, to be replaced by a variegated conception, involving both sensation and activity, and prominently including qualitative distinctions. It is for this reason that philosophers today typically find Mill more subtle and conceptually satisfactory than Bentham.

Modern philosophical discussion of pleasure follows Aristotle and Mill. In one of the best recent accounts, J. C. B. Gosling's (1969) book *Pleasure and Desire*, Gosling investigates three different views of what pleasure is: the sensation view (Bentham/Eudoxus), the activity view (Aristotle's first account), and what he calls the "adverbial" view (pleasure is a particular way of being active, a view closely related to Aristotle's second account). Uneasily, with much uncertainty, he opts, with Aristotle, for the adverbial view.

Now it is obvious that such debates influence the ways in which one would study pleasure empirically. If Aristotle, Mill, and Gosling are correct, it would not make sense to ask people to rank all their pleasures along a single quantitative dimension: this is just bullying people into disregarding features of their own experience that reflection would quickly reveal. People are easily bullied, particularly by prominent psychologists, and so they do answer such questions, rather than respond, "This question is ill-formed." If Mill and Aristotle are right, however, they would quickly agree on reflection that qualitative differences matter.

Moreover, any experiment that simply assumes pleasure to be a hedonic state, something like a sensation, would also be inadequate, say Mill and Aristotle, to the complexity of human experience, since people agree that activity matters: they would not think that the pleasure derived from being plugged into Robert Nozick's "experience machine" was equivalent to a pleasure associated with actually doing the activity oneself (Nozick 1974, pp. 42–45). 15

What Is Satisfaction with One's Life as a Whole?

Some of the most influential experiments ask not about pleasure or hedonic flow, but about satisfaction with one's life as a whole. Typical is the question posed by Kahneman, "Taking all things together, how satisfied are you with *your life as a whole* these days? Are you very satisfied, satisfied, not very satisfied, not at all satisfied?" (Kahneman and Krueger 2006, p. 7 n. 2, emphasis in the original). Notice here the bullying we encountered before: people are simply told that they are to aggregate experiences of many different kinds into a single whole, and the authority of the questioner is put behind that aggregation. There is no opportunity for them to answer something plausible, such as, "Well, my health is good, and my work is going well, but I am very upset about the Iraq war, and one of my friends is very ill." Not only is that opportunity not provided, but, in addition, the prestige of science—indeed of the Nobel Prize itself—is put behind the instruction to reckon all life elements up as a single whole. The fact that people answer such questions hardly shows that this is the way that they experience their lives.

If we bracket that difficulty, however, we arrive at another one. There is a deep ambiguity about the question being asked. The psychologists who pose this question take the question to be a request for a report of a subjective state of satisfaction, which is at least closely akin to the feeling of pleasure. (Kahneman treats this question and the hedonic flow question, on the whole, as different ways of getting at the same thing.) One might indeed hear the question that way. But one might also hear it in a very different way, as a request for a reflective judgment about one's life, which judgment might or might not be accompanied by feelings of satisfaction, contentment, or pleasure.

Consider J. S. Mill's last words: "You know that I have done my work" (Packe 1954, p. 507). Now I would say that this is in one way an answer to the overall satisfaction question: Mill is reporting, we might say, satisfaction with his life as a whole. He has done what he aimed to do. And yet it seems highly unlikely that Mill, on his deathbed, suffering from physical pain and from the fear of death that he acknowledges not being able to get rid of, is experiencing feelings of satisfaction or pleasure. (Mill once reports that the one great attraction of a belief in a life after death [which he finds himself ultimately unable to accept] is the hope it yields of being reunited "with those dear to him who have ended their earthly life before him"—a loss, he continues, that "is neither to be denied nor extenuated" [Mill 1998, p. 120]. So he would no doubt be struggling, on his deathbed, with the eternal loss of Harriet° in addition to his own demise.) While judging that his life is on balance successful, he is almost certainly not experiencing feelings of satisfaction or pleasure.

Since the psychologists who work with this question do not notice this ambiguity, they do nothing to sort things out, so we do not really know which question their subjects are answering. Probably some are answering one question, some the other. What would be needed to progress would be conceptual work to separate the feeling-conception from the judgment-conception, and then a set of questions designed to tease apart those distinct notions.

In my own case, the ambiguity produces something like a contradiction. That is, my own conception of a good life attaches a great deal of value to striving, longing, and working for a difficult goal. So, if I ever notice myself feeling feelings of satisfaction, I blame myself and think that, insofar as I have those feelings, I am like Mill's "pig satisfied" or Aristotle's "dumb grazing animals," and thus, reflectively, I report dissatisfaction with my life as a whole. Nor do I think that I am an unusual case. As I have indicated, Mill's contrast between Socrates and the pig reveals similar values, and anyone whose culture is deeply influenced by romanticism, with its exaltation of longing and yearning (or, indeed, by the more romantic varieties of Christianity, such as Augustine's), would have the same difficulty: insofar as one is feeling satisfied, thus far one's life is not a success. That is what Nietzsche° is getting at in my epigraph: having feelings of satisfaction as a goal, he thinks, is a rather base thing, something that he associates with the impoverishment of English culture, as contrasted with German romanticism. Zarathustra, asked whether he is happy, responds, "Do I strive after happiness? I strive after

Harriet: Harriet Taylor Mill (1807–1858), Mill's wife and an important influence on his thinking.
Nietzsche: Friedrich Nietzsche (1844–1900), German philosopher, critic of Christianity, and author of *Beyond Good and Evil* (1886) and *Thus Spake Zarathustra* (1883–1885) among other works.

my works."[5] Schiller, Beethoven, and Mahler might have said that they were satisfied with their life as a whole—in the reflective-judgment sense. They probably, however, did not report many feelings of satisfaction, and they would have worried about themselves if they had had such feelings. (Indeed, Mahler's Resurrection Symphony revolves precisely around the contrast between the herdlike feeling of satisfaction and the more exalted judgment that one's whole life is rich and meaningful—because it is governed by an active kind of love. The former is represented by the swoopy, aimless clarinet phrases of the third movement, the latter by the passionate heartbeat that the final movement associates with the wings of the soul.)[6]

What Is Happiness?

Bentham simply identifies happiness with pleasure. Kahneman on the whole agrees with Bentham. Some psychologists are more subtle. Seligman's conception of authentic happiness, for example, involves both positive emotion and valuable activity (Seligman 2002). But (to return to my question about Socrates and the pig) how are these two constituents related? Are they both necessary for happiness and jointly sufficient? Is one more important than the other? And must the positive emotion be suitably linked to the good activity, a kind of taking delight in one's good activity?

Here is what Aristotle thought: that activity is far and away the main thing, and that pleasure will normally crop up in connection with doing good activities without struggle, the way a virtuous person does them. Pleasure accompanies activity, and completes it, like, he says, the bloom on the cheek of a healthy young person. That example implies, too, that it would be totally mistaken to pry the pleasure apart from the activity and seek it on its own: for it would then not be the bloom on the cheek of a healthy person, it would be the rouge on the cheek of a person who has not bothered to cultivate health. And Aristotle also thought that sometimes the pleasure would not arrive: for example, the courageous person who is about to lose his life in battle is happy, but has no pleasant emotion, because he is losing everything. Wordsworth's° very Aristotelian poem, "Character of the Happy Warrior," tells a similar tale, describing the "happy warrior" as "happy" because he is active in accordance with

Wordsworth: William Wordsworth (1770–1850), a major English Romantic poet.

[5]See the excellent treatment of this passage in Birault (1985).
[6]See my analysis of the symphony in Nussbaum (2001b).

all the virtues, and yet he has little if any pleasure, and a good deal of pain.

Wordsworth is a useful interlocutor at this point, because we can see that the Aristotelian idea was dominant until Bentham's influence dislodged it, changing the very way that many people, at least, hear the English word "happiness." So powerful was the obscuring power of Bentham's oversimplification that a question that Wordsworth takes to be altogether askable, and which, indeed, he spends 85 lines answering—the question what happiness really is—soon looks to philosophers under Bentham's influence like a question whose answer is so obvious that it cannot be asked in earnest. Thus early twentieth-century philosopher Henry Prichard, albeit a foe of Utilitarianism, was so influenced in his thinking about happiness by Bentham's conception that he simply assumed that any philosopher who talks about happiness must be identifying it with pleasure or satisfaction. When Aristotle asks what happiness is, Prichard argued, he cannot really be asking the question he appears to be asking, since the answer to that question is obvious: happiness is contentment or satisfaction. Instead of asking what happiness consists in, then, he must really be asking about the instrumental means to the production of happiness.[7] Nietzsche, similarly, understands happiness to be (uncontroversially) a state of pleasure and contentment, and expresses his scorn for Englishmen who pursue that goal, rather than richer goals involving suffering for a noble end, continued striving, activities that put contentment at risk, and so forth. Apparently unaware of the richer English tradition about happiness represented in Wordsworth's poem, he simply took English "happiness" to be what Bentham said it was. So, much later, did Finnish sociologist Erik Allardt, when he wrote an attack on the idea that happiness was the end of social planning, entitling his book *Having, Loving, Being*—active things that he took to be more important than satisfaction, which Finns, heir of Nordic romanticism, typically think quite unimportant (Allardt 1975).[8] Like Nietzsche, he understood the "happiness" of the social scientists to be a state of pleasure or satisfaction. (He is correct about the social scientists, if not about "happiness.")

[7]Prichard (1935), famously discussed and criticized in Austin (1979). My account of Prichard follows Austin's, including his (fair) account of Prichard's implicit premises.

[8]A brief summary of some of the argument in English can be found in Allardt (1993). (The original language of the book is Swedish because Allardt is a Swedish-speaking Finn.)

Aristotle's richer conception is still present in our lives, and we can see that ideas like Seligman's idea of authentic happiness capture something of its spirit.[9] According to this Aristotelian tradition, what we all can agree about is that happiness (*eudaimonia*) is something like flourishing human living, a kind of living that is active, inclusive of all that has intrinsic value, and complete, meaning lacking in nothing that would make it richer or better. Everything else about happiness is disputed, says Aristotle, but he then goes on to argue for a conception of happiness that identifies it with a specific plurality of valuable activities, including activity in accordance with excellences[10] (valuable traits) of many sorts, including ethical, intellectual, and political excellences, and activities involved in love and friendship. Pleasure, as I have said, is not identical with happiness, but it usually (not always) accompanies the unimpeded performance of the activities that constitute happiness.

Something like this is the idea that Wordsworth is relying on, when he asks, in each of the many areas of life, what the character and demeanor of the "happy Warrior" would be, and answers that question. As J. L. Austin° (1979, p. 20) memorably wrote in a devastating critique of Prichard on Aristotle, "I do not think Wordsworth meant . . . : 'This is the warrior who feels pleased.' Indeed, he is 'Doomed to go in company with Pain / And fear and bloodshed, miserable train.' "

As Austin saw, the important thing about the happy warrior is that he has traits that make him capable of performing all of life's many activities in an exemplary way, and he acts in accordance with those traits. He is moderate, kind, courageous, loving, a good friend, concerned for the community, honest,[11] not excessively attached to honor or worldly ambition, a lover of reason, an equal lover of home and family. His life is happy because it is full and rich, even though it sometimes may involve pain and loss.

J. L. Austin (1911–1960): British philosopher of language and author of *How to Do Things with Words* (1962).

[9]For an excellent recent analysis, arguing that the Aristotelian view captures best our intuitive sense of what happiness is, see Nozick (1989, chap. 10).

[10]I thus render Greek *aretē*, usually translated "virtue." *Aretē* need not be ethical; indeed it need not even be a trait of a person. It is a trait of anything, whatever that thing is, that makes it good at doing what that sort of thing characteristically does. Thus Plato can speak of the *aretē* of a pruning knife.

[11]Here we see the one major departure from Aristotle that apparently seemed to Wordsworth required by British morality. Aristotle does not make much of honesty. In other respects, Wordsworth is remarkably close to Aristotle, whether he knew it or not.

So would Seligman agree with Aristotle and Wordsworth that the happy warrior is indeed happy? Or does he require pleasant emotion in addition to the good activity? If even Seligman's conception is underspecified, however, Kahneman does not get to the point of noticing a problem at all and simply goes along with Bentham.

(I note that the happy warrior is still happy because he is still able to act well; Aristotle believed, however, that more extreme calamities could "dislodge" one from happiness, by removing one's sphere of activity. His example is Priam° at the end of the Trojan War, who lost his children, his political freedom and power, and his personal freedom.)[12]

When we notice that happiness is complex, we are prepared to face yet a further question in connection with its proper analysis: does happiness require self-examination? All the ancient philosophers take issue with some of the popular accounts of *eudaimonia*° in their cultural setting, by arguing that no life is truly happy unless it is accompanied by reflection. As Socrates says in the *Apology*, "The unexamined life is not worth living for a human being." One sees clearly in Plato's dialogues how controversial this emphasis is. When people are asked to define a virtue (seen as a putative part of happiness), they never include this element of knowledge or reflection—until Socrates patiently shows them that any definition that leaves it out is inadequate. On reflection, however, they always agree with Socrates, and I would say that my contemporary students do as well when they think about it for a while. Aristotle gives a little more room than Plato does to the nonintellectual elements in virtue, including emotions as at least one part of what each virtue involves. But he, too, sticks to the Socratic commitment, saying that each and every virtue of character requires the intellectual virtue of practical wisdom. Much later, as we saw, J. S. Mill insists that it is better to be Socrates dissatisfied than a pig satisfied.

"When we notice that happiness is complex, we are prepared to face yet a further question in connection with its proper analysis: does happiness require self-examination?"

Wordsworth, as you can see, agrees with the Socratic tradition: the happy warrior's "law is reason." He "depends / Upon that law as on the

Priam: king of Troy in Homer's epic poem *The Iliad*.
***eudaimonia*:** a Greek word used by Aristotle. Its literal meaning is "good spirited"; its closest equivalent in English is "happiness."

[12]See my treatment of this passage in Nussbaum (2001a, chap. 10).

best of friends," and he strives to become ever "More skilful in self-knowledge."

The commitment to reflection is also a commitment to the ceaseless critical scrutiny of cultural beliefs and cultural authorities. Socrates interrogates everyone he meets, and nobody does very well, especially not received cultural authorities. Socrates himself does best only in the sense that he is aware of the incompleteness and fallibility of his knowledge of happiness. Although later Greek philosophers are more willing than Socrates to pronounce on what happiness is, they are no more trustful of their culture, and all are relentless critics of their cultures' dominant understandings of happiness. Aristotle excoriates the undue attention given to the accumulation of wealth, to pleasure, and to manly honor. The Stoics° have similar criticisms. And yet, they hold, not implausibly, that if people give it enough thought, they will agree with their proposal, because it honors something that people will understand to be deep in themselves, the source of their human dignity.

The omission of this reflective element in happiness is one of the most disturbing aspects of the conceptual breeziness of contemporary subjective-state psychology, insofar as it is laying the groundwork for normative recommendations. Our democracy has many of the vices Socrates identified in his: haste, macho posturing, an excessive deference to wealth and honor. We badly need the element of reflection, and if prestigious psychologists simply tell us again and again that reflection is not a necessary element of the happy life, we may begin to believe it.

What Emotions Are Positive?

The part of subjective-state measurement that focuses on moment-to-moment hedonic flow assumes that some emotions are positive and others are negative. Seligman makes a similar assumption and tells us somewhat more about what he is assuming, in keeping with his rather greater interest in philosophical matters. For Seligman, positive emotions, to put it somewhat crudely, are those that feel good. So love would be positive, anger and grief negative, and so forth.

The ancient thinkers adopt a very different account. Again, this issue deeply affects any normative recommendations that may ultimately be based on the conceptual assumptions.

Since the Greeks and Romans (along with the best work on emotions in contemporary cognitive psychology) believe that emotions embody 35

Stoics: believers in a philosophical school founded by Zeno of Citium (335–263 BCE). They believed that virtue and happiness came from an understanding of the true nature of things. See Epictetus's *Handbook* (p. 88).

appraisals or evaluations of things in the world, they think it is very important for those appraisals to be correct. Fear, for example, involves (in Aristotle's view) the thought that there are serious damages impending and that one is not entirely in control of warding them off. Anger (again in Aristotle's view) involves the thought that a serious and inappropriate damage has been willfully inflicted on me or someone or something one cares about, and also the thought that it would be good for that damage to be made good somehow.

So we can see that there are a number of things that can go wrong here. One might get the facts wrong, thinking that a danger was present when it was not, or that a wrong had been done when it had not. One might blame the wrong person for the wrong or might wrongly believe that the damage was blameworthy when it was in fact accidental. Finally, one can get the seriousness of the good or bad event wrong: one may get angry over trivia—Aristotle's example is when someone forgets your name, so you see the world has changed little. Or, again Aristotle's example, one might fear a mouse running across the floor.

Because emotions embody appraisals, one can get them to be appropriate only by getting appropriate appraisals. Thus, in the *Rhetoric,* Aristotle gives the aspiring orator recipes for provoking anger in an audience—by convincing them that their enemies have wronged them in some illicit way, for example—and also recipes for taking anger away and calming people down—by convincing them that they had not in fact been wronged in the way they thought, or that the thing was not of much importance.

For all the ancient thinkers, a necessary and sufficient condition of an emotion's being truly positive—in the sense of making a positive contribution toward a flourishing life—is that it be based on true beliefs, both about value and about what events have occurred. This is as true of good-feeling as of bad-feeling emotion. Many instances of good-feeling emotion are actually quite negative, inasmuch as they are based on false beliefs about value. Pleasure is only as good as the thing one takes pleasure in: if one takes pleasure in harming others, that good-feeling emotion is very negative; even if one takes pleasure in shirking one's duty and lazing around, that is also quite negative. If one feels hope, that emotion is good only if it is based on accurate evaluations of the worth of what one hopes for and true beliefs about what is likely.

By the same token, many negative-feeling emotions are appropriate, and even very valuable. Aristotle, like Wordsworth, stresses that the courageous person is not free from fear: indeed, he will appropriately feel more fear and pain at the prospect of losing his life in battle than the mediocre person, because his life, which is at risk, is a valuable life and he knows it. Anger is a sign of what we care intensely about and a spur to justice. Aristotle does not urge people to be angry all the time; indeed, he thinks that the appropriate virtue in this area should be called "mildness of temper," in order to indicate that the good person does not get angry too often. But if someone did not get angry at damages to loved ones or kin, he would be "slavish," in Aristotle's view. Again, compassion is painful, but it is extremely valuable, when based on true beliefs and accurate evaluations of the seriousness of the other person's predicament, because it connects us to the suffering of others and gives us a motive to help them. Grief when a loved one dies is extremely appropriate (although Plato, admiring self-sufficiency, tried to deny this).

The ancient philosophers also stress that happy and sad emotions are conceptually interconnected: to the extent that you value uncertain things that are in the control of chance, you cannot help having both fear and hope about them, since their prospects are in fact uncertain. Where you have love, you will also have anxiety—and, very likely, anger. Where you have gratitude (when someone does something importantly nice for you), there is also conceptual space for anger (if that same person should decide to treat you badly). The Stoics saw clearly that the only way to get rid of negative emotions was not to value the uncertain things of human life at all and to care only for one's own inner states. But Aristotle, and most modern readers of the texts, reject that solution. 40

Aristotle is correct here. That is, emotions are positive or negative, in the sense relevant to normative thinking, according to the correctness of the appraisals or evaluations they contain. And since human life contains, in fact, many bad accidents and much bad behavior, there is no way a person who values friends, loved ones, work, and political action can avoid having many painful-feeling emotions, such as grief, fear, and anxiety. These emotions are valuable in themselves, as expressions of correct evaluation, and also spurs to good action. Can one imagine a struggle for justice that was not fueled by justified anger? Can one imagine a decent society that is not held together by compassion for suffering? Can one imagine love that does not assume the risk of grief? I believe that C. Daniel Batson's excellent research on compassion (which, I note en passant, has a rare philosophical sophistication and precision) has shown that the painful emotion leads to helping; so it is extremely important not to set out to avoid painful emotional experiences (Batson 1991).

Seligman, in particular, thinks that it is good to promote good-feeling emotions and to minimize bad-feeling emotions, often by thinking hopeful thoughts. But sometimes having a hopeful "take" on the bad thing that has happened seems to trivialize it. The Stoics urged people to respond to the death of a loved one with constructive sentiments, such as "Everyone is mortal, and you will get over this pretty soon." But are they correct? Is this really the way to take the measure of love? It is very interesting to see how Cicero, who in his voluminous correspondence consoled his friends with positive sentiments like Seligman's, rejects them utterly when his beloved daughter Tullia dies. Among the most moving letters in history are his outpourings of desperate grief to his friend Atticus, to whom he says that he feels that he is in a dark forest, and whose injunctions to put an end to his mourning he angrily rejects, saying that he cannot do it, and moreover, he thinks that he should not, even if he could.

Today, Americans are often embarrassed by deep grief and tend to give Stoic advice too freely. A colleague in my university lost his son: a young man, troubled, who died either of a drug overdose or by suicide. I wrote him, saying that I thought this was the worst thing that could happen to someone and he had my sympathy. This man, whom I do not know very well, wrote back immediately, thanking me and saying, "I really dislike this American stuff about healing." (He is an American.) I inferred from that response that many other messages he had received had talked about healing, and he had gotten fed up with them. I am with him: it seems a deeply inappropriate way to think of the tragic death of a child.

So I would like to see psychology think more about positive pain, that is, the grief that expresses love, the fear that expresses a true sense of a threat directed at something or someone one loves, the compassion that shares the pain of a suffering person, the anger that says, "This is deeply wrong and I will try to right it."

References

Allardt, Erik. 1975. *Att ha, alska, att vara: Om valfard i Norden* (Having, loving, being: On welfare in the Nordic countries). Borgholm: Argos.

———. 1993. Having, Loving, Being: An Alternative to the Swedish Model of Welfare Research. Pp. 88–94 in *The Quality of Life*, edited by Martha Nussbaum and Amartya Sen. Oxford: Clarendon Press.

Austin, J. L. 1979. *Agathon* and *eudaimonia* in the *Ethics* of Aristotle. Pp. 1–31 in *Philosophical Papers*, edited by J. O. Urmson and G. J. Warnock. Oxford and New York: Oxford University Press.

Batson, C. Daniel. 1991. *The Altruism Question*. Hillsdale, N.J.: Lawrence Erlbaum.

Birault, Henri. 1985. Beatitude in Nietzsche. Pp. 219–31 in *The New Nietzsche*, edited by David Allison. Cambridge, Mass.: MIT Press.

Gosling, J. C. B. 1969. *Pleasure and Desire*. Oxford: Clarendon Press.

Gosling, J. C. B., and C. C. W. Taylor. 1982. *The Greeks on Pleasure*. Oxford and New York: Clarendon Press.

Kahneman, Daniel, and Alan B. Krueger. 2006. Developments in the Measurement of Subjective Well-Being. *Journal of Economic Perspectives* 20:3–24.

Mill, John Stuart. 1998. The Utility of Religion. Pp. 69–122 in *Mill: Three Essays on Religion*. Amherst, N.Y.: Prometheus Books.

Nozick, Robert. 1974. *Anarchy, State, and Utopia*. New York: Basic Books.

———. 1989. *The Examined Life*. New York: Simon & Schuster.

Nussbaum, Martha. 1994. *The Therapy of Desire: Theory and Practice in Hellenistic Ethics*. Princeton, N.J.: Princeton University Press.

———. 2001a. *The Fragility of Goodness: Luck and Ethics in Greek Tragedy and Philosophy*. Updated ed. Cambridge: Cambridge University Press.

———. 2001b. *Upheavals of Thought: The Intelligence of Emotions*. New York: Cambridge University Press.

———. 2004. Mill between Bentham and Aristotle. *Daedalus* 133(2):60–68.

Packe, Michael St. John. 1954. *The Life of John Stuart Mill*. New York: Macmillan.

Prichard, H. A. 1935. The Meaning of *agathon* in the *Ethics* of Aristotle. *Philosophy* 10:27–39.

Seligman, Martin. 2002. *Authentic Happiness: Using the New Positive Psychology to Realize Your Potential for Lasting Fulfillment*. New York: Free Press.

Taylor, C. C. W. 1976. *Plato: Protagoras*. Oxford: Clarendon Press.

Understanding the Text

1. Nussbaum takes it as her task to sort through many theories of happiness as a philosopher. Where do you hear her doing the work of philosophy, as you understand it?
2. Many theories of happiness appear in quick succession here. Make a list of the many thinkers Nussbaum cites. Next to each one, write a sentence describing what Nussbaum finds important about that person's views. This will serve as a kind of outline for the piece.
3. Why do you think Nussbaum divides the essay into the sections she includes here? Make a different chart, in which you explain what question each section of the piece asks and how that question is ultimately answered.

Reflection and Response

4. Nussbaum intends to clear up misconceptions of the current understanding of happiness. What misconceptions does she identify, and how does she correct them?
5. This piece is long and thoughtful. Choose one section and become an "expert reader." Look up the authors Nussbaum mentions; define any words you do not know. Make a chart of the argument for just this section. Then write three to five pages in which you summarize this section and offer thoughts for further exploration based on your outside research.

Making Connections

6. Nussbaum mentions many authors in this piece, but perhaps none so much as Aristotle. Write an essay in which you evaluate Nussbaum's overview of Aristotle. Is there anything she leaves out or misrepresents? How would you revise Nussbaum's overview?
7. Write an essay in which you discuss Nussbaum's argument about pleasure in relation to two of the authors in Chapter 5 of this book. How might these authors respond to Nussbaum's claims?
8. Although many of the authors Nussbaum refers to in this text are represented in this reader, several are not. Choose one of the authors in *Pursuing Happiness* that Nussbaum does not mention and write a few paragraphs about that person's article as it would appear in Nussbaum's essay. Be sure to note where you would include this piece when you revised Nussbaum's essay. (It might make the most sense to scatter your comments in the piece, just as Nussbaum does her comments about a few of the authors, including John Stuart Mill.)

Of What Sort of Proof the Principle of Utility Is Susceptible

John Stuart Mill

John Stuart Mill (1806–1873) was one of the most influential philosophers of the nineteenth century. His essay "On Liberty" remains a foundational statement of the principles of liberalism, arguing for the rights of the individual against interference by government and society.

Mill had no formal schooling; he was taught at home by his father, James Mill (1773–1836), a philosopher and an economist. He began learning ancient Greek at age three; by age 14, Mill had read most of the Greek and Roman classics in the original, and he soon began writing and publishing his own works. But at age 20 he suffered a nervous breakdown, apparently the result of the rigors and emotional deprivations of his upbringing. After a slow recovery, he became a more independent and original thinker.

Both father and son were greatly influenced by the philosopher Jeremy Bentham (1748–1832), a close family friend and the founder of Utilitarianism, a philosophy that argues that the right course of action is the one that produces the greatest benefit. John Stuart Mill adopted the Utilitarian position but, unlike Bentham, distinguished between higher pleasures and lower pleasures, between true happiness and mere feelings of contentment or satisfaction.

The following essay is the fourth chapter of Mill's book *Utilitarianism*, originally published in *Fraser's Magazine* as a series of three essays in 1861 and subsequently in book form in 1863.

It has already been remarked, that questions of ultimate ends° do not admit of proof, in the ordinary acceptation of the term. To be incapable of proof by reasoning is common to all first principles; to the first premises of our knowledge, as well as to those of our conduct. But the former, being matters of fact, may be the subject of a direct appeal to the faculties which judge of fact—namely, our senses, and our internal consciousness. Can an appeal be made to the same faculties on questions of practical ends? Or by what other faculty is cognizance taken of them?

Questions about ends are, in other words, questions [about] what things are desirable. The utilitarian doctrine is, that happiness is desirable, and the only thing desirable, as an end; all other things being only desirable as

ultimate ends: final goals or results.

means to that end. What ought to be required of this doctrine—what conditions is it requisite that the doctrine should fulfil—to make good its claim to be believed?

The only proof capable of being given that an object is visible, is that people actually see it. The only proof that a sound is audible, is that people hear it: and so of the other sources of our experience. In like manner, I apprehend, the sole evidence it is possible to produce that anything is desirable, is that people do actually desire it. If the end which the utilitarian doctrine proposes to itself were not, in theory and in practice, acknowledged to be an end, nothing could ever convince any person that it was so. No reason can be given why the general happiness is desirable, except that each person, so far as he believes it to be attainable, desires his own happiness. This, however, being a fact, we have not only all the proof which the case admits of, but all which it is possible to require, that happiness is a good: that each person's happiness is a good to that person, and the general happiness, therefore, a good to the aggregate of all persons. Happiness has made out its title as *one* of the ends of conduct, and consequently one of the criteria of morality.

But it has not, by this alone, proved itself to be the sole criterion. To do that, it would seem, by the same rule, necessary to show, not only that people desire happiness, but that they never desire anything else. Now it is palpable that they do desire things which, in common language, are decidedly distinguished from happiness. They desire, for example, virtue, and the absence of vice, no less really than pleasure and the absence of pain. The desire of virtue is not as universal, but it is as authentic a fact, as the desire of happiness. And hence the opponents of the utilitarian standard deem that they have a right to infer that there are other ends of human action besides happiness, and that happiness is not the standard of approbation and disapprobation.

But does the utilitarian doctrine deny that people desire virtue, or maintain that virtue is not a thing to be desired? The very reverse. It maintains not only that virtue is to be desired, but that it is to be desired disinterestedly, for itself. Whatever may be the opinion of utilitarian moralists as to the original conditions by which virtue is made virtue; however they may believe (as they do) that actions and dispositions are only virtuous because they promote another end than virtue; yet this being granted, and it having been decided, from considerations of this description, what *is* virtuous, they not only place virtue at the very head of the things which are good as means to the ultimate end, but they also recognise as a psychological fact the possibility of its being, to the individual, a good in itself, without looking to any end beyond it; and hold, 5 that the mind is not in a right state, not in a state conformable to Utility, not in the state most conducive to the general happiness, unless it does love virtue in this manner—as a thing desirable in itself, even although, in the individual instance, it should not produce those other desirable consequences which it tends to produce, and on account of which it is held to be virtue. This opinion is not, in the smallest degree, a departure from the Happiness principle. The ingredients of happiness are very various, and each of them is desirable in itself, and not merely when considered as swelling an aggregate. The principle of utility does not mean that any given pleasure, as music, for instance, or any given exemption from pain, as for example health, are to be looked upon as means to a collective something termed happiness, and to be desired on that account. They are desired and desirable in and for themselves; besides being means, they are a part of the end. Virtue, according to the utilitarian doctrine, is not naturally and originally part of the end, but it is capable of becoming so; and in those who love it disinterestedly it has become so, and is desired and cherished, not as a means to happiness, but as a part of their happiness.

To illustrate this farther, we may remember that virtue is not the only thing, originally a means, and which if it were not a means to anything else, would be and remain indifferent, but which by association with what it is a means to, comes to be desired for itself, and that too with the utmost intensity. What, for example, shall we say of the love of money? There is nothing originally more desirable about money than about any heap of glittering pebbles. Its worth is solely that of the things which it will buy; the desires for other things than itself, which it is a means of gratifying. Yet the love of money is not only one of the strongest moving forces of human life, but money is, in many cases, desired in and for itself; the desire to possess it is often stronger than the desire to use it, and goes on increasing when all the desires which point to ends beyond it, to be compassed by it, are falling off. It may be then said truly, that money is desired not for the sake of an end, but as part of the end. From being a means to happiness, it has come to be itself a principal ingredient of the individual's conception of happiness. The same may be said of the majority of the great objects of human life—power, for example, or fame; except that to each of these there is a certain amount of immediate pleasure annexed, which has at least the semblance of being naturally inherent in them; a thing which cannot be said of money. Still, however, the strongest natural attraction, both of power and of fame, is the immense aid they give to the attainment of our other wishes; and it is the strong association thus generated between them and all our objects of desire, which gives to the direct desire of them the intensity it often assumes, so as in some characters to surpass in strength all other desires. In these cases the means have become a part of the end, and a more important part of it than any of the things which they are means to. What was once desired as an instrument for the attainment of happiness, has come to be desired for its own sake. In being desired for its own sake it is, however, desired as *part* of happiness. The person is made, or thinks he would be made, happy by its mere possession; and is made unhappy by failure to obtain it. The desire of it is not a different thing from the desire of happiness, any more than the love of music, or the desire of health. They are included in happiness. They are some of the elements of which the desire of happiness is made up. Happiness is not an abstract idea, but a concrete whole; and these are some of its parts. And the utilitarian standard sanctions and approves their being so. Life would be a poor thing, very ill provided with sources of happiness, if there were not this provision of nature, by which things originally indifferent, but conducive to, or otherwise associated with, the satisfaction of our primitive desires, become in themselves sources of pleasure more valuable than the primitive pleasures, both in permanency, in the space of human existence that they are capable of covering, and even in intensity.

Virtue, according to the utilitarian conception, is a good of this description. There was no original desire of it, or motive to it, save its conduciveness to pleasure, and especially to protection from pain. But through the association thus formed, it may be felt a good in itself, and desired as such with as great intensity as any other good; and with this difference between it and the love of money, of power, or of fame, that all of these may, and often do, render the individual noxious to the other members of the society to which he belongs, whereas there is nothing which makes him so much a blessing to them as the cultivation of the disinterested love of virtue. And consequently, the utilitarian standard, while it tolerates and approves those other acquired desires, up to the point beyond which they would be more injurious to the general happiness than promotive of it, enjoins and requires the cultivation of the love of virtue up to the greatest strength possible, as being above all things important to the general happiness.

"Happiness is the sole end of human action, and the promotion of it the test by which to judge of all human conduct."

It results from the preceding considerations, that there is in reality nothing desired except happiness. Whatever is desired otherwise than as a means to some end beyond itself, and ultimately to happiness, is desired as itself a part of happiness, and is not desired for itself until it has

A baroque portrayal of earthly pleasures by Dutch painter Jan Steen (1674).
Feast in an Inn (oil on canvas), Steen, Jan Havicksz (1625/26–1679)/Louvre, Paris, France/ Bridgeman Images

become so. Those who desire virtue for its own sake, desire it either because the consciousness of it is a pleasure, or because the consciousness of being without it is a pain, or for both reasons united; as in truth the pleasure and pain seldom exist separately, but almost always together, the same person feeling pleasure in the degree of virtue attained, and pain in not having attained more. If one of these gave him no pleasure, and the other no pain, he would not love or desire virtue, or would desire it only for the other benefits which it might produce to himself or to persons whom he cared for.

We have now, then, an answer to the question, of what sort of proof the principle of utility is susceptible. If the opinion which I have now stated is psychologically true—if human nature is so constituted as to desire nothing which is not either a part of happiness or a means of happiness, we can have no other proof, and we require no other, that these are the only things desirable. If so, happiness is the sole end of human action, and the promotion of it the test by which to judge of all human conduct; from whence it necessarily follows that it must be the criterion of morality, since a part is included in the whole.

10 And now to decide whether this is really so; whether mankind do desire nothing for itself but that which is a pleasure to them, or of which the absence is a pain; we have evidently arrived at a question of fact and experience, dependent, like all similar questions, upon evidence. It can only be determined by practised self-consciousness and self-observation, assisted by observation of others. I believe that these sources of evidence, impartially consulted, will declare that desiring a thing and finding it pleasant, aversion to it and thinking of it as painful, are phenomena entirely inseparable, or rather two parts of the same phenomenon; in strictness of language, two different modes of naming the same psychological fact: that to think of an object as desirable (unless for the sake of its consequences), and to think of it as pleasant, are one and the same thing; and that to desire anything, except in proportion as the idea of it is pleasant, is a physical and metaphysical impossibility.

So obvious does this appear to me, that I expect it will hardly be disputed: and the objection made will be, not that desire can possibly be directed to anything ultimately except pleasure and exemption from pain, but that the will is a different thing from desire; that a person of confirmed virtue, or any other person whose purposes are fixed, carries out his purposes without any thought of the pleasure he has in contemplating them, or expects to derive from their fulfilment; and persists in acting on them, even though these pleasures are much diminished, by changes in his character or decay of his passive sensibilities, or are outweighed by the pains which the pursuit of the purposes may bring upon him. All this I fully admit, and have stated it elsewhere, as positively and emphatically as any one. Will, the active phenomenon, is a different thing from desire, the state of passive sensibility, and though originally an offshoot from it, may in time take root and detach itself from the parent stock; so much so, that in the case of an habitual purpose, instead of willing the thing because we desire it, we often desire it only because we will it. This, however, is but an instance of that familiar fact, the power of habit, and is nowise confined to the case of virtuous actions. Many indifferent things, which men originally did from a motive of some sort, they continue to do from habit. Sometimes this is done unconsciously, the consciousness coming only after the action: at other times with conscious volition, but volition which has become habitual, and is put into operation by the force of habit, in opposition perhaps to the deliberate preference, as often happens with those who have contracted habits of vicious or hurtful indulgence. Third and last comes the case in which the habitual act of will in the individual instance is not in contradiction to the general intention prevailing at other times, but in fulfilment of it; as in the case of the person of confirmed virtue, and of all who pursue deliberately and consistently any determinate end. The distinction between will and desire thus understood, is an authentic and highly important psychological fact; but the fact consists solely in this—that will, like all other parts of our constitution, is amenable to habit, and that we may will from habit what we no longer desire for itself, or desire only because we will it. It is not the less true that will, in the beginning, is entirely produced by desire; including in that term the repelling influence of pain as well as the attractive one of pleasure. Let us take into consideration, no longer the person who has a confirmed will to do right, but him in whom that virtuous will is still feeble, conquerable by temptation, and not to be fully relied on; by what means can it be strengthened? How can the will to be virtuous, where it does not exist in sufficient force, be implanted or awakened? Only by making the person *desire* virtue—by making him think of it in a pleasurable light, or of its absence in a painful one. It is by associating the doing right with pleasure, or the doing wrong with pain, or by eliciting and impressing and bringing home to the person's experience the pleasure naturally involved in the one or the pain in the other, that it is possible to call forth that will to be virtuous, which, when confirmed, acts without any thought of either pleasure or pain. Will is the child of desire, and passes out of the dominion of its parent only to come under that of habit. That which is the result of habit affords no presumption of being intrinsically good; and there would be no reason for wishing that the purpose of virtue should become independent of pleasure and pain, were it not that the influence of the pleasurable and painful associations which prompt to virtue is not sufficiently to be depended on for unerring constancy of action until it has acquired the support of habit. Both in feeling and in conduct, habit is the only thing which imparts certainty; and it is because of the importance to others of being able to rely absolutely on one's feelings and conduct, and to oneself of being able to rely on one's own, that the will to do right ought to be cultivated into this habitual independence. In other words, this state of the will is a means to good, not intrinsically a good; and does not contradict the doctrine that nothing is a good to human beings but in so far as it is either itself pleasurable, or a means of attaining pleasure or averting pain.

But if this doctrine be true, the principle of utility is proved. Whether it is so or not, must now be left to the consideration of the thoughtful reader.

Understanding the Text

1. What is the happiness principle that Mill describes?
2. What is Mill's understanding of the relationship between virtue and happiness?

Reflection and Response

3. Mill explores the relationships between desire and what it is that we desire. What does he say about this? Do you find his argument true to your own experiences of wanting and acquiring? Provide at least two examples to illustrate your point.
4. How does Mill understand the role of pleasure in our lives?

Making Connections

5. Write an essay in which you consider Mill's argument from the vantage point of two poets: John Keats ("Ode on Melancholy," p. 264) and Rumi ("How Should the Soul," p. 64). What can you learn from these two poets about how to interpret Mill's argument?
6. Consider Mill's discussion of habit in relation to the discussion of habit on Gretchen Rubin's Happiness blog. Do these writers share a similar position?

Happiness and Its Discontents

Daniel M. Haybron

Daniel Haybron is Associate Professor in the Department of Philosophy at Saint Louis University and the author of *Happiness: A Very Short Introduction* (2013) and *The Pursuit of Unhappiness: The Elusive Psychology of Well-Being* (2008). He holds a Ph.D. in philosophy from Rutgers University (2001). "My research focuses mainly on the psychology of well-being and its connections with issues in ethical and political thought, as well as empirical research on well-being." He is the author of the entry "Happiness" in the *Stanford Encyclopedia of Philosophy* (Fall 2011 ed.). In this article, which appeared in the "Opinionator" column in the *New York Times* in April 2014, Haybron examines what scholars mean when they write of "happiness," and he argues that the English language lacks terms for the precise kind of emotional state that scholars have in mind when they write about "happiness" as an enduring condition.

I

What does it mean to be happy?

The answer to this question once seemed obvious to me. To be happy is to be satisfied with your life. If you want to find out how happy someone is, you ask him a question like, "Taking all things together, how satisfied are you with your life as a whole?"

Over the past 30 years or so, as the field of happiness studies has emerged from social psychology, economics and other disciplines, many researchers have had the same thought. Indeed this "life satisfaction" view of happiness lies behind most of the happiness studies you've read about. Happiness embodies your *judgment* about your life, and what matters for your happiness is something for you to decide.

This is an appealing view. But I have come to believe that it is probably wrong. Or at least, it can't do justice to our everyday concerns about happiness.

5 One of the most remarkable findings in this area of psychology, for instance, is just how many poor people say they are satisfied with their lives—very often a majority of them, even in harsh environments like the slums of Calcutta. In a recent study of poor Egyptians, researchers asked them to explain why they were satisfied, and their responses often took something like this form: "One day is good and the other one is bad; whoever accepts the least lives." This sounds like resignation, not happiness. Yet these Egyptians were, in terms of life satisfaction, happy.

The problem is that life satisfaction doesn't really mean what we tend to think it means. For you can reasonably be satisfied with your life even if you think your life is going badly for you, and even if you feel bad. To be satisfied is just to regard your life as going well *enough*—it is satisfactory. You might think even a hard slog through a joyless existence is good enough. It sure beats being dead, and maybe you feel you have no right to complain about what God, or fate, has given you.

Similarly, you might be satisfied with a hard life because you care about things besides avoiding misery. Perhaps you are a dissident in an autocratic state and suffering dearly for it, yet you are satisfied with your life because you believe in what you are doing. But are you happy? Probably not.

I do not mean to suggest that life satisfaction studies can't give us useful information about how people are doing. But I am suggesting that it is misleading to equate satisfaction with happiness, even if it is perfectly ordinary to talk that way at times.

So how else might we define happiness? There is another approach popular among researchers—one that focuses on *feelings*. If you feel good, and not bad, you're happy. Feeling good may not be all that matters, but it certainly sounds like a more suitable candidate for happiness than a judgment that your life is good enough. Evidently, those Egyptians do not feel good, and that has a lot to do with why it seems unnatural to say that they are happy.

10 But what exactly is this "feeling good"? The standard view is this: Happiness is pleasure, and unhappiness is pain, or suffering. Philosophers call this view "hedonism" about happiness. If we think of happiness as pleasure, we can see why people value happiness so highly: Who really prefers misery to enjoyment? Lots of philosophers, like Epicurus, Jeremy Bentham and John Stuart Mill,° have thought that pleasure and suffering are all that ultimately matters. Hedonism about happiness has an obvious appeal. It is natural to think of happiness as a matter of feelings, and what else could this mean but having pleasant feelings?

"To be happy is to inhabit a favorable emotional state. On this view, we can think of happiness, loosely, as the opposite of anxiety and depression."

Epicurus, Jeremy Bentham, and John Stuart Mill: Epicurus (341–270 BCE) was a Greek philosopher who taught that the good is what gives pleasure and evil is what gives pain. Jeremy Bentham (1748–1832) was a British philosopher and founder of modern Utilitarianism. John Stuart Mill (1806–1873) was a British Utilitarian philosopher. See Mill's "Of What Sort of Proof the Principle of Utility Is Susceptible" (p. 123).

But I have come to believe that this approach is also probably wrong. When you look at the way researchers study this kind of happiness, you'll notice something peculiar: Their questionnaires almost always ask about emotions and mood states, and rarely ask directly about pleasure, pain or suffering. In fact, you might have thought that if happiness researchers were really interested in pleasure and pain, among their queries would be questions about *pain* ("Do you suffer from chronic pain?" and so on). Such pains make a tremendous difference in how pleasant our lives are, yet happiness surveys rarely ask about them.

Why not? Because, I would venture, these researchers aren't really thinking of happiness as pleasure, as they take themselves to be doing. Rather, they're tacitly thinking of happiness in another, more interesting way.

II

I would suggest that when we talk about happiness, we are actually referring, much of the time, to a complex emotional phenomenon. Call it emotional well-being. Happiness as emotional well-being concerns your emotions and moods, more broadly your emotional condition as a whole. To be happy is to inhabit a favorable emotional state.

On this view, we can think of happiness, loosely, as the opposite of anxiety and depression. Being in good spirits, quick to laugh and slow to anger, at peace and untroubled, confident and comfortable in your own skin, engaged, energetic and full of life. To measure happiness, we might use extended versions of existing questionnaires for anxiety and depression from the mental-health literature. Already, such diagnostics often ask questions about positive states like laughter and cheerfulness, or your ability to enjoy things.

The emotional-state theory of happiness has significant advantages over the hedonistic view. Consider, for starters, that we don't normally think of pain as an emotion or mood. It seems more natural, for example, to think of back pain as something that *causes* unhappiness, not as unhappiness itself. A more important point is that we are fundamentally emotional beings. Who we are is in great part defined by our emotional natures, by what ways of living make us happy. Yes, we have animal needs for food, shelter, clothing and the like. But we also have needs as *persons*, and happiness concerns the fulfillment of those needs. 15

What sorts of needs are we talking about? Among the most important sources of happiness are: a sense of security; a good outlook; autonomy or control over our lives; good relationships; and skilled and meaningful activity. If you are unhappy, there's a good chance that it's for want of something on this list.

Unhappiness is not just a brute physical or animal response to your life. It is *you*, as a person, responding to your life as being somehow deficient. Unhappiness, like happiness, says something about your personality. Whereas back pain does not: It is just a sensation, something that happens to you. Accordingly, Buddhists and Stoics° do not counsel us not to feel pain; their training aims, instead, at not letting pain and other irritants *get* to us.

Our language also marks the difference: You merely *feel* a pain, but you *are* depressed, anxious, melancholy or whatever. Similarly, you might have a depressive or anxious or cheerful personality. But we never talk of someone having a "painful" or "pleasureful" personality.

Note also how we don't worry about taking medicine for pain the way we often do about taking "happiness" pills like antidepressants. We worry that by artificially changing our mood we risk not being "us." But no one feels inauthentic because he took ibuprofen to relieve his back pain.

III

While the emotional-state view of happiness might seem commonsensical, it was barely discussed 20 years ago, and the differences between this approach and hedonism still are not widely acknowledged in the scientific literature on happiness. Why has it been so neglected? 20

The reason, I suspect, is that we tend to take a superficial view of the emotional realm. In the popular imagination, the rich tapestry of our emotional lives is reduced to nearly a point—or rather, two points for eyes, a "U" for a mouth and a circle enclosing them. But there is much more to happiness than the smiley-face emotion of feeling happy.

Our very language is deficient, and so we sometimes reach for other expressions that better convey the depth and richness of happiness: happiness as a matter of the psyche, spirit or soul. Researchers rightly tend to avoid such metaphors in their scholarly work, which demands clearly defined terminology. But even those of us who do not believe in immaterial souls often find this sort of language usefully evocative, as our technical vocabulary can be pretty feeble in expressing the complexities of

Stoics: believers in a philosophical school founded by Zeno of Citium (335–263 BCE). They believed that virtue and happiness came from an understanding of the true nature of things. See Epictetus's *Handbook* (p. 88).

human experience. At times, then, I have found it useful to employ terms like psychic affirmation or, for the truly thriving, psychic flourishing. We are not just talking about "being in a good mood."

So there is something specially human about happiness, something that speaks to our natures and needs as persons. And meeting our needs as persons—our spiritual needs, one might say—seems to have a special importance.

Why should these needs, these aspects of ourselves, be so important? There is a long history of philosophical thought, with roots stretching back at least to Plato and Aristotle in Greece, and the Vedas in India,° that conceives of human flourishing in terms of the fulfillment of the self. Human well-being, on this sort of view, means living in accordance with your nature, with who you are. On this way of thinking, we might regard happiness as a central part of self-fulfillment.

Furthermore, our emotional conditions may provide the single best indicator of how, in general, our lives are going. They don't simply track the moment-to-moment flow of events. If you are generally depressed, anxious or stressed, you will probably not find an answer to your problems by scrutinizing the day's events one by one. It may be wiser, instead, to consider whether the way you are living really makes sense. Often, the signals of the emotional self can set us on the path to better ways of living—and a happiness worthy of the name. 25

Plato and Aristotle in Greece, and the Vedas in India: Plato (428/427–348/347 BCE) and Aristotle (384–322 BCE) were the two most influential Western philosophers of the ancient world. The Vedas are the oldest Hindu scriptures.

Understanding the Text

1. Why are some cultures suspicious of happiness?
2. Compare Haybron's definitions of "happiness" and "satisfaction."

Reflection and Response

3. What is Haybron's position on the significance of differing cultural interpretations of happiness? Discuss the value and limitations of this way of thinking about happiness.
4. Would you argue that this article works to change our ideas about happiness? What is your estimation of what Haybron is trying to teach the audience? Is he convincing?

Making Connections

5. Haybron and David Brooks ("What Suffering Does," p. 284) might be said to have similar positions on happiness, but they reach very different conclusions. Discuss these two authors' ideas about happiness in relation to those of one author in Chapter 4 of this text.
6. Discuss Jennifer Michael Hecht's theories of happiness and ritual ("Remember Death," p. 233) in relation to the argument that Haybron offers here.

3 What Makes People Happy?

We wake up, get dressed, move through our day, do the work that we need to do, eat meals, share time with friends, enjoy some downtime by reading or looking at social media. But how do we feel? Are we happy? Sometimes the idea of happiness can feel like a mystery. But how is it that some people seem to be unhappy while others in similar circumstances express contentment with their lives?

Can we really measure happiness? If you look at the Oxford Happiness Questionnaire, you will see one version of how researchers have tried to quantify this difficult emotion. Complete the questionnaire to see what you think of the questions as ways of thinking about true happiness.

To study means of acquiring happiness, many people question the happiness of various groups in different places and phases of life. The National Academy of Sciences Global Well-Being Ladder provides a visual representation of the relationships between material wealth and personal happiness around the world.

Where does happiness come from? Sonja Lyubomirsky offers a model of measuring happiness that focuses on its origins: Is it genetic? Can we change our happiness destiny? Most important, how does our behavior influence our feelings of happiness? Stefan Klein explores the role of sensory pleasure in our definitions of happiness. How important are good food, alcohol, and massage to our sense of well-being? Ed Diener and Martin Seligman, in "Very Happy People," study how important social relationships can be in the levels of happiness in people's lives.

Many of these authors consider how material circumstances affect our happiness. Ed Diener and Robert Biswas-Diener as well as Mihaly Csikszentmihalyi explore the common idea that money leads to happiness. Can it be that one need only work to obtain as much money as possible and this will lead to a fulfilling life? If we listen to Diener and Biswas-Diener, we might agree.

And what can we do about the fact that so many people are deeply unhappy for seemingly insufficient reasons? Stu Horsfield, in his interview with Dr. Jordan McKenzie, discusses how he decided similarly that he would study happy people as a way of understanding how unhappy people might become happier.

If We Are So Rich, Why Aren't We Happy?

Mihaly Csikszentmihalyi

Mihaly Csikszentmihalyi (born in Fiume, Italy, now Rijeka, Croatia) is Distinguished Professor of Psychology and Management in the Division of Behaviorial and Organizational Sciences at Claremont Graduate University in California. With Martin Seligman, he is a founder of "positive psychology," a relatively new branch of psychology (dating from the late 1990s) that studies how people can lead happier, more fulfilled lives, rather than how mental disorders can be treated. He emigrated to the United States in 1956 and earned his Ph.D. from the University of Chicago in 1965. Author of eight books and more than 120 articles or book chapters, Csikszentmihalyi is best known as the originator of the concept of "flow," a mental state characterized by complete absorption in an activity, and often by a high level of productivity or creativity. That concept has been widely applied and referenced in areas as different as management, sport, music, and spirituality.

Ever since systematic thought has been recorded, the question of what makes men and women happy has been of central concern. Answers to this question have ranged from the materialist extreme of searching for happiness in external conditions to the spiritual extreme claiming that happiness is the result of a mental attitude. Psychologists have recently rediscovered this topic. Research supports both the materialist and the mentalist positions, although the latter produces the stronger findings. The article focuses in particular on one dimension of happiness: the flow experience, or the state of total involvement in an activity that requires complete concentration.

Psychology is the heir to those "sciences of man" envisioned by Enlightenment thinkers such as Giambattista Vico, David Hume, and the baron de Montesquieu.° One of their fundamental conclusions was that the

Giambattista Vico, David Hume, and the baron de Montesquieu: Giambattista Vico (1668–1744) was an Italian philosopher and author of *Scienza nuova* ("New Science," 1725). He argued that civilizations pass through recurring cycles of growth and decay. David Hume (1711–1776) was a Scottish philosopher and author of *A Treatise of Human Nature* (1739–1740). He applied the empirical method to the study of human nature. De Montesquieu (1689–1755) was a French political philosopher and author of *L'Esprit des lois* ("The Spirit of Laws," 1748). He argued that a separation of judicial, legislative, and executive powers was needed to safeguard individual liberty.

pursuit of happiness constituted the basis of both individual motivation and social well-being. This insight into the human condition was condensed by John Locke° (1690/1975) in his famous statement, "That we call Good which is apt to cause or increase pleasure, or diminish pain" (p. 2), whereas evil is the reverse—it is what causes or increases pain and diminishes pleasure.

The generation of utilitarian philosophers that followed Locke, including David Hartley, Joseph Priestley, and Jeremy Bentham,° construed a good society as that which allows the greatest happiness for the greatest number (Bentham, 1789/1970, pp. 64–65). This focus on pleasure or happiness as the touchstone of private and public life is by no means a brainchild of post-Reformation Europe. It was already present in the writings of the Greeks—for instance, Aristotle° noted that although humankind values a great many things, such as health, fame, and possessions, because we think that they will make us happy, we value happiness for itself. Thus, happiness is the only intrinsic goal that people seek for its own sake, the bottom line of all desire. The idea that furthering the pursuit of happiness should be one of the responsibilities of a just government was of course enshrined later in the Declaration of Independence of the United States.

Despite this recognition on the part of the human sciences that happiness is the fundamental goal of life, there has been slow progress in understanding what happiness itself consists of. Perhaps because the heyday of utilitarian philosophy coincided with the start of the enormous forward strides in public health and in the manufacturing and distribution of goods, the majority of those who thought about such things assumed that increases in pleasure and happiness would come from increased affluence, from greater control over the material environment. The great self-confidence of the Western technological nations, and especially of the United States, was in large part because of the belief

John Locke (1632–1704): English philosopher and author of *Two Treatises of Government* (1690). He argued for toleration in politics and religion and a "social contract" among citizens.

David Hartley, Joseph Priestley, and Jeremy Bentham: David Hartley (1705–1757) was an English physician and philosopher, and author of *Observations on Man, His Frame, His Duty, and His Expectations* (1749). He argued that the mind learns by associating new sensations with existing ideas. Joseph Priestley (1733–1804) was an English scientist who in 1774 discovered oxygen (or "dephlogisticated air"). Jeremy Bentham (1748–1832) was a philosopher and the founder of modern Utilitarianism, the view that the best course is the one that maximizes "utility," or the greatest benefit.

Aristotle (384–322 BCE): Greek philosopher whose works treat a wide range of subjects, including logic, rhetoric, ethics, natural science, and physics. See Aristotle's "Nicomachean Ethics," p. 82.

that materialism—the prolongation of a healthy life, the acquisition of wealth, the ownership of consumer goods—would be the royal road to a happy life.

However, the virtual monopoly of materialism as the dominant ideology has come at the price of a trivialization that has robbed it of much of the truth it once contained. In current use, it amounts to little more than a thoughtless hedonism, a call to do one's thing regardless of consequences, a belief that whatever feels good at the moment must be worth doing. 5

This is a far cry from the original view of materialists, such as John Locke, who were aware of the futility of pursuing happiness without qualifications and who advocated the pursuit of happiness through prudence—making sure that people do not mistake imaginary happiness for real happiness.

What does it mean to pursue happiness through prudence? Locke must have derived his inspiration from the Greek philosopher Epicurus,° who 2,300 years ago already saw clearly that to enjoy a happy life, one must develop self-discipline. The materialism of Epicurus was solidly based on the ability to defer gratification. He claimed that although all pain was evil, this did not mean one should always avoid pain—for instance, it made sense to put up with pain now if one was sure to avoid thereby a greater pain later. He wrote to his friend Menoeceus

The beginning and the greatest good . . . is prudence. For this reason prudence is more valuable even than philosophy: from it derive all the other virtues. Prudence teaches us how impossible it is to live pleasantly without living wisely, virtuously, and justly . . . take thought, then, for these and kindred matters day and night. . . . You shall be disturbed neither waking nor sleeping, and you shall live as a god among men. (Epicurus of Samos, trans. 1998, p. 48)

This is not the image of epicureanism held by most people. The popular view holds that pleasure and material comforts should be grasped wherever they can, and that these alone will improve the quality of one's life. As the fruits of technology have ripened and the life span has lengthened, the hope that increased material rewards would bring about a better life seemed for a while justified.

Now, at the end of the second millennium, it is becoming clear that the solution is not that simple. Inhabitants of the wealthiest industrial-

Epicurus (341–270 BCE) was a Greek philosopher who taught that the good is what gives pleasure and evil is what gives pain.

ized Western nations are living in a period of unprecedented riches, in conditions that previous generations would have considered luxuriously comfortable, in relative peace and security, and they are living on the average close to twice as long as their great-grandparents did. Yet, despite all these improvements in material conditions, it does not seem that people are so much more satisfied with their lives than they were before.

The Ambiguous Relationship between Material and Subjective Well-Being

The indirect evidence that those of us living in the United States today are not happier than our ancestors were comes from national statistics of social pathology—the figures that show the doubling, and tripling, of violent crimes, family breakdown, and psychosomatic complaints since at least the halfway mark of the century. If material well-being leads to happiness, why is it that neither capitalist nor socialist solutions seem to work? Why is it that the crew on the flagship of capitalist affluence is becoming increasingly addicted to drugs for falling asleep, for waking up, for staying slim, for escaping boredom and depression? Why are suicides and loneliness such a problem in Sweden, which has applied the best of socialist principles to provide material security to its people? 10

Direct evidence about the ambiguous relationship of material and subjective well-being comes from studies of happiness that psychologists and other social scientists have finally started to pursue, after a long delay in which research on happiness was considered too soft for scientists to undertake. It is true that these surveys are based on self-reports and on verbal scales that might have different meanings depending on the culture and the language in which they are written. Thus, the results of culturally and methodologically circumscribed studies need to be taken with more than the usual grain of salt. Nevertheless, at this point they represent the state of the art—an art that will inevitably become more precise with time.

Although cross-national comparisons show a reasonable correlation between the wealth of a country as measured by its gross national product and the self-reported happiness of its inhabitants (Inglehart, 1990), the relationship is far from perfect. The inhabitants of Germany and Japan, for instance, nations with more than twice the gross national product of Ireland, report much lower levels of happiness.

Comparisons within countries show an even weaker relationship between material and subjective well-being. Diener, Horwitz, and Emmons (1985), in a study of some of the wealthiest individuals in the United States, found their levels of happiness to be barely above that of individuals with average incomes. After following a group of lottery winners,

Brickman, Coates, and Janoff-Bulman (1978) concluded that despite their sudden increase in wealth, their happiness was no different from that of people struck by traumas, such as blindness or paraplegia. That having more money to spend does not necessarily bring about greater subjective well-being has also been documented on a national scale by David G. Myers (1993). His calculations show that although the adjusted value of after-tax personal income in the United States has more than doubled between 1960 and 1990, the percentage of people describing themselves as "very happy" has remained unchanged at 30% (Myers, 1993, pp. 41–42).

In the *American Psychologist*'s January 2000 special issue on positive psychology, David G. Myers (in press) and Ed Diener (in press) discuss in great detail the lack of relationship between material and subjective well-being, so I will not belabor the point here. Suffice it to say that in current longitudinal studies of a representative sample of almost 1,000 American adolescents conducted with the experience sampling method and supported by the Sloan Foundation, a consistently low negative relationship between material and subjective well-being has been found (Csikszentmihalyi & Schneider, in press). For instance, the reported happiness of teenagers (measured several times a day for a week in each of three years) shows a very significant inverse relationship to the social class of the community in which teens live, to their parents' level of education, and to their parents' occupational status. Children of the lowest socioeconomic strata generally report the highest happiness, and upper middle-class children generally report the least happiness. Does this mean that more affluent children are in fact less happy, or does it mean that the norms of their social class prescribe that they should present themselves as less happy? At this point, we are unable to make this vital distinction.

15

Yet despite the evidence that the relationship between material wealth and happiness is tenuous at best, most people still cling to the notion that their problems would be resolved if they only had more money. In a survey conducted at the University of Michigan, when people were asked what would improve the quality of their lives, the first and foremost answer was "more money" (Campbell, 1981).

Given these facts, it seems that one of the most important tasks psychologists face is to better understand the dynamics of happiness and to communicate these findings to the public at large. If the main justification of psychology is to help reduce psychic distress and support psychic well-being, then psychologists should try to prevent the disillusionment that comes when people find out that they have wasted their lives struggling to reach goals that cannot satisfy them. Psychologists should be able to provide alternatives that in the long run will lead to a more rewarding life.

Why Material Rewards Do Not Necessarily Make People Happy

To answer this question, I'll start by reflecting on why material rewards, which people regard so highly, do not necessarily provide the happiness expected from them. The first reason is the well-documented escalation of expectations. If people strive for a certain level of affluence thinking that it will make them happy, they find that on reaching it, they become very quickly habituated, and at that point they start hankering for the next level of income, property, or good health. In a 1987 poll conducted by the *Chicago Tribune*, people who earned less than $30,000 a year said that $50,000 would fulfill their dreams, whereas those with yearly incomes of over $100,000 said they would need $250,000 to be satisfied ("Pay Nags," 1987; "Rich Think Big," 1987; see also Myers, 1993, p. 57). Several studies have confirmed that goals keep getting pushed upward as soon as a lower level is reached. It is not the objective size of the reward but its difference from one's "adaptation level" that provides subjective value (e.g., Davis, 1959; Michalos, 1985; Parducci, 1995).

The second reason is related to the first. When resources are unevenly distributed, people evaluate their possessions not in terms of what they need to live in comfort, but in comparison with those who have the most. Thus, the relatively affluent feel poor in comparison with the very rich and are unhappy as a result. This phenomenon of "relative deprivation" (Martin, 1981; Williams, 1975) seems to be fairly universal and well-entrenched. In the United States, the disparity in incomes between the top percentage and the rest is getting wider; this does not bode well for the future happiness of the population.

The third reason is that even though being rich and famous might be rewarding, nobody has ever claimed that material rewards alone are sufficient to make us happy. Other conditions—such as a satisfying family life, having intimate friends, having time to reflect and pursue diverse interests—have been shown to be related to happiness (Myers, 1993; Myers & Diener, 1995; Veenhoven, 1988). There is no intrinsic reason why these two sets of rewards—the material and the socioemotional—should be mutually exclusive. In practice, however, it is very difficult to reconcile their conflicting demands. As many psychologists from William James° (1890) to Herbert A. Simon° (1969) have remarked, time is the ultimate

William James (1842–1910): American psychologist and philosopher. As a pragmatist, he believed that the value of a theory or belief should be measured by its usefulness or applicability in practice.
Herbert A. Simon (1916–2001): American social scientist, and author of *Administrative Behavior* (1947). He argued that business decisions have complex motives, not just the maximizing of profits. He won the Nobel Prize for Economics in 1978.

scarce resource, and the allocation of time (or more precisely, of attention over time) presents difficult choices that eventually determine the content and quality of our lives. This is why professional and business persons find it so difficult to balance the demands of work and family, and why they so rarely feel that they have not shortchanged one of these vital aspects of their lives.

Material advantages do not readily translate into social and emotional benefits. In fact, to the extent that most of one's psychic energy becomes invested in material goals, it is typical for sensitivity to other rewards to atrophy. Friendship, art, literature, natural beauty, religion, and philosophy become less and less interesting. The Swedish economist Stephen Linder was the first to point out that as income and therefore the value of one's time increases, it becomes less and less "rational" to spend it on anything besides making money—or on spending it conspicuously (Linder, 1970). The opportunity costs of playing with one's child, reading poetry, or attending a family reunion become too high, and so one stops doing such irrational things. Eventually a person who only responds to material rewards becomes blind to any other kind and loses the ability to derive happiness from other sources (see also Benedikt, 1999; Scitovsky, 1975). As is true of addiction in general, material rewards at first enrich the quality of life. Because of this, we tend to conclude that more must be better. But life is rarely linear; in most cases, what is good in small quantities becomes commonplace and then harmful in larger doses.

Dependence on material goals is so difficult to avoid in part because our culture has progressively eliminated every alternative that in previous times used to give meaning and purpose to individual lives. Although hard comparative data are lacking, many historians (e.g., Polanyi, 1957) have claimed that past cultures provided a greater variety of attractive models for successful lives. A person could be valued and admired because he or she was a saint, a bon vivant, a wise person, a good craftsman, a brave patriot, or an upright citizen. Nowadays the logic of reducing everything to quantifiable measures has made the dollar the common metric by which to evaluate every aspect of human action. The worth of a person and of a person's accomplishments are determined by the price they fetch in the marketplace. It is useless to claim that a painting is good art unless it gets high bids at Sotheby's, nor can we claim that someone is wise unless he or she can charge five figures for a consultation. Given the hegemony of material rewards in our culture's restricted repertoire, it is not surprising that so many people feel that their only hope for a happy life is to amass all the earthly goods they can lay hands on.

To recapitulate, there are several reasons for the lack of a direct relationship between material well-being and happiness. Two of them are sociocultural: (a) The growing disparity in wealth makes even the reasonably affluent feel poor. (b) This relative deprivation is exacerbated by a cultural factor, namely, the lack of alternative values and a wide range of successful lifestyles that could compensate for a single, zero-sum° hierarchy based on dollars and cents. Two of the reasons are more psychological: (a) When we evaluate success, our minds use a strategy of escalating expectations, so that few people are ever satisfied for long with what they possess or what they have achieved. (b) As more psychic energy is invested in material goals, less of it is left to pursue other goals that are also necessary for a life in which one aspires to happiness. None of this is intended to suggest that the material rewards of wealth, health, comfort, and fame detract from happiness. Rather, after a certain minimum threshold—which is not stable but varies with the distribution of resources in the given society—they seem to be irrelevant. Of course, most people will still go on from cradle to grave believing that if they could only have had more money, or good looks, or lucky breaks, they would have achieved that elusive state.

Psychological Approaches to Happiness

If people are wrong about the relation between material conditions and how happy they are, then what *does* matter? The alternative to the materialist approach has always been something that used to be called a "spiritual" and nowadays we may call a "psychological" solution. This approach is based on the premise that if happiness is a mental state, people should be able to control it through cognitive means. Of course, it is also possible to control the mind pharmacologically. Every culture has developed drugs ranging from peyote to heroin to alcohol in an effort to improve the quality of experience by direct chemical means. In my opinion, however, chemically induced well-being lacks a vital ingredient of happiness: the knowledge that one is responsible for having achieved it. Happiness is not something that happens to people but something that they make happen.

In some cultures, drugs ingested in a ritual, ceremonial context appear to have lasting beneficial effects, but in such cases the benefits most likely result primarily from performing the ritual, rather than from the chemicals per se. Thus, in discussing psychological approaches to happiness, I focus exclusively on processes in which human consciousness uses its self-organizing ability to achieve a positive internal state through

zero-sum: Whatever is lost on one side is gained on the other side.

its own efforts, with minimal reliance on external manipulation of the nervous system.

There have been many very different ways to program the mind to increase happiness or at least to avoid being unhappy. Some religions have done it by promising [that] an eternal life of happiness follows our earthly existence. Others, on realizing that most unhappiness is the result of frustrated goals and thwarted desires, teach people to give up desires altogether and thus avoid disappointment. Still others, such as Yoga and Zen,° have developed complex techniques for controlling the stream of thoughts and feelings, thereby providing the means for shutting out negative content from consciousness. Some of the most radical and sophisticated disciplines for self-control of the mind were those developed in India, culminating in the Buddhist teachings 25 centuries ago. Regardless of its truth content, faith in a supernatural order seems to enhance subjective well-being: Surveys generally show a low but consistent correlation between religiosity and happiness (Csikszentmihalyi & Patton, 1997; Myers, 1993).

25

Contemporary psychology has developed several solutions that share some of the premises of these ancient traditions but differ drastically in content and detail. What is common to them is the assumption that cognitive techniques, attributions, attitudes, and perceptual styles can change the effects of material conditions on consciousness, help restructure an individual's goals, and consequently improve the quality of experience. Maslow's (1968, 1971) *self-actualization,* Block and Block's (1980) *ego-resiliency,* Diener's (1984, in press) *positive emotionality,* Antonovsky's (1979) *salutogenic approach,* Seeman's (1996) *personality integration,* Deci and Ryan's (1985; Ryan & Deci, in press) *autonomy,* Scheier and Carver's (1985) *dispositional optimism,* and Seligman's (1991) *learned optimism* are only a few of the theoretical concepts developed recently, many with their own preventive and therapeutic implications.

The Experience of Flow

My own addition to this list is the concept of the *autotelic*° *experience,* or *flow,* and of the autotelic personality. The concept describes a particular kind of experience that is so engrossing and enjoyable that it becomes

Yoga and Zen: Yoga is an Indian tradition of spiritual discipline that includes meditation and breath control as well as the practice of postures. Zen is a Japanese school of Buddhism that emphasizes spiritual awakening through intuition as well as the practice of meditation.
autotelic: having its purpose or goal (*telos*) within itself (*auto*).

autotelic, that is, worth doing for its own sake even though it may have no consequence outside itself. Creative activities, music, sports, games, and religious rituals are typical sources for this kind of experience. Autotelic persons are those who have such flow experiences relatively often, regardless of what they are doing.

Of course, we never do anything purely for its own sake. Our motives are always a mixture of intrinsic and extrinsic considerations. For instance, composers may write music because they hope to sell it and pay the bills, because they want to become famous, because their self-image depends on writing songs—all of these being extrinsic motives. But if the composers are motivated only by these extrinsic rewards, they are missing an essential ingredient. In addition to these rewards, they could also enjoy writing music for its own sake—in which case, the activity would become autotelic. My studies (e.g., Csikszentmihalyi, 1975, 1996, 1997) have suggested that happiness depends on whether a person is able to derive flow from whatever he or she does. A brief selection from one of the more than 10,000 interviews collected from around the world might provide a sense of what the flow experience is like. Asked how it felt when writing music was going well, a composer responded,

You are in an ecstatic state to such a point that you feel as though you almost don't exist. I have experienced this time and time again. My hand seems devoid of myself, and I have nothing to do with what is happening. I just sit there watching in a state of awe and wonderment. And the music just flows out by itself. (Csikszentmihalyi, 1975, p. 44)

This response is quite typical of most descriptions of how people feel when they are thoroughly involved in something that is enjoyable and meaningful to the person. First of all, the experience is described as "ecstatic": in other words, as being somehow separate from the routines of everyday life. This sense of having stepped into a different reality can be induced by environmental cues, such as walking into a sport event, a religious ceremony, or a musical performance, or the feeling can be produced internally, by focusing attention on a set of stimuli with their own rules, such as the composition of music.

Next, the composer claims that "you feel as though you almost don't exist." This dimension of the experience refers to involvement in the activity being so demanding that no surplus attention is left to monitor any stimuli irrelevant to the task at hand. Thus, chess players might stand up after a game and realize that they have splitting headaches and must run to the bathroom, whereas for many hours during the game they had excluded all information about their bodily states from consciousness. 30

The composer also refers to the felt spontaneity of the experience: "My hand seems devoid of myself . . . I have nothing to do with what is happening." Of course, this sense of effortless performance is only possible because the skills and techniques have been learned and practiced so well that they have become automatic. This brings up one of the paradoxes of flow: One has to be in control of the activity to experience it, yet one should not try to consciously control what one is doing.

As the composer stated, when the conditions are right, action "just flows out by itself." It is because so many respondents used the analogy of spontaneous, effortless flow to describe how it felt when what they were doing was going well that I used the term flow to describe the autotelic experience. Here is what a well-known lyricist, a former poet laureate of the United States, said about his writing:

You lose your sense of time, you're completely enraptured, you are completely caught up in what you're doing, and you are sort of swayed by the possibilities you see in this work. If that becomes too powerful, then you get up, because the excitement is too great. . . . The idea is to be so, so saturated with it that there's no future or past, it's just an extended present in which you are . . . making meaning. And dismantling meaning, and remaking it. (Csikszentmihalyi, 1996, p. 121)

This kind of intense experience is not limited to creative endeavors. It is reported by teenagers who love studying, by workers who like their jobs, by drivers who enjoy driving. Here is what one woman said about her sources of deepest enjoyment:

[It happens when] I am working with my daughter, when she's discovered something new. A new cookie recipe that she has accomplished, that she has made herself, an artistic work that she's done and she is proud of. Her reading is something that she is really into, and we read together. She reads to me and I read to her, and that's a time when I sort of lose touch with the rest of the world. I am totally absorbed in what I am doing. (Allison & Duncan, 1988, p. 129)

This kind of experience has a number of common characteristics. First people report knowing very clearly what they have to do moment by moment, either because the activity requires it (as when the score of a musical composition specifies what notes to play next), or because the person sets clear goals every step of the way (as when a rock climber decides which hold to try for next). Second, they are able to get immediate feedback on what they are doing. Again, this might be because the activity provides information about the performance (as when one is playing tennis and after each shot one knows whether the ball went where it was supposed to go), or it might be because the person has an internalized standard that makes it possible to know whether one's actions meet the standard (as when a poet reads the last word or the last sentence written and judges it to be right or in need of revision).

Another universal condition for the flow experience is that the person feels his or her abilities to act match the opportunities for action. If the challenges are too great for the person's skill, anxiety is likely to ensue; if the skills are greater than the challenges, one feels bored. When challenges are in balance with skills, one becomes lost in the activity and flow is likely to result (Csikszentmihalyi, 1975, 1997). 35

Even this greatly compressed summary of the flow experience should make it clear that it has little to do with the widespread cultural trope of "going with the flow." To go with the flow means to abandon oneself to a situation that feels good, natural, and spontaneous. The flow experience that I have been studying is something that requires skills, concentration, and perseverance. However, the evidence suggests that it is the second form of flow that leads to subjective well-being.

"The prerequisite for happiness is the ability to get fully involved in life. . . . Lack of wealth or health need not prevent one from finding flow in whatever circumstances one finds at hand."

The relationship between flow and happiness is not entirely self-evident. Strictly speaking, during the experience people are not necessarily happy because they are too involved in the task to have the luxury to reflect on their subjective states. Being happy would be a distraction, an interruption of the flow. But afterward, when the experience is over, people report having been in as positive a state as it is possible to feel. Autotelic persons, those who are often in flow, tend also to report more positive states overall and to feel that their lives are more purposeful and meaningful (Adlai-Gail, 1994; Hektner, 1996).

The phenomenon of flow helps explain the contradictory and confusing causes of what we usually call happiness. It explains why it is possible to achieve states of subjective well-being by so many different routes; either by achieving wealth and power or by relinquishing them; by cherishing either solitude or close relationships; through ambition or through its opposite, contentment; through the pursuit of objective science or through religious practice. *People are happy not because of what they do, but because of how they do it.* If they can experience flow working on the assembly line, chances are they will be happy, whereas if they don't have flow while lounging at a luxury resort, they are not going to be happy. The same is true of the various psychological techniques for achieving positive mental health: If the process of becoming resilient or self-efficacious is felt to be boring or an external imposition, the technique is unlikely to lead to happiness, even if it is mastered to the letter. You have to enjoy mental health to benefit from it.

Making Flow Possible

The prerequisite for happiness is the ability to get fully involved in life. If the material conditions are abundant, so much the better, but lack of wealth or health need not prevent one from finding flow in whatever circumstances one finds at hand. In fact, our studies suggest that children from the most affluent families find it more difficult to be in flow—compared with less well-to-do teenagers, they tend to be more bored, less involved, less enthusiastic, less excited.

At the same time, it would be a mistake to think that each person should be left to find enjoyment wherever he or she can find it or to give up efforts for improving collective conditions. There is so much that could be done to introduce more flow in schools, in family life, in the planning of communities, in jobs, in the way we commute to work and eat our meals—in short, in almost every aspect of life. This is especially important with respect to young people. Our research suggests, for instance, that more affluent teenagers experience flow less often because, although they dispose of more material possessions, they spend less time with their parents, and they do fewer interesting things with them (Hunter, 1998). Creating conditions that make flow experiences possible is one aspect of that "pursuit of happiness" for which the social and political community should be responsible.

40

Nevertheless, flow alone does not guarantee a happy life. It is also necessary to find flow in activities that are complex, namely, activities that provide a potential for growth over an entire life span, allow for the emergence of new opportunities for action, and stimulate the development of new skills. A person who never learns to enjoy the company of others and who finds few opportunities within a meaningful social context is unlikely to achieve inner harmony (Csikszentmihalyi, 1993; Csikszentmihalyi & Rathunde, 1998; Inghilleri, 1999), but when flow comes from active physical, mental, or emotional involvement—from work, sports, hobbies, meditation, and interpersonal relationships—then the chances for a complex life that leads to happiness improve.

The Limits of Flow

There is at least one more important issue left to consider. In reviewing the history of materialism, I have discussed John Locke's warnings about the necessity of pursuing happiness with prudence and about the importance of distinguishing real from imaginary happiness. Are similar caveats applicable to flow? Indeed, flow is necessary to happiness, but it is not sufficient. This is because people can experience flow in activities that are enjoyable at the moment but will detract from enjoyment in the long run. For instance, when a person finds few meaningful opportunities for action in the environment, he or she will often resort to finding flow in activities that are destructive, addictive, or at the very least wasteful (Csikszentmihalyi & Larson, 1978; Sato, 1988). Juvenile crime is rarely a direct consequence of deprivation but rather is caused by boredom or the frustration teenagers experience when other opportunities for flow are blocked. Vandalism, gang fights, promiscuous sex, and experimenting with psychotropic drugs° might provide flow at first, but such experiences are rarely enjoyable for long.

Another limitation of flow as a path to happiness is that a person might learn to enjoy an activity so much that everything else pales by comparison, and he or she then becomes dependent on a very narrow range of opportunities for action while neglecting to develop skills that would open up a much broader arena for enjoyment later. A chess master who can enjoy only the game and a workaholic who feels alive only while on the job are in danger of stunting their full development as persons and thus of forfeiting future opportunities for happiness.

In one respect, the negative impact on the social environment of an addiction to flow is less severe than that of an addiction to material rewards. Material rewards are zero-sum: To be rich means that others must be poor; to be famous means that others must be anonymous; to be powerful means that others must be helpless. If everyone strives for such self-limiting rewards, most people will necessarily remain frustrated, resulting in personal unhappiness and social instability. By contrast, the rewards of flow are open-ended and inexhaustible: If I get my joy from cooking Mediterranean food, or from surfing, or from coaching Little League, this will not decrease anyone else's happiness.

Unfortunately, too many institutions have a vested interest in making people believe that buying the right car, the right soft drink, the right watch, the right education will vastly improve their chances of being happy, even if doing so will mortgage their lives. In fact, societies are 45

psychotropic drugs: drugs that affect brain function.

usually structured so that the majority is led to believe that their well-being depends on being passive and contented. Whether the leadership is in the hands of a priesthood, of a warrior caste, of merchants, or of financiers, their interest is to have the rest of the population depend on whatever rewards they have to offer—be it eternal life, security, or material comfort. But if one puts one's faith in being a passive consumer—of products, ideas, or mind-altering drugs—one is likely to be disappointed. However, materialist propaganda is clever and convincing. It is not so easy, especially for young people, to tell what is truly in their interest from what will only harm them in the long run. This is why John Locke cautioned people not to mistake imaginary happiness for real happiness and why 25 centuries ago Plato wrote that the most urgent task for educators is to teach young people to find pleasure in the right things. Now this task falls partly on our shoulders. The job description for psychologists should encompass discovering what promotes happiness, and the calling of psychologists should include bringing this knowledge to public awareness.

References

Adlai-Gail, W. (1994). Exploring the autotelic personality. Unpublished doctoral dissertation, University of Chicago.

Allison, M. T., & Duncan, M. C. (1988). Women, work, and flow. In M. Csikszentmihalyi & I. Csikszentmihalyi (Eds.), *Optimal experience: Psychological studies of flow in consciousness* (pp. 118–137). New York: Cambridge University Press.

Antonovsky, A. (1979). *Health, stress, and coping*. San Francisco: Jossey-Bass.

Benedikt, M. (1999). *Values*. Austin: The University of Texas Press.

Bentham, J. (1970). *An introduction to the principles of morals and legislation*. Darien, CT: Hafner. (Original work published 1789)

Block, J. H., & Block, J. (1980). The role of ego-control and ego-resiliency in the organization of behavior. In W. A. Collins (Ed.), *The Minnesota Symposium on Child Psychology* (Vol. 13, pp. 39–101). Hillsdale, NJ: Erlbaum.

Brickman, P., Coates, D., & Janoff-Bulman, R. (1978). Lottery winners and accident victims: Is happiness relative? *Journal of Personality and Social Psychology*, 36, 917–927.

Campbell, A. (1981). *The sense of well-being in America*. New York: McGraw-Hill.

Csikszentmihalyi, M. (1975). *Beyond boredom and anxiety*. San Francisco: Jossey-Bass.

Csikszentmihalyi, M. (1993). *The evolving self*. New York: HarperCollins.

Csikszentmihalyi, M. (1996). *Creativity: Flow and the psychology of discovery and invention*. New York: HarperCollins.

Csikszentmihalyi, M. (1997). *Finding flow*. New York: Basic Books.

Csikszentmihalyi, M., & Larson, R. (1978). Intrinsic rewards in school crime. *Crime and Delinquency*, 24, 322–335.

Csikszentmihalyi, M., & Patton, J. D. (1997). Le bonheur, l'expérience optimale et les valeurs spirituelles: Une étude empirique auprès d'adolescents [Happiness, the optimal experience, and spiritual values: An empirical study of adolescents]. *Revue Québécoise de Psychologie*, 18, 167–190.

Csikszentmihalyi, M., & Rathunde, K. (1998). The development of the person: An experiential perspective on the ontogenesis of psychological complexity. In R. M. Lemer (Ed.), *Handbook of child psychology* (5th ed., Vol. 1). New York: Wiley.

Csikszentmihalyi, M., & Schneider, B. (in press). *Becoming adult: How teenagers prepare for work*. New York: Basic Books.

Davis, J. A. (1959). A formal interpretation of the theory of relative deprivation. *Sociometry*, 22, 289–296.

Deci, E., & Ryan, M. (1985). *Intrinsic motivation and self-determination in human behavior.* New York: Plenum.

Diener, E. (1984). Subjective well-being. *Psychological Bulletin*, 95, 542–575.

Diener, E. (in press). Subjective well-being: The science of happiness, and a proposal for a national index. *American Psychologist*.

Diener, E., Horwitz, J., & Emmons, R. A. (1985). Happiness of the very wealthy. *Social Indicators*, 16, 263–274.

Epicurus of Samos. (1998). Achieving the happy life. *Free Inquiry*, 18, 47–48.

Hektner, J. (1996). Exploring optimal personality development: A longitudinal study of adolescents. Unpublished doctoral dissertation, University of Chicago.

Hunter, J. (1998). The importance of engagement: A preliminary analysis. *North American Montessori Teachers' Association Journal*, 23, 58–75.

Inghilleri, P. (1999). *From subjective experience to cultural evolution*. New York: Cambridge University Press.

Inglehart, R. (1990). *Culture shift in advanced industrial society*. Princeton, NJ: Princeton University Press.

James, W. (1890). *Principles of psychology* (Vol. 1). New York: Holt.

Linder, S. (1970). *The harried leisure class*. New York: Columbia University Press.

Locke, J. (1975). *Essay concerning human understanding*. Oxford, England: Clarendon Press. (Original work published 1690)

Martin, J. (1981). Relative deprivation: A theory of distributive injustice for an era of shrinking resources. *Research in Organizational Behavior*, 3, 53–107.

Maslow, A. (1968). *Towards a psychology of being*. New York: Van Nostrand.

Maslow, A. (1971). *The farthest reaches of human nature*. New York: Viking.

Michalos, A. C. (1985). Multiple discrepancy theory (MDT). *Social Indicators Research*, 16, 347–413.

Myers, D. G. (1993). *The pursuit of happiness*. New York: Avon.

Myers, D. G. (in press). The funds, friends, and faith of happy people. *American Psychologist*.

Myers, D. G., & Diener, E. (1995). Who is happy? *Psychological Science*, 6, 10–19.

Parducci, A. (1995). *Happiness, pleasure, and judgment*. Mahwah, NJ: Erlbaum.

Pay nags at workers' job views. (1987, October 18). *Chicago Tribune*, IOB.

Polanyi, K. (1957). *The great transformation*. Boston: Beacon Press.

Rich think big about living well. (1987, September 24). *Chicago Tribune*, 3.

Ryan, R. M., & Deci, E. L. (in press). Self-determination theory and the facilitation of intrinsic motivation, social development, and well-being. *American Psychologist*.

Sato, I. (1988). Bozozoku: Flow in Japanese motorcycle gangs. In M. Csikszentmihalyi & I. Csikszentmihalyi (Eds.), *Optimal experience* (pp. 92–117). New York: Cambridge University Press.

Scheier, M. F., & Carver, C. S. (1985). Optimism, coping, and health: Assessment and implications of generalized outcome expectancies. *Health Psychology*, 4, 210–247.

Scitovsky, T. (1975). *The joyless economy*. New York: Random House.

Seeman, T. E. (1996). Social ties and health: The benefits of social integration. *Annals of Epidemiology*, 6, 442–451.

Seligman, M. E. P. (1991). *Learned optimism*. New York: Random House.

Simon, H. A. (1969). *Sciences of the artificial*. Boston: MIT Press.

Veenhoven, R. (1988). The utility of happiness. *Social Indicators Research*, 20, 333–354.

Williams, R. M., Jr. (1975). Relative deprivation. In L. A. Coser (Ed.), *The idea of social structure: Papers in honor of Robert K. Merton* (pp. 355–378). New York: Harcourt Brace Jovanovich.

Understanding the Text

1. Csikszentmihalyi offers "flow" as one of a number of solutions to the problem of happiness in affluent countries today. What is the evidence, according to the author, that such a problem exists? How was this evidence gathered?
2. What exactly is "flow"? What are its elements? How does Csikszentmihalyi define it so that it includes a certain type of experience and excludes others?
3. Why, according to Csikszentmihalyi, is "flow" so important to a good quality of life? What does "the autotelic experience" contribute to the happy life?

Reflection and Response

4. Describe in detail one or two experiences that, in your view, fit Csikszentmihalyi's criteria for "flow." Explain why and how these experiences fit the criteria (they might not fit every single one perfectly). Were these experiences positive, "happy" ones? What can these experiences teach us about "flow," about the achievement of happiness, and about how a person might live a happy life?
5. Imagine you are a guidance counselor or career counselor speaking to a class of college students. You have read Csikszentmihalyi's article and found it persuasive. Write a speech in which you offer advice on how

college students should choose a major and make career choices, using Csikszentmihalyi's ideas as your guide.

6. In your view, is a happy life possible without the sort of experience that Csikszentmihalyi describes as "flow"?

Making Connections

7. Both Gretchen Rubin ("July: Buy Some Happiness," p. 291) and Csikszentmihalyi discuss the importance of structure in the journey toward happiness. Do they describe the same kinds of structures as key? How would you compare their approaches to the relationships between structure and freedom?
8. Csikszentmihalyi identifies "prudence" as a key element in ancient thinking about the pursuit of happiness. How do the selections by Aristotle ("Nicomachean Ethics," p. 82) and Epictetus ("Handbook," p. 88) argue for this virtue? How do their ideas about the achievement of happiness differ from Csikszentmihalyi's?
9. Aristotle, Rubin, and Csikszentmihalyi all consider practical aspects of the question of happiness in some way. Drawing from each of these essays, construct your theory of what happiness is and what it is not.

157

l Well-Being
r

National Academy of Sciences

The following graph appeared as Figure 4 in the article "A Snapshot of the Age Distribution of Psychological Well-Being in the United States" by researchers Arthur Stone, Joseph Schwartz, Joan Broderick, and Angus Deaton, in *Proceedings of the National Academy of Sciences* (*PNAS*), May 17, 2010.

The article reports the results of a 2008 telephone survey, conducted by the Gallup Organization, of 340,847 people in the United States between ages 18 and 85. Interviewees were asked to give an overall assessment of their well-being, "including . . . aspirations, achievements, and current circumstances." The graph below reports the results to the following question: "Please imagine a ladder with steps numbered from 0 at the bottom to 10 at the top. The top of the ladder represents the best possible life for you, and the bottom of the ladder represents the worst possible life for you. On which step of the ladder would you say you personally feel you stand at this time?"

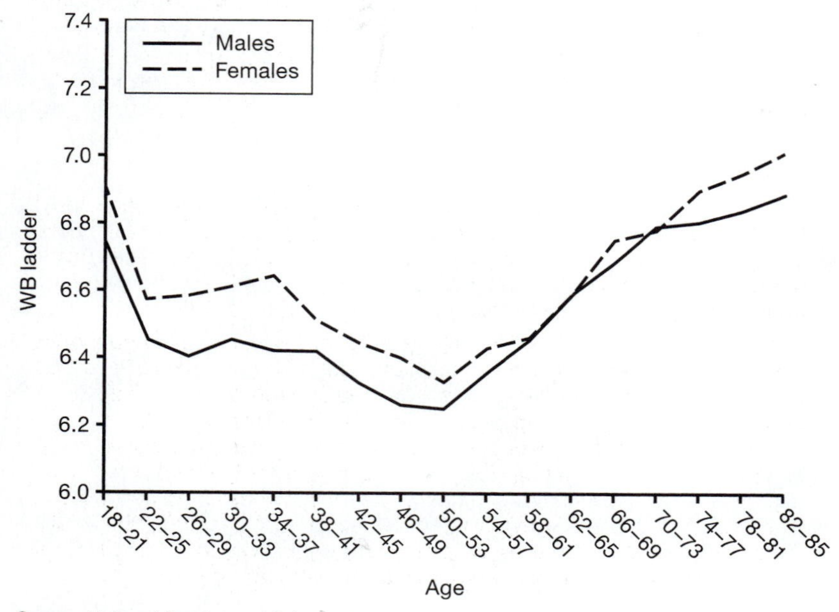

Source: National Academy of Sciences.

Although the results differed somewhat for women (the dashed line) and men (the solid line), both have a roughly similar U-shape that is consistent with other studies of self-reported well-being. Self-reported well-being rises in the late twenties and early thirties after a precipitous drop in the early twenties. Then a steady decline sets in until about age 53. Perhaps surprisingly, self-reported well-being rises steadily thereafter, with the highest levels of well-being being reported by individuals in their eighties.

Understanding the Text

1. What do the numbers on the vertical axis refer to? What is the range of mean average responses — that is, what is the numerical difference between the lowest mean reported and the highest?
2. At what point is the difference greatest between well-being as reported by females and well-being as reported by males? At what point is it smallest?

Reflection and Response

3. How would you answer the researchers' question (see headnote), if you were asked it today? In a few paragraphs, explain your answer.
4. Consider carefully the precise wording of the question asked by the researchers (see headnote). Might the words and phrases they chose have influenced the results in any way? For example, might younger people think about the "best possible life" and "worst possible life" differently than older people? Or might younger people and older people imagine the "ladder" of possibilities differently? Do you see any significant differences between "well-being" as reported in this survey and "happiness" or "contentment" in some other sense?

Making Connections

5. In "Who Is the Happy Warrior? Philosophy Poses Questions to Psychology" (p. 106), Martha C. Nussbaum raises questions about the concept of "well-being" used by psychologists. What questions might she raise about this survey? How might such questions complicate, alter, or influence your understanding of this graph and its meaning?
6. The graph plots mean averages for how respondents of various age groups assessed their well-being in relation to the best and worst possibilities, as they conceived them. In "How Happy Are You and Why?" (p. 179), Sonja Lyubomirsky explains "set-point theory" (see "The Happiness Set Point," p. 186). She states, "the present-day consensus among researchers, based on a growing number of twin studies, is that the heritability of happiness is approximately 50 percent . . ." (p. 188). Assuming that *most* respondents to the survey were unfamiliar with set-point theory, how might the theory complicate or alter our understanding of the survey's results? Or does it make no difference at all? Explain your conclusions.

Can Money Buy Happiness?

Ed Diener and Robert Biswas-Diener

Ed Diener is Joseph R. Smiley Distinguished Professor Emeritus of Psychology at the University of Illinois. His research focuses on the psychology of "subjective well-being" — that is, an individual's own evaluation of his or her quality of life at a given moment or over a period of time. Much of his research seeks to identify the factors that have the greatest impact on subjective well-being, such as temperament, income, and health. He is one of the founders of the *Journal of Happiness Studies* and coauthor, with his son, the psychologist Robert Biswas-Diener, of *Happiness: Unlocking the Mysteries of Psychological Wealth* (2008). In the following chapter from that book, the authors review psychological research on the relationship between money and happiness, and argue that the relationship is more complex than we might imagine.

Recently, a journalist from a well-known news magazine contacted us by email to find out the answer to a question that has fascinated people for centuries: Does money buy happiness? He told us that although scientists like to hedge their answers and give convoluted replies full of disclaimers, he wanted a simple yes or no answer. "Does money buy happiness?" he demanded to know, followed by "Please reply immediately." We thought about his question, and then deleted his email. It was a bit like demanding a yes or no answer to the question "Is Chinese food better than Mexican food?"

In the real world, where many processes influence the outcomes we care about, the answer to the burning question of money and happiness is more complex than a simple yes or no. If it were that easy, people wouldn't be asking the question at all; the answer would be obvious to all of us. If, however, we were pressed by a friendly journalist to reduce the answer as simply as possible, we would respond to the question by saying, "Yes, money buys happiness, but there are important exceptions."

When you think of money and happiness, you probably recall all the things money can buy—a nice house and car, fun vacations, and a good education for your kids. More money can help us get better medical care and a more comfortable retirement. There are intangibles, such as status, that wealthy people tend to receive. Therefore, it seems natural to assume that rich people will be happier than others. But money is only one part of psychological wealth, so the picture is complicated. Rich people may sacrifice other types of wealth to get money, and sometimes develop unhappy attitudes on their way to making their fortunes. Money can be a help in attaining psychological wealth, but it must be considered in the bigger picture of what makes people genuinely rich.

The issue of money's influence on happiness is, perhaps, one of the most talked-about and hotly debated in the history of happiness. Some insist that the rich suburbs are sinks of dissatisfaction, while others scoff at the idea that the poor could be anything but miserable. But what does the evidence say about how money affects psychological wealth? Is it a necessity or a curse?

> "The answer to the burning question of money and happiness is more complex than a simple yes or no. If it were that easy, people wouldn't be asking the question at all."

Money Makes the World Go Round

The question of whether money buys happiness is a timely one because there are more rich people alive today than at any other time in history. In the old days, wealth was largely reserved for those with noble blood or in command of large armies. Today, however, riches are more accessible to common people. Newspapers and magazines are full of stories of small-town boys and girls who grow up to be rich movie stars, musicians, television personalities, professional athletes, lottery winners, politicians, business owners, and bestselling novelists. 5

The number of millionaires is growing rapidly, with more than 8 million in the United States alone. However, poverty is still with us, and the gap between rich and poor is growing in the wealthiest nations. Even in rich Western countries, homelessness and financial marginalization are pressing concerns. As the income gap between rich and poor widens daily, it makes sense to wonder which economic group—the rich or the poor—is the greater inheritor of happiness.

Wealthy People

In the mid-1980s, when Ed's happiness research was starting to gain momentum, he decided to investigate the topic of money and well-being by analyzing the happiness of the superrich. He sent off questionnaires to a hundred of those fabulously wealthy souls who had secured a spot for themselves on the prestigious Forbes list of richest Americans, these people whose net worth was, at the time, $125 million or more. These were people who owned jets, private islands, and large companies. Surprisingly, these economic juggernauts were not too busy to respond to a happiness survey, and forty-nine of them completed and returned it. Some of the wealthy participants even followed up with a phone call. Now, before we get to the punch line, take a moment and make a guess about the results. Were the extremely wealthy happy, or were they anxious and dissatisfied?

It turns out that forty-seven of the forty-nine rich people who responded to Ed's survey were satisfied with their lives, significantly more than a control sample of average Americans taken from the same geographic locations. But, according to the participants in this study, it wasn't money that brought their happiness. None of the Forbes group listed vacation homes, swimming pools, or designer clothing as the major contributor to their emotional well-being. Instead, they mentioned the types of things you might expect from mere financial mortals: pleasing family relationships, helping the world, and fulfillment and pride from their work and accomplishments. The Forbes group wasn't wildly happy, just a bit more satisfied than regular folks.

The notion that money boosts happiness is not a phenomenon confined to people with private jets and impressive mansions. Data collected from everyday citizens in Germany show much the same trend. Our colleagues Richard Lucas and Ulrich Schimmack analyzed many years of happiness data from an enormous German sample and found that life satisfaction increases with income. Figure 3.1 presents these data on a

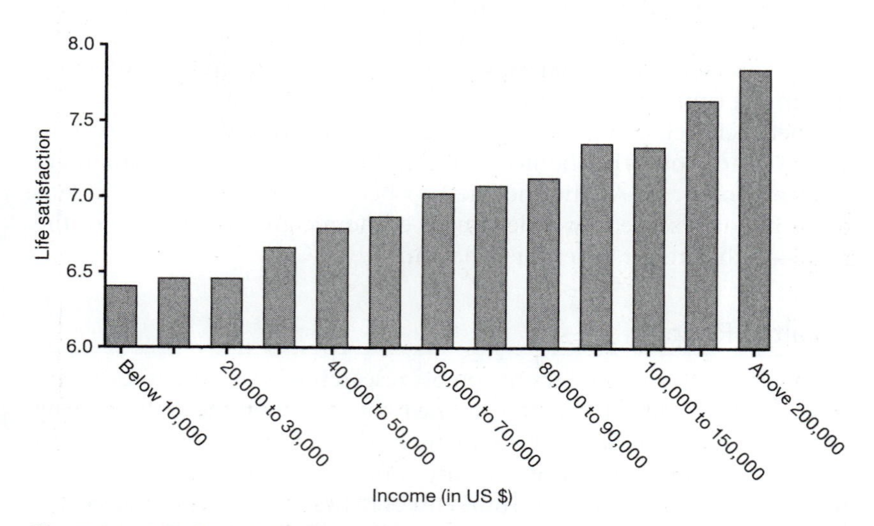

Figure 3.1 **Life Satisfaction, Income**
Source: From Lucas and Schimmack (n.d.).

1–10 scale of life satisfaction. We found in past studies that once an individual is earning a middle-class income, money bought little additional happiness. However, Lucas and Schimmack did not confirm this trend. Folks earning $80,000 a year were more satisfied than their counterparts earning $60,000, and those earning more than $200,000 were significantly more satisfied than the middle class.

Wealthy Nations

When we later examine the happiness of nations, we will see that all of the societies with the highest life satisfaction are wealthy ones, such as Ireland and Denmark, and most of the unhappiest nations are extremely poor ones, such as Sierra Leone and Togo. Indeed, the wealth of nations is one of the strongest, if not the strongest, predictors of the life satisfaction in societies.

10

Figure 3.2 shows the relation between the wealth of nations and the "ladder of life" score from Gallup's 2006 World Survey. The scale asks respondents to say where they currently stand on the steps of a ladder, shown below, which goes from zero, the worst possible life one can imagine for

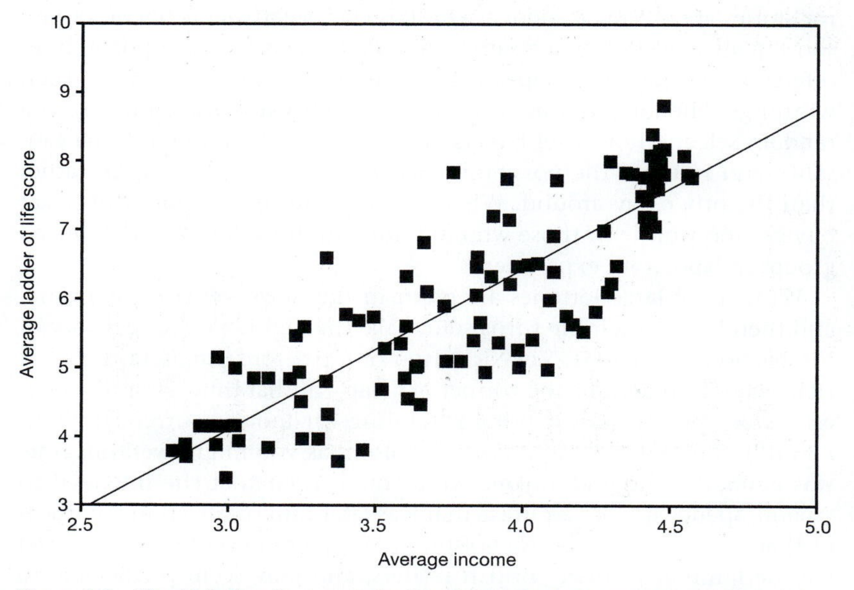

Figure 3.2 **The Relation between the Wealth of Nations and the "Ladder of Life" Score**
The scales ask respondents to say where they currently stand on the steps of a ladder.

oneself, to ten, the best possible life one can imagine for oneself. As can be seen, there are a few somewhat poor nations with fairly high ladder scores. But all of the extremely poor nations are low on the ladder, and most of the extremely wealthy nations are high. There is no nation with an average income of less than $2,000 a year that has a life satisfaction as high as any nation with an income of more than $20,000 a year. For those of you who understand statistics, the Pearson correlation° between income and happiness is .82, which is about as high as correlations ever get in happiness research! In other words, rich nations are, on average, satisfied, and very poor nations tend not to be. As we will see later, although money matters, other factors also influence the happiness of nations, and this is revealed by the fact that figure 3.2 does not show a perfectly straight line between money and life satisfaction.

Lottery Winners

Rich people and nations are happier than their poor counterparts; don't let anyone tell you differently. But another way to analyze the effect of money on happiness is to examine the emotional well-being of those lucky souls who have won a large lottery. Most of us have heard the horror stories about how a sudden windfall can negatively influence a person's quality of life. At the same time, most of us find the possibilities offered by a lottery win appealing and few of us would turn down such winnings. The lottery is interesting to study because the winners are a random selection of ticket buyers, and so scientists can determine causality and rule out the possibility that happiness led to wealth, rather than the other way around. When we compare the happiness of ticket buyers who won with those who did not win, they are like randomized groups in laboratory experiments.

Winners of large lotteries are often in the news—first for winning, and then later if their life turns sour. Take the highly publicized story of Viv Nicholson. In 1961, Viv Nicholson of Castleford, England, struck it rich. Nicholson became the winner of what—at that time—was the largest lottery pool in Great Britain, totaling (in today's currency) about £3 million (roughly $6 million). Nicholson, as you might well imagine, was euphoric. She told anyone who would listen that she intended to "spend, spend, spend," a phrase that was later immortalized in a musical of that name inspired by Nicholson's life. The sad events that followed will be familiar to many British readers, and may seem predictable to

Pearson correlation: a measure of the correlation between two variables, where 0 equals no correlation and 1 equals total correlation.

others. Nicholson had a difficult time coping with her new circumstances, and became increasingly estranged from her friends. In a 1999 article in the British newspaper the *Independent*, Nicholson recalled this time: "Even my old friends left me. They didn't want people saying they were going about with me because I had money." Her life became a series of drinking and shopping sprees that, ultimately, landed Nicholson in financial dire straits. At one point, she escaped to Malta, but was deported for assaulting a police officer. Nicholson filed for bankruptcy, was married five times (once for only thirteen weeks), and eventually wound up working as a stripper and drinking heavily.

But the story does not end there. Viv Nicholson found religion, became an active member of the Jehovah's Witnesses, and began a new, more wholesome life. In the same article in the *Independent*, Nicholson described her new state of affairs: "I'm quite happy with my lot. I'm a happy chappy. I can make any situation happy. You don't have to have money to be happy." Whether she learned important lessons, or whether her newfound religion has given her renewed meaning, Nicholson appeared to be living a much more fulfilling life.

As Nicholson's story illustrates, it is a bit difficult to draw firm conclusions about the money-happiness relationship from isolated instances. It might be argued that her lottery wins caused her grief, or it might be said that they ultimately led her to a place of satisfaction. Perhaps we should examine another winner. The American Jack Whittaker won $314 million in the Powerball lottery in 2002, and hoped to make a positive impact on society by starting a charitable foundation. Jack's granddaughter died of a drug overdose after he lavished money on her, and he was sued by a gambling casino for bouncing checks. Like Viv, Jack did not seem to find happiness with his lottery win. Two years later, Jack had two arrests for driving under the influence, had been the victim of multiple burglaries, was estranged from his wife, had been arrested for assault, and had to close down his foundation. The problem with these sensational cases is that they might not represent average lottery winners; the media may find lottery winners newsworthy only when they make a mess of their lives. When lottery winners live happily ever after, we might never hear of them. What does the science say about the average lottery winner? Are lottery winners on average miserable or are our two examples exceptions to the rule that lottery winners are happy? Fortunately, several studies now have been conducted with this fascinating group. 15

In one study, conducted in Illinois, winners of moderate-size lotteries—those who won about $400,000 on average—were happier than folks in a control group, but the difference was small and not statistically significant. This study is quoted frequently to indicate that money does not help happiness. In a more intensive lottery study, however, the sociologists Stephen Smith and Peter Razzell found that people who had won large lotteries in the United Kingdom were happier than other people. These pools require an individual to guess a large number of soccer game wins for that week. When they were interviewed, the pool winners in the study sometimes mentioned problems that came with the money, such as losing a few of their old friends. But on the whole the winners' happiness was higher than that of a similar group of people who had not won lotteries.

In two other studies, conducted by the economists Jonathan Gardner and Andrew Oswald, the researchers found the same trend: people receiving small to medium windfalls were clearly happier, and this effect persisted over time. In their study, Gardner and Oswald used data from thousands of people who were being questioned time and again over a period of years. From this group, the researchers identified individuals who won lotteries during the course of the study. After analyzing the data, Gardner and Oswald found that two years after winning the lottery, people reported less unhappiness than they had before winning. In a second study, Gardner and Oswald found that those who inherited significant sums of money showed significant increases in happiness.

The Case That Money Does Not Equal Happiness

Despite individual instances where money seems to harm people, with data like the happiness of multimillionaires and lottery winners, as well as the life satisfaction differences between rich and poor, why would anyone doubt that money is on average important to well-being? It turns out that there are also findings that point in other directions. For one thing, people in some poor societies are reasonably happy, at least above the neutral point. For another, it seems that rising desires for goods and services to some degree cancel the effects of greater income. Finally, we know that materialism can be toxic to happiness. We will describe these findings that indicate that money does not always equal happiness, and explore the costs as well as the benefits of money to explain why it is sometimes related to happiness and sometimes not.

City of Joy: The Happiness of the World's Poorest Citizens

The data from samples of rich people and lottery winners paint a positive picture of money and life satisfaction. At the other end of the spectrum, can homeless people and others living in impoverished conditions be satisfied with their lives, or are they doomed to an existence of psychological poverty as well? Some of our most interesting research was conducted with a sample of the poorest citizens in the world. In 2000, one of the authors, Robert, went to Kolkata, formerly known as Calcutta, to learn about the happiness levels of people living in dire poverty. Kolkata is a wonderful city, but is notorious for its widespread poverty, crowding, and noise. By some counts, there are more than a hundred thousand homeless children in the city, and as many as half of the 15 million inhabitants live below the poverty line. Many visitors to the city are overwhelmed by the vast destitution, and on occasions foreigners break down crying on the street. On the other hand, Kolkata has a reputation for inspiring heroism. Mother Teresa, the saintly nun who spent her life caring for the poor and dying, suggested that there is something worthwhile in every corner of life, no matter how humble. Dominique Lapierre wrote the famous novel *City of Joy*, in which the slum-dwelling protagonists fight valiantly against the crush of poverty.

In collecting data in India, Robert spoke with the street people and pavement dwellers of Kolkata. He visited people in makeshift shelters and spoke with women in blackened, windowless kitchens heavy with the smell of kerosene. He posed questions about happiness to sex workers and tea hawkers, to rickshaw pullers and people burdened with leprosy. He heard stories about foraging for scraps of cardboard to light a fire for cooking, and of police harassment. It is easy to imagine that these people were miserable. The data showed, instead, that they were slightly negative to slightly positive on scales of life satisfaction. While this certainly isn't the romantic notion of the joyful poor, it also contradicts the idea of a legion of despondent have-nots with an unmitigated black outlook on life. 20

We replicated the life satisfaction finding using three samples of homeless people: one from Kolkata; one from Fresno, California; and one from Dignity Village, a tent camp in Portland, Oregon. We collected happiness data from men and women in these locations and found that the two American samples were, on average, slightly dissatisfied with their lives, while their Indian counterparts were mildly satisfied. When we asked about satisfaction with specific life domains such as food, health, intelligence, and friends, we similarly found variation in the amount of satisfaction these people experienced. These results are both informative and reason for optimism. In short, this research indicates that, overall, being extraordinarily poor has a negative influence on happiness, but that some very poor individuals are, in fact, somewhat satisfied, and even extremely poor people are usually not depressed.

Which brings us back to the question: "Does money buy happiness?" How is it that many rich people are not extremely happy, and how can it be that some poor people are happy? The answers lie, in part, in the fact that there are many other influences on happiness, such as a cheery

America's Happiest (and least happy) States

2012 Rank	2013 Rank
1. Hawaii	1. North Dakota
2. Colorado	2. South Dakota
3. Minnesota	3. Nebraska
4. Utah	4. Minnesota
5. Vermont	5. Montana
6. Montana	6. Vermont
7. Nebraska	7. Colorado
8. New Hampshire	8. Hawaii
9. Iowa	9. Washington
10. Massachusetts	10. Iowa
11. Maryland	11. New Hampshire
12. South Dakota	12. Utah
13. Wyoming	13. Massachusetts
14. Virginia	14. Wisconsin
15. Washington	15. Maine
16. Connecticut	16. Alaska
17. Kansas	17. California
18. California	18. Maryland
19. North Dakota	19. Arizona
20. Wisconsin	20. Kansas
21. Maine	21. Texas
22. Idaho	22. Illinois
23. Arizona	23. New Jersey
24. Oregon	24. Virginia
25. New Mexico	25. Oregon
26. Delaware	26. Nevada
27. Texas	27. Georgia
28. Illinois	28. Delaware
29. Pennsylvania	29. Idaho
30. New York	30. Florida
31. Alaska	31. Connecticut
32. New Jersey	32. North Carolina
33. Georgia	33. New Mexico
34. Florida	34. Wyoming
35. North Carolina	35. New York
36. Michigan	36. Pennsylvania
37. Rhode Island	37. Michigan
38. Missouri	38. South Carolina

2012 Rank	2013 Rank
39. Nevada	39. Rhode Island
40. South Carolina	40. Indiana
41. Oklahoma	41. Louisiana
42. Indiana	42. Oklahoma
43. Louisiana	43. Missouri
44. Ohio	44. Tennessee
45. Alabama	45. Arkansas
46. Arkansas	46. Ohio
47. Tennessee	47. Alabama
48. Mississippi	48. Mississippi
49. Kentucky	49. Kentucky
50. West Virginia	50. West Virginia

Source: Gallup/Healthways Well-Being Index.

genetic disposition and having supportive relationships. That is, they may have the other components of psychological wealth even if they are missing money. And what of rich people who are unhappy? There are factors that can cancel the beneficial effects of money on happiness if people are not careful.

Wanting It All: Aspirations and Happiness

Money is more than a fixed amount of legal tender. Wealth is, in part, also about your desires. Being satisfied with your paycheck, just like being satisfied with your life, is about your point of view. We have one friend who leads wilderness trips. He lives in a simple cabin, spends much of his time outdoors, and only uses about $5,000 a year. Contrast this with another friend of ours who once spent $30,000 on a single hotel stay. Obviously, money and comfort don't mean the same thing to these two people. To better understand how money adds and subtracts from happiness, and why it does so idiosyncratically from person to person, it is important to consider aspirations. Take the following example.

We know two young couples in which both the wife and husband are professors in universities. One couple, whom we will call the Johnsons, earns a combined income of $90,000 a year, and the other couple, the Thompsons, earns $200,000 a year. The Johnsons are quite satisfied with their income, and feel it is adequate to their wants and needs. The richer Thompsons, making more than twice the money of the first couple, constantly feel strapped for cash and frequently argue over finances. The problem is that the Thompsons want more expensive luxuries and experiences, and thus end up feeling poorer. This is a perfect illustration of the research findings of the psychologists Wendy Johnson and Robert Krueger. The researchers studied the incomes and happiness of twins, which meant that they could parse out those pesky genetic influences that often contaminate research on happiness. What they found was surprising: the amount of money a person made only modestly predicted whether or not she was satisfied with her income. Some people with a lot of money could not meet their desires, and others with little money were able to do so.

This brings us to the famous formula:

25

$$\text{Happiness} = \frac{\text{What we have (attainments)}}{\text{What we want (aspirations)}}$$

This formula makes sense. It means that it doesn't matter so much if you make $20,000 a year or $100,000, if you drive a new BMW or an old Chevrolet—what matters more is that your income is sufficient for your desires. Of course, we know from the bulk of the research that it is generally better to have more, rather than less, money. But individual variation in desire helps explain why some poor folks are happy and some wealthy people are not.

Returning to the couples we described earlier, we can see that differences in aspirations lead to very different amounts of happiness. The couple with the middle-class income are quite pleased because they have modest desires. They are content with their large but old home. They drive a Toyota that runs well, and one spouse usually takes the bus to work. If the weather permits, the husband rides his bike to the university. Their leisure time is spent gardening, watching DVDs, driving to see relatives in nearby cities, and attending their children's extracurricular events. By contrast, the wealthier couple pine for expensive trips to Aspen and to Europe, lease new cars every two years, eat at expensive restaurants, dress themselves in the latest fashions, and own an enormous home on which they carry an equally large mortgage. Let's plug the two couples' incomes and aspirations into the happiness formula.

On a scale ranging from zero to ten, here is how the couples stack up in happiness:

Happiness of professors with high income:

$$\frac{\$200{,}000}{\$400{,}000} = .5 \text{ or Unhappiness}$$

Desires: Foreign travel, luxury cars, expensive house, the latest electronic gadgets, private schools

Happiness of professors with good income: 30

$$\frac{\$100,000}{\$50,000} = 2.0 \text{ or High Happiness}$$

Desires: Modest house and car, some travel, social leisure, health insurance, and inexpensive lessons for their children

The "poorer" example is four times as happy with their money because they have more than their desires require. In contrast, the well-off couple has enough money to meet only half of their desires, and therefore they feel poorer. We saw a perfect illustration of the influence of aspirations when we conducted research with Amish people living in the American Midwest. The Amish are a group of German-speaking Christians who eschew many worldly goods and technologies. They farm without the use of tractors, use horses and buggies instead of automobiles, and choose kerosene lanterns over electricity in their homes. Most do not own televisions, computers, or telephones. The Amish live, in other words, a simple life centered around religion, hard work, and a sense of tight-knit community. They are famous for their frolics, or barn raisings, in which the community joins together to work on a communal building project.

We spent months in Amish country, interviewing the locals and collecting happiness data. Although the Amish live a more technologically simple existence than most readers of this book, they reported being satisfied with their lives. In fact, despite large families and relatively low earnings, the Amish reported being quite satisfied with their income, housing, food, and other material goods. Sophisticated urbanites probably look down their noses at simple Amish pastimes like quilting and donkey basketball, and may prefer instead Dom Pérignon after an evening at the theater. But who is to say which one produces more happiness? It may be that they are both happiness producers for the same reasons—sharing common experiences with friends, in a pursuit that alters the rhythm of everyday life.

Clearly, there are well-off people who feel they don't have enough money, and there are people of modest means who feel that they have enough. The lesson here is that no matter how much money you earn, you can always want more, and feel poor along the way. Even if you make a million dollars a year, you will find that your desires have a way of slowly ballooning over time. You were once pleased with the studio apartment you and a friend shared in college. Then you were proud of your tiny ranch-style house. As you earned more, you graduated to a beautiful turn-of-the-century home in a fashionable part of town. Soon thereafter you found yourself wanting a vacation home at the beach. We see this same pattern of rising desires across the wealthy nations of the world.

Although incomes have increased dramatically since World War II, people are not a lot happier. Why not? As the industrialized world has become more affluent, the average level of aspirations has also risen. What was once seen as luxury—owning two cars, for instance—has become a "necessity" for many in modern times. With this kind of luxury fever, people can always feel poor. Each of us must ask ourselves whether we have become a victim of our rising material desires.

Buyer Beware: The Toxic Effects of Materialism

Having high aspirations is not always bad, especially if they match your [35] level of income. However, when aspirations run out of control, and are too heavily focused on physical comfort and luxury items, we brand this "materialism." Materialism, simply put, is wanting money and material goods more than you want other things, such as love or leisure time. Of course, we all want a good income, but materialistic people think money is the most important thing in life. How happy are materialists? Most studies show that materialistic people are less happy than others. That's right: although having money proves to be a boon to happiness, wanting money too much can detract from it!

Take a look at some results from a study on materialism and happiness conducted with college students. In figure 3.3, we show the life satisfaction of people with different levels of income. There are two lines—one for those who said money was not important, and another line for those who said money was extremely important. As can be seen, the material-

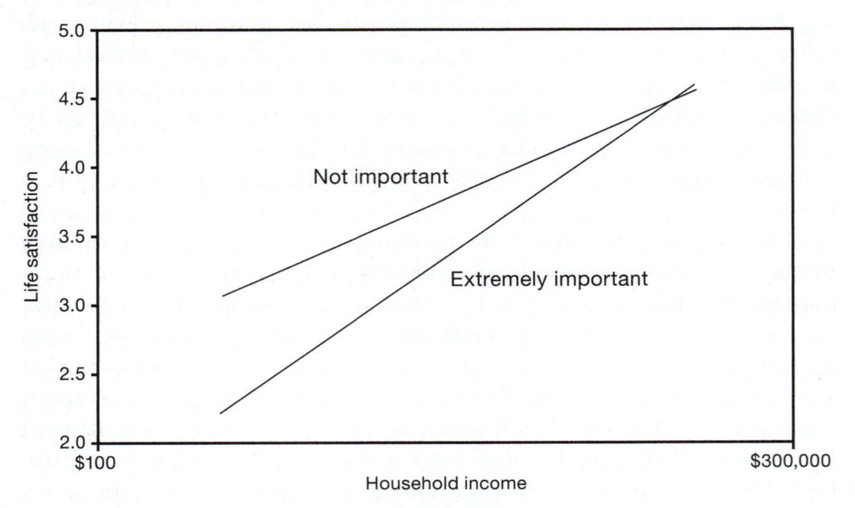

Figure 3.3 **Life Satisfaction for People Varying in Valuing Money**

istic people are less satisfied with their lives at each level of income, except for the highest level of wealth, where they finally catch up.

The happiness of materialists can suffer because their pursuit of money distracts them from other important aspects of life, such as relationships. Huge sums of cash require hard work, and materialists tend to put in extra time at the office and miss out on quality time at home. Although many people enjoy their work, too much of it can harm happiness if the person then has little time left for family and friends. In addition, materialists tend to be dissatisfied because their aspirations are so high, and constantly trend higher. In this way, materialism is a neverending pursuit, with one materialistic goal being quickly replaced with another. No matter the income level, there is always a more expensive car, house, vacation, jet, or private island for which a person can strive. Because materialists tend to earn more money than others, some of the toxic effects of materialism on psychological wealth are damped. However, it is harder for materialists on average to be happy at the same level of income as nonmaterialists because they very often feel as though they need more money, no matter how much they have.

Some readers still may not be convinced that heavily valuing money is toxic to happiness. After all, how can a plasma screen television, a PlayStation game console, or a new set of golf clubs be harmful? Aren't these examples of fun recreational pursuits that can be enjoyed with friends? As it turns out, some clever research illustrates both the benefits and downsides of money. Kathleen Vohs and her colleagues were interested to discover how money, and even reminders of money, affects people psychologically. To do this, they primed the concept of money by leaving subtle reminders around the research laboratory. For instance, they placed a flying dollar as the screen saver on a computer screen in the room, or put a framed dollar bill on the wall. Amazingly, research participants who were exposed to these small monetary cues felt more self-confident than those who were not. They also were able to persevere longer at a difficult task without asking for help than folks in the no-money condition. The effects of money, however, were not all positive in Vohs's study. The people in the money-cue condition were also less likely to be sociable later on, preferring to wait for the experimenters alone rather than with others, sitting farther away from others in a waiting room, and opting for solitary rather than group activities when offered the choice. The money-primed participants were also less helpful to a confederate who appeared to accidentally have dropped his belongings, and they donated less of their experimental earnings to charity when given the opportunity to do so. Thus, the merest hint of money led to a tendency for folks to feel confident, but also to feel more distant from others.

Understanding the Text

1. Explain the happiness formula that the authors provide in this text.
2. The authors cite studies from around the world as evidence of a connection between money and happiness. How do they conceptualize individual happiness compared to national happiness? Which pieces of evidence are most persuasive to you? Which are less persuasive?
3. What do Diener and Biswas-Diener suggest as the correlation between happiness and desire? Identify examples from the reading. Relate this to an example from your own life that supports or refutes their theory. In your view, to what extent is their postulation accurate?

Reflection and Response

4. Diener and Biswas-Diener state that the relationship between happiness and money is too complicated and cannot be understood with a simple explanation because there are many complex variables involved. Describe in detail one or two experiences that, in your view, suggest a link between happiness and money. To what extent do these experiences confirm or challenge the theories presented in this reading?
5. Diener and Biswas-Diener state, "The happiness of materialists can suffer because their pursuit of money distracts them from other important aspects of life, such as relationships" (par. 37). In this sense, the authors would not support the act of shopping as a means to create and sustain happiness. Discuss what they argue about this American obsession. How might you analyze their argument in relation to what you understand about consumer culture today?
6. What examples of uses, abuses, or both of the happiness formula might you provide from our current cultural climate? Cite evidence from social media, newspapers, and periodicals as you make your case.

Making Connections

7. Analyze your own history with money. How important has your material wealth been to you? Discuss the elements of this essay that seem most relevant to your experience. Has your view on the relationship between money and happiness changed after reading this passage? Do you anticipate a shift in your relationship to money in the future?
8. Perform your own mini-study of the relationship between money and happiness using a sample of five or more people. What conclusions might you draw regarding a relationship between wealth and happiness? Discuss your study with regard to this essay. How do your findings compare with those in this piece?
9. Discuss how two authors from Chapter 1 might respond to the remarks in this essay. How might their views contradict those offered here?

The Sociology of Happiness and Contentment: An Interview with Dr. Jordan McKenzie

Stu Horsfield

The following interview appeared in *Nucleus*, the student newspaper of the University of New England in Armidale, Australia, on March 12, 2014. The interviewer, Stu Horsfield, was one of the newspaper's editors. Dr. Jordan McKenzie is a lecturer in the School of Behavioural Cognitive and Social Sciences at the university. He holds a Ph.D. from Flinders University, Australia, and specializes in social and critical theory. Here, McKenzie discusses his own research within the larger context of recent work in happiness studies.

Can you say a bit about your work on happiness, and what your definition of happiness would be?

Defining happiness I think is really problematic in this area. There are a lot of different definitions floating around, and if you look at studies from economics, psychology, sociology and so on, you'll see terms like "happiness," "subjective wellbeing," "contentment," and "satisfaction"; they not only mean different things within a single study, they can often mean quite different things from study to study. So, what one group might refer to as "happiness" may be closer to "wellbeing" for a different group, and so on.

You might be interested to know that the far majority of happiness research is actually done by economists, which I think is really peculiar. There is a journal called *The Journal of Happiness Studies* which publishes a lot on this topic. From memory I think about 75–80% of it is written by economists, and most of the remaining 20% is psychologists. So for sociology, and even philosophy, I think it's interesting to note that especially in journal publications, their voice is really missing from the area.

My research in the sociology of happiness and contentment is interested in looking at a number of things: how societies construct or think about happiness; and how we can think about different forms of happiness depending on whether they are socially derived or perhaps more personally experienced. In my PhD thesis I was trying to set up the distinction of happiness as a personal experience and contentment as a social emotion, or at least a socially dependent emotion. In order to feel content about something I think you need to feel as though it is in line with your expectations; that it's in line with social standards, norms and values. So, something might make you feel really happy, but if it's socially deviant it might be hard for that to produce a kind of lasting contentment.

As a result that means that contentment is an aspect of your relationship with society and how you understand yourself through connecting with society, rather than a purely personal, individualistic thing. So in that sense, you could say that happiness and contentment both change over time. 5

You mentioned the problematic nature of happiness, in what sense is it problematic?

I think one of the reasons happiness is a bit problematic today is really tied to expectations. If you look at a lot of the data and research on happiness levels, it does appear in a lot of this research that happiness is in decline. There is this thing that's referred to as the "Easterlin paradox"° which this very famous researcher discovered, which suggests that as disposable income goes up in advanced first world countries, the number of people reporting that they're very happy actually goes down. This paradox has been argued about since the 70s I think, but it does still seem to be happening.

I think the reason why we're seeing this perceived decline is around this idea of expectations; we have come to expect a lot. I expect my TV shows to be instantly available online when I want them to be, I want the latest bits of information on my phone, instantly and smoothly, I expect technology to work. We expect to be able to get from one place to another faster and cheaper. We derive a sense of what we ought to expect from our social life. Not just through socialisation, education, and so on, but also through comparing ourselves to our friends, colleagues and family members.

We develop these ideas about where we ought to be up to, what we ought to have accomplished, and these expectations are really tricky, because we live in a world that is increasingly unpredictable and kind of chaotic. It's a bit like, you're setting up these life goals, but by the time you're ready to accomplish them the goal posts have moved.

You might be doing a university degree, and then at the end of the three or four years it takes you to finish the degree, maybe that career doesn't really exist in the way it existed when you started the degree. This is something that we all feel strangely familiar about, but at the same time we all expect to have these great careers and to accomplish a great deal. That can be really challenging emotionally, to live with that 10

Easterlin paradox: named for its author, economist Richard Easterlin (b. 1926).

kind of instability and impermanence, but at the same time have these high expectations for the possibilities of what might happen.

It sounds kind of depressing, but at the same time the reason I'm so interested in this area is that I think there are a lot of really valuable lessons that can be extracted out of sociology that can help us better understand happiness.

Does happiness emerge from contentment? Or are they different things?

I think they're quite different. One of the funny things about happiness when you look at it in the long term is that often the times in our lives that we look back on as being the happiest were not actually terribly enjoyable while we were doing them. There's a great line from Theodor Adorno° in *Minima Moralia* where he says that happiness only really exists in memories, because when we are doing things that make us happy, it's often not really pleasurable.

"Happiness only really exists in memories, because when we are doing things that make us happy, it's often not really pleasurable."

As an undergraduate student, you might think back to a time when you were writing an essay and it was just painful, it was really tough and you doubted yourself, stressed, worried, and panicked. And then you get a really high grade for it and you look back on this 10 years later as being this great time in your life where you accomplished something fantastic, but at the time you just wanted to crawl back into bed and hide from everything. And that's of course perfectly normal. That highlights one of the challenges with our thinking about happiness.

I think modernity promises happiness to be this kind of instant gratification, we live in this kind of instant consumer society, and so I think there are aspects of modernity that make promises about happiness that it actually can't keep. You know, "if you do this or that you'll be happy," if you get this new car or new outfit and so on. And that teaches us that happiness is something that should be gained instantly, that you should get something for nothing, or get more than you put in. I don't think happiness really works that way. That leads back to the point I was making before about expectations, that we expect things to be instantly satisfying. 15

Would you say that happiness, and to an extent contentment, involves an element of hard work?

Theodor Adorno (1903–1969): German philosopher and sociologist, and a key figure in the Frankfurt School of critical theory.

Yeah, unfortunately. This is an argument that has been going on for a long time. Do we need a degree of unpleasantness in order to help us contextualise pleasantness? I definitely think we need a variety.

Part of that is accepting that a certain degree of unpleasantness or sadness is actually perfectly natural. I think we live in a society that doesn't think that way. A few hundred years ago we would think about melancholia as being something that highly intelligent people had. The great composer or the great mathematician would go through a period of melancholia and it was admirable. It was like an athlete punishing their body in order to accomplish a physical task. An intellectual would go through melancholia to accomplish some great piece of work. This is something that people really were in awe of, and now it's something that has to be cured.

Of course, I have to be absolutely clear: my work is more about happiness and sadness in the majority of people. In terms of cases where people are suffering from something quite radically different I'll hold back from commenting because it's not my area. I'm not looking at people who are suffering from an illness, I'm looking at people who fit within what we might call "normal," but who, in day to day life will feel happy and feel sad. I think there is definitely a wider scope for thinking about normal amounts of happiness and sadness than we sometimes give credit for. But the idea that sadness necessarily has to be fixed and cured, I don't buy into that idea.

Understanding the Text

1. Why is it so hard to define happiness, according to McKenzie?
2. What is the attitude of Horsfield, the interviewer? How would you describe the tone of the interview?

Reflection and Response

3. Reflect on the relationships between personal and social definitions of happiness. How do these two realms interact, according to McKenzie? Is this true in your experience?
4. McKenzie speaks about the experience of a university student. Does his assessment of the life of the university student align with your experience?

Making Connections

5. Write an essay in which you consider McKenzie's comments from the vantage point of Gretchen Rubin ("July: Buy Some Happiness," p. 291). Does Rubin share McKenzie's point of view on happiness?
6. McKenzie discusses hard work and instant gratification as polar opposites in our culture. Find examples of people working for happiness and write an essay about their work, citing McKenzie as you make your case.

How Happy Are You and Why?

Sonja Lyubomirsky

Sonja Lyubomirsky is professor of psychology at the University of California, Riverside. Born in Russia, she earned a Ph.D. in social psychology from Stanford University in 1994. She is the author of *The How of Happiness: A New Approach to Getting the Life You Want* (2008) and *The Myths of Happiness: What Should Make You Happy, but Doesn't, What Shouldn't Make You Happy, but Does* (2013). She has also published more than eighty articles and book chapters. Her research focuses on the development of "sustainable" happiness and cultural influences on the pursuit of happiness. The following chapter from *The How of Happiness* draws on a wide range of scientific research to consider steps that individuals can take to increase their level of happiness.

Have you ever known someone who is deeply and genuinely happy? A person who truly has the ability to see the world through rose-colored glasses? Someone who appears composed and untroubled even in the face of adversity? Perhaps it is a friend or a coworker or even a member of your family. It's hard not to envy such people. How do they do it? Why aren't they bothered or distraught by the strains and ordeals of everyday life, like most of us?

It's especially frustrating and perplexing to be around such individuals when they're in the same difficult or troubling situation as we are but seem happy in spite of it. Say, for example, that you both share a tormenting boss, a screamer who is never satisfied with your work. Or you both are in the first year of law school and are loaded down with a crushing amount of reading and homework. Or you both are new parents and overwhelmed with the sleep deprivation, anxiety, and drudgery of caring for a newborn. Such situations drag you down, making you moody, nerve-racked, and sometimes even terribly unhappy and low. But this happy person you know seems able to brush off the frustrations, the stresses, the hardships, and the disappointments, to pick herself up each time and to put on a positive face. She sees challenge where you see only threat. She takes an uplifting, optimistic perspective when you feel distrustful and beaten down. She is galvanized to take action, while you are sluggish and passive.

Such individuals may be mind-boggling and intimidating and, yes, even off-putting at times. They can be demoralizing because they make us wonder about our own dispositions. How can we be more like them? Can we ever be as happy as they are? I've asked myself these questions too and decided that the only way to find out is to do some research, to study genuinely happy people systematically and intensively. By closely observing them, we can learn a great deal not just about them but about ourselves.

In my interviews and experiments with very happy people, I've even found a few who remain happy or are able to recover their happiness fairly quickly after tragedies or major setbacks. Take the cases of Angela and Randy.

Angela

Angela is thirty-four and one of the happiest people that I ever interviewed. You wouldn't guess it, however, from all she's had to bear. When Angela was growing up in Southern California, her mother was emotionally and physically abusive to her, and her father did nothing to intervene. In addition to what she endured at home, she was overweight as a teenager and stigmatized at school. When Angela was in eleventh grade, her mother was diagnosed with breast cancer, and the physical abuse ended. However, the emotional abuse got only worse, until Angela couldn't stand it any longer and moved out to marry a man she'd known for just three months. She and her husband moved up north and lived there for four years. Soon after the birth of their daughter, Ella, they divorced, and Angela moved back to California, where she still lives.

Angela is currently a single mother. Things are hard financially. Her ex-husband doesn't visit his daughter and pays no child support. To provide for her small family, Angela has taken a crack at several careers. During her last career change she felt as though she had finally found her dream job (as an aesthetician), but she was fired unexpectedly, her hopes and finances in ruins. She had to file for bankruptcy and go on welfare for a time. Right now she is back in college full-time, working toward a degree in nursing.

Still, with all that has happened and all the challenges that have come to pass, Angela considers herself a very happy person. Her daughter, Ella, to whom she is extremely close, brings her endless joy. They relish reading *The Chronicles of Narnia* together, going to free concerts, and snuggling in bed watching videos. As Angela sees it, Ella doesn't always have what the other kids have, but she gets more love than she could possibly want. Angela also has an infectious sense of humor, and when she laughs about her troubles—the time on welfare, the day she lost her beloved job—it's impossible not to laugh along with her. She has made many friends—indeed, formed a whole community of like-minded people—and they are a pleasure and a support to her. She finds deep satisfaction in helping others heal from their own wounds and traumas, for as she reasons, "It's virtually impossible to face one's shadows alone."

Randy

Like Angela, Randy endured a lot as a child. He lost two people close to him to suicide, at age twelve his father and at age seventeen his best friend. When he was in fifth grade, his mother left his father and moved the family out of state and away from everyone he knew in order that she could live with her boyfriend, Roy. Although Randy's bond with his mother was, and still is, strong, Roy belittled Randy, and their relationship was strained. Interestingly, much like Angela, Randy escaped his home life by marrying too soon and too young. His marriage was fraught with difficulty and finally ended when he discovered the extent of his wife's infidelities. Still, he was devastated initially by the breakup and felt that he had had more than his share of loss and death.

Today Randy is one of those happy people who make everyone around them smile and laugh. He picked himself up after his divorce, moved to another city, found work as a safety engineer, and eventually remarried. He is now forty-three, remarried for three years, and stepfather to three boys. How did he do it? Randy is an eternal optimist and claims that seeing the "silver lining in the cloud" has always been his key to survival. For example, although some of his coworkers find their jobs frustrating and stressful, he says that his allows him "to think outside the box." Moreover, while a friend of his struggles with stepchildren, Randy is overjoyed by "the opportunity to be a dad." Indeed, one of his favorite activities is watching his sons play football. Others might look back on their childhoods with bitterness, but he remembers the good times.

Where Do You Fit In?

10 Although they may appear unique, there are quite a few Randys and Angelas around. Of course, there are many very unhappy individuals as well. All of us can identify people who are exactly the opposite—that is, people who never seem to be happy, even during the good times, who are chronically sullen and sour, who accentuate the negative and focus on the downside of everything, and appear to be unable to find much joy in life.

Shannon

One such person I interviewed is Shannon. At twenty-seven Shannon is studying for a certificate to teach English as a second language. She has a boyfriend, who's in school in Italy, and when he returns in two months, they plan to move in together. Growing up, Shannon had an uneventful childhood, a stable and modest home, and several close friends.

Her family did a lot of traveling all over the United States. Shannon told me that when she was in eighth grade, her mother gave her a dog, Daisy, still alive today. Shannon considers the dog one of her best friends.

But despite the lack of tragedy or trauma in her life, Shannon seems to turn everything into a crisis. She found the transition from high school to college extremely stressful and often felt crushed and overwrought about the harder and less familiar workload. In the dormitory, she shared a room with a roommate, who was generally a nice person but who had irritating habits, like turning up the volume on the TV. Shannon was incredibly bothered by this and grew more and more distant and hostile toward her roommate. When Shannon finally was able to switch to a new roommate whom she liked and admired, she was ecstatic at first but then became hurt that the other girl "was never around."

Today Shannon is very active. She rock climbs and Rollerblades in the summer and snowboards and skis in the winter. She also told me that she enjoys teaching and thinks there is mutual growth between the children she currently tutors and herself. On the surface, her life is quite good. She has a promising and enjoyable career ahead of her, a boyfriend, a stable family life, even a dog she loves. However, Shannon sees herself as a generally unhappy person. Although she is pleased with her academic achievements, she believes that she can't truly enjoy those achievements because of a lack of self-confidence. Indeed, she minimizes any success by explaining it away as caused by luck or persistence. Sometimes she even is haunted by the feeling that she should have chosen a different career. Overall, Shannon feels very alone and believes her life to be unsteady and her relationships unreliable. She remembers her childhood fondly, as the only time she knew "true happiness" and felt self-assured and carefree. Today she depends a great deal on her boyfriend for positive feelings of self-worth, and she experiences life as "very lonely" when he's not around. She is prone to overspend and overeat at such times. When Shannon feels particularly insecure and hopeless, everything seems dark, and she finds herself sinking into dejection and gloom.

The Happiness Continuum

Human happiness, like height or temperature or IQ, lies on a continuum, a numerical scale that ranges from very, very low to very, very high. Shannon represents the lower end of the happiness continuum. Randy and Angela are at the high end. All of us fit somewhere on that scale, and it is critical to find out where exactly that may be. No matter whether you are deeply depressed or are simply not as happy as you'd like to be, before you can begin the process of becoming happier, you need to deter-

SUBJECTIVE HAPPINESS SCALE

INSTRUCTIONS: For each of the following statements or questions, please circle the number from the scale that you think is most appropriate in describing you. (Carefully take note of the labels, or anchors, for the 1 to 7 scales, as they differ for each of the four items.)

(1) In general, I consider myself:

1	2	3	4	5	6	7
not a very happy person						a very happy person

(2) Compared with most of my peers, I consider myself:

1	2	3	4	5	6	7
less happy						more happy

(3) Some people are generally very happy. They enjoy life regardless of what is going on, getting the most out of everything. To what extent does this characterization describe you?

1	2	3	4	5	6	7
not at all						a great deal

(4) Some people are generally not very happy. Although they are not depressed, they never seem as happy as they might be. To what extent does this characterization describe you?

1	2	3	4	5	6	7
a great deal						not at all

HOW TO CALCULATE YOUR SCORE:

STEP 1: Total = Item 1:___ + Item 2:___ + Item 3:___ + Item 4:___ = _____

STEP 2: Happiness score = Total (from above)_____ divided by 4 = _____

Date: ____________________

Happiness score (2nd administration): ___ Date: ____________________

Happiness score (3rd administration): ___ Date: ____________________

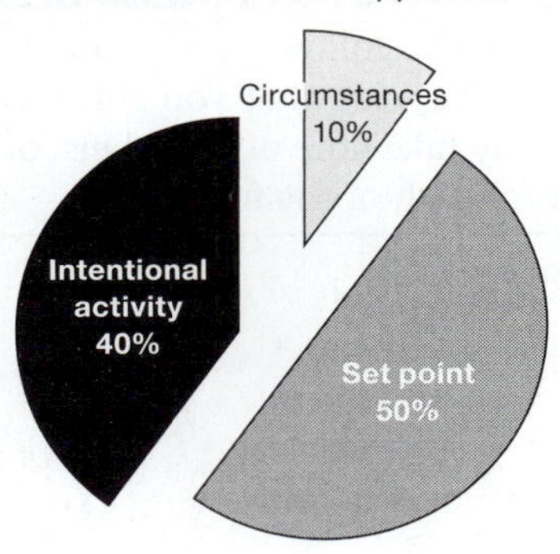

mine your present personal happiness level, which will provide your first estimate of your happiness set point.

15 From the Greek philosopher Aristotle to the father of psychoanalysis Sigmund Freud to *Peanuts* creator Charles Schulz, writers and thinkers have offered wide-ranging definitions of happiness. Aristotle wrote that happiness is "an expression of the soul in considered actions," Freud noted that it's a matter of *lieben und arbeiten*—to love and to work—and Schulz famously proclaimed, "Happiness is a warm puppy." Most of us, however, are well aware of what happiness is and whether we are happy. To paraphrase the late U.S. Supreme Court Justice Potter Stewart, happiness is like obscenity: We can't define it, but we know it when we see it.

I use the term *happiness* to refer to the experience of joy, contentment, or positive well-being, combined with a sense that one's life is good, meaningful, and worthwhile. However, most of us don't need a definition of happiness because we instinctively know whether we are happy or not. Academic researchers prefer the term *subjective well-being* (or simply *well-being*) because it sounds more scientific and does not carry the weight of centuries of historical, literary, and philosophical subtexts. I use the terms *happiness* and *well-being* interchangeably.

So, how do you measure the degree to which you are a happy or an unhappy person? Because no appropriate happiness thermometer exists, researchers generally rely on self-reports. In much of my research with human participants, I have used a popular simple four-item measure of overall happiness that I developed and call the Subjective Happiness Scale. The title is fitting, inasmuch as happiness is inherently subjective and must be defined from the perspective of the person. No one but you knows or should tell you how happy you truly are. So reply to the four items [in the Subjective Happiness Scale] to determine your current happiness level, which you need to know before you can estimate your set point. (More on that later.)

Myth No. 1: Happiness Must Be "Found"

The first myth is that happiness is something that we must *find*, that it's out there somewhere, a place just beyond our reach, a kind of Shangri-la. We could get there, yes, but only if the right things would come to pass: if we'd marry our true loves, secure our dream jobs, purchase elegant houses. Don't be the person who is waiting for this, that, or the other thing to happen before she can be happy. There's a cartoon in which a little boy on a tricycle says to a playmate holding a kite, "I can't wait to grow up and be happy." If you're not happy today, then you won't be happy tomorrow unless you take things into your own hands and take action. To understand that 40 percent of our happiness is determined by intentional activity is to appreciate the promise of the great impact that you can make on your own life through intentional strategies that *you* can implement to remake yourself as a happier person.

"Happiness, more than anything, is a state of mind, a way of perceiving and approaching ourselves and the world in which we reside."

Happiness is not out there for us to find. The reason that it's not *out* there is that it's *inside* us. As banal and clichéd as this might sound, happiness, more than anything, is a state of mind, a way of perceiving and approaching ourselves and the world in which we reside. So, if you want to be happy tomorrow, the day after, and for the rest of your life, you can do it by choosing to change and manage your state of mind. These steps lie at the heart of this book.

Myth No. 2: Happiness Lies in Changing Our Circumstances

Another big fallacy is the notion that if only something about the circumstances of our lives would change, then we would be happy. This kind of thinking is what I call "I would be happy IF ______" or "I will be happy WHEN ______." This logic is shared by some of us who remember periods in our lives when we experienced real happiness but think that we could never recapture the exact set of circumstances that brought this real happiness about. Perhaps these were the college years (as they were for me, at least in hindsight), or when we fell in love for the first time, or when our children were young, or when we lived abroad. The reality is that the elements that determined our happiness in the past, and can make for future happiness, are with us right now and are right here waiting to be taken advantage of. As we can see from the pie chart [on p. 184], 20 changes in our circumstances, no matter how positive and stunning, actually have little bearing on our well-being.

Myth No. 3: You Either Have It or You Don't

One day my brother, who's an electrical engineer, told me that he had read an article about Buddhist monks who taught themselves to be happy through meditation. "What a new concept!" he exclaimed. "I never thought you could *teach* yourself to be happy. I thought you either have it or you don't." This notion—that we are born happy or unhappy—is ubiquitous. Many of us, especially those of us who are not very happy, believe that our unhappiness is genetic and there's really nothing we can do about it. To the contrary, growing research demonstrates persuasively that we can overcome our genetic programming. . . .

The Happiness Set Point

I hope that you have now accepted the fact that the specifics of your life circumstances, unless they are truly dire, are really not the crux of your unhappiness. If you're unhappy with your job, your friends, your marriage, your salary, or your looks, the first step you should take toward reaching greater lasting happiness is to put those things aside in your mind for now. Hard as it is, try not to reflect on them. Keep reminding yourself that these things are really not what is preventing you from getting happier. It will take a great deal of discipline and self-control, and you may lapse, but it's important to unlearn this commonly held but false belief.

One of my guilty pastimes is reading newspaper advice columns. Some months ago a woman wrote in to my local paper, complaining about every job that she's ever had. At her first job she was plagued by spiteful, gossipy coworkers, at her second it was an overbearing boss, at her third it was utter monotony, and so on. She appealed for help in finding a job she likes. The wise advice columnist's blunt reply was something like this: "It's not the colleagues or the boss or the nature of the work; it's something that *you're* doing!"

If the cause of your unhappiness is really not your circumstances, then surely it must be that you were just born this way. This is also a fallacy, the myth of "you either have it or you don't." Challenging the veracity of this belief is trickier because you see, it is partly true. As the pie chart illustrates, your genetically determined predisposition for happiness (or unhappiness) accounts for 50 percent of the differences between you and everyone else. Notably, a susceptibility to clinical depression has also been found to be partly rooted in our genetic makeups. Before we

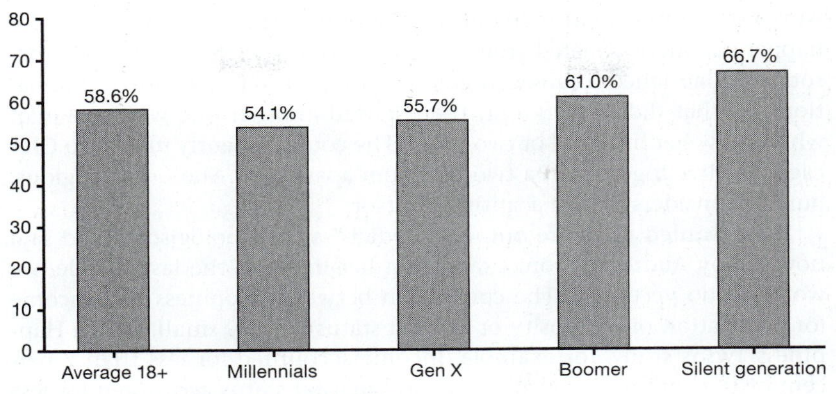

Source: Data from Proper Insights & Analytics.

get depressed about being born depressed, however, I'd like to highlight one vital implication of these findings: that those of us who wish we were a great deal happier should be a little less hard on ourselves. We are, after all, dealing with a stacked deck to some extent. Another critical step in clearing the way to committing to becoming happier is to appreciate the fact that 50 percent is a long way from 100 percent, and that leaves ample room for improvement. So how exactly do we know that the happiness set point accounts for 50 percent?

Helen and Audrey

The strongest evidence for the set point comes from a series of fascinating studies done with identical and fraternal twins. The reason that studying twins reveals so much about the genetics of happiness is that twins share specifically known portions of their genetic material; identical twins share 100 percent, and fraternal twins (like regular siblings) 50 percent. So, by measuring the degree to which twins are similar in their happiness levels, we can infer how much of their happiness is likely rooted in their genes. 25

One of the most famous twin studies, the Happiness Twins study, was carried out by behavior geneticists David Lykken, Auke Tellegen, and colleagues at the University of Minnesota. Using data from the Minnesota Twin Registry, they have followed a large number of mostly Caucasian twins born in Minnesota. Let's consider two participants from their study, Helen and Audrey, who are thirty years old and identical twins, born in St. Paul. Suppose our task was to guess how happy Audrey is, and we are given information about her life during the past ten years. A lot happened: She graduated from Carleton College in Northfield, Minnesota, and launched a career in graphic design; she had a long-term relationship that didn't work out, then started another one with the man who is now her husband of two years. The couple recently moved to Chicago and live together in a two-bedroom apartment. She's not religious, but she considers herself a spiritual person.

If we wanted to figure out (or "predict," as psychologists would say) how happy Audrey is from examining her life over the last decade, we wouldn't do very well. The correlation between happiness and income (or occupation or religiosity or marital status) is very small. In the Happiness Twins study, for example, income accounted for less than 2 percent of the variance in well-being, and marital status accounted for less than 1 percent. However, if we tried to guess how happy Audrey is by considering the happiness level of her twin sister, Helen, who still lives in St. Paul, we'd be much more accurate. In fact, if we considered Helen's happiness level ten years ago—at age twenty!—that level would be very close to Audrey's happiness today.

In other words, the average happiness of your identical twin (even if assessed ten years earlier) is a much more powerful clue to your happiness today than *all the facts and events* of your life!

However, to be completely sure of their striking findings of the comparable levels of the happiness of identical twins, researchers had to compare the happiness of fraternal twins as well. Recall that fraternal twins are one-half as genetically similar to each other as are identical twins. Interestingly, the researchers found that if Helen and Audrey had been fraternal twins and thus no more alike than any two sisters, you could *not* guess Audrey's happiness from knowing Helen's. Whether or not your fraternal twin (or any other sibling) is happy or unhappy implies nothing about how happy or unhappy you might be. This fact—that identical twins (but not fraternal ones) share similar happiness levels—suggests that happiness is largely genetically determined. Indeed, the present-day consensus among researchers, based on a growing number of twin studies, is that the heritability of happiness is approximately 50 percent; hence the 50 percent slice of the pie on my pie chart.

Separated at Birth

There's a significant problem with such twin studies, however. To make [30] conclusions from them, the researchers must assume that both types of twins—identical and fraternal—experience similar family environments. But is this really true? Unlike identical twins, fraternal twins of the same sex often look and behave quite differently. Thus their parents, teachers, and friends are likely to treat them differently, and the twins themselves are likely to emphasize their uniqueness. So the environment and upbringing of fraternal twins are not really as closely shared as those of identical twins.

Fortunately, this problem can be addressed by doing a different kind of study altogether. Researchers can compare twins raised together with twins separated in infancy and raised apart. This is a tough-to-find sample, but one researcher managed to assemble a set of such twins who had already reached middle age and asked them to complete measures of well-being. Their findings have been deemed a classic in psychology. The identical twins were extremely similar to each other in their happiness scores, and remarkably, the similarity was no smaller if the twins had been raised apart! The happier one identical twin was, the happier the other was—no matter whether they grew up under the same roof or on different coasts. Interestingly, however, regardless of whether they were raised together or apart, the happiness levels of the *fraternal* twins were completely uncorrelated. Like any siblings, fraternal twins do not resemble each other in their average levels of happiness. Again, these findings are fascinating, underscoring the conclusion that happiness is, to a large extent, influenced by genetic factors, that each one of us inherits a pre-programmed set point. But the research also shows us that yes, while 50 percent of the differences among our happiness levels is determined by set points (and 10 percent, let's not forget, by circumstances), fully 40 percent is still available to us to mold.

I've probably come across the twins data a dozen times, yet they freshly surprise me each time I see them. I picture two little identical twin boys separated at birth and growing up to be teenagers and then men with different parents and siblings, in different homes, schools, and cities. I imagine them meeting each other for the first time in their thirties or forties and being floored at how similar they are. The Minnesota Twin Registry has documented many such meetings, and the stories are probably familiar enough to have entered the national consciousness. The most famous case is that of two men—both named James—who encountered each other for the first time at age thirty-nine. The day they met, both were six feet tall and weighed exactly 180 pounds. Each smoked Salems, drank Miller Lite, and habitually bit his fingernails. When they discussed their life histories, some incredible coincidences emerged. Both had married women named Linda, had divorced them, and then remarried women named Betty. Each James enjoyed leaving love notes to his wife throughout the house (though perhaps both Lindas didn't appreciate it enough). Their firstborn sons were also named James, one James Alan and the other James Allen, and both men had named their dogs Toy. Each James had owned a light blue Chevrolet and had driven it to the same beach in Florida (Pass-a-Grille Beach) for family vacations. I would bet anything that they were equally happy (or unhappy).

Do Genes Predestine Us to Be Happy or Unhappy?

No matter which way we look at it, the empirical data from the Happiness Twins study led to the conclusion that the genetic basis for happiness is strong—very strong. It appears that each of us is born with a happiness set point, a characteristic potential for happiness throughout our lives. The magnitude of that set point may originate from the sunny maternal side of our family or our depressive paternal side, or roughly equally from both; we'll never know. The essential point is that even if major life changes, like a new relationship or a car accident, might push our happiness level up or down, we tend to revert to this genetically determined set point. Evidence for this phenomenon comes from studies that follow people over time as they react to good and bad things happening in their lives. For example, one study tracked Australian citizens every two years from 1981 to 1987 and found that positive and negative life events (e.g., "made lots of new friends," "got married," "experienced serious problems with children," or "became unemployed") influenced their feelings of happiness and satisfaction as we would expect. But after the events had passed, their feelings returned to their original baselines. Another study conducted in the United States with undergraduates showed essentially the same thing. The big and small events experienced by these students boosted or deflated their well-being, but only for about three months. So, although you may be made temporarily ecstatic or miserable by what comes to pass, it seems that you can't help eventually returning to your set point. And as far as anyone knows, this set point *cannot be changed.* It is fixed, immune to influence or control.

But just because your happiness set point cannot be changed doesn't mean that your happiness level cannot be changed.

In *The African Queen,* Katharine Hepburn declares to Humphrey Bogart, "Nature, Mr. Allnut, is what we are put in this world to rise above!" We can rise above our happiness set points, just as we can rise above our set points for weight or cholesterol. Although on the face of it, the set point data appear to suggest that we all are subject to our genetic programming, that we all are destined to be only as happy as that "programming" allows, in actuality they do not. Our genes do not *determine* our life experience and behavior. Indeed, our "hard wiring" can be dramatically influenced by our experience and our behavior. This is illustrated, as I describe in detail later, by the notion that there's a great deal of room to improve our happiness by the things we *do*, our intentional activities. Even the most heritable traits like height, which has a heritability level of .90 (relative to about .50 for happiness), can be radically modified by environmental and behavioral changes. For example, since the 1950s the average height of Europeans has been growing at a rate of two centimeters per decade, in part because of better overall nutrition.

Or take the case of a rare condition known as phenylketonuria. PKU stems from a mutation in a single gene on chromosome 12 and, without treatment, leads to brain damage, resulting in mental retardation and premature death. PKU is said to have a heritability of 1, because it is *entirely* genetically determined. But this doesn't mean that an infant born with the gene that causes PKU is doomed to its lethal effects. If the parents ensure that the infant's diet is free of an amino acid called phenylalanine, which is found in such common foods as eggs, milk, bananas, and NutraSweet, the brain damage may be entirely prevented. It's important to note that the infant's genetic endowment doesn't change—she will always carry the mutant gene—but the expression of her genetic endowment *can* change.

I make much the same case for happiness. If you are born with a low set point for happiness, the genes coding for that set point will always be a part of you. However, for those genes to be fully expressed, they must encounter the appropriate, fitting environment, much the way a seed requires a particular soil to grow. In fact, there is a powerful study that shows just what a dramatic effect one particular environmental factor can have on whether or not people who have a "depression gene" actually succumb to depression. That environmental factor is severe stress.

The Case of the "Depression Gene"

When I was an undergraduate, I was a research assistant for a psychology professor named Paul Andreassen. Paul was a good friend of another professor, Avshalom Caspi, who dropped by our lab on a regular basis. At the time I was in awe of research, of professors, indeed of anything having to do with Harvard, and I remember Avshalom as a dark, striking figure with long hair and an Israeli accent. Little did I know that years later and a continent away, along with his future wife and collaborator, Terri Moffitt, he would conduct a truly groundbreaking study. Caspi, Moffitt, and their colleagues at King's College in London were interested in the relationship between stress and depression. Why do stressful life experiences, like being evicted from one's apartment or losing a pregnancy, trigger depression in some people but not in others?

It turns out that depression is associated with a particular gene, called the 5-HTTLPR, which comes in two forms, the long and the short. The short allele° is undesirable to have, because it rids the brain of a substance needed to fend off depressive symptoms. Caspi tracked the presence of this so-called bad gene in a sample of 847 infants born in New Zealand and learned that more than half carried it. At the time of the study, because those infants were now twenty-six years old, the researchers were able to identify the number of stressful or negative life events the participants had experienced during the past five years (since age twenty-one), as well as evidence of depression during the past year (at age twenty-six). A quarter (26 percent) reported having experienced three or more adverse life events, and 17 percent had had major depressive episodes.

Not surprisingly, overall the more stress and trauma the New Zealanders had experienced during their last five years, the more likely they were to become depressed. The critical finding, however, was that the stressful experiences led to depression *only* among those participants who carried the "bad" short allele of the 5-HTTLPR gene. Interestingly, the same result was found for stress suffered in childhood. Those participants who were maltreated between ages three and eleven were more likely to become depressed at age twenty-six, but again, *only* if they carried the ill-fated short allele. 40

So, our genes play an important role in depression, as they do in happiness, but they need to be "expressed"—or turned on or off. The findings of the New Zealand study, which was voted by the editorial board of *Science* magazine as the second-biggest finding of that year (the biggest was on the origins of life!), suggest that the short allele variant of the 5-HTTLPR gene is activated by an environmental trigger—namely, stress. Similarly, the long "good" allele appears to *protect* us from responding to a stressful experience by becoming depressed—that is, by making us resilient. The fact that many of us may carry genes for a particular vulnerability (be it PKU or cardiovascular disease or depression or happiness) therefore does not mean that we will express that vulnerability in our lives. If the New Zealanders with the short "bad" allele of the 5-HTTLPR gene were able to avoid highly stressful situations or to engage psychotherapists or supportive confidants when they anticipated stress, their genetic propensity for depression might never be triggered. Furthermore, new research has shown that individuals unfortunate enough to possess the "bad" gene yet fortunate to have had either supportive family environments *or* sev-

allele: one of two or more alternate forms of the same gene.

eral present-day positive life experiences do *not* become depressed. In order to express or *not* to express themselves, genes need a particular environment (e.g., a happy marriage or job layoff) or a particular behavior (e.g., seeking out social support). This means that no matter what your genetic predisposition, whether or not that predisposition is expressed is in *your* hands.

What Electrodes Can Teach Us

A better understanding of the happiness set point comes from perhaps the most exciting laboratory right now in the area of well-being, that of Richard Davidson at the University of Wisconsin–Madison. Like the behavior geneticists, Davidson argues that each of us has a natural set point, which he defines as a baseline of activity in the prefrontal cortex (front part) of the brain. In a fascinating discovery, he noticed that happy people show greater activity in one side of their brain than the other, and unhappy people show the reverse pattern.

Davidson uses the procedure called electroencephalography (EEG) to measure a person's brain activity. He finds that happy people, those who smile more, and who report themselves to be enthusiastic, alert, and engaged in life show a curious asymmetry in their brain activity; they have more activity in their *left* prefrontal cortex than in the right. Although no researcher would claim that the left side of the front region of the brain is the "happiness center," clearly this region is associated with positive emotion. Even newborns who are given something nice to suck display increased activation in the left sides of their brains, and so do adults who are shown funny film clips. The right prefrontal region, by contrast, is activated during unpleasant states and negative emotions.

What does it mean to any of us that the left side of a happy person's brain lights up more than the right side? Perhaps only something as seemingly ineffable as the fact that happiness appears to be hardwired in the neural circuitry. Thus, although Davidson's work doesn't offer proof for the notion of a happiness set point, it certainly supports it. If the set point is genetically determined, it's presumably rooted in our neurobiology.

Implications for You

45 Some of us simply possess higher set points for happiness, more cheerful dispositions, and higher potentials for well-being. Perhaps "the sun shines more brightly for some persons than others." Having a high set point may feel as if more of our days were sunny ones. It may mean never having to work very hard at being happy. But this is not the situation facing most of us. So let's start with the premise that we may have a disappointingly

low set point and then ask ourselves: First, precisely how low *is* that set point, and second, what can we do about it?

To address the first question, it's impossible to know exactly what your set point is unless you evaluate it over time. You need to record the date that you first completed the Subjective Happiness Scale (see p. 183). Your score on that scale is your *preliminary estimate* of your set point. The reason it's preliminary is that it's somewhat sensitive to what's happening around you. For example, your score could have been influenced by a recent event, by your stress level that day, even by the weather. You will need therefore to fill out the Subjective Happiness Scale again, ideally at least two weeks after initially taking it but *before* you begin the happiness building program. . . . If you intend to begin straightaway, then retake the scale the day before you start; the *average* of your two scores (or three scores, if you take it three times, and so on) will serve as the estimate of your set point. The more often you take the Subjective Happiness Scale, and the further apart in time you take it, the more reliable the estimate of your set point.

What can you do if your happiness set point is lower than you like? (Although the average is around five, your own hoped-for yardstick may be a lot higher or a lot lower.) To begin with, I must stress that if you desire to become lastingly happier, the answer is not to try to change your set point. By definition, the set point is constant, immune to influence, and wired in your genes. Analogously, if you are born with brown eyes, your eyes will forever remain truly brown. However, as you saw earlier, you are not doomed to obey the directives of your genes, because your genes need a specific environment, a particular set of life experiences, in order to be expressed. Many of these life experiences are indeed under your control, and their potential for influencing your happiness lies in the activities and strategies that make up the large 40 percent of our happiness "pie." Through these activities we can change our happiness *levels*, if not our set points, much as we can change our eye colors (through tinted contact lenses), if not the innate colors of our eyes.

The Promise of Intentional Activity

> Happiness consists in activity. It is a running stream, not a stagnant pool.
>
> —JOHN MASON GOOD

Many are familiar with the Serenity Prayer, written by German philosopher Reinhold Niebuhr and widely adopted for use in twelve-step programs: "God, grant me the serenity to accept the things I cannot change, the courage to change the things I can, and the wisdom to know the difference." But how *can* you know the difference?

It should be obvious by now where the secret to happiness does *not* lie. The fountain of happiness lies *not* in changing our genetically determined set points, for they are, by definition, resistant to change, influence, or control. We are also unlikely to find lasting happiness by changing our life circumstances. Although we may achieve temporary boosts in well-being by moving to new parts of the country, securing raises, or changing our appearances, such boosts are unlikely to be long-lasting. The primary reason, as I have argued, is that people readily and rapidly adapt to positive circumstantial changes. I would furthermore be remiss if I failed to point out other reasons why circumstantial changes may prove unsuccessful in making us permanently happier: because they can be very costly, often impractical, and sometimes even impossible. Does everyone have the money, resources, or time to change her living situation, her job, her spouse, her physical appearance?

If the secret to happiness does not lie in increasing our set points or in positively impacting the circumstances of our lives, what is left? Is it possible to attain greater happiness and sustain it? To be sure, most of us do become happier at some point during our lives. Indeed, contrary to popular belief, people actually get happier with age. A twenty-two-year study of about two thousand healthy veterans of World War II and the Korean War revealed that life satisfaction increased over the course of these men's lives, peaked at age sixty-five, and didn't start significantly declining until age seventy-five. . . . 50

Conclusion

The media are constantly telling us about the latest newfangled strategy shown to "really" work in boosting health and well-being. These strategies keep changing, each one evidently bested by the next, such that every new pronouncement becomes harder to believe. If the new kind of yoga or meditation or marital therapy technique were as effective as the reports claim, then wouldn't everyone be doing it and benefiting from it? Well, no. Any major life-changing endeavor must be accompanied by considerable sustained effort, and I would speculate that the majority of people do not or cannot continue putting out that kind of effort. What's more, all new happiness-enhancing or health-boosting strategies have something in common; each one bestows on the person a specific *goal*, something to do and to look forward [to]. Moreover, as I explain later on, having goals in and of themselves is strongly associated with happiness and life satisfaction. That's why—at least for a time—any new happiness strategy does work!

In a nutshell, the fountain of happiness can be found in how you behave, what you think, and what goals you set every day of your life. "There is no happiness without action." If feelings of passivity and futility overcome you whenever you face up to your happiness set point or to your circumstances, you must know that a genuine and abiding happiness is indeed within your reach, lying within the 40 percent of the happiness pie chart that's yours to guide.

Understanding the Text

1. Lyubomirsky opens with four interviews in which she discusses happiness, and later in the reading she studies "myths" about happiness. What connections does she offer between her interviews and her discussion of "myths"? How might you expand on parts of this conversation?
2. There are two questionnaires in this chapter, the "Subjective Happiness Scale" in this selection and the "Oxford Happiness Questionnaire" (p. 221). First, fill them out. Then assess how you believe your performance in these questionnaires was influenced by the way Lyubomirsky sets up the cases. How would you argue that reading this passage has shaped your view on happiness?
3. What is the role of genetics in Lyubomirsky's definition of happiness?

Reflection and Response

4. Money plays an important role in Lyubomirsky's argument about the myths and truths of happiness. Analyze two advertisements that illustrate the money myths that she discusses; then provide one example that challenges her argument.
5. This reading contains many pieces of advice about acquiring a happier disposition. Discuss these pieces of advice in greater detail. To what extent does Lyubormirsky expand on the correlation between actions and attitudes in these pieces of advice? To what extent would you agree with this argument?

Making Connections

6. Using concepts and terms from Daniel Gilbert ("Paradise Glossed," p. 96), analyze the way that Lyubomirsky builds her argument. How might Gilbert comment on the argument presented by this piece? To what extent would you argue that Lyubomirsky's argument affects the reader's opinion?
7. Using three sources from Chapter 1, evaluate and challenge Lyubomirsky's position. In your view, does spiritual tradition present a parallel to what Lyubomirsky argues in this reading? Cite sentences from this reading to support your claim.
8. Write an essay in which you discuss a relationship between beauty and happiness. What are the benefits to this connection, and what might some critiques be? Use Lyubomirsky and Eric G. Wilson ("Terrible Beauty,"

p. 247) as your sources. How do they support your argument, and how might they oppose it?

9. Compare the "Subjective Happiness Scale" in this selection to the "Oxford Happiness Questionnaire" (p. 221). Do the two questionnaires produce very different results? What are the advantages and disadvantages of the more simple and direct approach of the "Subjective Happiness Scale"?

Enjoyment

Stefan Klein

Stefan Klein is a science writer whose work focuses on the social implications of science. He studied physics and analytical philosophy at the University of Munich and Grenoble, and theoretical biophysics at the University of Freiburg. He left academia in 1996 to become science editor at the German newsmagazine *Der Spiegel*, and in 1999 he turned full time to freelance writing. His first book, *The Science of Happiness: How Our Brains Make Us Happy — and What We Can Do to Get Happier* (2002, trans. Stephen Lehmann), brought together research in the fields of neuroscience, social psychology, and philosophy to explain how feelings of happiness arise in the human brain. Subsequent books include *The Secret Pulse of Time: Making Sense of Life's Scarcest Commodity* (2007) and, most recently, *Survival of the Nicest: How Altruism Made Us Human and Why It Pays to Get Along* (2014). The following chapter from *The Science of Happiness* examines the brain chemistry that produces feelings of contentment and pleasure.

Wanting and liking are two different matters. How often do we go to a party, although we're fairly sure that we won't feel comfortable? There'll just be a lot of boring people clutching their beer bottles, and, frankly, we're not even close to the hosts. Why bother? And yet we want to go, though we can't really explain why. It's as if we're afraid of missing something exciting. But as usual, once we're there, nothing happens, and for a few hours we stand around in a kind of small-talk hell. We swear we'll never again waste an evening in this way . . . until the next time.

Smokers, too, know the difference between wanting and liking. A cigarette can be wonderful. The smoke caresses the nose and tickles the throat like a thousand tender feathers. On its way down, its pleasant bite unfolds as it releases a flavor that is both austere and soft. But by the day's eighth or ninth cigarette . . . ? "Difficult to describe precisely . . ." wrote Jay McInerney in his novel on smoking, ". . . a mix of ozone, blond tobacco and early-evening angst on the tongue."

In such moments a chain smoker begins to hate himself for his dependency and weakness. He despises his cigarettes, and yet he wants them — so much so that he runs to the store in the pouring rain when his pack is empty.

We aren't accustomed to distinguishing between wanting and liking, for very often the two come to the same thing. You probably won't order something off a menu if you know you won't like it. But to confuse the two impulses can be a source of unhappiness, as the bored partygoer and the desperate chain smoker demonstrate. In the worst case, it can lead to serious addictions.

On the other hand, the opposite can happen as well: we can like something without wanting it. After a seven-course meal, you'd still like the dessert, but you wouldn't want to order it. 5

Positive feelings come about in two different ways: when we want something, or when we've gotten something that gives us pleasure. The brain creates the two sets of impulses—wanting/enjoyment, liking/anticipation—in different ways. The Harvard neuroscientist Hans Breiter was even able to show that they activate different parts of the brain. Anticipation activates a center in the forebrain—the *nucleus accumbens*, "the leaning center," so called because it is angled like the Leaning Tower of Pisa. It's controlled by dopamine, the molecule of pleasure, and plays an important role in remembering positive experiences. But when we enjoy something, the areas of the cerebrum responsible for conscious perception are also activated. And the transmitter here isn't dopamine, but opioids, natural substances that resemble opium.

The Transmitters of Euphoria

Every enjoyment is a kind of rush. Whether it's a hot shower on a winter morning, a massage, a good meal, or sex—the same mechanism is at work, and the same synapses in the brain are responsible. And they have the same chemistry: opioids are involved in the creation of every experience of pleasure. At their core all pleasures are the same. What distinguishes the delights of a massage, therefore, from the enjoyment of a cold beer on a hot summer day isn't the melody in the brain, but the different instruments on which it's played. In the one case, signals come from the pressure-sensitive sensors on the skin, in the other, from the tongue and gums. Once the stimuli reach the brain, however, the resulting pleasure is the same.

Maybe the French poet Charles Baudelaire suspected these connections when he exhorted his readers: "You should always be drunk. Everything depends on it. If you don't want to feel the awful burden of Time breaking your shoulders and pressing you to the ground, you must be ceaselessly drunk. But on what? On wine, poetry, virtue . . . whatever you want. But get drunk."

The frenzy of enjoyment interrupts the flow of time—the idea isn't as odd as we might think, since opioids chemically alter our experience of time. During orgasm, for example, the clock seems to stop. Baudelaire recognized that all intoxicants have the same effect and, what's more, that we don't even need artificial stimulants to get intoxicated. The

Luncheon of the Boating Party, Pierre-Auguste Renoir (1881).
Phillips Collection/Washington, D.C./Superstock

equation of "good" and "bad" states of intoxication seemed a monstrous thought at the time. Baudelaire's volume of poetry *Les Fleurs du Mal* (*The Flowers of Evil*) caused a scandal when it was published in 1857. And his collection of prose poems that includes "But get drunk" wasn't published until after his death.

More than a hundred years later, neuroscientists provided the biological basis for Baudelaire's bold claim. In 1973, three research groups determined independently that neurons in the human brain contain receptors—chemical docking stations—for opiates, among them morphine and heroin. To what evolutionary purpose? Certainly not for people to yield to the pleasures of the poppy! 10

Scientists searched feverishly for answers and discovered that the brain can create morphinelike substances that fit exactly onto the mysterious receptors: the first natural opiates—drugs that the body itself creates—had been found. They were called endorphins, a neologism forged from the Greek prefix "endo," for "inner," and "morphine." Soon more such substances were identified: the enkephalins. Finally dynorphins, which have exactly the opposite effect from the endorphins, were discovered—instead of pleasure, they stimulate repugnance. Today all these substances—endorphins, enkephalins, and dynorphins—are brought together under the term "opioids." Opioids are neuropeptides, molecules that are much bigger and have a more complicated structure than dopamine.

After scientists discovered these chemicals in the human brain, it didn't take them long to find the transmitters for pleasure in other animals as well. Opioids flow in the brains of dogs, rodents, and insects, and even in the simple nervous system of the rainworm. Does this mean that all of nature is moved to search for happiness?

Embracing the Whole World

Without endorphins and enkephalins the world would be terribly gray. Just how gray we know in cases where medications cause these transmitters to temporarily lose their effectiveness. Naloxon is such a medication. It is taken to cure heroin addiction, but it also kills the taste for food, stifles laughter, and transforms one's perception of the environment into something resembling soulless machinery, peopled by robots. Sex loses its appeal entirely, although the body still has all the normal physiological responses to orgasm. Without opioids, people seem to be perfectly capable of copulating—they just don't experience pleasure.

The situation gets even worse when the field is left to the endorphins' opponents, the dynorphins. The misery caused by the resulting feelings [is] hard to describe. Experimental subjects who have ingested substances related to dynorphins report chills, insane thoughts, physical weakness, and a complete loss of self-control. Some of them found the experience so terrible that they wanted to jump out a window.

Rats reacted similarly when researchers removed the part of the midbrain controlled by opioids. Everything disgusted them. When they were given sweets that they had especially favored before the operation, they spat them out. If they hadn't been fed intravenously, they would have starved. 15

But what joy we feel when the endorphins and enkephalins are circulating in our heads! We suddenly notice an entire fireworks display of flavors when eating a perfectly normal dish. Our appetite grows and persists even when we're actually full—a reason why pleasure in eating can lead to overweight. Everything seems bright and friendly. If we could, we'd embrace the whole world. We beam when we encounter perfect strangers, not only because we're feeling so good, but because they really seem nice. Our happiness is spilling over—would that we could share it!

When people are under the influence of this substance, they seem to be incapable of sadness. Even Helen of Troy knew after the Trojan War that her relatives needed an intoxicating drink to help ease their sense of loss. In the fourth book of the *Odyssey*° we read:

> Into the mixing-bowl from which they drank their wine
> she slipped a drug, heart's ease, dissolving anger,
> magic to make us all forget our pains . . .
>
> No one who drank it deeply, mulled in wine,
> could let a tear roll down his cheeks that day,
> not even if his mother should die, his father die . . .

Neuropharmacologists today assume that this mixture contained opium, and, indeed, into the nineteenth century treating anxiety and depression with opium was considered best medical practice. "For the relief of the psychic pains nothing equals opium," wrote the author of an American medical textbook of the time. "It is almost as specific in its action in relieving the mental suffering and depression . . . "

Given its addictiveness, no one today would advise us to smoke opium to assuage our sadness. But the brain naturally creates a substance, beta-endorphin, which is much more effective than opium. As harmless as it is effective, it is produced by a gland of the midbrain, the hypophysis cerebri. Sometimes all it takes is a good meal.

Taste, Source of Pleasures

"The close relationship between happiness and roast turkey is a marvel, as is the heart's resilience when a bottle of Marcobrunn parries its every beat," wrote the German novelist Theodor Fontane. Since Fontane wasn't one to drown his sorrows in liquor, and German white wine is not all that potent, the explanation for this phenomenon lies in something other than alcohol. Tasting roasted meat and wine releases beta-endorphins, which scatter sadness to the winds. 20

But good feelings don't come from opioids alone. The entire body is set up for enjoyment. Nothing demonstrates this as clearly as the pleasure we get from food. Nourishment is a necessity of life, but eating is one of life's great pleasures. And because our enjoyment of food is such an elementary happiness, it is the best and also the best-researched example of all sensual pleasures. The machinery of taste shows the extent

the *Odyssey*: Greek epic poem in twenty-four books attributed to Homer, concerning the travels of Odysseus returning from the Trojan War. Composed around the eighth century BCE.

to which human beings are built for happiness and how useful enjoyment can be.

If, as many religions believe, the body is God's temple, then the mouth is its gateway. It is equipped with about three thousand taste buds, tiny little nubs a few hundredths of a millimeter high, mainly on the tongue. Each of these little bumps contains about fifty sense cells that respond to the different tastes.

The taste sensors are the reason some people like spinach, for example, while others don't. A quarter of the population consists of so-called supertasters, who perceive bitterness and sweetness more intensely than the rest of us. Just what the combination of genes is that ruins the taste for spinach we don't yet know. Two groups of scientists, however, have recently identified hereditary factors that are responsible for the sense of sweetness.

"Nature invented positive feelings to seduce us into useful behavior."

Altogether, more than a hundred thousand nerve strands, bundled into two cords, pass taste information from the tongue to the brain. In addition, there are sensors that report heat and cold, and others that identify texture—whether it's soft or crunchy, moist or dry. Cotton candy tastes different from caramel, although both are made of sugar. Finally, there are those sensors that register burning and thus respond to the spiciness of chilies. Every bite and every movement of the tongue sets off an entire firework display of electric signals.

But the signals don't translate into pleasure until they've been received in the brain. As I explained in the first chapter, nature invented positive feelings to seduce us into useful behavior. The pleasure we derive from taste serves to control our energy supply, as experimental psychobiologists have demonstrated on rats. If the rats—who'd been given nothing to eat—wanted to receive nourishment, they had to press a lever, which would release a nutrient solution that flowed through a tube directly into their stomachs, completely bypassing the taste/pleasure circuit. Although they could ingest as much as they wished, after a few weeks they lost almost a third of their weight. The pleasure that eating gives us is anything but a luxury. 25

There is another reason "a thousand things are indifferent to touch, hearing and sight, but nothing is indifferent to taste," as Jean-Jacques Rousseau° observed. As omnivores, humans are not limited to a small menu—unlike dogs, for example, who eat little except meat, or cows,

Jean-Jacques Rousseau (1712–1778): French philosopher (born in Switzerland) and author of *The Social Contract* (1762).

which feed only on grass and herbs. So humans are constantly having to try out unknown foods, which we evaluate with our sense of taste. Pleasure and distaste indicate what is likely to be good for us, and what not. Taste, however, doesn't always lead us to the correct conclusion. Notorious counterexamples are the pleasing taste of the deadly amanita mushroom, or the Japanese blowfish, on which more than one gourmet has feasted to death.

Incidentally, humans do not recognize only four kinds of taste, but in all likelihood five, as scientists have recently discovered: sweetness, saltiness, sourness, bitterness, and savory, also known by its Japanese name, *umami*. This signal is released by certain amino acids, like glutamate, which are found in meat but also in foods like mushrooms, cheese, and tomatoes.

Unsalted food tastes bland because the body needs salt to function, just as it also needs protein. But we tolerate bitter and sour tastes only moderately—a warning, for most poisons are bitter, and many sour fruits aren't ripe. Instead, we devour anything sweet, for sugar is straight energy. Thus the dieter's dilemma: evolution hadn't foreseen diets. It made its creatures to absorb as much nourishment as possible—as a precaution against bad times. The addiction to cake and ice cream is inscribed in our brains.

The Appeal of Massages

With the help of opioids, the brain evaluates everything that we experience, just as it does with food. When something good happens to us, it releases endorphins. But when bad things happen, it's the dynorphins that give the signal. In this way evolution gets its creatures to do what they should do, and to do it gladly. Mammals have to care for their young. Because they're under the influence of opioids, mothers pursue this task with enthusiasm. Endorphins and enkephalins sweeten responsibility: Reward and pleasure are always better motivators than force and fear of punishment. It is precisely those things that are most pleasant that are most necessary for the survival of the species. Sex is a good example: since nature wants us to pass on our genetic inheritance, opioids flow at orgasm.

People also like to be stroked. And not only humans, but monkeys, cats, and guinea pigs are calmed by touch. Even birds, when touched, release opioids in their brain. Interestingly, the surge of opioids brought on by physical contact seems to be less about creating desire than assuaging fear and calming individual members of a group when they feel abandoned or frightened. When young animals are touched, they immediately

30

stop making unhappy sounds. If they're given opiates from an external source, their need for physical contact is diminished. People who are satisfied require less reassurance than those who aren't. And a massage can do miracles when we feel lonely or depressed.

The Path to Harmony

Enjoyment is a signal that the organism is getting what it needs. But what do we need? That depends. When we're thirsty, water. When we're hungry, food. When we're sad, solace. When we're thirsty, the first gulps taste the best, and after a strenuous hike, an otherwise so-so campfire meal tastes superb. Desperate times, desperate measures—but these sometimes turn out to be rather appealing.

Whenever life's basic needs are missing, the body ascertains a deficit. When we're hungry, for example, there's an imbalance between the need for energy and the intake of nourishment. The body releases dynorphin, the opioid of discomfort, which is responsible for our perceiving hunger as unpleasant.

An impulse is set in motion to do something against the unpleasantness. We become restless, irritable, on our guard. We look for a signal to compensate for the deficiency.

We see a goal: a roast chicken! The brain releases beta-endorphin that gives a foretaste of the desired pleasure and signals that the food before us should benefit the organism. At the same time the brain very quickly releases dopamine, the molecule of desire. The circuits for wishing and wanting are closely connected. Under the influence of dopamine we become optimistic and more alert, and we make an effort to satisfy our desires.

We smell the odor of meat, bite into the drumstick, and enjoy the flavor. [35] Still more endorphin floods the brain and signals to the organism that its needs have been met and that it is returning to a state of equilibrium: it's full, and it's comfortable. We relax. Life is good.

In this way, enjoyment accompanies the return to physiological balance. If it's good for you, you'll like it. But the organism's hedonistic principle has another side: pleasure cannot last. As soon as everything is back in order, the sense of pleasure dissipates.

Enjoyment is a signal that we are moving from a worse to a better condition. Positive feelings depend, therefore, on circumstance and timing. Everything has its moment. When it's hot, you'll seek shade, and when you're freezing, you want nothing so much as a seat in front of a fireplace, or at least a cozy wool blanket. It's not the temperature as such that's so essential for our well-being, but its relation to the previous condition of the body. After all, the same cold shower that we find refreshing on a humid summer afternoon takes on a very different quality after a day on the ski slopes.

Every Hollywood director knows this. Most of us no more enjoy a film in which everyone is nice to everyone else than we do one where there is only murder and mayhem. A good plot takes the spectator on a roller coaster of feelings. In the first half hour, we fall in love with the hero. Just when we're sunning ourselves in the glow of his beautiful life and the warmth of his charismatic appeal, he finds himself in terrible danger. Horrible things happen—and we suffer with him. The greater is our joy when everything works out in his favor. The dramatists of ancient Greece called this moment *catharsis*: terror gives way to relief. They, too, knew that contrast is a key to enjoyment.

When Pain Abates

This is why positive feelings come about when pain abates. People have always intuited a connection between pain and pleasure. But it was left to neuropharmacology of the past two decades to show just how closely they're connected.

We perceive pain in the brain, but, as we've learned, the brain is also [40] able to block pain. If I cut my finger, pain sensors, responding to the injury, send electric signals through special bundles of fibers in the spinal cord to the brain. This information is processed in the thalamus, a center in the midbrain: we feel pain. But when it's necessary, the neighboring hypothalamus can order the release of opioids. Enkephalins or endorphins or even the bad dynorphins—all work to neutralize pain, for they interrupt the transmission of signals in the spinal cord. This is why morphine, which resembles natural opiates, is the strongest painkiller of all.

There is a precise and apt expression for the jogger's good spirits: *runner's high*. Releasing endorphins and enkephalins when we're about to be overcome by exhaustion helps the organism to run past the pain. Euphoria suppresses the sense of weakness and goads the runner on to exert himself even further.

It isn't difficult to guess why nature created this mechanism. When an animal is attacked and wounded, its instinct would normally be to lie down in order to save energy. But if opioids have stopped the pain, it can still run for its life. There are other kinds of stress besides the attack of a predator that stimulate the brain's production of opioids. Some of our busy colleagues might be looking for exactly this effect when they keep piling on the work: Stress, too, can be pleasurable. Seen in terms of evolution, this is an old mechanism. The German neuroscientist Randolf

Menzel discovered that even bees have the ability to turn off pain under stress.

Thanks to natural opiates women are able to endure the pain of childbirth. Natural opiates also account for the relaxed, almost beatific glow on the face of many mothers shortly after labor. When acupuncture eases pain, the likely explanation is that the minor pain induced by the needles releases very large amounts of opioids. There is even speculation (as yet unproven) that some people value the spiciness of chilies because they want to savor the rush of the opioids that follows the burning pain in the mouth.

There is nothing in which pain and pleasure are as entwined as in sexuality. One explanation for some masochistic sexual practices might be that endorphins offer a kind of reward for the endurance of pain, thus intensifying the pleasure. Among other effects, endorphins cause dopamine to be released in the brain, which might explain how the enjoyment of pain could lead to a further fanning of desire. But until now, even the most creative neuropsychologists have stayed away from a closer examination of sadomasochistic sexual practices.

The Seesaw of Positive Feelings

The cat plays with the mouse before killing it. Sometimes appetite is more pleasurable than the food itself. In love, too, it can happen that the greatest appeal lies in the games, the flirting, the detours, and the delays. He who seeks to reach his goal by the fastest route is not a good lover. "Good things shouldn't come cheaply," explains Valmont, the practiced and sinister seducer in Choderlos de Laclos' epistolary novel *Dangerous Liaisons*. He is afraid of losing the pleasure of the long erotic contest if he gets to his goal too quickly. 45

Desire and enjoyment are closely connected, but they are also opposed to one another. They're like children on the seesaw: sometimes one is up, sometimes the other. To be in a state of desire means not enjoying the present to the fullest. And to reach and enjoy one's goal is also to experience the extinction of desire, at least for the moment. The urge to exert oneself is inherent in desire, whereas enjoyment is sufficient unto itself. Someone who enjoys eating a good meal, falling in love, or simply sitting in the sun is not leading armies. At that moment he isn't even fit for the small battles of daily life.

In extreme cases, enjoyment can lead to total paralysis. Rats that have been given opiates in high doses are so apathetic that their bodies become waxen and can be shaped like a ball of dough into almost any position. It has been shown neurochemically that when opioids are administered above a certain quantity, the dopamine level can temporarily sink again. The neuropsychologist Jaak Panksepp at Bowling Green State University suspects that this explains the drop in energy and drive after we experience pleasure.

But we can't endure this pleasant laziness for too long, for the effect of opioids lasts only a short while—between a few minutes and a few hours, depending on the situation. After all, enjoyment serves as a signal. When the message has been delivered, the messenger has no more to say.

This is the shadow side of pleasure. If the efficacy of the happiness drug wanes, our "normal" mood returns, and after the prior euphoria this can be perceived as an intolerable decline. Recognition of the sadness that can follow lovemaking is as old as the expression of feeling itself. And the Old Testament describes the emptiness that King Kohelet felt after having amassed more property and enjoyed more delights than any king before him: "Then my thoughts turned to all the fortune my hands had built up, to the wealth I had acquired and won—and oh, it was all futile and pursuit of wind; there was no real value under the sun! . . . And so I loathed life."

50 Desiring a goal and pursuing it, on the other hand, might last for hours, days, and years. Sometimes the banquet may be better than the hunt, and the rush of enjoyment can surpass the itch of anticipation. Anticipation, on the other hand, lasts much longer. Many people try to spare themselves the letdown by doing everything more or less consciously to avoid the fulfillment of their longings. "The way is the goal," might be their motto. There were entire epochs characterized by unfulfilled desire. The German Romantic poets went into raptures over the *blue flower,* which could never be found and thus eternally sought. The medieval bards worshipped married women, who remained, of necessity, forever elusive. A troubadour couldn't hope for more than a few quickly written lines and a stolen smile—enough to keep his longing alive, too little to ever fulfill it.

Understanding the Text

1. What is the difference between anticipation and pleasure as Klein explains it? Give two examples of your own to show your understanding of what he means.
2. Klein argues that the body has its own "happiness drugs." Expand on Klein's understanding of these natural and artificial drugs. How might they affect our construction of happiness? In your view, is Klein correct in his understanding of how the body responds to these drugs?
3. What is the relationship between pleasure and pain in Klein's analysis? What conclusions does Klein draw based on this correlation?

Reflection and Response

4. As evidence of the role that pleasure plays in the act of eating, Klein cites a study of rats that lost weight when a part of their brains was removed. In this light, he relates this pleasure in eating to an organism's survival. Consider three food advertisements of your choice. How do these ads contribute to a culture of eating that promotes human survival?
5. List the works of literature Klein cites as examples to support his argument. Revise two paragraphs from Klein's essay, replacing his examples with your own.
6. Klein concludes this essay with a few paragraphs about the concept of longing. Write a short essay in which you explore the idea of longing by considering examples from literature, film, and social media. How, in your view, might longing and "desire" relate to a person's own construction of happiness?

Making Connections

7. Klein argues that the relationship between pleasure and pain is contextually dependent. Compare his argument about context and human pleasure seeking with Daniel Gilbert's ("Paradise Glossed," p. 96) analysis of the contextual basis of all meaning-making. In what ways do Klein and Gilbert relate to each other in their arguments, and in what ways do they differ?
8. All of the authors in Chapter 3 focus on cognitive processes that are involved in the making of happiness. Find an author in this text who argues that happiness is not a matter of cognition. What are the differences in the two approaches?
9. Collect two or more birth narratives from people you know, books you've read, or another source (for example, Alice McDermott's in *Someone*, Margaret Atwood's 1977 story "Giving Birth," or from the Birth Narratives Oral History Project at birthnarrativeproject.org). Using Klein's arguments about pain and pleasure as your lens, write an essay in which you discuss "birth and happiness." What can you conclude from using these stories as data?

Very Happy People

Ed Diener and Martin Seligman

Martin E. P. Seligman is Zellerbach Family Professor of Psychology and Director of the Positive Psychology Center at the University of Pennsylvania. He is the author of 20 books and more than 250 publications. Much of his research has focused on depression and "learned helplessness," a concept that he pioneered in the 1960s and 1970s. Since 2000, his work has concentrated on the field of "positive psychology," and his widely read books *Authentic Happiness* (2002) and *Flourish* (2011) have made a significant impact in the psychology of well-being. Ed Diener is Joseph R. Smiley Distinguished Professor Emeritus of Psychology at the University of Illinois. A more extensive biography of Diener can be found on page 160. In the following article from *Psychological Science*, Seligman and Diener report on the results of a study of 222 college students, which identified certain common characteristics among the happiest 10 percent.

Abstract

A sample of 222 undergraduates was screened for high happiness using multiple confirming assessment filters. We compared the upper 10% of consistently very happy people with average and very unhappy people. The very happy people were highly social, and had stronger romantic and other social relationships than less happy groups. They were more extraverted, more agreeable, and less neurotic, and scored lower on several psychopathology scales of the Minnesota Multiphasic Personality Inventory. Compared with the less happy groups, the happiest respondents did not exercise significantly more, participate in religious activities significantly more, or experience more objectively defined good events. No variable was sufficient for happiness, but good social relations were necessary. Members of the happiest group experienced positive, but not ecstatic, feelings most of the time, and they reported occasional negative moods. This suggests that very happy people do have a functioning emotion system that can react appropriately to life events.

Investigations of very unhappy individuals, such as people with anxiety and mood disorders, abound in the psychological literature (Myers, 2000). In contrast, investigations of happy people are rare, and investigations of very happy people do not exist. This imbalance probably stems from clinical psychology's historic emphasis on pathology, coupled with the belief that understanding abnormal processes can illuminate normal processes. We have the complementary belief: that understanding "supranormal" individuals can illuminate normal processes, and that knowing how very happy people function might provide information on how to buffer very unhappy people against psychopathology (Seligman & Csikszentmihalyi, 2000). We report here the first study of the behavioral and personality correlates of high happiness.

In this study, we examined some factors that seem likely to influence high happiness: social relationships, personality and psychopathology, and variables (e.g., religiosity and exercise) that have been related to subjective well-being in correlational studies. In addition to examining how the happiest respondents compared with the average and with very unhappy respondents on these variables, we examined the patterns of necessity and sufficiency. For a variable to be sufficient for happiness, all persons with that variable should be happy (i.e., if *X*, always happy)—and therefore virtually no unhappy people should possess the variable. For a variable to be necessary for happiness, virtually every happy person should possess that variable (i.e., if happy, then *X*). Thus, in these analyses, we examined whether there is a "key" to happiness—a variable that is both necessary and sufficient for happiness.

A third purpose of the study was to examine the moods and emotions of the happiest individuals. Did they experience mostly euphoric feelings or only moderate positive emotions on most occasions? Did they experience occasional unpleasant emotions? If the happiest people never experienced negative emotions and were locked into euphoric feelings, the state might be dysfunctional because these individuals would not react to the events happening to them and would not receive calibrated feedback from their emotions.

Method

The primary sample for this study emerged from a semester-long intensive study of 222 college students at the University of Illinois. This sample was screened for high happiness using combined filters: First, very happy individuals, average, and the least happy individuals were identified by an aggregate based on peer reports of affect,° global self-reports of life satisfaction and affect collected on several occasions separated by months, and daily reports of affect over 51 days. Next, the placement of individuals in these groups was refined using three additional measures.

affect: emotion or desire.

The following measures were used initially to divide respondents into groups: 5

- *Satisfaction With Life Scale:* This scale was administered on three occasions—early, middle, and late semester. Scores on the scale range from 5 to 35 (5 = *extreme dissatisfaction*, 20 = *neutral*, and 35 = *extreme satisfaction*; Diener, Emmons, Larsen, & Griffin, 1985). The mean average of these scores is reported in Results.
- *Global self-reported affect balance:* Self-reported affect was measured by asking the students on two occasions (middle and late semester) how often they felt each of 8 positive emotions and 16 negative emotions (each emotion reported on a scale from 1 = *none* to 7 = *always*) in the past month. Global affect balance was calculated as the mean frequency of the positive emotions minus the mean frequency of the negative emotions (see Diener, Smith, & Fujita, 1995).
- *Informant affect balance:* Affect was also measured by asking informants to rate how often the participants experienced positive and negative emotions (using the same mood adjectives as for self-reported affect). On average, five informants rated each participant. The score for each participant was calculated by subtracting the mean for negative adjectives from the mean for positive adjectives.
- *Daily affect balance:* Respondents reported their affect each day for 51 days. Daily affect balance was calculated as the mean frequency of positive-mood adjectives minus the mean frequency of negative-mood adjectives across an individual's quotidian reports.

These four measures were standardized, and the *z* scores° for each individual were added. The highest and lowest 10% were then selected on the basis of this distribution, and the remaining respondents were divided into three groups of roughly equal size.

Next, we used a discriminant function° with three alternate measures to refine the assignments to the middle, lowest, and highest groups (omitting the second and fourth groups). We determined whether these three measures would lead to the same group assignments as the first four, and

z scores: the number of standard deviations above the mean; that is, the difference between a subject's happiness score and the average happiness score for the sample.
discriminant function: a method for sorting subjects into groups of similar types.

as a result of this analysis discarded from the very happy group 1 individual who was classified differently by the additional measures. The three measures used for this second stage of filtering were as follows:

- *Memory event recall balance:* Each respondent was given 2 min each to recall positive events from the past year, positive events from his or her lifetime, negative events from the past year, and negative events from his or her lifetime. Positive event recall balance was calculated as the total number of positive events recalled minus the total number of negative events recalled (Sandvik, Diener, & Seidlitz, 1993).
- *Trait self-description:* Respondents completed a forced-choice task in which they selected adjectives that described themselves. The score on this measure was calculated as the probability of selecting happy emotion adjectives over equally desirable nonemotional

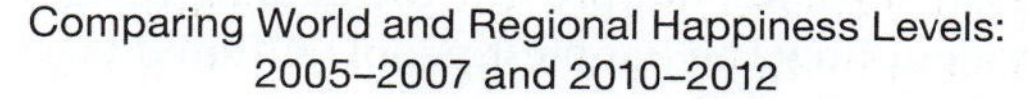

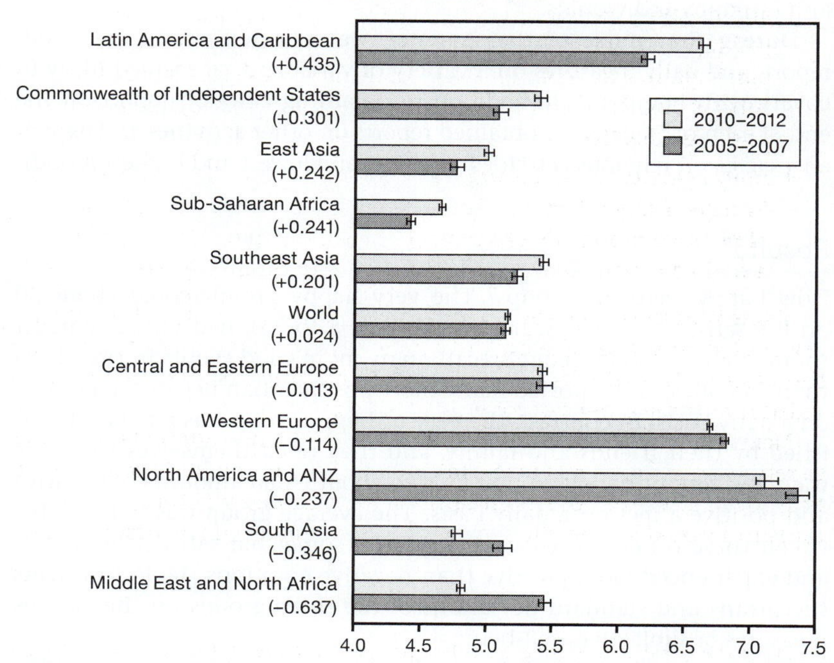

Source: Data from United Nations Sustainable Development Solutions Network, *World Happiness Report, 2013*.

positive personality adjectives minus the probability of selecting unhappy emotion adjectives over equally undesirable nonemotional negative personality adjectives (Sandvik et al., 1993).

- *Interview suicide measure:* Scores on this measure of suicidal thoughts and behavior could range from 0 (*have never thought of committing suicide*) to 5 (*have made active attempts to commit suicide*).

The discriminant function accurately predicted membership in the very happy group 96% of the time, indicating the strong validity of the initial division into groups. The 1 respondent whose group membership was not accurately predicted scored low on two of the additional measures and was discarded from the very happy group, leaving 14 women and 8 men in the group.

We compared the happiest 10% of people according to these criteria ($n = 22$), the unhappiest 10% ($n = 24$), and the average group, which constituted the middle 27% of the sample ($n = 60$). We also conducted continuous regression analyses, but present the data by categories for clarity, and to make evident how the happiest people differed from both average and unhappy individuals.

During the course of the semester, we collected peer, global self-report, and daily measures on a variety of variables that seemed likely to covary with happiness. In addition to obtaining emotion reports at the end of each of 51 days, we obtained reports on other activities and experiences (e.g., on religious activities, exercise, and lowest and highest mood). 10

Results

How happy were the groups? The very happy group scored about 30 on life satisfaction (the scale ranged from 5 to 35), had virtually never thought about suicide, could recall many more good events in their lives than bad ones, and reported many more positive than negative emotions on a daily basis. In contrast, the very unhappy group was rated as dissatisfied by their friends and family, and they rated themselves the same way. The very unhappy group reported about equal amounts of negative and positive affect on a daily basis. The average group was halfway between these other two groups; they were somewhat satisfied with life, and experienced more positive than negative emotions. Table 1 presents the means and standard deviations of the three groups on the various measures of subjective well-being.

The very happy group differed substantially from the average and the very unhappy groups in their fulsome and satisfying interpersonal lives. The very happy group spent the least time alone and the most time

Table 1 **Means (and standard deviations) of the Three Groups on Measures of Subjective Well-Being**

Measure (possible range)	Group		
	Unhappy	Average	Very Happy
Satisfaction with life	15.7	25.7	29.4
(5 to 35)	(3.8)	(3.3)	(2.6)
Global self-reported affect balance	0.1	1.8	3.5
(−6 to +6)	(0.8)	(0.5)	(0.5)
Informant affect balance	0.8	1.9	3.0
(−6 to +6)	(0.7)	(0.7)	(0.5)
Daily affect balance	0.3	1.6	3.7
(−6 to +6)	(0.7)	(0.4)	(0.5)
Memory event recall balance	0.9	4.1	10.5
(unrestricted)	(4.1)	(4.4)	(4.7)
Trait self-description	−.3	.1	.3
(−1.0 to +1.0)	(.2)	(.3)	(.4)
Interview suicide measure	1.7	0.7	0.2
(0 to 5)	(1.5)	(1.3)	(0.5)

socializing, and was rated highest on good relationships by themselves and by informants. Table 2 presents the means for the three groups on these interpersonal variables. Although these statistical relations are strong (the eta-squared values° indicate that large portions of variance between the groups can be predicted by social relationships), no one of the variables was sufficient for high happiness: Some members of the very unhappy group reported satisfactory family, interpersonal, and romantic relationships, and frequent socializing. The lack of sufficiency was true for every variable, with some unhappy people scoring well on each predictor variable. Good social relationships might be a necessary condition for high happiness, however; all members of the very happy group reported good-quality social relationships.

There were personality and psychopathology differences among the three groups as well. The psychopathology scores from the Minnesota Multiphasic Personality Inventory (MMPI) tended to be lowest, most of them significantly so, for the very happy group, except for the Hypomania°

eta-squared values: refers to the proportion of a variance (in this case, happiness) that can be attributed to an effect (in this case, social relationships). In Table 2, this is the column with the heading "η^2."
Hypomania: mild mania marked by hyperactivity and elation or irritability.

Table 2 **Social Relationships of the Three Groups**

Measure (possible range)	**Group** Very Unhappy	Middle	Very Happy	η^2
Self-rating of relationships (1 to 7)[a]				
Close friends	4.1a	5.2b	6.3c	.24
Strong family relationships	3.7a	5.8b	6.4b	.36
Romantic relationship	2.3a	4.8b	6.0c	.38
Peer rating of target's relationships (1 to 7)[a]	4.2a	5.3b	6.1c	.44
Daily activities (1 to 10)[b]				
Mean time spent alone	5.8a	5.0ab	4.4b	.12
Mean time spent with family, friends, and romantic partner	3.6a	4.5b	5.1c	.28

Note: The overall Wilks's lambda° for the multivariate analysis of variance (MANOVA) was significant, $p < .001$. All individual dependent variables in the MANOVA are significant at $p < .01$ or less. Within each dependent variable, groups with different letters differ significantly from one another at $p < .05$ or less.

[a]On the rating scale, 1 represented *much below the average University of Illinois student*, and 7 represented *much above the average University of Illinois student*.

[b]On the rating scale, 1 represented *no time*, and 10 represented *8 hr/day*.

score. The very happy group virtually never scored in the clinical range (T = 65 and above) on the MMPI scales (except for 6 individuals who scored high on the Hypomania scale), whereas almost half the individuals in the very unhappy group did so. Again, there was a necessary but not sufficient pattern: The very happy group virtually always had normal scores, although members of the very unhappy group also often scored in the normal range. In addition, the very happy group was more extraverted, had lower neuroticism scores, and had higher agreeableness scores than the other two groups. Personality dimensions that failed to significantly distinguish the very happy group included conscientiousness, openness to experience, and affect intensity. Table 3 presents the main findings for personality and psychopathology variables.

Although the very happy group had a slight advantage on a number of other variables, they did not differ significantly from the average group on these factors: their perception of how the amount of money they had compared with what other students had, the number of objectively positive and negative events they had experienced, grade point average (from

Wilks's lambda: a test statistic used in multivariate analysis of variance to measure differences in the mean averages of multiple variables between groups.

Table 3 **Personality of the Three Groups**

Measure	Group: Very Unhappy	Middle	Very Happy	η^2
Self-reports				
Affect intensity	150.2a	158.2a	161.1a	n.s.
Big Five				
NEO Extraversion	104.9a	120.4b	132.9c	.25
NEO Neuroticism	113.8a	90.7b	72.2c	.32
NEO Agreeableness	41.2a	44.6a	50.9b	.12
NEO Conscientious[ness]	38.2a	44.6b	40.8ab	.07
NEO Openness	124.2a	115.4a	120.1a	n.s.
Minnesota Multiphasic Personality Inventory Pathology scales (with K corrections)				
Hypochondriasis	15.0a	13.7b	12.1b	.06
Depression	26.9a	19.8b	15.9c	.39
Hysteria	23.0a	22.0a	20.0a	n.s.
Psychopathic	28.8a	24.3b	21.0c	.22
Paranoia	12.3a	10.1b	8.8b	.14
Psychasthenia	35.8a	29.7b	25.8c	.31
Schizophrenia	37.1a	29.9b	25.0c	.28
Hypomania	23.9a	23.9a	24.5a	n.s.
Family Conflict	8.5a	6.3b	4.8c	.22

Note: The overall Wilks's lambdas for the multivariate analyses of variance (MANOVAs) of both sets of variables were significant, $p < .001$. Where etas are shown, groups differ overall on that dependent variable by $p < .05$ or less. Within each dependent variable, groups with different letters differ significantly from one another at $p < .05$ or less. The affect-intensity measure was from Larsen and Diener (1987). NEO = NEO Personality Inventory (Costa & McCrae, 1985).

college transcripts), objective physical attractiveness (rated by coders from pictures), use of tobacco and alcohol (from daily recording over 51 days), and time spent (based on daily recordings) sleeping, watching television, exercising, and participating in religious activities.

Were the very happy people ecstatic? No. We sampled them on 92 moments, but the members of the very happy group never reported their mood to be "ecstatic" or at the very top of the 10-point scale. They did, however, frequently assign their moods a rating of 7 or 8, and often even 9. Were they always happy? No again. All members of the very happy group at least occasionally reported unhappiness or neutral moods; on about

15

half the days, the happiest people experienced a negative mood, but only 7% of the time did they report a very negative mood (1 or 2 on the 10-point scale). Their average mood was 7.7, between "mildly happy" (7) and "spirits high, feeling good" (8).

Discussion

Our study's conclusions are limited by the sample and by its correlational method; broader samples and longitudinal methods will be very desirable in the future. However, we did use strong and thorough measures of happiness, and examined a number of theoretical issues for the first time. To the best of our knowledge, this is the first report to focus on very happy individuals. In addition, we included daily measures of many of our variables over a span of almost 2 months. Therefore, the findings are intriguing, despite being limited to a sample of college students measured in cross section.

"High happiness seems to be like beautiful symphonic music — necessitating many instruments, without any one being sufficient for the beautiful quality."

Our findings suggest that very happy people have rich and satisfying social relationships and spend little time alone relative to average people. In contrast, unhappy people have social relationships that are significantly worse than average. One might conjecture that good social relationships are, like food and thermoregulation, universally important to human mood. Because our data are cross-sectional, we do not know if rich social lives caused happiness, or if happiness caused rich social lives, or if both were caused by some third variable. It is interesting, however, that social relationships form a necessary but not sufficient condition for high happiness—that is, they do not guarantee high happiness, but it does not appear to occur without them. In addition, extraversion, low neuroticism, and relatively low levels of psychopathology form necessary, but not sufficient, conditions for high happiness. Thus, there appears to be no single key to high happiness that automatically produces this state. Instead, high happiness appears to have a number of necessary preconditions that must be in place before it occurs. High happiness seems to be like beautiful symphonic music—necessitating many instruments, without any one being sufficient for the beautiful quality.

Being very happy does not seem to be a malfunction (Alloy & Abramson, 1979). The very happiest people experience unpleasant emotions not infrequently. Although they feel happy most of the time, their ability to feel unpleasant emotions at certain times is undoubtedly functional. Similarly, the happiest people rarely feel euphoria or ecstasy. Instead, they feel medium to moderately strong pleasant emotions much of the time. Again, this pattern seems to be functional in that even very happy people have the ability to move upward in mood when good situations present themselves, and are able to react with negative moods when something bad occurs.

Our findings are limited by the fact that the sample was restricted to college students. Nonetheless, we have replicated the necessity of satisfying social relationships for high happiness in an unpublished analysis of a multination survey based on large probability samples of adults. It could be, however, that variables such as religiosity and exercise will show a greater influence in broader samples of adults.

A useful five-step research strategy for investigating the negative end of personality has developed over the past 40 years: (a) isolate a group of individuals at the extreme negative end (e.g., depressive disorder) and study them intensively, (b) measure their personality and lifestyle, (c) track them longitudinally to understand naturally occurring increases or decreases in their well-being, (d) intervene behaviorally or pharmacologically to improve their well-being, and (e) assess the outcomes of these interventions. We suggest that exactly the obverse strategy is likely to illuminate the causes and building blocks of human well-being, and we present this study as a first attempt. 20

References

Alloy, L., & Abramson, L. (1979). Judgment of contingency in depressed and nondepressed students: Sadder, but wiser. *Journal of Experimental Psychology: General, 108*, 441–485.

Costa, P. T., & McCrae, R. R. (1985). *The NEO Personality Inventory*. Odessa, FL: Psychological Assessment Resources.

Diener, E., Emmons, R. A., Larsen, R. J., & Griffin, S. (1985). The Satisfaction With Life Scale. *Journal of Personality Assessment, 49*, 71–75.

Diener, E., Smith, H., & Fujita, F. (1995). The personality structure of affect. *Journal of Personality and Social Psychology, 69*, 130–141.

Larsen, R. J., & Diener, E. (1987). Emotional response intensity as an individual difference characteristic. *Journal of Research in Personality, 21*, 1–39.

Myers, D. (2000). The funds, friends, and faith of happy people. *American Psychologist, 55*, 56–67.

Sandvik, E., Diener, E., & Seidlitz, L. (1993). Subjective well-being: The convergence and stability of self-report and non-self-report measures. *Journal of Personality, 61*, 317–342.

Seligman, M. E. P., & Csikszentmihalyi, M. (2000). Positive psychology: An introduction. *American Psychologist, 35*, 5–14.

Understanding the Text

1. How was this happiness study designed? Who participated? What was measured and how? Be specific about the methods the authors used.
2. This "research report" follows a format that is widely used in the natural sciences. Note the section headings and all the other elements, such as the abstract and tables. What seems to be the function of each section and element? How do these sections and elements help readers understand and evaluate the authors' findings?

Reflection and Response

3. According to the authors, what are the differences between happy people and unhappy people in terms of social relationships? Discuss what you think these results tell us about the role of interpersonal interactions in people's lives.
4. What kind of study do these authors believe might change the lives of unhappy people? Do you agree with their assessment of the problem with prevailing methods? Write an essay in which you interpret the findings of this study and describe how its application might be used to improve overall human happiness.

Making Connections

5. Construct an informal happiness study of your own, using the same measures and scales used by the authors of this article. Invite a number of friends or acquaintances to participate. Compare your results with those of the authors.
6. Reread the "Discussion" section of this article carefully. Then read Daniel Haybron's "Happiness and Its Discontents" (p. 131). Haybron is a philosopher, whereas Diener and Seligman are psychologists. Are Haybron's views inconsistent with Diener and Seligman's findings? Or do they lead, in your view, to similar conclusions about the way to achieve exceptional happiness?

The Oxford Happiness Questionnaire

Michael Argyle and Peter Hills

The Oxford Happiness Questionnaire was developed in 2001 by psychologists Peter Hills and Michael Argyle of Oxford Brookes University, England, as a compact instrument for measuring subjective well-being. It was designed to be a simpler and more reliable substitute for the Oxford Happiness Inventory, a test that used multiple-choice responses rather than a Likert scale (a 6-point answer scale, ranging from strongly disagree to strongly agree). The Oxford Happiness Inventory was modeled on the Beck Depression Inventory (1961). While the Oxford Happiness Questionnaire is not the only test that measures levels of subjective well-being or happiness — see, for example, the Short Happiness and Affect Research Protocol (Stones, Kozma, Hirdes, & Gold, 1996), the Subjective Happiness Scale (Lyubomirsky & Lepper, 1999), and the Depression-Happiness Scale (Joseph & Lewis, 1998; McGreal & Joseph, 1993) — it is perhaps the most widely administered of such tests and is a representative example of instruments that rely on self-reporting rather than external observation. Being easy to understand and quite concise, it has been used in research involving a wide variety of populations — though none more extensively than college undergraduates, a readily accessible population for academic researchers to enlist.

Instructions

Below are a number of statements about happiness. Please indicate how much you agree or disagree with each by entering a number in the blank after each statement, according to the following scale:

1 = strongly disagree
2 = moderately disagree
3 = slightly disagree
4 = slightly agree
5 = moderately agree
6 = strongly agree

Please read the statements carefully, because some are phrased positively and others negatively. Don't take too long over individual questions; there are no "right" or "wrong" answers (and no trick questions). The first answer that comes into your head is probably the right one for you. If you find some of the questions difficult, please give the answer that is true for you in general or for most of the time.

The Questionnaire

1. I don't feel particularly pleased with the way I am. (R) _____
2. I am intensely interested in other people. _____
3. I feel that life is very rewarding. _____
4. I have very warm feelings towards almost everyone. _____
5. I rarely wake up feeling rested. (R) _____
6. I am not particularly optimistic about the future. (R) _____
7. I find most things amusing. _____
8. I am always committed and involved. _____
9. Life is good. _____
10. I do not think that the world is a good place. (R) _____
11. I laugh a lot. _____
12. I am well satisfied about everything in my life. _____
13. I don't think I look attractive. (R) _____
14. There is a gap between what I would like to do and what I have done. (R) _____
15. I am very happy. _____
16. I find beauty in some things. _____
17. I always have a cheerful effect on others. _____
18. I can fit in (find time for) everything I want to. _____
19. I feel that I am not especially in control of my life. (R) _____
20. I feel able to take anything on. _____
21. I feel fully mentally alert. _____
22. I often experience joy and elation. _____
23. I don't find it easy to make decisions. (R) _____
24. I don't have a particular sense of meaning and purpose in my life. (R) _____
25. I feel I have a great deal of energy. _____
26. I usually have a good influence on events. _____
27. I don't have fun with other people. (R) _____
28. I don't feel particularly healthy. (R) _____
29. I don't have particularly happy memories of the past. (R) _____

Calculate Your Score

Step 1. Items marked (R) should be scored in reverse:

If you gave yourself a "1," cross it out and change it to a "6."
Change "2" to a "5."
Change "3" to a "4."
Change "4" to a "3."
Change "5" to a "2."
Change "6" to a "1."

Step 2. Add the numbers for all 29 questions. (Use the converted numbers for the 12 items that are reverse scored.)

Step 3. Divide by 29. So your happiness score = the total (from step 2) divided by 29.

Interpretation of Score

I suggest you read all the entries below regardless of what score you got, because I think there's valuable information here for everyone.

1–2: Not happy. If you answered honestly and got a very low score, you're probably seeing yourself and your situation as worse than it really is. I recommend taking the *Depression Symptoms test* (CES-D Questionnaire) at the University of Pennsylvania's "Authentic Happiness" Testing Center. You'll have to register, but this is beneficial because there are a lot of good tests there and you can re-take them later and compare your scores.

2–3: Somewhat unhappy. Try some of the exercises on this site like the *Gratitude Journal & Gratitude Lists,* or the *Gratitude Visit*; or take a look at the "Authentic Happiness" site mentioned immediately above.

3–4: Not particularly happy or unhappy. A score of 3.5 would be an exact numerical average of happy and unhappy responses.

4: Somewhat happy or moderately happy. Satisfied. This is what the average person scores.

4–5: Rather happy; pretty happy. Check other score ranges for some of my suggestions.

5–6: Very happy. Being happy has more benefits than just feeling good. It's correlated with benefits like health, better marriages, and attaining your goals.

6: Too happy. Yes, you read that right. Recent research seems to show that there's an optimal level of happiness for things like doing well at work or school, or for being healthy, and that being "too happy" may be associated with lower levels of such things.

Reference

Hills, P., & Argyle, M. (2002). The Oxford Happiness Questionnaire: A compact scale for the measurement of psychological well-being. *Personality and Individual Differences*, 33, 1073–1082.

Understanding the Text

1. What can you discern about the view of happiness represented by these questions?
2. Place the questions into categories. What aspects of human experience are represented?

Reflection and Response

3. After completing the questionnaire, discuss your reactions to this assessment of your happiness. Is it accurate in your view? Are any significant aspects of your happiness quotient not being tested by these questions? Which ones?
4. Compare these questions to questions on another kind of questionnaire about happiness that you have taken or can find. What is the relationship between the two kinds of questions? Does each questionnaire construct an idea of a human being even as it questions him or her? How?

Making Connections

5. Create your own happiness questionnaire. Explain why you designed it in the way that you did.
6. What is the philosophy of this questionnaire as Martha Nussbaum ("Who Is the Happy Warrior?," p. 106) might assess it? Discuss how Nussbaum's argument might relate to this document.

© Jean Louis Aubert/Getty Images

4 Do We Deserve to Be Happy?

Do humans really deserve happiness? Is happiness a human right? The authors in this chapter discuss the idea that happiness might not be something that every person can expect of his or her life. Maybe the need for happiness conflicts with the need for basic necessities, such as food, water, and shelter. Or perhaps it is a goal more strongly sanctioned in some cultures than in others. Or perhaps it is simply not the highest good, not the greatest thing we can aspire to.

Some of these authors question whether pursuing happiness is unnecessary, out of our control, or irrational. In "Aversion to Happiness across Cultures: A Review of Where and Why People Are Averse to Happiness," we learn that some cultures do not hold the pursuit of happiness to be the primary goal in life; in fact, some avoid it as positively dangerous. And Jennifer Michael Hecht asks us to remember a fact that no culture or person can avoid: death. If we acknowledge this fact, she suggests, we must work to make our happiness while we can.

Millions of people suffer from depression: facing days, months, and even years when happiness seems as remote an idea as any. On the one hand, Giles Fraser contends that offering pills to those who are sad or depressed may mask the fact that unhappy feelings come with the human condition. On the other, Dürer's engraving *Melencolia I* ("melancholy") and John Keats's "Ode on Melancholy" both celebrate a kind of sadness, one that has often been considered, paradoxically, a kind of pleasure.

And what if choosing your own happiness harms someone else? C. S. Lewis discusses whether his friend's decision to leave his wife reveals the friend's erroneous understanding of the importance of his own happiness. Perhaps the word "happiness" provides a mask for egotism?

In fact, as David Brooks points out, perhaps it is unhappiness rather than happiness that defines us as human. Eric G. Wilson eloquently explores the sorrowful life of John Keats, capturing the depths of his suffering in the midst of his awakening to the beauty of human expression and experience.

photo: © Jean Louis Aubert/Getty Images

We Have No Right to Happiness

C. S. Lewis

Clive Staples Lewis (1898–1963) was a scholar of medieval and Renaissance literature at Oxford and Cambridge Universities and the author of more than a dozen novels, including *The Chronicles of Narnia* (1950–1956) and *The Screwtape Letters* (1942). As a young man, Lewis was an atheist, but he converted to Christianity in 1931, influenced in part by his friend J. R. R. Tolkien. Many of his writings reflect, either directly or indirectly, his deep faith in the doctrines of the Church of England. On the fiftieth anniversary of his death, in 2013, his memory was honored in Poets' Corner, Westminster Abbey. The following essay, which examines the moral basis of the pursuit of happiness, was the last he published; it appeared in *The Saturday Evening Post* in 1963.

"After all," said Clare, "they had a right to happiness."

We were discussing something that once happened in our own neighborhood. Mr. A. had deserted Mrs. A. and got his divorce in order to marry Mrs. B., who had likewise got her divorce in order to marry Mr. A. And there was certainly no doubt that Mr. A. and Mrs. B. were very much in love with one another. If they continued to be in love, and if nothing went wrong with their health or their income, they might reasonably expect to be very happy.

It was equally clear that they were not happy with their old partners. Mrs. B. had adored her husband at the outset. But then he got smashed up in the war. It was thought he had lost his virility, and it was known that he had lost his job. Life with him was no longer what Mrs. B. had bargained for. Poor Mrs. A., too. She had lost her looks—and all her liveliness. It might be true, as some said, that she consumed herself by bearing his children and nursing him through the long illness that overshadowed their earlier married life.

You mustn't, by the way, imagine that A. was the sort of man who nonchalantly threw a wife away like the peel of an orange he'd sucked dry. Her suicide was a terrible shock to him. We all knew this, for he told us so himself. "But what could I do?" he said. "A man has a right to happiness. I had to take my one chance when it came."

I went away thinking about the concept of a "right to happiness." 5

At first this sounds to me as odd as a right to good luck. For I believe—whatever one school of moralists may say—that we depend for a very great deal of our happiness or misery on circumstances outside all human control. A right to happiness doesn't, for me, make much more sense than a right to be six feet tall, or to have a millionaire for your father, or to get good weather whenever you might want to have a picnic.

I can understand a right as a freedom guaranteed me by the laws of the society I live in. Thus, I have a right to travel along the public roads because society gives me that freedom; that's what we mean by calling the roads "public." I can also understand a right as a claim guaranteed me by the laws and correlative to an obligation on someone else's part. If I have a right to receive $100 from you, this is another way of saying that you have a duty to pay me $100. If the laws allow Mr. A. to desert his wife and seduce his neighbor's wife, then, by definition, Mr. A. has a legal right to do so, and we need bring in no talk about "happiness."

But of course that was not what Clare meant. She meant that he had not only a legal but a moral right to act as he did. In other words, Clare is—or would be if she thought it out—a classical moralist after the style of Thomas Aquinas, Grotius, Hooker and Locke.° She believes that behind the laws of the state there is a Natural Law.

I agree with her. I hold this conception to be basic to all civilization. Without it, the actual laws of the state become an absolute, as in Hegel.° They cannot be criticized because there is no norm against which they should be judged.

The ancestry of Clare's maxim, "They have a right to happiness," is august. In words that are cherished by all civilized men, but especially by Americans, it has been laid down that one of the rights of many is a right to "the pursuit of happiness." And now we get to the real point. 10

What did the writers of that august declaration mean?

It is quite certain what they did not mean. They did not mean that man was entitled to pursue happiness by any and every means—including, say, murder, rape, robbery, treason and fraud. No society could be built on such a basis.

Thomas Aquinas, Grotius, Hooker, and Locke: Thomas Aquinas (1225–1274) was a philosopher and theologian whose works constitute the basis of Roman Catholic theology. He argued that human reason as well as divine revelation can lead to the truth. Hugo Grotius (1583–1645, also known as Hugo de Groot) was a philosopher and jurist whose work furnished the basis of international law. Richard Hooker (1554–1600) was an English priest and theologian whose ideas about the relation between reason and scripture became central to the theology of the Church of England. John Locke (1632–1704) was an English philosopher and one of the chief founders of empiricism and political liberalism; his work helped launch the Age of Enlightenment.
Hegel: G. W. F. Hegel (1770–1831) was a German philosopher whose system of "absolute idealism" and dialectical view of history was widely influential. Among many others, Karl Marx drew on his ideas.

They meant "to pursue happiness by all lawful means": that is, by all means which the Law of Nature eternally sanctions and which the laws of the nation shall sanction.

Admittedly, this seems at first to reduce their maxim to the tautology that men (in pursuit of happiness) have a right to do whatever they have a right to do. But tautologies, seen against their proper historical context, are not always barren tautologies. The declaration is primarily a denial of the political principles which long governed Europe: a challenge flung down to the Austrian and Russian empires, to England before the Reform Bills, to Bourbon France.° It demands that whatever means of pursuing happiness are lawful for any should be lawful for all: that "man," not men of some particular caste, class, status or religion, should be free to use them. In a century when this is being unsaid by nation after nation and party after party, let us not call it a barren tautology.

But the question as to what means are "lawful"—what methods of pursuing happiness are either morally permissible by the Law of Nature or should be declared legally permissible by the legislature of a particular nation—remains exactly where it did. And on that question I disagree with Clare. I don't think it is obvious that people have the unlimited "right to happiness" which she suggests. 15

For one thing, I believe that Clare, when she says "happiness," means simply and solely "sexual happiness." Partly because women like Clare never use the word "happiness" in any other sense. But also because I never heard Clare talk about the "right" to any other kind. She was rather leftist in her politics, and would have been scandalized if anyone had defended the actions of a ruthless man-eating tycoon on the ground that his happiness consisted in making money and he was pursuing his happiness. She was also a rabid teetotaler; I never heard her excuse an alcoholic because he was happy when he was drunk.

A good many of Clare's friends, and especially her female friends, often felt—I've heard them say so—that their own happiness would be perceptibly increased by boxing her ears. I very much doubt if this would have brought her theory of a right to happiness into play.

Clare, in fact, is doing what the whole Western world seems to me to have been doing for the last 40-odd years. When I was a youngster, all the progressive people were saying, "Why all this prudery? Let us treat sex just as we treat all our other impulses." I was simple-minded enough

Bourbon France: The Bourbon family ruled France from 1589 to 1792, when the monarchy was overthrown during the French Revolution, and again from 1815 to 1848. The extravagant autocracy of Louis XIV and Louis XV helped precipitate the French Revolution.

to believe they meant what they said. I have since discovered that they meant exactly the opposite. They meant that sex was to be treated as no other impulse in our nature has ever been treated by civilized people. All the others, we admit, have to be bridled. Absolute obedience to your instinct for self-preservation is what we call cowardice; to your acquisitive impulse, avarice. Even sleep must be resisted if you're a sentry. But every unkindness and breach of faith seems to be condoned provided that the object aimed at is "four bare legs in a bed."

It is like having a morality in which stealing fruit is considered wrong—unless you steal nectarines.

And if you protest against this view, you are usually met with chatter about the legitimacy and beauty and sanctity of "sex" and accused of harboring some Puritan prejudice against it as something disreputable or shameful. I deny the charge. Foam-born Venus . . . golden Aphrodite . . . Our Lady of Cyprus° . . . I never breathed a word against you. If I object to boys who steal my nectarines, must I be supposed to disapprove of nectarines in general? Or even of boys in general? It might, you know, be stealing that I disapproved of. 20

"To be in love involves the almost irresistible conviction that one will go on being in love until one dies and that possession of the beloved will confer, not merely frequent ecstasies, but settled, fruitful, deep-rooted, lifelong happiness."

The real situation is skillfully concealed by saying that the question of Mr. A.'s "right" to desert his wife is one of "sexual morality." Robbing an orchard is not an offense against some special morality called "fruit morality." It is an offense against honesty. Mr. A.'s action is an offense against good faith (to solemn promises), against gratitude (toward one to whom he was deeply indebted) and against common humanity.

Our sexual impulses are thus being put in a position of preposterous privilege. The sexual motive is taken to condone all sorts of behavior which, if it had any other end in view, would be condemned as merciless, treacherous and unjust.

Now though I see no good reason for giving sex this privilege, I think I see a strong cause. It is this.

It is part of the nature of a strong erotic passion—as distinct from a transient fit of appetite—that it makes more towering promises than any

Foam-born Venus . . . golden Aphrodite . . . Our Lady of Cyprus: names for the goddess of love and sexuality in ancient Greece and Rome.

other emotion. No doubt all our desires make promises, but not so impressively. To be in love involves the almost irresistible conviction that one will go on being in love until one dies and that possession of the beloved will confer, not merely frequent ecstasies, but settled, fruitful, deep-rooted, lifelong happiness. Hence *all* seems to be at stake. If we miss this chance we shall have lived in vain. At the very thought of such a doom we sink into fathomless depths of self-pity.

Unfortunately these promises are found often to be quite untrue. 25 Every experienced adult knows this to be so as regards all erotic passions (except the one he himself is feeling at the moment). We discount the world-without-end pretensions of our friends' amours easily enough. We know that such things sometimes last—and sometimes don't. And when they do last, this is not because they promised at the outset to do so. When two people achieve lasting happiness, this is not solely because they are great lovers but because they are also—I must put it crudely—good people: controlled, loyal, fair-minded, mutually adaptable people.

If we establish a "right to (sexual) happiness" which supersedes all the ordinary rules of behaviors we do so not because of what our passion shows itself to be in experience but because of what it professes to be while we are in the grip of it. Hence, while the bad behavior is real and works miseries and degradations, the happiness which was the object of the behavior turns out again and again to be illusory. Everyone (except Mr. A. and Mrs. B.) knows that Mr. A. in a year or so may have the same reason for deserting his new wife as for deserting his old. He will see himself again as the great lover, and his pity for himself will exclude all pity for the woman.

Though the "right to happiness" is chiefly claimed for the sexual impulse, it seems to me impossible that the matter should stay there. We thus advance toward a state of society in which not only each man but every impulse in each man claims *carte blanche*. And then, though our technological skill may help us survive a little longer, our civilization will have died at heart and will be swept away.

Understanding the Text

1. Lewis discusses the idea of having a "right to happiness." What are some of his critiques of this "right," and what are some of the benefits and advantages? In your view, which argument is more compelling?
2. How is Lewis's position regarding "the right to happiness" related to the idea of desire? Can one base a "right to happiness" on sexual desire?

Reflection and Response

3. Lewis writes, "We . . . advance toward a state of society in which not only each man but every impulse in each man claims *carte blanche*. And then, though our technological skill may help us survive a little longer, our civilization will have died at heart and will be swept away" (par. 27). What does this mean? To what extent would you agree with this statement? What arguments might you present to challenge Lewis?

Making Connections

4. Would you argue that happiness is a natural right? Write an essay in which you use three essays from this chapter to support your position.
5. Several authors in this book discuss how desire may influence the way a person determines his or her own standard of happiness. Choose three of them to use as you construct your own essay. To help you make your case, find three examples in the media that suggest that a "right to happiness" is determined by personal desire.
6. Imagine you are asked to represent one of the four divorced people discussed in the opening of this article. How might you defend their "right to happiness" with the arguments offered by Lewis and Sonja Lyubomirsky ("How Happy Are You and Why?," p. 179)? Would you offer different approaches to constructing happiness in the light of each person's circumstances?

Remember Death

Jennifer Michael Hecht

Jennifer Michael Hecht is a poet, historian, and philosopher whose books include *Doubt: A History* (2003), which is a history of atheism, and *Stay: A History of Suicide and the Philosophies against It* (2013). She earned her Ph.D. in the history of science and European cultural history from Columbia University in 1995, and she continues to live and work in New York. Her contrarian book *The Happiness Myth: Why What We Think Is Right Is Wrong* (2007) argues that many popular beliefs about the sources of happiness are mistaken — that, for example, money can buy happiness and that certain drugs, taken in moderation, may increase happiness. In this chapter from that book, she examines the modern habit of "death denial," arguing that paying more attention to death might actually make us happier.

All the great graceful-life philosophies and all the great religions counsel people to remember death. Today we tend to want to forget death: our supermarkets make it seem like meat grows on white Styrofoam, almost bloodless, always pink. Dying happens elsewhere. We catch and release fish, then go have hamburgers. Human dying occurs in hospices, alone at night. Most people have not seen someone die, whereas, in past centuries, even young children were brought to deathbeds to witness a period of sometimes agonized dying, and then the much respected moment of transformation. This moment was as sacred and revered as the modern-day birth. Men of a century ago saw no births, or recordings of births, but they saw many deaths and recordings of deaths. Deathbed scenes were commonplace in literature and theater, magazine essay, and Sunday sermon. The idea was to educate people to have a good death and to help other people have one. For instance, an etching might show how the departing man or woman might reach up to God, and how the many guests should respond—for instance, that it was okay for some to look away, some to gaze with fixed attention, and for very young children to play beneath the chairs. Verbal descriptions of death offered a variety of models for how to behave in one's suffering, how to make peace and find forgiveness, and how to commend oneself to God. We have childbirth classes where you see and hear about a splendid array of births; they had essays and sermons that described an endless parade of deaths. In the future, classes for dying might look very much the same as childbirth classes, showing some breathing methods to manage pain and fear, and showing the partner, or "death coach," different ways of soothing the dying one. But instruction on death is not part of mainstream culture today. Indeed, studying it seems morbid, rebellious, adolescent. Valuing birth as a site for study and reverence and hiding death as a kind of profane, dark, secret, gross thing is, of course, a cultural trance. Cemeteries were often at the center of small towns and part of the life of the village; people picnicked there and daily visited their defunct friends and family. Even only a century ago, there were all sorts of customs around death that would seem bizarre and morbid today—for example, wearing a broach made out of elaborately twisted strands of your dead sister-in-law's hair. It is also true that until recently, much of history considered the execution of criminals to be an edifying and entertaining spectacle. Death denial may have reached its height at the middle of the twentieth century, a time when revelations about the Holocaust and memory of two world wars may have occasioned a general psychological shutdown on the issue. In a famous little essay of 1955 (it was two short pages!), "The Pornography of Death," sociologist Geoffrey Gorer pointed out that as the nineteenth century treated sex, so his time now treated death, and vice versa. Wrote Gorer,

I cannot recollect a novel or play of the last twenty years or so which has a "death-bed scene" in it, describing in any detail the death "from natural causes" of a major character; this topic was a set piece for most of the eminent Victorian and Edwardian writers, evoking their finest prose and their most elaborate technical effects to produce the greatest amount of pathos or edification.

One of the reasons, I imagine, for this plethora of death-bed scenes—apart from their intrinsic emotional and religious content—was that it was one of the relatively few experiences that an author could be fairly sure would have been shared by the vast majority of his readers. Questioning my old acquaintances, I cannot find one over the age of sixty who did not witness the agony of at least one near relative; I do not think I know a single person under the age of thirty who has had a similar experience.

Gorer's guess about why this transformation occurred was that "belief in the future life as taught in the Christian doctrine is very uncommon today even in the minority who make church-going or prayer a consistent part of their lives," and that without such a belief, death and decomposition "have become too horrible to contemplate or discuss." An interesting theory, but what counted most was the observation itself: we were avoiding the subject. There were other calls for attention to death. Elizabeth Kübler-Ross's 1969 *On Death and Dying* generated a whole new vocabulary. Her five stages of grief gave us a way to talk about discreet parts of the experience of dying. She later explained that she did not intend her list—denial, anger, bargaining, depression, acceptance—to be understood as a neat series of events, just as you could write up the drama of falling in love as five stages but wouldn't expect a consistent one-to-one correlation when looking at real people's experiences. The fact that our culture has so mightily seized on her ideas, and for so long, tells us how desperate we are for some kind of script.

Gorer's comments about the deathbed scenes of theater bring to mind Margaret Edison's 1999 Pulitzer Prize–winning play, *Wit*, in which a brilliant scholar of the poet John Donne° deals with her cancer and death open to the gaze of the audience. What makes that play work is decidedly not that the viewers had all seen this sort of thing in their real lives. The play is part of a change that took place in response to Gorer and Kübler-Ross, wherein the wise once again try to get us to stop averting our gaze. People seem to find this offer almost titillating. The HBO series *Six Feet Under* invited people to look at a corpse's journey from death to burial, and it was enthusiastically embraced by television audiences.

Even with the changes toward more direct conversation about death, the age-old advice to remember death, to keep it in the forefront of our minds for the sake of bettering the life we lead now, is still rather lost in our culture of youth, competition, and vigor. There is, however, one modern-day conviction about the life benefits of remembering death: the axiom that survivors of an almost-fatal experience are understood to be happier than other people.

5 The idea is that the cancer survivor lives every day in exquisite gratitude. What happens seems so fundamental as to suggest that there is a biological component to it, a change in brain pathways, or chemistry, or something of the sort. Let's call it "posttraumatic bliss." There are feelings in this life—good and bad—that cannot be conquered by intellect or force of will. Some are potentially blissful, like romantic love. Most are rough: the sudden loss of a family member, a violent personal assault, a brutal accident—or maybe something you did to someone else—soldier's remorse, for instance. Trauma flashes back. I am suggesting that almost dying can realign you in a way that is the positive incarnation of trauma: posttraumatic bliss. Throughout history we have tried to induce posttraumatic bliss by reminding ourselves of death. By this downright physiological interpretation, some aspect of self-induced posttraumatic bliss has been thought possible throughout the ages. People have tried to give themselves a jolt of the positive incarnation of trauma by traumatizing themselves with thoughts of death. Of course, the injunction to

John Donne (1572–1631): foremost English Metaphysical poet and a churchman famous for his spellbinding sermons.

remember death is also intellectual; it is supposed to help you come to understand death in a way that won't distress you. But the way they tell you to study a skull reveals that it is more about shocking yourself into a post-near-death good mood. Consider a few brief and insightful attestations.

The Buddha wrote: "Of all mindfulness meditations, that on death is supreme." Koheleth in Ecclesiastes° added this beautiful tangle of thoughts: "It is better to go to the house of mourning, than to go to the house of feasting: for that is the end of all men; and the living will lay it to his heart. Sorrow is better than laughter: for by the sadness of the countenance the heart is made better. The heart of the wise is in the house of mourning; but the heart of fools is in the house of mirth." The great Epicurus held that the "true understanding of the fact that death is nothing to us renders enjoyable the mortality of existence, not by adding infinite time but by taking away the yearning for immortality." The crowning insight comes from Aurelius:° If, instead of fearing death, "you shall fear never to have begun to live according to nature—then you will be a man worthy of the universe that has produced you, and you will cease to be a stranger in your native land, and to wonder at things that happen daily as if they were something unexpected, and to be dependent on this or that." Pay attention to living fully and you won't worry about death.

When Christianity arose, the wisdom to remember death was very well established. St. Gregory (329–388) was forever quoting Plato's° advice to practice regular "meditation upon death." Ash Wednesday is a holiday devoted to remembering death. Each year, on the day after Mardi Gras, or Fat Tuesday, the priest takes ashes (from burning last year's Palm Sunday palms, and then mixing with a little olive oil to make them sticky) and rubs them on people's foreheads, in the shape of a cross. It used to be that clerics, who all wore what we think of as monk's tonsures (a shaved top of the head), would get their ashes in the tonsure. It must have been eerie to talk to a man, then see him turn to go and be confronted with this reminder that he was a man marked for death. Whether you get it coming or going, the minister of the rite marks you with ash

Koheleth in Ecclesiastes: known in the Christian Bible as "Ecclesiastes," the book is known in the Hebrew Bible by the name of its author "Koheleth," a word that means "teacher" or "gatherer."

Aurelius: Marcus Aurelius (121–180) was a Roman emperor and the author of *Meditations*, an influential work of Stoic philosophy.

Plato (429–348/347 BCE): Greek philosopher, disciple of Socrates, and teacher of Aristotle.

and says, "Remember, man, that you are dust, and to dust you shall return." Catholics fast that day and don't wash off the smudge until after nightfall.

Plato would have loved it. He warned against poetic fantasies, so we generally think he would have found the promise of a Christian afterlife a little silly, but he loved the idea of enacting one's philosophy in ritual. The ancient philosophers always said that remembering death took active meditations and gestures. Ash Wednesday leads up to Easter, a holiday whose meaning is a fantasy of resurrection. But in and of itself, the holiday is philosophical and somber. Ash Wednesday arose from Christianity's two greatest sources: the Jewish influence came from the Jews' remembrance of death in a day of fasting on Yom Kippur. On this holiday Jews concentrate their minds on death, and rhythmically beat their fist against their heart. The Greek influence was in part as a supposed bad example: the holiday of Lent was set up as a specific refusal to join in the wild party of the Sacred Mysteries.

Christians also persisted in citing ancient calls to remember death. St. John Climacus, who wrote in the late 500s, advised people to "let the memory of death sleep and awake with you," and St. Benedict's guidebook for monasteries, known as his *Rule* (c. 530), advised monks to "see death before one daily." Eventually, Christianity formulated the idea of death as the time of reckoning, and of either torture or reward. Still, the fundamental message was that the contemplation of death was itself curative. Whatever you believe about your soul, your flesh is going to leave your bones. It is a potent notion. In medieval times, monks often had *memento mori* in their cells, objects kept because they remind one of death—usually, real human skulls or images of skeletons. The great Renaissance sculptor Bernini designed a memorial for Pope Urban VIII in bas-relief: a tremendous bronze and marble skeleton, with awesome wings, holding a banner upon which the pope's name is written. The skeleton is in the midst of ripping the banner in two. Bernini found a spot on the dim church wall that was occasionally hit by a beam of light from a high window, and had the monument placed there so that it would be nearly invisible until it was revealed in brilliant glory. The image was so striking that people had it copied for their own monuments, and these too became known as *memento mori*. Much of the history of remembering death is comprehensible as a kind of posttraumatic bliss. It is not easy to invoke, but it works. It can make you feel mellow and happy.

10 In other cases, the call to remember death is more an intellectual argument than a technique for internal transformation, and its result is

not mellow gratitude for the life you have but revved-up desire for more life. The thesis runs as follows: remember that you should fill your days with exotic action, because you could die at any time. In 1922 a French journal asked a range of noted people to answer a question—one of the main literary-magazine devices of the nineteenth century (another was the essay contest). This time the question was: "An American scientist announces that the world will end. . . . If this prediction were confirmed, what do you think would be its effects on people . . .?" I love the gratuitous note that the scientist is American; it borrows our scientific clout to help sell the scenario, but it also feels a little like a premonition that American science itself may bring disaster. Anyway, here's how Marcel Proust° responded:

I think that life would suddenly seem wonderful to us if we were threatened to die, as you say. Just think of how many projects, travels, love affairs, studies, it—our life—hides from us, made invisible by our laziness which, certain of a future, delays them incessantly. But let all this threaten to become impossible forever, how beautiful it all becomes again. Ah! if only the cataclysm doesn't happen this time, we won't miss visiting the new galleries of the Louvre, throwing ourselves at the feet of Miss X, making a trip to India. The cataclysm doesn't happen, we don't do any of it, because we find ourselves back in the heart of normal life, where negligence deadens desire.

Proust then reminds himself and his reader that simple human mortality ought to be enough to get us in gear but, oddly, isn't. In his own life, Proust neither visited museums, nor threw himself at anyone's feet, nor even seemed vaguely interested in a trip to India. He liked to stay home in bed under heavy covers, eat stewed fruits, take tea and other drugs, and write his books. He did in fact die only a few months after he wrote this, not having gone much of anywhere. I do not agree with his own assumption that this was laziness. A lazy person could not even read the monumental *À la recherche du temps perdu*, let alone write it. The man made choices about how he wanted to fill his days. We know exactly what he would do if he had three months left to live: answer a magazine question, write his book, and generally take part in the great literary drama of humanity.

The idea that we need to remember death so that we will go to the Louvre almost sounds like there is a deathbed scorecard, or even an after-

Marcel Proust (1871–1922): French novelist and essayist.

life scorecard. There is not. There's a wonderfully silly country music song, "Not a Moment Too Soon," big in 2005, that claims that if we found out we were dying, we'd go skydiving, we'd go "Rocky Mountain climbing," we'd go "two-point-seven seconds on a bull named Fu Manchu." There is some truth to it. But remember, too, that we choose the things we do on a regular basis at least in part because we like doing them. Just because I'm dying I should suddenly feel like riding a mechanical bull? No. It is all metaphorical. We worry about death because we worry we aren't living. Living can be enhanced by doing exotic things, but that's not really so important. Noticing death may challenge you to do unordinary stuff. But noticing that you are especially wracked with fear of death—that should challenge you to think about what you wish were going on in your ordinary life.

Today *memento mori* are seen as a bit gruesome. If you are Catholic and you go to church or to your parents' house, you will see a statue of a dead or dying man. The rest of the time, like most everyone else, you live in a world that doesn't show you artistic images of a dead or dying person. The rituals of remembering death have largely disappeared, from communal chest beating to ash wearing. Yet despite the way natural death is concealed in the daily lives of Americans, images of death have snuck back into our lives and nearly taken over.

We live with constant images of death. The news photographs are not billed as *memento mori,* but with a little consideration of the idea, it becomes clear that they are. There have been inquiries into what we are doing when we photograph the affliction of others, and publish it, and purchase it, recycle the paper, and do it again. Susan Sontag's final book, *On the Suffering of Others,* is in part a recantation of her famous moral indictment of such photography of the early part of her career. She came to believe that looking at these pictures is more politically active than she had originally allowed. I am arguing that beyond politics, there is an old psychological need being filled. Given how often humanity has devised ways to look upon death in order to achieve happiness, and given how much we have sanitized our lives to free them of images of death, consider that the images of dead people that we see in the news, which is driven by our desires, are there to help us be happy. We shield children from news, but we still tell them to remember death. Think of classic fairy tales, and of Edward Gorey's doomed boys and girls. Think, too, of the dead parents of James of the Giant Peach, Lemony Snicket's Baudelaire children, and Harry Potter—all orphans. Children are going to think about death anyway, and it is much easier to think about death directly than it is to host the monsters that roam your head (and bedroom closet) when you try not to think about it.

Montaigne° knew that thoughts of death could bring insight and liberation, but could be depressing in the short run. "It is certain that to most people preparation for death has given more torment than the dying." He blames philosophy for making us think of death so much and then rushing in like a hero to save us from our fatalism: 15

Philosophy orders us to have death ever before our eyes, to foresee and consider it before the time comes, and afterward gives us the rules and precautions to provide against our being wounded by this foresight and this thought. That is what those doctors do who make us ill so that they may have something on which to employ their drugs and their art . . . They may boast about it all they please: "The whole life of a philosopher is a meditation on death" (Cicero). But it seems to me that death is indeed the end, but not therefore the goal, of life.

Remembering death seemed to be something that intellectuals fretted over, while the less schooled managed the issue in a more natural, more relaxed way:

I never saw one of my peasant neighbors cogitating over the countenance and assurance with which he would pass this last hour. Nature teaches him not to think about death except when he is dying. And then he has better grace about it than Aristotle, whom death oppresses doubly, by itself and by a long foreknowledge.

Only the educated think of death when they are healthy, "dine worse for it," and go looking for opportunities "to frown at the image of death." More-common people stand in need of no preparatory consolation and rather just take in the shock "when the blow comes."

Knowledge of death makes us human, and great knowledge of death can make us great humans. Still, I cannot help but agree with Montaigne that there is also the possibility of too much exposure to death, and too much acceptance of death. For some of us, it is hard enough to get our cleats into life. Remembering death is like switching to skates. The only historically defensible conclusion is this: Life does not seem like it is going to end. It is, though, and for your own happiness, you have to train yourself to accept it and keep it in mind. Only if you can cozy up to this peculiar fact can you be mature and happy, because otherwise you will

Montaigne: Michel Eyquem de Montaigne (1533–1592) was a French writer and politician who is widely considered the inventor of the modern essay.

be in worse trouble than normal if someone close to you dies; also because death lends life a gravitas and a sweetness; and finally, because the work of denying death will keep you as busy as a full-time job. But once you school yourself in the awareness and acceptance of death, you have to try to forget it again. Consciousness of death makes it too hard to invest effort in the present or the future. With knowledge of the sun's eventual expansion and absorption of the earth, the future is not what it once was. I am joking, as no one really needed science to get to nihilism. Over two thousand years ago, Koheleth said that everyone is forgotten. Want to know how forgotten we will be? I know you know all four of your grandparents' names, and that you may love them, and see them as your connection to your family's past. Good. Now list the names of your grandparents' mothers. I casually surveyed a bevy of Americans of greatly varied ages, and only a tiny minority could name even two or three of their four great-grandmothers. These are the mothers of people you have loved, spent days with, and possibly mourned. Koheleth was right. We are not going to be remembered.

Once we learn to remember death, how can we care about the future? The answer turns out to be romantic and moral; it is about our children most of all, but not only. Could I abide it if, after my death, someone burned the New York Public Library? I work my way back into existence from there. You want to be able to work your way back. Again, the way out of this happiness trap is to teach yourself to remember death, a long and laborious process, and then, though it will be almost as difficult, teach yourself to forget death again. As with controlling desire, remember that the Buddha said his method was a raft you use to get to the other side of the river; once you have gotten where you needed to go, you can stop doing the practice. Make yourself face death and become familiar with it. Effect within yourself a transformation. Seek out a state of posttraumatic bliss. But once you have done that, you have to firmly guide your attention back to life. Don't justify life and help it stand up to the paradoxes posed by eternity. Just walk your mind away from the dark edge of the beautiful springtime field and into its lovely center. Search a clover patch for a sprout with extra leaves, or roll over and look at the cloud-scattered sky.

"Make yourself face death and become familiar with it. Effect within yourself a transformation. Seek out a state of posttraumatic bliss."

Any time is all time. As he lay dying, the Buddha told his students not to grieve. He explained, "If I were to live in the world for a whole eon, my 20 association with you would still come to an end, since a meeting with no parting is an impossibility." Also know that Seneca° tried to stop Nero from killing his rivals by telling him, "No matter how many you slay, you cannot kill your successor." Someone is coming, because, sooner or later, we are going.

Listen to our very motivated Shaw° again: "Life is no brief candle to me. It is a sort of splendid torch which I have got a hold of for the moment, and I want to make it burn as brightly as possible before handing it on to future generations." Of course, he's arguing with Shakespeare, through Macbeth. Macbeth sighed that life was so short we almost might as well extinguish it now, that it hardly mattered. "Out, out brief candle." He knows how an abyss yawns on either side of this tiny life, and these abysses make our stretch of life so tiny that the difference of years or decades loses all meaning. That's not how Shaw wants it. Not a "brief candle," he protests, but a splendid torch! We'll leave them comparing candles; it is a game even good men take to when they are scared of the dark. What's so bad about the threat of the dark, though? Neither Shaw nor Shakespeare must have ever been to high school or to a faculty meeting. They must never have tried to get home in the rain or had morning sickness. How could they have missed how slow life is?

To those dogged by a nagging fear of death, it is like you are at a carnival with four lousy rides and a three-gag funhouse, playing rigged midway games, occasionally winning something and henceforth having to carry it around—and meanwhile, you spend a lot of time staring at the exit sign and worrying over eventually having to go home. Jeez, closing time is the least of your troubles.

As I mentioned earlier, I wrote this section, and really this whole book, as a way to develop an answer to Montaigne's challenge to wisdom. What I have come to believe might best be explained by a porcine romp through history. We follow the pig. In 334 BCE, Pyrrho of Elis joined the court of Alexander the Great. (Aristotle had finished his eight years as Alexander's teacher about a year earlier.) Pyrrho traveled with Alexander to India, where he studied with philosophers and ascetics. While at Alexander's court Pyrrho also came in contact with various Greek philosophers. When he came back, he became the founder of a

Seneca: Lucius Annaeus Seneca (4 BCE–65 CE), known as Seneca the Younger, was a Roman philosopher, statesman, and playwright, as well as a tutor to the future emperor Nero (37–68).
Shaw: George Bernard Shaw (1856–1950) was an Irish playwright and writer.

new and powerful school of thought, Skepticism. In his hands, the gist of it was that every argument has a counterargument and that our senses and our reason frequently lie to us. Others would make more epistemological arguments based on Pyrrho's idea, but for him the point was that we should find Eastern calm in the realization that truth cannot be known. Once, when Pyrrho was at sea, a terrible storm tossed his ship around, and the passengers panicked and screamed. Pointing to a pig that was munching away on deck and looking at the waves without fear, Pyrrho told his fellow humans that the pig had the right idea. They all survived, and so did the story.

Listen to Montaigne, almost two thousand years later:

But even if knowledge would actually do what they say, blunt and lessen the keenness of the misfortunes that pursue us, what does it do but what ignorance does much more purely and more evidently? The philosopher Pyrrho, incurring the peril of a great storm at sea, offered those who were with him nothing better to imitate than the assurance of a pig that was traveling with them, and that was looking at this tempest without fear. Philosophy, at the end of her precepts, sends us back to the examples of an athlete or a muleteer, in whom we ordinarily see much less feeling of death, pain, and other discomforts, and more firmness than knowledge ever supplied to any man who had not been born and prepared for it on his own by natural habit.

25 Knowledge might be forgiven this failing if it were easy to acquire, but it demands supreme effort, over long periods of time, all the while promising consolation even as we can see, with our own eyes, that philosophers sometimes jump out of high windows, just like everybody else. They have meaningless weeping jags. We have heard of those who are rude to waiters, toady up to horrific political leaders, shove a chattering but innocent neighbor down the stairs, cultivate personal wretchedness, starve themselves to death, and allow their children to suffer deprivation and death. Some mock the poor and the worker, some have been racist, some have kept slaves, and most have been so vicious about women's minds and abilities as to constitute a gross inner failure in themselves. Even the Buddha didn't give women full access to fairyland. With Montaigne, I have to say, "Wisdom, my friend, I am not impressed." Yet, the next thought must always be, "Ignorance, I am even less impressed; indeed, I am appalled." There is a big difference between those who try to be broadly humane and those who indulge and coddle their self-centered fantasies. Knowledge and wisdom are a lot better than ignorance and immaturity.

In 1861 John Stuart Mill° wrote: "It is better to be a human being dissatisfied than a pig satisfied; better to be Socrates dissatisfied than a fool satisfied. And if the fool, or the pig, are of a different opinion, it is because they only know their own side of the question. The other party to the comparison knows both sides." Remember this the next time someone asks why we support fine arts that do not quite support themselves. This whole pig-versus-philosopher debate is pretty hilarious, yes? The upshot is that the wise can get wiser by watching the innocent. But that doesn't mean the wise want to switch places. What I have come to believe about all these paeans to wisdom flanked by all this despair about wisdom is this: everything has to be learned twice. In childhood we have ignorant happiness, and we must lose this happiness if we are ever to get beyond it. Repression is not the same as transcendence. Between these states of calm ignorance and calm knowing, there has to be some half-wise screaming. Some few people actually grow wise by acting wise, but most grow wise by acting foolish, by accruing a variety of experiences, by taking chances (and thus learning about chance, our constant companion), and by making errors. Voltaire's Candide said that we should cultivate our own gardens, but he concluded this only after he was no longer the naïf his name implies. By then, he had gone on many travels, seen a fine woman return from a voyage with but one buttock, seen the great philosopher of optimism lose one extremity after another until he was a mere nub of optimism, and seen kind men do as much terrible harm as cruel ones. What if all these characters had instead stayed home, cultivating their gardens, and had kept their buttocks, limbs, and innocence? They would have remained children. Or, as so many adult children are, pigs. Spinoza° quoted Ecclesiastes' saying that whoever increases knowledge increases sorrow. But he was explicit in his opinion that, though both fools and wise people have happiness, they do not have the same happiness. As Spinoza put it, both a human and a horse have lust, but a horse lusts for a horse and a human for a human. Just so, Spinoza explained, the happiness of a drunkard is not the happiness of the wise. Knowledge and wisdom are worth it.

According to the great philosophers, your worst barrier against happiness is you, your own wrong thinking. Your four problems are these: You cannot see yourself or much about the world you live in. You are ruled by desire and emotion. You will not take your place or rise to your role. You

John Stuart Mill (1806–1873) was an English political philosopher and economist (see p. 123).
Spinoza: Baruch Spinoza (1632–1677) was a Dutch philosopher who rejected the mind/body dualism of René Descartes (1596–1650).

are alternately oblivious to death and terrified of it. As such, your job is to master these four errors in yourself. If you do, you will be happy and more free to love, work, and play the way you wish you could. None of this comes easily; it has to be practiced a great deal, and it never works completely. However, there is no useful alternative to the effort. As Epicurus° reminds us, "We must exercise ourselves in the things which bring happiness, since, if that be present, we have everything, and, if that be absent, all our actions are directed towards attaining it."

The wisdom literature I have been discussing addressed itself to the question of how to live, but it is worth noticing, in closing, that the core of our lives is love and work, and these wisdom instructions also apply in these more specific realms. If you want your love and your work to be successful, actively apply yourself to knowing yourself, controlling your desires, taking what is yours, and remembering that love and work can both end abruptly—remembering to the extent that you cherish them both—and learn to let them flow. Actively applying yourself means doing something different in the service of these goals and seeking out information about what it is you need to learn. We acknowledge only some parts of the great store of happiness advice, and the most important idea that we have lost is that happiness takes study. Secular happiness requires the same kind of meditative work that religion requires: the solace works only if you rehearse, daily, weekly, and on special days, reading over and over the phrases and arguments that seem most persuasive.

Epicurus (341–270 BCE): Greek philosopher, the founder of Epicureanism, which held the belief that pleasure is the greatest good and should be pursued with intelligence and self-discipline.

Understanding the Text

1. To what extent does Hecht discuss the conceptualization of dying in the light of the conceptualization of living? How does she draw parallels between the two? Would you agree that our society promotes the very same parallels?
2. Define the term "posttraumatic bliss" (par. 5). What examples, her own and those from other sources, does Hecht provide to reflect on this term? In what ways, if any, does Hecht connect this idea to ideas of happiness?
3. What effect does "remembering death" have on your ideas about happiness? Does the awareness of death undercut or destroy the possibility of true happiness? Or does it qualify or even deepen your sense of what it means to be happy?

Reflection and Response

4. Describe a way in which our culture applies Hecht's meaning of dying to our routine of living. Explain the similarities and differences between your example and Hecht's. Does this example serve as what Hecht would consider an appropriate model for deriving happiness from dying?
5. Hecht states, "According to the great philosophers, your worst barrier against happiness is you, your own wrong thinking" (par. 27). She continues by suggesting ways in which people could conduct meaningful work to create happiness in themselves. List some examples of ways Hecht suggests creating this sense of happiness. Which ways, if any, are most applicable to your life today?
6. Think of yourself in ten years, then twenty, then thirty, and so on. Which parts of Hecht's article would you consider applying to the ways in which you are living? Would this change for you with more experience and age?

Making Connections

7. In Eric G. Wilson's "Terrible Beauty" (p. 247), he discusses the ways Keats saw beauty in life by having an understanding of death and dying. To what extent is this argument relevant for the discussion presented by Hecht? What if Hecht were to discuss Keats in her piece? What would she say?
8. Hecht cites several works of "wisdom literature" that teach readers how to "remember death" and how to live with death. Several of the authors she cites (for example, the Buddha, John Stuart Mill, and Aristotle) are represented in this book. Reread one of them with the theme of death in mind: what role does an awareness of death play in their wisdom? Choose specific passages that support your claims.

Terrible Beauty

Eric G. Wilson

Eric Wilson is Thomas H. Pritchard Professor of English at Wake Forest University, where he teaches the literature of Romanticism and film. He earned a Ph.D. in English from the City University of New York in 1996. He is the author of eleven books, including his most recent, *Everyone Loves a Good Train Wreck: Why We Can't Look Away* (2012). In *Against Happiness: In Praise of Melancholy* (2008), Wilson argues that melancholy — or pensive sadness — is underrated and that our contemporary, superficial notion of happiness is likewise greatly overrated. Indeed, creativity and inventiveness may thrive on melancholy.

> Melancholy is at the bottom of everything, just as at the end of all rivers is the sea. Can it be otherwise in a world where nothing lasts, where all that we have loved or shall love must die? Is death, then, the secret of life? The gloom of an eternal mourning enwraps, more or less closely, every serious and thoughtful soul, as night enwraps the universe.
>
> —HENRI FRÉDÉRIC AMIEL

On November 30, 1820, as the autumn orange decayed into earth's winter muck, John Keats,° suffering from the tuberculosis that killed his mother and his brother Tom, sat down to draft a letter to his good friend Charles Brown. This was to be his last known correspondence. Between horrific bouts of coughing—coughing that stained his tongue with blood—Keats recovered himself enough to write these striking lines: "I have an habitual feeling of my real life having past, and that I am leading a posthumous existence." At the age of twenty-five, when he should have been relishing multitudinous opportunities for love and for growth, for summer's larks and pretty girls, Keats already felt like a corpse. It seemed to him as though he were already in the grave and therefore looking back on his days as one would witness a character in a finished story. There he was, composing, viewing the world with a dead man's eyes.

While he was creating this epistle, Keats no doubt brooded over his brief life. When he was but nine years old, his father, while riding home from a visit, fell from his horse and died the very next day. After only a

John Keats (1795–1821) was an English poet. See p. 264.

few years had passed, his mother was, as I've mentioned, diagnosed with tuberculosis. Though Keats nursed her assiduously, sitting up with her all hours of the night, cooking for her, reading to her, she succumbed in 1810, during Keats's fifteenth year. Orphaned, Keats was assigned to a guardian and soon after taken from a beloved boarding school and required to apprentice as an apothecary. Keats found the work to be tedious, for during these years, his late teen years, he was awakening to the grandeurs of poetry, especially the verse of Spenser° and Shakespeare. To complete his training, Keats had to learn surgery during the years 1815 and 1816. Day after day he toiled in a hospital, malodorous and bloody, where he witnessed nothing but suffering. As he increasingly turned from surgery and toward poetry, he completed his first substantial poem, *Endymion*, which he published in 1818. Two of the leading literary magazines of the time attacked the poem for not making sense. Around this time Keats's brother Tom died after a long and painful period of illness. While attending Tom, Keats met the love of his life, Fanny Brawne. He became engaged to her in 1819. However, he soon realized that he would never be able to marry her because he himself was doomed to fall prey to the same disease that killed his family members. He knew he would die without ever consummating his ardent love.

One would think that Keats's tragic life would have fostered in him an extreme bitterness, a petulance born of persistent unfairness. But Keats, much to his credit and almost miraculously, remained generous in the face of his difficulties. Indeed, he weathered life's blows as though he were in a sense already dead, posthumous, someone who could somehow transcend suffering and despair even as he underwent the horrific calamities.

This is the essence of his announcement that he felt "posthumous." The statement suggests that Keats near the end of his life was not rancorous toward his misfortunes. Rather, as he approached his demise, he was strangely detached from life's perpetual ills. He could basically say that he was in the race and out of the race at the same time, both engrossed by the sense of his impending death and disjoined from this same sensibility. He could endure the bludgeons of time while at the same time not caring about the contusions.

5 To be sure, it says something about Keats that he didn't flee to the usual escapes that offered themselves in the early nineteenth century:

Spenser: Edmund Spenser (1552/53–1631), English poet whose long allegorical poem *The Fairie Queene*, written in the Spenserian stanza, is thought one of the greatest in the English language.

Christianity or opium, drink or dreaming. Though he unsurprisingly underwent pangs of serious melancholia (who wouldn't, faced with his disasters?), he nonetheless remained sturdy in the face of his abiding woe. He never fell into self-pity or self-indulgent sorrow. In fact, he consistently transformed his gloom, grown primarily from his experiences with death, into a vital source of beauty. Things are gorgeous, he often claimed, *because* they die. The porcelain rose is not as pretty as the one that decays. Melancholia over time's passing is the proper stance for beholding beauty. Mourning makes the dead dawn brightly shine.

Why would Keats do such a seemingly perverse thing? Why would he actually embrace decay and the consequent heartaches? He did so because he understood that suffering and death are not aberrations to be cursed but necessary parts of a capacious existence, a personal history attuned to the plentiful polarity of the cosmos. To deny calamity and the corpse would be to live only a partial life, one devoid of creativity and beauty. Keats welcomed his death so that he could live.

Taking this double stance—suffering death while transcending death—Keats was in his pain and above his pain. He could refuse it and hold it at once. He could at the same time loathe it and love it. He could fear it and see the beauty in it. Keats developed this interplay between detachment and attachment in one of his most famous letters, the one on the "vale of Soul-making." In this 1819 epistle, penned at the bleak nadir of his tragic life, Keats asks the following question: "Do you not see how necessary a World of Pains and troubles is to school an Intelligence and make it a Soul?" He's here implying that an abstract mind can develop into a full-hearted person only through enduring long periods of sadness and pain. Only a person who could accept the world as it is, a place of sorrow as much as joy, would say such a thing. Keats is acutely aware of the difficulty of becoming a human being in this world, but he also realizes, as though he were beyond the agony, that the pain is absolutely necessary.

In another famous letter, this one from 1818, Keats compares a human's life with a "large Mansion of Many Apartments." He states that the only way to engage the great mysteries of life is to suffer "Misery and Heartbreak, Pain, Sickness and oppression." Undergoing these troubles, one moves from the "Chamber of Maiden Thought," the room of innocence, into darker passages, the regions of profound experience. In this latter place, one finds the inspiration for poetry, poetry that explores the mysterious burdens of life. In this case, too, Keats shows himself to be intensely aware of the painful world but also keenly willing to embrace this same pain. It's as if once more he were somehow in the world but not of it, able to suffer the troublous gloom but also able to see beyond it. He's able to see beyond it, we soon learn, because this pain is the muse of beauty.

• • •

Keats makes this point in a poem, "Ode on Melancholy," from 1819. [See page 264.] This poem begins with Keats calling us to hold hard to our melancholy moods. He urges us not to alleviate our blues with befuddling chemicals. He also calls on us not to escape our suffering through suicide. Finally, he makes a plea for us not to become so melancholy that all that we can think of are yewberries,° death-moths, and morbid owls. If we do any of these things, then we'll dull the edge of melancholia. We'll "drown the wakeful anguish of the soul."

Keats next explores the result of keeping our melancholy keen. Remaining conscious of our dark moods, we might fall into a "melancholy fit," a deep experience of life's transience but also of its beauty. Fittingly, this melancholy fit is a mixed affair. It falls from heaven like a "weeping cloud, / That fosters the droop-headed flowers all." That is, this fit is a blend of gloom—clouds and wilting flowers—and of vitality: rain and nourishment. Indeed, this cloud "hides the green hill in an April shroud." This strongly suggests that the melancholy fit is a meeting of fertility and decay. 10

What can we call this fit but a meaningful experience of generative melancholy, of that strange feeling that sadness connects us to life's vibrant pulses? Alienated from home and happiness, we sense what is most essential: not comfort or contentment but authentic participation in life's grim interplay between stinking corpses and singing lemurs. This experience is a "fit." It shivers our souls.

In this tense mood we are in a position to understand the relationship between beauty and death. Keats urges us while in this condition to "glut" our sorrow on a "morning rose" or "on the rainbow of the salt sand-wave" or "on the wealth of globed peonies." He then says that if our "mistress" shows "rich" anger, we should take her hand and let her "rave" and "feed deep, deep upon her peerless eyes."

What do these recommendations have in common? Each features the melancholy soul experiencing something beautiful but also something

yewberries: The yew tree is traditionally associated with death; its berries are deadly poisonous.

transient, a quick rose or an ephemeral rainbow or peonies that perish or a mistress's flashing eyes. The suggestion appears to be this: there is a connection among melancholy, beauty, and death.

Keats makes this connection clear in the next sequence. He tells us that this mistress and, by implication, those roses and rainbows and peonies all dwell with beauty, beauty "that must die." These elements also live with joy, "whose hand is ever at his lips / Bidding adieu; and aching Pleasure nigh, / Turning to poison while the bee-mouth sips." Indeed, in the "temple of Delight, / Veiled Melancholy has her sovran shrine." No one can witness this shrine but the person "whose strenuous tongue" has "burst Joy's grape against his palate fine." This person will taste the "sadness" of melancholy's "might." He will be among her "cloudy trophies hung."

15 These associations make for several conclusions. The "wakeful anguish" of sharp melancholia can lead to a shuddering experience, a "fit." This vital moment grows from an insight into the nature of things: life grows from death; death gives rise to life. This insight animates melancholy, makes it vibrant. But it also intensifies the pain, for it emphasizes this: everything, no matter how beautiful, must die. Rather than flee from this difficult position, the melancholic appreciates things all the more *because* they die. Appreciating these things, the melancholic enjoys their beauty. In enjoying the beauty of the world, the melancholic himself wants to create beauty, to become a trophy that commemorates his resplendent experience of earth's transient gorgeousness.

• • •

Melancholia empowers us to experience beauty. When I say beauty, I don't mean the Hallmark beauty, prettiness, really: those perfect sunsets on the coastal horizon or those tranquil panoramas from the rounded top of a mountain or those perfectly airbrushed faces, wrinkle free and vacant. The beauty I have in mind is something much wilder: the violent ocean roiling under the tepidly peaceful beams or the dark and jagged peaks that bloody the hands or those unforgettable faces, striking because of a disproportionate nose or mouth that somehow brings the whole visage into a uniquely dynamic harmony.

Think of it. All pretty things are almost exactly alike, while all beautiful events are distinct. Prettiness, the manifestation of American happiness, is devoted to predictability and smoothness. The pretty view has no dangerous edges; the pretty face features no unexpected distortions. Don't all postcards give off a similar idea, that nature is a tranquil scene merely to be enjoyed by humans? Don't all supermodels look almost exactly alike, as if they were produced on some perfumed assembly line? We can go further: pretty things suggest a kind of emptiness. The mountain range reduced to a harmlessly fungible square of paper seems devoid of portentous power and foreboding threat. The human face is painted as a deserted gaze corresponding to the untenanted skull within; the bland expression is an extension of bland thoughts. Prettiness, then, with its halfhearted focus on sleekness and blankness, is finally a denial of the organic world—that serrated mess, that community that's craggy. And being a denial of organicity, this same prettiness is really an avoidance of death, a feeble hope that one can somehow escape the lacerations of time.

Beauty, on the other hand, is organic. The beautiful object is unpredictably mottled, scabrous, and fractured. The beautiful vista is indeed teeming with ominous waves and cloud-rending peaks. Likewise, the beautiful face from certain angles looks even homely, what with its lines and its asymmetries, but then, suddenly, in the right light, it all comes together into a ravishing vision. These interesting events, motley and slightly aberrant, seem to be expressions of equally interesting powers. The rough sea appears to manifest some magnificently afflicted organic principle. The intricate face in the same way probably corresponds to a nimble and flexible mind within. This ocean, this face: both are ultimately beautiful because they reveal the death within them. The turbulent sea threatens destruction as much as creation; the pied visage shows decay as well as growth.

Indeed, you can experience beauty only when you have a melancholy foreboding that all things in this world die. The transience of an object makes it beautiful, and its transience is manifested in its fault lines, its expressions of decrepitude. To go in fear of death is to forgo beauty for prettiness, that flaccid rebellion against corrosion. To walk with death in your head is to open the heart to peerless flashes of fire.

"To go in fear of death is to forgo beauty for prettiness, that flaccid rebellion against corrosion. To walk with death in your head is to open the heart to peerless flashes of fire."

20 So, it should by now be obvious you can't discover beauty when you join the vacationing masses in search of poster aesthetics. Indeed, these folks—almost all of them happy types—can't really perceive beauty at all. All that they see is their expectation of the picture-perfect shot, pretty and presentable. They go to the mountains or the coast with numerous images downloaded into their heads. When they reach their

destinations, they're not out to experience the strange terrain, the uncanny upsurges of gorgeous weirdness. They're rather in search only of occurrences that match their paper-thin minds. In this way, these scenery freaks don't get the world at all. All they notice is what they expect to witness, static shots of a Photoshopped globe.

The novelist Walker Percy, probably with Blake's take on the particular somewhere in his mind, discusses precisely this problem. In his essay "The Loss of the Creature" (1954), Percy argues that most go through life witnessing not the actual world but their preconceptions of it. Millions each year go to the Grand Canyon hoping for a sublime vision of nature's grandeur. However, these same millions have for years studied the canyon from afar, in postcards, posters, and photographs. These simulations of reality eventually encode in the many brains ideal images of the scene. When these masses finally muster the energy to go to the Grand Canyon, they never truly get to see the vast chasm. Instead, all they really perceive is their prefabricated picture of the place, their safely sentimental rendering. Indeed, many of these tourists come away from the actual canyon disappointed. They feel that the real canyon didn't quite measure up to their internal portrait. They feel that they didn't get the experience they really wanted. They feel cheated, slightly disdainful.

This same problem occurs in many contexts. Most students go to their biology classes believing that they will learn something about basic anatomy. Their professor gives them frogs to dissect. As the students go to work with their scalpels, they don't actually see frogs at all. All they perceive are the abstract anatomical relationships that the frogs exemplify. The particular frog is not a being in and of itself, a spotted olive sheen from which protrude indifferent eyes; it is simply a "specimen" of anatomy. The same occurs in English classes. Students arrive thinking that they might come to understand the nature of the sonnet. The professor distributes one day Keats's first great poem, a sonnet, "On First Looking into Chapman's Homer." Along with the professor, the students quickly try to learn just how this poem serves as a sonnet, is a "specimen" of a sonnet. Doing so, these students miss the unrepeatable concreteness of Keats's work, its striking idiosyncrasies, its images that are unforgettable, its eventful rhymes.

Percy offers a useful recommendation: biology teachers should one day surprise their students with sonnets, and English instructors should of a day startle their classes with dead frogs. Such unorthodox behavior would shock students out of their complacency, their dependence on safe abstractions, and force them to stare at things unadorned—beautiful and strange. Denuded of their habitual internal images, these students would have nothing to protect them from the world's gorgeous weirdness. Once overwhelmed with this torqued upsurge, these same students would likely work for the remainder of their days to surprise themselves, to strain through their familiar grids. They would go to the Louvre in hopes of breaking through their years of T-shirts and postcards and actually experience the enigmatic wantonness of the *Mona Lisa*. They would travel to Mont Blanc dreaming of the vertigo of altitudinous snow.

But these students, perhaps poor and pining with love, would prove the rare exception. Sadly, the loss of the real affects millions of folks every year. It's as if the masses had decided to eat menus instead of real food or consume money instead of what it can buy. They probably relinquish the world in hopes of remaining contented, safe, untroubled by the eerie dawn, the preternatural twilight. They wish for their lives to be one long vacation; they want to be perennial tourists. Remaining safely behind the objects of the gift shop, they stay separated from that shocking and tottering world that would depress them as much as buoy them, that would remind them of their own beautiful ugliness and their own living deaths.

All of us, obviously, go through the world with expectations. We face each day hoping that certain experiences will occur. However, we melancholy types, stoked on Keats and committed to learning, are aware that our preconceptions can block our access to the outlandishly novel world. Like those poor students at the Louvre or on Mont Blanc, we try as hard as we can to let go of our prefabricated grids and behold the world devoid of ourselves. When we do, we are amazed at what we find, a world whose deathly deformities cohere into durable pulchritude. Finding this, we begin to feel our own deaths pulsing in our veins. We realize that it is precisely these deaths that give us our unique and comely appearance. We try to embrace, then, the sad fact that the world most wants to forget: we all die, and in our dying is, paradoxically, our living. 25

• • •

America is obsessed with forgetting this sad fact. Think of the country's collective, 85 percent of the people wearing a pretty grin to cover the beautiful grind of life. After a while, most come to think of this painted smile as the real thing. Doing so, the majority are rather easily able to reduce earth's tragedies into safe clichés, lazy chitchat.

An example of this flattening of the vital real to the boring idle is this: happy types tend to reduce the world's terrible tragedies—its wars, its hungers—to mindless talk on a television screen. While the earth struggles under its burdens, happy types tune in to pundits thundering over which side is right, the conservatives or the liberals, the war supporters or the peace lovers. The real issues are lost in all the talk. This is comforting, though, to happy types, who, after watching the shouting politicos, always have something to say about the worst crises. Reflecting the thoughts of the collective, those bent on happiness can pretend to understand and control barely bearable complexities. These types can always take a side and have something seemingly important to say.

Happy types tend to boil down their own problems in the same way. When they experience those terrible longings for what has been lost, when they feel those difficult hatreds toward what can never come back, then they fall into some clichéd affirmation about how they're good people and deserve to be happy. Or they recite some smarmy poem like Mary Stevenson's "Footprints in the Sand." Or they pray to some kind presence sitting idly in the sky. Or they take down their favorite book on happiness, or a devotional manual, or that bestseller on the wisdom of children. They pull themselves once more into that contented feeling. They go out into the world again beaming with all their might.

If only these types could learn to sit long with their inevitable anxieties. Regardless of how much they repress or ignore or forget, they must feel in their bones what all of us feel, fear of their own demise. This ubiquitous anxiety besets every conscious individual. There's no escaping it. When we think even for a minute about the nature of the universe, we remember that everything is rushing toward annihilation, and we become anxious about our own deaths. Surprised by this sudden anxiety, we can do one of two things. We can quickly flee from this feeling into the land of indolent babble, that flatland where everything ultimately is good. Or we can sit with our anxiety and let it pervade our hearts and thus honestly encounter our own finitude.

30 Anxiety indeed pushes us to consider the relative shortness of our lives. What are we always anxious about, either directly or indirectly, but our own end? Whether we are careworn over losing our jobs or being bereft of control or becoming alienated from a loved one, we always ultimately fear pain, and what is pain but a precursor to the last pain, death? When we are forced to face the fact that our existences are but mere blips on the scale of cosmic time, we realize how absolutely precious every instant is. We understand that we have only a very short time remaining to us and that we'd better make the best of it. In this way, just when we experience our extreme limitation, we also become aware of our grand possibilities. We want, more than anything, to live hard and full, to do what we've never done but only dreamed.

Feeling, in our nerves, this finitude, we enjoy, perhaps for the first time, beauty. Death like a slow-burning fire is consuming our very hearts. We sense its vital force consuming our ventricles and our aortas, illuminating them, stimulating them, even as it eats them away. Every single beat becomes to us a miracle, one more stay against the final thump before the silence. Desperate for each pulsation of fresh oxygen, we look around, bewildered, until our eyes light on something living to die: a crocus, drooping, or a Maine coon cat. These beings suddenly become to us what they are—self-contained lights, revelations of the quick hum and buzz of life: visions. There they stand, the purplish crocus and the wild-eyed feline.

It is now that we understand the great profundity of the old idea of the *memento mori* (remember that you will die). Meditative souls of the Middle Ages often adorned their tables with skulls or kept close by etchings of skeletons engaged in the danse macabre. Later, during the early Renaissance, funeral art featured grim reapers or skull and bones. Even later large clocks had engraved upon them mottoes, such as ultima forsan (perhaps the last) or vulnerant omnes, ultima necat (they all wound, and the last kills) or, perhaps the best known, tempus fugit (time flies). Seen in the light of Keats's linkage of melancholy, death, and beauty, these motifs do not appear to be morbid but rather celebratory, vibrant gestures toward life's ambrosial finitude.

When I embrace this theme—and it's extremely difficult to do so—I feel as though my anxiety were an invitation to participate in the great rondure of life. Though my anxiety over death initially makes me feel alone, separated from everything else and forced to face my own unique possibilities, this same feeling eventually encourages me to sense my solidarity with all other living things. I know that we all are this minute, with every new breath, driving toward death. Knowing this, I for an instant penetrate the mysteries of the cosmos's organisms. I sound ambiguous depths. I realize that beneath the surfaces of my very self are the same rhythms that drive the round earth and the stars that seem still. I feel at one with what I can only call Being—beautiful and robust.

Encountering this unity, I feel as though I were authentic, true, alive. All fakeness falls away, and I am at the core of life. This is death's boon, sorrowful yet sonorous, the call to authenticity. What is authenticity but accepting that melancholy death is the muse of my existence, the sweet inspiration that reminds me of who I am and what I can do, that saves me from the masses and keeps me honest? This is indeed authenticity. It is that feeling that my deepest anxieties over passing things makes me who I really am: this unique and unrepeatable possibility, this quivering node of individuality, this miraculous breath of Being. It is further that feeling that this sudden separation from the collective, this delving into my own-most potency, is paradoxically an experience of unity with all organisms, with their sweet contracting and expanding. It, authenticity, is finally that feeling that all of this weird planet, distant yet so intimate, is beautiful in its passing, is so gorgeous, with its desperate starlings and its stark mica, that we want to weep.

Understanding the Text

1. What does Wilson mean when he uses the term "posthumous" (par. 3)? How does Wilson apply this term to John Keats ("Ode on Melancholy," p. 264)? What does this statement suggest about the quality of one's life?
2. Describe Wilson's dichotomy between suffering death and transcending death. How does this relate to Keats's representation of the relationship between detachment and attachment? Draw on Wilson's discussion of Keats's letters to discuss the ways in which Keats conceptualized happiness in the world around him.
3. Wilson discusses at great length the relationship between beauty and dying. Why does Wilson think this connection is important? In what ways does this relationship determine criteria for one's personal happiness?

Reflection and Response

4. Describe a time in your own life when you conceptualized life similarly to the ways Wilson suggests. Did you consider the act of dying when you were conceptualizing living? Did factors of "beauty" or "anxiety," or both, determine a criterion for happiness? Discuss this example in terms of Wilson's views. Does your example support his position? Do you agree with his argument? Why or why not?
5. To what extent, if any, do you consider melancholia a factor in determining your happiness? Would you agree that one cannot truly find the beauty in the world without recognizing the sorrow as well?
6. Wilson provides several literary examples that relate the beauty in life to the conceptualization of death and sorrow. Discuss some of these examples at greater length. How applicable do you find these examples to your own definition of happiness?

Making Connections

7. Wilson discusses Keats's construction of happiness in terms of his conceptualization of death. Discuss Keats's poem "Ode on Melancholy" (p. 264). First, copy two or three lines from the poem that you believe illuminate Wilson's argument. Then translate these lines into your own words. Based on Keats's writing, would you agree or disagree with Wilson's argument?

8. Draw on two readings from earlier chapters in this book. How do these readings support the connection provided by Wilson in relation to the construction of happiness? Alternatively, you may discuss readings in which the authors directly oppose statements provided by Wilson.
9. Think of examples from popular song lyrics today that present ideas similar to those offered by poets such as Keats. Write an essay in which you compare the meaning behind the song lyrics to the meaning behind Wilson's and Keats's words. How does our culture today conceptualize these ideas in different outlets?

Melencolia I

Albrecht Dürer

The engraving *Melencolia I* by the German artist Albrecht Dürer (1471–1528) has fascinated and puzzled viewers for centuries. Printed in appropriately heavy black ink in 1514, it depicts a very solid-looking angel surrounded by an array of objects and figures, each of which symbolizes some aspect of the condition known as melancholia. In

ibusca/Getty Images

premodern medicine, melancholy was one of the four temperaments, or "humors"; it was associated with "black bile," a substance that was thought to stimulate not only sadness or depression but also thoughtfulness, intellectual activity, and creativity. The other humors are sanguine (associated with the blood), phlegmatic (phlegm), and choleric (yellow bile). Scholars in the Renaissance period often thought of melancholy as a disease of intellectuals and artists.

Detailed analyses of the engraving have been attempted by a number of art historians. Erwin Panofsky, in a famous analysis in his study *The Life and Art of Albrecht Dürer* (1943), suggested that the iconography was based on Heinrich Cornelius Agrippa's *De Occulta Philosophia* (composed 1509–1510, printed 1533). But any viewer can respond to the rich details and speculate about their significance: the craftsman's tools, the magic square (in which the numbers in every direction add up to 34), the hourglass, the sleeping hound, and so on.

Understanding the Text

1. Describe what you see in this engraving. Simply make a list.
2. What do you conclude from the number of observations you have made about the engraving in question 1? What is this engraving trying to show us?

Reflection and Response

3. Some have argued that this is an allegorical work. Is it? What do you think is its main purpose, either allegorical or otherwise?
4. It is also popular to read this work autobiographically. Imagine that this engraving tells us a lot about Dürer. What do we know after studying it closely?

Making Connections

5. Consider this engraving in relation to Keats's "Ode on Melancholy" (p. 264). Your essay should discuss the theories of melancholy embodied in each piece. Do not forget to discuss their different forms.
6. Dürer engraved this in the sixteenth century. Do you see any signs that this engraving could just as easily be made today? Find a contemporary piece of any kind that speaks to the same issues as this engraving. In your essay, consider Dürer's engraving and the piece you have chosen in an exhibit entitled something like "Centuries of Melancholia."

Taking Pills for Unhappiness Reinforces the Idea That Being Sad Is Not Human

Giles Fraser

The Reverend Doctor Giles Fraser is a priest of the Church of England and formerly the Canon Chancellor (the priest responsible for education and outreach) of St. Paul's Cathedral. He resigned in October 2011 over the City of London's decision to remove Occupy protesters forcibly from the cathedral steps, and he currently serves as the parish priest of St. Mary's, Newington, in London. He writes a weekly column for the *Guardian* newspaper. Fraser holds a degree in philosophy from the University of Newcastle and a Ph.D. from the University of Lancaster. He studied theology at Oxford University.

I was trouble at school. "Like a monkey at the zoo, Giles is intent on displaying himself from his least flattering angle," said one teacher in my term report, a document strewn with words like "disruptive" and "unfocused." Thank God this was in the early 80s, otherwise I bet someone would have suggested Ritalin.° For, since the mid 80s, society has decided that adolescent trouble-making is some sort of medical condition. We have given it a scientific-sounding classification, ADHD, securing a sense that a messy adolescence is pathological, some sort of chemical imbalance. Thus the scientists are called in to reinforce generally conservative norms of appropriate behavior. In the US, between 1987 and 2007, there was a 35-fold increase in the number of children being classified as having some form of mental deficiency.

Of course, there are alternative narratives of my trouble-causing. I hated school because I wanted to live by a different story to the one proposed by the British public school system. Or, maybe, I preferred having fun to reading Chaucer. That may be a less noble account, but hardly pathological, or in need of some medical classification. But deviation from social conformity is increasingly seen to be something in need of a pill. In the UK in 1999, there were 158,000 prescriptions written for Ritalin. In 2010 it was 661,463.

Ritalin: one of several trade names for the stimulant methylphenidate, used to treat attention-deficit/hyperactivity disorder among other conditions.

The same thing has happened with depression and drugs like Prozac; though calling it depression is already to classify a particular kind of experience as something quasi-medical, thus leading one to think in terms of medical treatment. Sometimes I am just sad. Sometimes pissed off. Sometimes smothered in darkness. But we often lump all these experiences together simply because pharmaceutical companies have developed a certain sort of treatment. And, once you have a hammer in your hand, it is convenient to see every problem in terms of its being a nail. We have found the solution, now let's make the problem fit the solution we have available. It's a form of reverse engineering.

"If we translate misery into some sort of chemical imbalance then someone can make big money out of it. But unhappiness is often a perfectly proper response to the state of the world."

It is significant that psychoactive drugs were originally developed for other purposes. Drugs such as Thorazine, Miltown and Marsilid were developed in the 50s as ways to treat infections. But they were also seen to have mood-altering side-effects—though scientists had no idea why or how. So, as several writers have pointed out, "instead of developing a drug to fit an abnormality an abnormality was postulated to fit a drug." Thus we are encouraged to think of our problems in terms of the lucrative solutions to problems we didn't know we had. In this way, the pharmaceutical companies are responsible for the very conditions they propose to alleviate.

Forget the fact that some people are miserable because they are struggling on zero-hours contracts, or have lost their partner or have been watching the news too much—if we translate misery into some sort of chemical imbalance then someone can make big money out of it. But unhappiness is often a perfectly proper response to the state of the world. If you have a shit job or a shit home life, being unhappy is hardly inappropriate. At best, many of the drugs we are popping only deal with the symptoms of all this, not the causes. At worst, they pathologize deviations for normalcy, thus helping to police the established values of consumer capitalism, and reinforcing the very unhappiness that they purport to cure.

Yes, there are some for whom happiness can be reclaimed by doing a bit more exercise or being more sociable. This sounds healthier than pills. But for those for whom these are not solutions, let's not make it worse by insisting upon the compulsory happiness of the smiley face. For, like the drugs, this can be just another way of shutting people up.

Understanding the Text

1. Fraser claims that pharmaceuticals such as Prozac may not always be the right response to depression or sadness, and that "unhappiness is often a perfectly proper response to the state of the world." Does that mean that unhappiness must be accepted as an inevitability, or does Fraser suggest other ways of alleviating unhappiness? If so, what are those other ways, and where does Fraser hint at them?
2. Fraser uses his own experience as an example here. Why does he do this? Do you think this and other evidence he offers effectively supports his case? Why or why not?

Reflection and Response

3. Fraser makes a case against pills to treat what he sees as normal social deviancies. Discuss how Fraser's assessment confirms or contradicts what you have learned about people and pills. Feel free to cite other sources as you make your case.
4. What is Fraser's point about the place of unhappiness in human life? Do you agree? Why or why not?

Making Connections

5. Write an essay in which you consider Fraser's argument in relation to a few articles on ADHD that you find in the *New York Times* from the last decade.
6. Which entries from Chapter 1 would support Fraser's argument? Write an essay in which you consider spiritual alternatives to the pill-popping model.

Ode on Melancholy

John Keats

John Keats (1795–1821) died at age 26, having published only fifty-four poems in his short life, yet he ranks among the most admired and influential of English poets. He trained to become a surgeon, but increasingly felt drawn to poetry and published his first volume, *Poems*, in 1817. The poems for which he is most famous, a series of lyric odes, were written two years later. The "Ode on Melancholy," inspired partly by Robert Burton's encyclopedic *Anatomy of Melancholy* (1621), characteristically extols intense experience and keen feeling, in verse so evocative that it arouses the very emotions it describes. Keats died of tuberculosis in Rome, Italy.

1

No, no, go not to Lethe,° neither twist
    Wolf's-bane,° tight-rooted, for its poisonous wine;
Nor suffer thy pale forehead to be kiss'd
    By nightshade, ruby grape of Proserpine;°
Make not your rosary of yew-berries,° 5
    Nor let the beetle, nor the death-moth be
        Your mournful Psyche,° nor the downy owl
A partner in your sorrow's mysteries;
    For shade to shade will come too drowsily,
        And drown the wakeful anguish of the soul. 10

2

But when the melancholy fit shall fall
    Sudden from heaven like a weeping cloud,
That fosters the droop-headed flowers all,
    And hides the green hill in an April shroud;

Lethe: a river in Hades, the dwelling place of the dead in ancient Greek mythology. Drinking its water caused total loss of memory of life on earth.
Wolf's-bane: a flowering plant with poisonous roots (once used to poison wolves).
Proserpine: Roman goddess, abducted by the god of the underworld and eventually rescued by her mother, Ceres.
yew-berries: The yew tree is traditionally associated with death; its berries are deadly poisonous.
Psyche: a personification of the soul in Greek and Roman mythology. *The Golden Ass* by Apuleius tells the allegorical story of Psyche's love of Cupid.

Then glut thy sorrow on a morning rose, 15
Or on the rainbow of the salt sand-wave,
Or on the wealth of globed peonies;
Or if thy mistress some rich anger shows,
Emprison her soft hand, and let her rave,
And feed deep, deep upon her peerless eyes. 20

3

She dwells with Beauty—Beauty that must die;
And Joy, whose hand is ever at his lips
Bidding adieu; and aching Pleasure nigh,
Turning to poison while the bee-mouth sips:
Ay, in the very temple of Delight 25
Veil'd Melancholy has her sovran shrine,
Though seen of none save him whose strenuous tongue
Can burst Joy's grape against his palate fine;
His soul shall taste the sadness of her might,
And be among her cloudy trophies hung. 30

Understanding the Text

1. Paraphrase this poem. Write it in your own words. For every word Keats uses, choose one that has a similar meaning. You may leave the articles and conjunctions as is ("the," "an," "and," etc.).
2. We might consider each stanza as a piece of a three-part argument. What is the argument of each stanza? How does it progress from one to the next?
3. Make a chart of the different vocabularies in this poem. Place the words in columns. For example, "rose," "peonies," and "shade" might go in a nature column. How many vocabularies can you name?

Reflection and Response

4. We might argue that this is a poem about desire. What is its speaker saying about desire?
5. Imagine that the speaker of this poem is talking just to you. What is the message of each line? Translate it into your own words.
6. Consider Keats's figurative language. Why does he use the words he uses? Look, for example, at his verbs. What is he trying to make happen? Now look at his adjectives. How does he weave his message?

Making Connections

7. Write an essay in which you compare the views of Keats and Epictetus ("Handbook," p. 88) on pain and suffering.
8. Keats's speaker uses the emphatic "no" and the implied "yes" to move the audience from one position to another. Write a new stanza for this ode in which the language is mostly "maybe."
9. Would you consider Keats's ode as a foil to Noelle Oxenhandler's "Ah, But the Breezes . . ." (p. 314)? Write an essay in which you consider their positions as opposites, or not.

Aversion to Happiness across Cultures: A Review of Where and Why People Are Averse to Happiness

Mohsen Joshanloo and Dan Weijers

The following selection contains excerpts from an article that appeared in the June 2014 issue of the *Journal of Happiness Studies*. It is the first review of scholarship that examines why some cultures seem to be, in varying degrees, "averse to happiness." People in Europe and the United States tend to assume that personal happiness is the supreme goal in life; however, people in non-Western cultures (and even some in Western cultures) often carry very different assumptions. At the time of their research, Mohsen Joshanloo and Dan Weijers were postdoctoral students at Victoria University, Wellington, Australia. Joshanloo is currently a postdoctoral fellow in psychology at Chungbuk National University, Korea; Weijers currently teaches philosophy at California State University, Sacramento.

Introduction

In contemporary psychological literature, scientific analysis of individuals' well-being is focussed on subjective well-being, and is mainly undertaken in the well-established field of happiness studies. Subjective well-being is believed to consist of life satisfaction, the presence of positive affect, and the absence of negative affect (Diener et al. 1999). Ever since the Enlightenment, Westerners have responded to the ideas of liberal modernity, hedonism, and romantic individualism (Christopher and Hickinbottom 2008) by believing in the sovereignty of individuals over their personal happiness (Haybron 2008), and the importance of positive mood and affect balance as ingredients of a good life (Christopher 1999; Tatarkiewicz 1976). Indeed, Western culture and psychology seem to take for granted that happiness is one of the most important values guiding individuals' lives, if not *the* most important. Western culture and psychology also seem to take for granted that happiness is best understood as a personal concept, such that an individual's happiness is not directly constituted (but may be affected) by the success, health, or psychological well-being of others. In this paper, any unqualified use of the term "happiness" refers to the Western concept of personal happiness that is characterized by satisfaction with life and a preponderance of positive over negative emotions.

Contrary to this Western view, our survey of some less-studied aspects of various cultures reveals that many individuals possess negative views about happiness, and are sometimes averse to it. In this paper the aversion to happiness, and particularly different reasons why different cultures are averse to happiness, are analyzed through a brief review of relevant theoretical and empirical literature on happiness from a variety of cultures and academic disciplines. We find that there are many claimed justifications for being averse to happiness, and that at least some people from all cultures are likely to be averse to some kind of happiness for these reasons. We conclude that this important aspect of human culture should be given consideration in future studies on happiness, and that such consideration is likely to produce more informed results, especially in cross-cultural studies. . . .

Reasons for Aversion to Happiness across Cultures

In this section we provide cultural and empirical evidence of people being averse to happiness, or believing that people should be averse to happiness, for the following reasons: being happy makes it more likely that bad things will happen to you, being happy makes you a worse person, expressing happiness is bad for you and others, and pursuing happiness is bad for you and others.

Being Happy Makes It More Likely That Bad Things Will Happen to You

Our research has shown us that many people are averse to happiness because bad things, such as unhappiness, suffering, and death, tend to happen to happy people. Since these negative conditions are often seen as being more negative than being happy is positive (Baumeister et al. 2001), belief that happiness causes, or tends to be followed by, these negative conditions is enough to make people averse to happiness (preferring a roughly neutral state). Furthermore, since different emotional states, such as happiness and unhappiness, are valued differently by different cultures (e.g., Diener et al. 2003, p. 412), we should expect to find cultural differences in the extent to which people are averse to happiness because of the negative conditions it can cause.

East Asian cultures are somewhat under the influence of Taoism (Ho 1995). In Taoism, it is posited that things tend to revert to their opposite (Chen 2006; Peng et al. 2006). Happiness (best understood in this context as success or experiencing fortune and pleasantness) tends to be accompanied by and then outweighed by unhappiness and vice versa. For example, in the Tao-Te-Ching we read: "Misery!—happiness is to be

5

found by its side! Happiness!—misery lurks beneath it! Who knows what either will come to in the end?" (Lao Tse 2008, p. 106). Furthermore, Ji et al. (2001) showed that Chinese were more likely than Americans to predict a reversal in their happiness status when shown graphs showing various trends over the life course, with the Chinese participants much more likely to choose graphs in which the happiness trend reverted or oscillated.

> "Being happy makes it more likely that bad things will happen to you, being happy makes you a worse person, expressing happiness is bad for you and others, and pursuing happiness is bad for you and others."

One half of this dialectical view of happiness—that happiness tends to cause, or be followed by, sadness—seems to be a very widespread belief. For example, in Korea, there is a lay cultural belief that if an individual is happy now, he or she is likely to be less happy in the future (Koo and Suh 2007). Furthermore, in a qualitative study, Uchida and Kitayama (2009) found that Japanese participants believed that happiness could lead to negative consequences because happiness made them inattentive to their surroundings. Sayings expressing the same sentiment (e.g., "crying will come after laughing," "we laughed a lot, then we will come to its harms," and "laughing loudly wakes up sadness") are also often heard in Iran.

The belief that happiness causes, or is likely to be followed by, unhappiness is also present, albeit to a lesser degree, in Western cultures (Ho 2000). Noting Western adages and proverbs, such as the following ones: "happiness and a glass vessel are most easily shattered," "after joy, sorrow," "sorrow never comes too late and happiness too swiftly flies" (Tatarkiewicz 1976, p. 249), Tatarkiewicz concludes that some people naturally expect happiness to be followed by unhappiness. Taking this idea further, Holden (2009) claims that fearing happiness because it is likely to lead to unhappiness is also the meaning behind the popular Western sayings: "after happiness, there comes a fall" and "what goes up must come down" (p. 111). Furthermore, Gilbert et al. (2012) argue that happiness can be "frightening" if you believe that "when I feel happy I am always waiting for something bad to happen" (p. 375). Ben-Shahar (2002, p. 79) and Holden (2009) agree, arguing that people might be averse to happiness because they fear the devastating loss of newly-attained happiness more than they value the actual attainment of it. Indeed, Epicurus (c. 341–271 BCE) warned that intense pleasures, which many Westerners now associate with happiness, are to be avoided because they are likely to result in painful unsatisfiable desires for more and better of the same (Weijers 2011).

While some might be averse to all degrees of happiness, others are only averse to extreme happiness. Extreme or intense happiness has most or all of the consequences that lower intensities of happiness have and some that they do not. Similarly to above, in Japanese culture, extreme happiness (or good fortune) is thought to lead to suffering (Minami 1971), echoed by the Chinese proverb: "extreme happiness begets tragedy" (Bryant and Veroff 2007, p. 39). Pflug's (2009) qualitative study revealed the same idea in a Western culture, finding that some German students mentioned that intense happiness leads to unhappiness in their responses to open-ended questions about happiness. Western philosopher, Joel Kupperman (2006), argues that extreme happiness might lead to negative consequences because it causes carelessness, which can result in catastrophic misfortune, including death.

A separate empirical line of research on the concept "fear of emotion" has reached a similar conclusion; some individuals are afraid of certain affects, including positive affects, particularly when they are strong. Such individuals fear strong affective states because they are concerned that they will lose control over their emotions or their behavioral reactions to emotions (e.g., Berg et al. 1998; Melka et al. 2011). Along similar lines, Holden (2009) has argued that people fear achieving extremely high levels of happiness because they worry that they will lose control of their lives in a narrative sense; that is, they will lose sense of who they are, and consequently feel alien in their own minds.

But happiness having negative consequences *in life* is not the only reason to be averse to it. In traditional Christianity, if happiness (perhaps best understood as a combination of worldly success, a positive state of mind, and occasional merriment in this context) is not accompanied by salvation and grace, it might draw a true Christian away from God, something which could be greatly feared. Indeed, the danger of happiness, for medieval Christians, lurked more in the possibility that it would lead to eternal damnation than in any suffering it might lead to in life (Tatarkiewicz 1976). This perceived danger of happiness resulted in cultural forces that created an aversion to happiness by inculcating most Western children with the idea "that to be happy is to be doing wrong" up till the second half of the nineteenth century (George M. Beard; c.f. Sicherman 1976, p. 904). More recently, Arieti and Bemporad (1980, c.f. Gilbert et al. 2012, p. 377) noted that some depressed patients are "fearful of feeling happy" because they have a "taboo on pleasure," probably because of an upbringing in a hard line puritanical Christian family.

Although these ideas no longer seem to be widespread in the contemporary era, it is not unreasonable to assume that they linger among some Christians to some extent (possibly in modified forms).

In sum, there is evidence from a variety of cultures that people are averse to happiness because they believe that happiness and especially extreme happiness lead to unhappiness and other negative consequences that outweigh the benefits of being happy.

Being Happy Makes You a Worse Person

People aren't just averse to happiness because it might lead to something bad, however; some individuals and some cultures tend to believe that happiness is worthy of aversion because being happy can make someone a worse person (both morally and otherwise). Again, we found evidence for this belief in both non-Western and Western cultures. First we discuss beliefs that happiness is worthy of aversion because it can make someone a morally worse person, and then we discuss beliefs that happiness is worthy of aversion because it can make someone less creative.

Generally speaking, Islam is critical of people that are perceived to be very happy (best understood as experiencing regular and intense positive emotions and few, if any, negative emotions in this context). Prophet Muhammad is cited as saying that "were you to know what I know, you would laugh little and weep much" and "avoid much laughter, for much laughter deadens the heart" (Chittick 2005, p. 133, see also Quran, 5:87). Good and Good (1988) note that ever since the 1979 Islamic Revolution in Iran, under the influence of the Shiite ideology, happiness has been associated with shallowness, foolishness, and vulgarity. Happy people are also seen as being distracted from God, making them morally and spiritually deficient (in Islamic cultures, true happiness is considered to be an inner peace derived from devotion to God; Joshanloo 2013). In contrast, sad people are often defined as serious and deep. Since Islam is relatively widespread, aversion to happiness for the reason that it can make you a bad person is likely to be equivalently widespread. Similarly, but on a smaller scale, Holden (2009, p. 110) observes that some Westerners are averse to happiness because they consider happy people to be superficial "intellectual lightweights" as opposed to "serious-minded" people who "lament the hopeless suffering of the world." Naturally, happiness doesn't necessarily cause ignorance about the hopeless suffering of the world (it is more likely the other way around), but some people nevertheless worry that happiness might preoccupy their minds, leaving them little time for deep reflection on important (e.g., political or religious) issues.

Ahmed (2007, p. 135) has pointed out that, at different times in the West, members of marginalized groups (e.g., women, immigrants, and homosexuals) have had an important reason to kill joy, avoid happiness, and cling to unhappiness: because to be happy in proximity to the injustice they suffer could make them weak in the face of oppression. So, perhaps even in the West, certain members of cultural subgroups have been averse to happiness because being happy might make them less motivated to fight for justice, thereby making them morally worse people. Furthermore, Ben-Shahar (2002, p. 79) and others (e.g., Holden 2009, p. 107) argue that people might fear happiness because they would feel unworthy and guilty if they were to attain it; they would feel like bad people for being happy when they know that more deserving people are suffering.

Similarly, there exists a cultural myth that portrays unhappy people as more creative than sad people (Fredrickson et al. 2000), leading some aspiring artists to fear happiness as they would fear writer's block. For example, when Edvard Munch, the depressive author of the famous painting *The Scream*, was asked why he did not do something about his emotional ailments, he retorted: "They are part of me and my art. They are indistinguishable from me, and it would destroy my art. I want to keep those sufferings." (c.f. Layard 2005, p. 220). Holden (2009, p. 110) reports that this fear—the worry that being happy will lead to a loss of creative and artistic faculty—is widespread among actors and artists. Indeed, Glück (1996, pp. 579–580), herself an artist, has reported that the thought of being happy was terrifying to her because it represented itself as a "vision of desolate normalcy" and threatened to eradicate her desire and capacity to produce good art. Perhaps the fears of these artistic types can be explained by the idea that being happy is bad for you because being happy is boring and being boring is the characteristic most reviled by artists. In this vein, Wilson (2008, p. 7) argues that happiness makes people bland because interesting lives include agony and dejection, not just a preponderance of positive emotions.

In sum, some people and some cultures tend to be averse to happiness not just for what it leads to, but also for what it means about the person who is happy. In both Western and non-Western cultures, evidence points [to] an aversion to happiness based on the belief that being happy makes you a worse person (morally or otherwise).

Expressing Happiness Is Bad for You and Others

In addition to being averse to *being* happy, individuals in many cultures have issued warnings about *expressing* happiness (often understood as success in the following examples) because of the negative consequences for the expresser and those around her. Expressing happiness usually comes in the form of explicit verbal statements, such as "I am so happy today!," excited and extroverted behavior, and copious smiling and laughing. Happiness, understood as satisfaction, can also be expressed, albeit it in less physically obvious ways, such as demonstrating unflappable smugness when questioned about one's life. Even though not expressing happiness is sometimes seen as a reason for concern in Western cultures, we found evidence for the belief that expressing happiness should be avoided in many non-Western and Western cultures.

According to Uchida and Kitayama (2009), in Eastern cultures, expressing happiness or outwardly displaying success can arouse envy, such that the positive feelings associated with happiness might be offset by the negative feelings of guilt and disharmony. Indeed, a Miyamoto et al. (2010) experimental study revealed that East Asians' concern about the interpersonal consequences of their actions, such as causing unhappiness in others by expressing happiness, makes what would probably be positive experiences for Westerners become bittersweet. Furthermore, in another study in which researchers asked participants to report different aspects, features, or effects of happiness, the Japanese participants frequently mentioned negative social consequences of expressing happiness, such as arousing others' envy, while American participants did so rarely (Uchida and Kitayama 2009). These findings help to explain why the simultaneous experience of negative and positive emotions in pleasant settings is more prevalent in East Asian cultures than Western cultures (e.g., Goetz et al. 2008; Leu et al. 2010; Miyamoto et al. 2010).

Similarly, Lyubomirsky (2000) observes that the expressions of happiness or success in Russia are often perceived as inviting envy, resentment, and suspicion, at least partly because there is a cultural belief in Russia that anyone who is happy or successful might have used immoral means for achieving these states. A similar perspective is taken in some other cultures. In Micronesia, Lutz (1987) demonstrated that in Ifaluk culture happiness is discouraged as too individualistic for the communal good of the tribe because for the Ifaluk, happiness is associated with showing off, overexcitement, and failure at doing one's duties. Since the envy and resentment of your neighbors can have severely negative consequences for you, it makes sense to be averse to anything that might cause neighborly envy and resentment, such as overt displays of happiness or success. Even in the West, as Holden (2009, pp. 109–110) observes, it is common to try to avoid expressing happiness, and especially extreme happiness, in many situations because it annoys, and attracts the envy of, others and even invites possible attack from them.

In many cultures, even people with the power to resist attacks from their mortal peers apparently have reason to avoid expressing happiness. Lyubomirsky (2000) mentions that, in Russia, the expression of happiness or success is often perceived as inviting the ire of the devil. And, in the United States, Holden (2009) observes that some people fear extreme happiness because "you fear that God is going to single you out and make you die because things are going too well" (p. 112). Perhaps for such people the attainment of extreme happiness seems so unnatural to them, that they believe the force in control of nature would have no choice but to correct the anomaly if they ever attained extreme happiness. There is also belief in the "evil eye," prevalent in Iran and neighboring countries, which is believed to damage people who fail to hide their happiness and achievements (Moshiri Tafreshi 2009). Perhaps in an attempt to avoid the gaze of the evil eye, when Iranians talk about something good that has happened or is going to happen to them, they may also invoke this ritual saying: "may the devil's ear be deaf" (which is similar to the English proverb "do not tempt fate"). It is perhaps no coincidence that many of these lay beliefs apply to outward signs of both happiness and success, since these beliefs are likely to have evolved in a time when happiness was synonymous with success. 20

In sum, there are individuals and cultures that tend to be averse to expressing happiness because they worry that their peers, or a supernatural deity, might resent them for it, resulting in any number of severe consequences.

Pursuing Happiness Is Bad for You and Others

Individuals in many cultures have also issued warnings about actively pursuing happiness (particularly of the individualistic and immediate pleasure-based kind) because of the negative consequences for the pursuer and those around him. These warnings could plausibly result in individuals and cultures tending to be averse to the pursuit of personal happiness (as opposed to pursuing the happiness of others); something we found considerable evidence for in both non-Western and Western cultures.

Many East Asian cultures are influenced by Buddhism. In a Buddhist context pursuing personal happiness is seen as misguided: "And with the very desire for happiness, out of delusion they destroy their own well-being as if it were their enemy" (Shantideva 1997, p. 21, as cited in Wallace and Shapiro 2006). Furthermore, Ricard (2011) argues that the desire for pleasure-based happiness is nearly always centered on the self, which can make a person more selfish and thereby have negative effects on the well-being of others. Indeed, Buddhists tend to argue that the narrow pursuit of happiness can lead to such mental states as cruelty, violence, pride, and greed, and hence have negative consequences for the pursuer of personal happiness and those around him (Ricard 2011). In addition to actively causing harm to others, Buddhists also tend to view the pursuit of happiness in a negative light because it may lead to the passive harm of others through neglect. Similarly, striving for personal pleasure-based happiness was seen as misguided and shameful in traditional Chinese culture because contributing to society was considered as better for oneself and everyone else (Lu 2001).

Many Western writers have also found reasons to despise the pursuit of happiness in its individualistic sense because of its negative effects on both the individuals pursuing happiness and on those around them (e.g., Bruckner 2012; Hochschild 1996). Indeed, that the pursuit of happiness (at least in its dogged, unreflective, or extreme forms) is worrying precisely because it often results in a lose–lose situation, with the pursuers ending up dissatisfied and burnt-out while those around them get disaffected and just generally burnt.

Regarding the negative effects of the direct pursuit of personal happiness on the pursuer, Bruckner (2012) has argued that the industry of happiness, and the notion that health is required for happiness, has led to such an abundance of devices and strategies for monitoring and improving happiness that the active pursuit of happiness requires constant effort in such a way that no pursuer of happiness has the time or carefree attitude required to appreciate happiness. Bruckner's argument is a version of the paradox of happiness—that the direct pursuit of happiness is likely to lead to unhappiness (see, e.g., Martin 2008)—an idea with a lengthy history in Western thought that goes back at least as far as Epicurus (discussed above). The usual advice offered by authors in this Western tradition is to directly pursue activities, such as acting morally, that tend to bring about happiness as a by-product (e.g., Locke 1991).

For fear of the resulting negative effects, Westerners have also brought many warnings against the increasing self-inflation and radical individualism in contemporary Western cultures that have resulted from the widespread pursuit of the American Dream. Envisaging the American dream as the achievement of happiness through (particularly material) success, Hochschild (1996) points out that the American dream is based on radical individualism, the importance of personal achievement, and indifference to society as a whole. Hochschild believes that this highly materialistically oriented and self-centered ideology is flawed because it leaves little room for other personal values or the value of other people. Indeed, Hochschild concurs with Thomas Hooker (1586–1647, a prominent puritan colonial leader) who said: "For if each man may do what is good in his owne eyes, proceed according to his own pleasure, so that none may crosse him or control him by any power; there must of necessity follow the distraction and desolation of the whole . . ." (c.f. Clinton 1952, p. 481). Indeed, Binkley (2011, p. 384) agrees that the pursuit of personal happiness leads to actions that are self-interested and "not in service to any vision of the social good." Along similar lines, Rehberg (2000) investigated the fear of, and skepticism towards, happiness in the works of prominent European philosophers expressing similar concerns (e.g., Max Scheler, Helmut Plessner, Arnold Ghlen, and Friedrich Nietzsche). Likewise, Holden (2009, p. 109) has observed that some people fear happiness because they think it will make them selfish and insensitive to the needs of others in a way that will offend or otherwise harm them.

Writers in critical psychology and cultural studies warn us that "the direct pursuit of security and happiness seems progressively to erode our capacity for devotion even to the best modern ideals of justice and the freedom of all" (Richardson and Guignon 2008, p. 618); a phenomenon that might be explained by the idea that pursuing happiness is bad for us because it weakens our critical capacities in a way that makes us less free to make our own value judgments (Ewen 1976; Binkley 2011, p. 385). Schumaker (2006, p. 9) concurs, arguing that the pursuit of happiness embodied in the American Dream is a "wild goose chase" that is bad for us because it diverts us from the path to authentic happiness—a happiness that arises from loving relationships and other meaningful pursuits.

In sum, considerable evidence exists (in both Western and non-Western cultures) for individual voices and cultural norms that warn against the perils of pursuing happiness because of the damage it can cause to the pursuer and those around her. These warnings are most prominent against the direct pursuit of individualistic, immediate, hedonistic, and material concepts of happiness. Given these voices and norms it is not surprising that some people are averse to pursuing happiness because of the likely negative effects on themselves and those around them.

Summary

Throughout history, it is perhaps impossible to find a culture wherein an aversion to the direct pursuit, or attainment, of some kind of happiness is entirely absent. Indeed, our review revealed that aversion to happiness has assumed many forms and has been based on many different premises. The core themes of these beliefs are that happiness, particularly its extreme forms, causes bad things to happen, including: making you unhappy, making you selfish, careless, shallow, complacent, and boring, and making others unhappy by gaining at their expense, ignoring their plights, disrupting social harmony, and making them envious. It appears that these beliefs are more strongly endorsed in non-Western cultures, while Western culture is more strongly animated by an urge to maximize happiness and minimize sadness (e.g., Christopher and Smith 2006; Eid and Diener 2001; Lyubomirsky 2000). We wrap up this section by making the important observation that, considering the inevitable individual differences in regards to even dominant cultural trends (Markus and Hamedani 2007), we expect no culture to unanimously hold any of these beliefs.

It should be noted that the culmination of this evidence does little to cast doubt on the intrinsic value of most kinds of happiness. Indeed, while happiness and the pursuit of certain kinds of happiness are widely believed to have negative effects for some people in some cases, happiness is, in and of itself, still a positive experience for most people and according to most of the common conceptions of happiness. Furthermore, some of the beliefs about the negative consequences of happiness seem to be exaggerations, often spurred by superstition, of timeless advice on how to enjoy a pleasant or prosperous life. Nevertheless, it should not be in doubt that many individuals and cultures do tend to be averse to some forms of happiness, especially when taken to the extreme, for many different reasons.

Conclusion and Implications

It seems that, in Western contexts, personal happiness (best understood as being satisfied with life and experiencing a preponderance of positive over negative emotions) is often emphasized, and failing to be happy is viewed negatively. Western (in particular Anglo-American) psychology and social sciences are influenced by the ethos of contemporary Western culture. Happiness is regarded by some Western scholars "as a basic building block, a value in terms of which other values are justified" (Braithwaite and Law 1985, p. 261). The zeitgeist of happiness is reflected by research on positive psychology and subjective well-being, which dominate contemporary research on happiness. However, our survey across time and cultures indicates that many of the ways in which people are averse to different kinds of happiness, and their reasons for these aversions, have gone relatively unnoticed in the contemporary happiness literature.

Our review of contemporary and historical psychological, philosophical, cultural, and religious research revealed that: aversion to some form of happiness or other is probably widespread (albeit with varying degrees of influence in different cultures), and there are several different beliefs that underpin people's aversion to happiness. The main cultural differences might be fruitfully explained by referring to both the extent to which happiness is valued in different cultures and the extent to which personal happiness is valued compared to collective values.

Perhaps the most important implication of aversion to happiness (and the beliefs that underpin that attitude) is the doubt it casts on claims that all forms of happiness are universally beneficial or worthy of direct pursuit. Some beliefs underpinning people's aversions to happiness do not contradict the idea that happiness is the greatest good, such as the belief that extreme happiness should be avoided because it will lead to extreme unhappiness, but others do cast some doubt on that idea. Indeed, some beliefs about why we should be averse to happiness are motivated by different individual and cultural views about what the best life for an individual consists in, including views where happiness is considered bad for the individual (e.g., some traditional versions of Christianity) and even something that makes a person bad (e.g., Iranian conceptions of happy people as superficial, foolish, and vulgar). These considerations show that equating happiness with *the* supreme universal good is dangerous unless each culture (or individual!) were to create and be assessed by its own definition of happiness. What remains unclear is whether there exists a definition of happiness that would universally be considered intrinsically good for the one experiencing it. Happiness defined as satisfaction with life and a preponderance of positive over negative emotions might be able to play this role conceptually, but once it is operationalized into a multi-item survey the assumptions made (e.g., about which emotions are positive) are likely to make the definition inappropriate for some individuals and cultures. Therefore, cross-cultural research on happiness should not assume that national subjective well-being scores are reporting on something that everyone values highly, and certainly not equally.

The existence of cultural differences in the extent of aversion to happiness also has important implications for the debate about whether international differences in levels of reported subjective well-being are mainly due to cultural reporting biases or actual differences in functioning in different cultures. That is, it stands to reason that a person with an aversion to expressing happiness (understood as subjective well-being) may report lower subjective well-being than they would otherwise. This would result in a response bias with the consequence that cross-cultural reports of subjective well-being would be less useful unless the bias could be corrected for. However, it is also likely that an aversion to happiness would lead an individual to engage in different behaviors and activities (e.g., suppressing positive feelings and avoiding joyous activities) with the result that they experience less positive emotion in their lives. Therefore, aversion to being happy might make individuals less happy, providing reason to think that the differences in levels of reported subjective well-being across cultures might reflect actual differences instead of cultural response biases. This is a potential avenue for further research. Most important in this line of research would be experimental studies designed to examine how much of the variance in subjective well-being scores is real and how much can be regarded as reporting bias. That part of the variance in reported subjective well-being is contributed by such cultural attitudes as aversion to happiness should not be ignored in future well-being studies, particularly when the subjective well-being scores are used to evaluate the functioning of nations.

References

Ahmed, S. (2007). Multiculturalism and the promise of happiness. *New Formations, 63*, 121–137.

Arieti, S., & Bemporad, J. (1980). *Severe and mild depression: The psychotherapeutic approach*. London: Tavistock.

Baumeister, R. F., Bratslavsky, E., Finkenauer, C., & Vohs, K. D. (2001). Bad is stronger than good. *Review of General Psychology, 5*(4), 323–370.

Ben-Shahar, T. (2002). *The question of happiness: On finding meaning, pleasure, and the ultimate currency*. New York: Writers Club Press.

Berg, C. Z., Shapiro, N., Chambless, D. L., & Ahrens, A. H. (1998). Are emotions frightening? II: An analogue study of fear of emotion, interpersonal conflict, and panic onset 1. *Behaviour Research and Therapy, 36*(1), 3–15.

Binkley, S. (2011). Happiness, positive psychology and the program of neoliberal governmentality. *Subjectivity, 4*(4), 371–394.

Braithwaite, V. A., & Law, H. (1985). Structure of human values: Testing the adequacy of the Rokeach Value Survey. *Journal of Personality and Social Psychology, 49*(1), 250.

Bruckner, P. (2012). The pursuit of happiness. In S. Vandamme (Ed.), *Geluk: Drang of dwang?* (pp. 59–66). Gent: Academia Press.

Bryant, F. B., & Veroff, J. (2007). *Savoring: A new model of positive experience*. Mahwah, NJ: Lawrence Erlbaum.

Chen, Y. H. (2006). The way of nature as a healing power. In T. P. Wong & C. J. Wong (Eds.), *Handbook of multicultural perspectives on stress and coping* (pp. 91–103). New York: Springer.

Chittick, W. C. (2005). Weeping in classical sufism. In K. C. Patton & J. S. Hawley (Eds.), *Holy tears: Weeping in the religious imagination* (pp. 132–144). New Jersey: Princeton University Press.

Christopher, J. C. (1999). Situating psychological well-being: Exploring the cultural roots of its theory and research. *Journal of Counseling and Development, 77*, 141–152.

Christopher, J. C., & Hickinbottom, S. (2008). Positive psychology, ethnocentrism, and the disguised ideology of individualism. *Theory and Psychology, 18*(5), 563–589.

Christopher, J. C., & Smith, A. (2006). A hermeneutic approach to culture and psychotherapy. In R. Moody & S. Palmer (Eds.), *Race, culture and psychotherapy: Critical perspective in multicultural practice* (pp. 265–280). New York: Brunner/Routledge.

Clinton, R. (1952). Thomas Hooker. *The New England Quarterly, 25*(4), 459–488.

Diener, E., Oishi, S., & Lucas, R. E. (2003). Personality, culture, and subjective well-being: Emotional and cognitive evaluations of life. *Annual Review of Psychology, 54*(1), 403–425.

Diener, E., Suh, E. M., Lucas, R. E., & Smith H. L. (1999). Subjective well-being: Three decades of progress. *Psychological Bulletin, 125*(2), 276–302.

Eid, M., & Diener, E. (2001). Norms for experiencing emotions in different cultures: Inter- and intranational differences. *Journal of Personality and Social Psychology, 81*(5), 869–885.

Ewen, S. (1976). *Captains of consciousness*. New York: Basic Books.

Fredrickson, B. L., Mancuso, R. A., Branigan, C., & Tugade, M. M. (2000). The undoing effect of positive emotions. *Motivation and Emotion, 24*, 237–258.

Gilbert, P., McEwan, K., Gibbons, L., Chotai, S., Duarte, J., & Matos, M. (2012). Fears of compassion and happiness in relation to alexithymia, mindfulness, and self-criticism. *Psychology and Psychotherapy: Theory, Research and Practice, 85*(4), 374–390.

Glück, L. (1996). Fear of happiness. *Michigan Quarterly Review, XXXV*(4), 579–585.

Goetz, J. L., Spencer-Rodgers, J., & Peng, K. (2008). Dialectical emotions: How cultural epistemologies influence the experience and regulation of emotional complexity. In R. M. Sorrentino & S. Yamaguchi (Eds.), *Handbook of motivation and cognition across cultures* (pp. 517–538). Amsterdam: Elsevier.

Good, M. J., & Good, B. J. (1988). Ritual, the state, and the transformation of emotional discourse in Iranian society. *Culture, Medicine and Psychiatry, 12*(1), 43–63.

Haybron, D. M. (2008). Philosophy and the science of subjective well-being. In M. Eid & R. J. Larsen (Eds.), *The science of subjective well-being* (pp. 17–43). New York, NY: Guilford Press.

Ho, D. Y. F. (1995). Selfhood and identity in Confucianism, Taoism, Buddhism, and Hinduism: Contrasts with the West. *Journal for the Theory of Social Behaviour, 25*(2), 115–139.

Ho, D. Y. F. (2000). Dialectical thinking: Neither Eastern nor Western. *American Psychologist, 55*(9), 1064–1065.

Hochschild, J. L. (1996). *Facing up to the American dream: Race, class, and the soul of the nation*. Princeton, NJ: Princeton University Press.

Holden, R. (2009). *Be happy: Release the power of happiness in you*. New York: Hay House Inc.

Ji, L. J., Nisbett, R. E., & Su, Y. (2001). Culture, change, and prediction. *Psychological Science, 12*(6), 450–456. doi:10.1111/1467-9280.00384.

Joshanloo, M. (2013). A comparison of western and Islamic conceptions of happiness. *Journal of Happiness Studies, 14*(6), 1857–1874.

Koo, J., & Suh, E. (2007). Is happiness a zero-sum game? Belief in fixed amount of happiness (BIFAH) and subjective well-being. *Korean Journal of Social and Personality Psychology, 21*(4), 1–19.

Kupperman, J. (2006). *Six myths about the good life: Thinking about what has value.* Indianapolis: Hackett Publishing.

Lao Tse. (2008). *Tao Te Ching: Or the Tao and its characteristics* (James Legge, Trans.). The Floating Press.

Layard, R. (2005). *Happiness: Lessons from a new science.* New York: Penguin Books.

Leu, J., Mesquita, B., Ellsworth, P. C., ZhiYong, Z., Huijuan, Y., Buchtel, E., et al. (2010). Situational differences in dialectical emotions: Boundary conditions in a cultural comparison of North Americans and East Asians. *Cognition and Emotion, 24*(3), 419–435.

Locke, J. (1991). *An essay concerning human understanding.* Oxford: Clarendon.

Lu, L. (2001). Understanding happiness: A look into the Chinese folk psychology. *Journal of Happiness Studies, 2*(4), 407–432.

Lutz, C. (1987). Goals, events, and understanding in Ifaluk emotion theory. In N. Quinn & D. Holland (Eds.), *Cultural models in language and thought.* New York: Cambridge University Press.

Lyubomirsky, S. (2000). *In the pursuit of happiness: Comparing the U.S. and Russia.* Paper presented at the Annual Meeting of the Society of Experimental Social Psychology, Atlanta, Georgia. (Symposium titled "Happiness, Hope, Optimism and Maturity: Social Psychological Approaches to Human Strengths").

Markus, H. R., & Hamedani, M. G. (2007). Sociocultural psychology: The dynamic interdependence among self systems and social systems. In S. Kitayama & D. Cohen (Eds.), *Handbook of cultural psychology* (pp. 3–39). New York: Guilford Press.

Martin, M. W. (2008). Paradoxes of happiness. *Journal of Happiness Studies, 9*(2), 171–184.

Melka, S. E., Lancaster, S. L., Bryant, A. R., Rodriguez, B. F., & Weston, R. (2011). An exploratory and confirmatory factor analysis of the Affective Control Scale in an undergraduate sample. *Journal of Psychopathology and Behavioral Assessment, 33*, 501–513.

Minami, H. (1971). *Psychology of the Japanese people.* Tokyo: University of Tokyo Press.

Miyamoto, Y., Uchida, Y., & Ellsworth, P. C. (2010). Culture and mixed emotions: Co-occurrence of positive and negative emotions in Japan and the United States. *Emotion, 10*(3), 404.

Moshiri Tafreshi, M. (2009). Evil eye: About contemporary society. *Chista, 259*, 108–116. [in Persian].

Peng, K., Spencer-Rodgers, J., & Nian, Z. (2006). Naïve dialecticism and the tao of Chinese thought. In U. Kim, K.-S. Yang, & K.-K. Hwang (Eds.), *Indigenous and cultural psychology: Understanding people in context* (pp. 247–262). Berlin: Springer.

Pflug, J. (2009). Folk theories of happiness: A cross-cultural comparison of conceptions of happiness in Germany and South Africa. *Social Indicators Research, 92*(3), 551–563.

Rehberg, K. S. (2000). The fear of happiness anthropological motives. *Journal of Happiness Studies, 1*(4), 479–500.

Ricard, M. (2011). The Dalai Lama: Happiness from within. *International Journal of Wellbeing, 1*(2), 274–290.

Richardson, F. C., & Guignon, C. B. (2008). Positive psychology and philosophy of social science. *Theory and Psychology, 18*(5), 605–627.

Schumaker, J. F. (2006). *In search of happiness: Understanding an endangered state of mind*. Auckland: Penguin Books.

Shantideva. (1997). *A guide to the bodhisattva way of life* (V. A. Wallace & B. A. Wallace, Trans.). Ithaca, NY: Snow Lion.

Sicherman, B. (1976). The paradox of prudence: Mental health in the gilded age. *The Journal of American History, 62*(4), 890–912.

Tatarkiewicz, W. (1976). *Analysis of happiness.* Warsaw: Polish Scientific Publishers.

Uchida, Y., & Kitayama, S. (2009). Happiness and unhappiness in east and west: Themes and variations. *Emotion, 9*(4), 441.

Wallace, B. A., & Shapiro, S. L. (2006). Mental balance and well-being: Building bridges between Buddhism and Western psychology. *American Psychologist, 61*(7), 690.

Weijers, D. (2011). Hedonism. *Internet Encyclopedia of Philosophy.* http://www.iep.utm.edu/hedonism/.

Wilson, E. G. (2008). *Against happiness: In praise of melancholy.* New York: Farrar, Straus and Giroux.

Understanding the Text

1. Why are some cultures suspicious of happiness? What are some of the goals or values that some individuals place more highly than personal happiness?
2. In their conclusion, Joshanloo and Weijers note that one way to explain the different attitudes toward happiness is to look at how cultures see personal values in comparison to collective values. What are these "collective values," and how do they come into play when individuals think about their own happiness and about happiness as a personal goal?

Reflection and Response

3. Is "aversion to happiness" caused purely by superstition and fear? Or do you find valid reasoning, philosophical insight, or wisdom in any of this mistrust of happiness? Explain.
4. How might the findings of Joshanloo and Weijers modify the way scholars approach the study of happiness? For example, if happiness is not necessarily the most important goal for all people, how might psychologists and economists adjust or complicate their objectives?

Making Connections

5. C. S. Lewis ("We Have No Right to Happiness," p. 227) and David Brooks ("What Suffering Does," p. 284) also question whether personal happiness should be our singular goal and purpose. Compare their arguments to the "aversions" described by Joshanloo and Weijers. Are the arguments fundamentally similar or fundamentally different?
6. Joshanloo and Weijers write that "East Asian cultures are somewhat under the influence of Taoism" (par. 5). Read the selection from the *Tao Te Ching* (p. 10). In your view, how do these verses enrich, complicate, or qualify the overview of the Taoist's attitude to happiness as presented in the sentences that follow the quotation above?

What Suffering Does

David Brooks

Since 2003, David Brooks has written a regular opinion column for the *New York Times*. He also appears regularly as a commentator on National Public Radio's *All Things Considered* and on the PBS *NewsHour*. Born in Toronto, Canada, in 1961, he grew up in New York City and earned a B.A. in history from the University of Chicago (1983). His career as a journalist took him to the *National Review*, the *Washington Times*, the *Wall Street Journal*, and the *Weekly Standard*. He has written five books, including *Bobos in Paradise: The New Upper Class and How They Got There* (2000) and *The Social Animal: The Hidden Sources of Love, Character, and Achievement* (2011), and has taught at Duke University and Yale University. Although he occupies a moderately conservative position on the political spectrum, his thinking is flexible and informed, and he often surprises audiences by taking unorthodox positions on controversial issues.

Over the past few weeks, I've found myself in a bunch of conversations in which the unspoken assumption was that the main goal of life is to maximize happiness. That's normal. When people plan for the future, they often talk about all the good times and good experiences they hope to have. We live in a culture awash in talk about happiness. In one three-month period last year, more than 1,000 books were released on Amazon on that subject.

But notice this phenomenon. When people remember the past, they don't only talk about happiness. It is often the ordeals that seem most significant. People shoot for happiness but feel formed through suffering.

Now, of course, it should be said that there is nothing intrinsically ennobling about suffering. Just as failure is sometimes just failure (and not your path to becoming the next Steve Jobs) suffering is sometimes just destructive, to be exited as quickly as possible.

But some people are clearly ennobled by it. Think of the way Franklin Roosevelt came back deeper and more empathetic after being struck with polio. Often, physical or social suffering can give people an outsider's perspective, an attuned awareness of what other outsiders are enduring.

5 But the big thing that suffering does is it takes you outside of precisely that logic that the happiness mentality encourages. Happiness wants you to think about maximizing your benefits. Difficulty and suffering sends you on a different course.

V-J Day in Times Square, Alfred Eisenstaadt (1945).
Alfred Eisenstaadt/Getty Images

First, suffering drags you deeper into yourself. The theologian Paul Tillich° wrote that people who endure suffering are taken beneath the routines of life and find they are not who they believed themselves to be. The agony involved in, say, composing a great piece of music or the grief

Paul Tillich (1886–1965) was a German-American Christian theologian and philosopher, author of *The Courage to Be* (1925) and many other books.

of having lost a loved one smashes through what they thought was the bottom floor of their personality, revealing an area below, and then it smashes through that floor revealing another area.

Then, suffering gives people a more accurate sense of their own limitations, what they can control and cannot control. When people are thrust down into these deeper zones, they are forced to confront the fact they can't determine what goes on there. Try as they might, they just can't tell themselves to stop feeling pain, or to stop missing the one who has died or gone. And even when tranquillity begins to come back, or in those moments when grief eases, it is not clear where the relief comes from. The healing process, too, feels as though it's part of some natural or divine process beyond individual control.

People in this circumstance often have the sense that they are swept up in some larger providence. Abraham Lincoln suffered through the pain of conducting a civil war, and he came out of that with the Second Inaugural. He emerged with this sense that there were deep currents of agony and redemption sweeping not just through him but through the nation as a whole, and that he was just an instrument for transcendent tasks.

"Recovering from suffering is not like recovering from a disease. Many people don't come out healed; they come out different."

It's at this point that people in the midst of difficulty begin to feel a call. They are not masters of the situation, but neither are they helpless. They can't determine the course of their pain, but they can participate in responding to it. They often feel an overwhelming moral responsibility to respond well to it. People who seek this proper rejoinder to ordeal sense that they are at a deeper level than the level of happiness and individual utility. They don't say, "Well, I'm feeling a lot of pain over the loss of my child. I should try to balance my hedonic account by going to a lot of parties and whooping it up."

The right response to this sort of pain is not pleasure. It's holiness. I don't even mean that in a purely religious sense. It means seeing life as a moral drama, placing the hard experiences in a moral context and trying to redeem something bad by turning it into something sacred. Parents who've lost a child start foundations. Lincoln sacrificed himself for the Union. Prisoners in the concentration camp with psychologist Viktor Frankl° rededicated themselves to living up to the hopes and expecta- 10

Viktor Frankl (1905–1997): psychotherapist and concentration-camp survivor, and author of *Man's Search for Meaning* (1959).

tions of their loved ones, even though those loved ones might themselves already be dead.

Recovering from suffering is not like recovering from a disease. Many people don't come out healed; they come out different. They crash through the logic of individual utility and behave paradoxically. Instead of recoiling from the sorts of loving commitments that almost always involve suffering, they throw themselves more deeply into them. Even while experiencing the worst and most lacerating consequences, some people double down on vulnerability. They hurl themselves deeper and gratefully into their art, loved ones and commitments.

The suffering involved in their tasks becomes a fearful gift and very different than that equal and other gift, happiness, conventionally defined.

Understanding the Text

1. What is Brooks's argument about the relationship between happiness and suffering?
2. Name the different things that suffering teaches us, according to Brooks.

Reflection and Response

3. Brooks strongly opposes some aspects of what we might call "the happiness culture." Do you find his argument persuasive? Is this opinion piece against happiness? Explain.
4. What is Brooks's argument about the nature and function of the individual experience of suffering? Does his argument hold true in your historical moment as you see it?

Making Connections

5. Consider how Brooks's piece relates to Matthieu Ricard's "The Alchemy of Suffering" (p. 34) and the Gospel of Matthew (p. 59).
6. Brooks does not often write about happiness or suffering. Read five of his columns from the past year. How does this piece fit into what you would argue are Brooks's preoccupations and methods as a writer?

5 Can We Create Our Own Happiness?

Gretchen Rubin set out to write *The Happiness Project* when she realized that her life seemed to provide all the necessary elements for happiness, but she was not happy. Spending a year focusing on what she thought could help her appreciate and savor her current life circumstances and relationships, she led an entire movement of people who simplify, praise, reorganize, and even eat differently in order to achieve a sense of contentment with their lives. Today, thousands of people read her blog, follow her year-of-happiness plan, or even take "a year of happiness."

Rubin chose to focus on a different means of making happiness each month, but for her and many others, achieving life satisfaction truly demands less rather than more. Graham Hill shows that removing almost all of the things he once thought essential to his daily life provided a sense of contentment he could not have anticipated. Daniel Mochon, Michael I. Norton, and Dan Ariely study exercise and ritual as ways of "Getting Off the Hedonic Treadmill." Vincent van Gogh's much-loved painting *Sunflowers* brims with energy and optimism, but is far from being a simple or unalloyed depiction of happiness. Finally, Noelle Oxenhandler's "Ah, But the Breezes . . ." examines the relationship between happiness and suffering as a personal and practical matter, though informed by philosophical and spiritual teaching.

July: Buy Some Happiness

Gretchen Rubin

Gretchen Craft Rubin was raised in Kansas City, Missouri, and now lives in New York. Her 2009 book *The Happiness Project: Or Why I Spent a Year Trying to Sing in the Morning, Clean My Closets, Fight Right, Read Aristotle, and Generally Have More Fun* became an international bestseller, and led to a follow-up book, published in 2012: *Happier at Home: Kiss More, Jump More, Abandon a Project, Read Samuel Johnson, and My Other Experiments in the Practice of Everyday Life.* Rubin is also the author of a popular blog, *The Happiness Project* (www.happiness-project.com), where she writes about her adventures as she test-drives various studies and theories about how to be happier.

The relationship between money and happiness was one of the most interesting, most complicated, and most sensitive questions in my study of happiness. People, including the experts, seemed very confused.

As I did my research, Gertrude Stein's° observation frequently floated through my mind: "Everyone has to make up their mind if money is money or money isn't money and sooner or later they always do decide that money is money." Money satisfies basic material needs. It's a means and an end. It's a way to keep score, win security, exercise generosity, and earn recognition. It can foster mastery or dilettantism. It symbolizes status and success. It buys time—which can be spent on aimless drifting or purposeful action. It creates power in relationships and in the world. It often stands for the things that we feel are lacking: if only we had the money, we'd be adventurous or thin or cultured or respected or generous.

Before I could figure out my resolutions for the month, I had to clarify my thinking about money. I was skeptical of much of what I read. In particular, I kept seeing the argument "Money can't buy happiness," but it certainly seemed that people appear fairly well convinced about the significance of money to their happiness. Money is not without its benefits, and the opposite case, though frequently made, has never proved widely persuasive. And in fact, studies show that people in wealthier countries *do* report being happier than people in poorer countries, and within a particular country, people with more money *do* tend to be happier than those with less. Also, as countries become richer, their citizens

Gertrude Stein (1874–1946): American avant-garde writer who lived in Paris from 1903. She was the author of *The Autobiography of Alice B. Toklas* (1933) and many other works.

become less focused on physical and economic security and more concerned with goals such as happiness and self-realization. Prosperity allows us to turn our attention to more transcendent matters—to yearn for lives not just of material comfort but of meaning, balance, and joy.

Within the United States, according to a 2006 Pew Research Center study, 49 percent of people with an annual family income of more than $100,000 said they were "very happy," in contrast to 24 percent of those with an annual family income of less than $30,000. And the percentages of reported happiness increased as income rose: 24 percent for those earning under $30,000; 33 percent for $30,000 to under $75,000; 38 percent for $75,000 to under $100,000; and 49 percent for more than $100,000. (Now, it's also true that there may be some reverse correlation: happy people become rich faster because they're more appealing to other people and their happiness helps them succeed.)

5

Also, it turns out that while the *absolute level* of wealth matters, *relative ranking* matters as well. One important way that people evaluate their circumstances is to compare themselves with the people around them and with their own previous experiences. For instance, people measure themselves against their age peers, and making more money than others in their age group tends to make people happier. Along the same lines, research shows that people who live in a neighborhood with richer people tend to be less happy than those in a neighborhood where their neighbors make about as much money as they do. A study of workers in various industries showed that their job satisfaction was less tied to their salaries than to how their salaries compared to their coworkers' salaries. People understand the significance of this principle: in one study, a majority of people chose to earn $50,000 where others earned $25,000, rather than earn $100,000 where others earned $250,000. My mother grew up feeling quite well-to-do in my parents' little hometown of North Platte, Nebraska, because her father had a highly coveted union job as an engineer on the Union Pacific Railroad. By contrast, a friend told me that he had felt poor growing up in New York City because he lived on Fifth Avenue above 96th Street—the less fashionable section of a very fashionable street.

The proponents of the "Money can't buy happiness" argument point to studies showing that people in the United States don't rate their quality of life much more highly than do people living in poverty in Calcutta—even though, of course, they live in vastly more comfortable circumstances. Most people, the world over, rate themselves as mildly happy.

It's admirable that people can find happiness in circumstances of poverty as well as in circumstances of plenty. That's the resilience of the human spirit. But I don't think that a particular individual would be indifferent to the disparities between the streets of Calcutta and the ranch houses of Atlanta. The fact is, people aren't made deliriously happy by the luxuries of salt and cinnamon (once so precious) or electricity or air-conditioning or cell phones or the Internet, because they come to accept these once-luxury goods as part of ordinary existence. That doesn't mean, however, that because people have learned to take clean water for granted, it no longer matters to their quality of life. Indeed, if that were true, would it mean it would be pointless to bother to try to improve the material circumstances of those folks in Calcutta?

But as I went deeper into the mystery of money, I was pulled toward research and analysis suitable for an entirely different book, away from my most pressing interest. Sure, I wanted to "Go off the path" to a point, and maybe one day I would devote an entire book to the topic, but for the moment, I didn't have to solve the enigma of money. I just needed to figure out how happiness and money fit together.

So was I arguing that "Money *can* buy happiness"? The answer: no. That was clear. Money alone can't buy happiness.

But, as a follow-up, I asked myself, "Can money *help* buy happiness?" 10 The answer: yes, used wisely, it can. Whether rich or poor, people make choices about how they spend money, and those choices can boost happiness or undermine it. It's a mistake to assume that money will affect everyone the same way. No statistical average could say how a particular *individual* would be affected by money—depending on that individual's circumstances and temperament. After a lot of thinking, I identified three factors that shape the significance of money to individuals:

It depends on what kind of person you are.

Money has a different value to different people. You might love to collect modern art, or you might love to rent old movies. You might have six children and ailing, dependent parents, or you might have no children and robust parents. You might love to travel, or you might prefer to putter around the house. You might care about eating organic, or you might be satisfied with the cheapest choices at the grocery store.

It depends on how you spend your money.

Some purchases are more likely to contribute to your happiness than others. You might buy cocaine, or you might buy a dog. You might splurge on a big-screen TV, or you might splurge on a new bike.

It depends on how much money you have relative to the people around you and relative to your own experience.

One person's fortune is another person's misfortune.

Developing and applying a three-factor test brought back pleasant memories of being a law student, and it was a helpful framework, but it was complex. I wanted a more cogent way to convey the relationship between money and happiness.

As I was mulling this over, one afternoon I picked up Eleanor the wrong way as I leaned over her crib, and the next morning, I woke up with agonizing back pain. For almost a month, I couldn't sit for long, I found it hard to type, I had trouble sleeping, and of course I couldn't stop picking up Eleanor, so I kept reaggravating the injury.

"You should go see my physical therapist," urged my father-in-law, who had suffered from back problems for years. "There's a lot they can do."

"I'm sure it will get better on its own," I kept insisting.

One night as I struggled to turn over in bed, I thought, "Ask for help! Bob says that physical therapy works; why am I resisting?" 15

I called Bob at work, got the information, made an appointment at the physical therapist's office, and two visits later, I was 100 percent better. It felt like a miracle. And one day after my pain was gone, I took my health for granted once again—and I had the Epiphany of the Back Spasm. *Money* doesn't buy happiness the way *good health* doesn't buy happiness.

When money or health is a problem, you think of little else; when it's not a problem, you don't think much about it. Both money and health contribute to happiness mostly in the negative; the lack of them brings much more unhappiness than possessing them brings happiness.

Being healthy doesn't guarantee happiness. Lots of healthy people are very unhappy. Many of them squander their health or take it for granted. In fact, some people might even be better off with some physical limitation that would prevent them from making destructive choices. (I once went on vacation with a group that included the most wild and reckless guy I'd ever met, and I was quite relieved when he broke his foot during an early escapade, because the mishap prevented him from getting up to much more mischief.) Ditto, money. But the fact that good health doesn't *guarantee* happiness doesn't mean that good health doesn't *matter* to happiness. Similarly, money. Used wisely, each can contribute greatly to happiness.

The First Splendid Truth° holds that to think about happiness, we should think about *feeling good, feeling bad, and feeling right, in an atmosphere of growth*. Money is most important for happiness in the "feeling

The First Splendid Truth: Earlier in her book *The Happiness Project* (Chapter 2, "February"), Rubin reported that she arrived at a formula that "struck me as so important that I named it the First Splendid Truth. . . : *To be happy, I needed to think about feeling good, feeling bad, and feeling right, in an atmosphere of growth*" (67).

bad" category. People's biggest worries include financial anxiety, health concerns, job insecurity, and having to do tiring and boring chores. Spent correctly, money can go a long way to solving these problems. I was extremely fortunate to be in a position where money wasn't a source of *feeling bad*. We had plenty of money to do what we wanted—even enough to feel secure, the toughest and most precious thing for money to buy. I resolved to do a better job of spending money in ways that could boost my happiness by supporting the other three elements of happiness.

Indulge in a Modest Splurge

I didn't spend enough time thinking about how money could buy me happiness. 20

I'd always had a vague sense that spending money was self-indulgent and that I should avoid spending money whenever possible. I once spent six very satisfying months living in San Francisco on $5 a day (except when I had to use the Laundromat). Now, however, I decided to find ways to spend to further my happiness goals. Studies show that people's basic psychological needs include the need to feel secure, to feel good at what they do, to be loved, to feel connected to others, and to have a strong sense of control. Money doesn't *automatically* fill these requirements, but it sure can help. People at every level of income can choose to direct their spending in ways that take them closer to happiness—or not.

I wanted to spend money to stay in closer contact with my family and friends; to promote my energy and health; to create a more serene environment in my apartment; to work more efficiently; to eliminate sources of boredom, irritation, and marital conflict; to support causes that I thought important; and to have experiences that would enlarge me. So, category by category, I looked for ways to spend money to support my happiness goals—within reason, of course.

For health and energy: in January, I'd already found a way to spend money to get better exercise. My strength-training workouts were expensive, but I was happy to know that I was doing something important for my long-term health. I also started spending more for food when I had to grab lunch outside our apartment. I'd always congratulated myself when I ducked into a deli to buy a bagel, because it was such a cheap and quick meal, but I stopped that. Instead, I gave myself a mental gold star for getting a big salad or soup and fruit, even though those choices were much more expensive.

For relationships: I'd give a party for my sister's wedding. It would be a major expenditure but also a major source of happiness. My relationship with my sister—and now with her fiancé—were among the most important in my life, but the fact that they lived in Los Angeles was a challenge. Hosting a party would be a way to make my own contribution to the wedding weekend.

For work: I bought some pens. Normally, I used makeshift pens, the kind of unsatisfactory implements that somehow materialized in my bag or in a drawer. But one day, when I was standing in line to buy envelopes, I caught sight of a box of my favorite kind of pen: the Deluxe Uniball Micro.

"Two ninety-nine for one pen!" I thought. "That's ridiculous." But after a fairly lengthy internal debate, I bought four.

It's such a joy to write with a good pen instead of making do with an underinked pharmaceutical promotional pen picked up from a doctor's office. My new pens weren't cheap, but when I think of all the time I spend using pens and how much I appreciate a good pen, I realize it was money well spent. Finely made tools help make work a pleasure.

For others: I wrote a check to the New York Public Library's Library Cubs program. I was already donating my time and energy to helping form this group, which supports the children's rooms in library branches. Time and energy helped the library; money was also useful.

For happy memories: I bought those file boxes in April—an excellent modest splurge. Also, I've never forgotten an older friend's observation: "One of my regrets about my children's childhoods is that I didn't have more professional photographs taken." As luck would have it, I know a terrific photographer. I arranged to have pictures taken of our children, and I was thrilled with the results. These photographs were far better than any snapshot I could take, and I bought several for us and for the grandparents, too. Remembering happy times gives a big boost to happiness, and looking at photographs of happy times helps make those memories more vivid. The money I spent on the photographs will strengthen family bonds, enhance happy memories, and capture fleeting moments of childhood. That's a pretty good return on the happiness investment.

I pushed a friend to "Buy some happiness" when I stopped by her apartment to admire her new baby (in keeping with my June resolution to "Show up").

"One thing is really bothering me," she said. "As a child, I was close to my grandparents, but my in-laws, who live nearby, aren't very interested in the baby. They already have seven grandchildren. My mother would love to see the baby all the time, but she lives in Cleveland and only comes to New York once a year."

"Well," I suggested, "at least until your son is in school, why don't you go to Cleveland every few months?"

She laughed. "That's way too expensive."

"Have you ever tried buying lots of stuff?"

This tongue-in-cheek cartoon originally appeared in the May 18, 2009, issue of *The New Yorker.*

Matt Diffee/The New Yorker Collection/The Cartoon Bank

"It's a lot of money, but it's important to you. Could you afford it?" I knew she could.

"Well, yes, I guess," she admitted, "but it would be such a hassle to fly with a baby."

"You could tell your mother you'll buy her plane tickets if she'll come to New York more often. Would she come?"

"You know . . . I bet she would!" my friend said. This solution shows both the importance of thinking about how money can buy happiness and also the importance of my Eighth Commandment: "Identify the problem." What was the problem? Finding a way for grandmother and grandson to spend time together.

Money, spent wisely, can support happiness goals of strengthening relationships, promoting health, having fun, and all the rest. At the same time, the emotions generated by sheer buying, by acquisition, are also powerful. Happiness theory suggests that if I move to a new apartment or buy a new pair of boots, I'll soon become accustomed to my new possession and be no happier than I was before. Nevertheless, many people make purchases for the fleeting jolt of happiness they get from the very act of gain.

Now, you might say—that's not true happiness; true happiness comes from doing good for others, being with friends and family, finding flow, meditating, and so on. But when I look around, I certainly see many people who look and act happy as they do their buying. The fact that the happiness boost that hits at the cash register isn't particularly admirable doesn't mean that it's not real—or that it doesn't shape people's behavior. Research and everyday experience show that receiving an unexpected present or being surprised by a windfall gives people a real boost; in one study, in fact, when researchers wanted to induce a good mood in their subjects to study the effects, the way they accomplished this good mood was to arrange for those subjects to find coins in a telephone booth or to be given bags of chocolates. For some people, the rush of happiness that accompanies gain is so seductive that they spend more money than they can afford and are hit by remorse and anxiety once they get their bags home. The quick fix of happiness turns into a longer-lasting unhappiness.

40 The happiness that people get from buying stuff isn't attributable only to consumerist indulgence. Any kind of gain creates at least a momentary atmosphere of growth, and there are a lot of reasons why people love to make a purchase: to keep their home in good repair, attractive, and well stocked; to provide for loved ones or strangers; to master something new (such as the latest gadget); to possess an admired object; to teach their children; to live as their peers live; to live differently from their peers; to beautify themselves; to maintain a collection; to keep up with fashion; to defy fashion; to support a hobby or expertise; to benefit others; to justify the enjoyment of shopping as an activity; to offer and return hospitality; to give gifts and support; to win or maintain status; to establish dominance and control; to express personality; to celebrate; to maintain traditions; to break traditions; to make life more convenient, healthier, or safer; to make life more challenging, adventurous, or risky.

I myself rarely feel cash register happiness. Quite the opposite. I'm usually hit by buyer's remorse when I spend, a feeling that I call "shop shock." Perhaps that's why I really notice other people's enthusiasm. Nevertheless, even for me, indulging in a modest splurge could bring a lot of happiness, if I made my purchases wisely. . . .

[O]ne of my favorite "modest splurges" was something that wouldn't appeal to most people—but for me meant getting my hands on something I'd coveted for years. I called Books of Wonder, a famous children's bookstore in Manhattan, and ordered the "Wizard's Super Special," the complete set of the fifteen Oz books by L. Frank Baum. Two weeks later, I got a huge thrill when I opened the large box. The hardback set had a unified design, with matching spines, gorgeous covers, and the original color illustrations.

Now, positive psychologists might argue that I'd adapt to my purchase. Soon I'd be accustomed to owning these books, they'd sit on a shelf and gather dust, and I'd be no better off than I was before. I disagree. Because I have a real passion for children's literature, I knew these books would give me a boost every time I saw them. After all, I keep a big stack of the old, beat-up *Cricket* magazines I had as a child, and just seeing them on the shelf makes me happy.

As always, the secret was to "Be Gretchen" and to choose wisely. What makes me happy is to spend money on the things *I* value—and it takes self-knowledge and discipline to discover what *I* really want, instead of parroting the desires of other people. One of the purchases that made my father happiest was a pinball machine. He'd played hours of pinball as a boy, and one of his childhood dreams was to have his own so he could play whenever he wanted, for free. This isn't a purchase that would have made everyone happy, but it made him extremely happy.

While I was thinking hard about the relationship between money and happiness, I struck up a conversation with a fellow guest at a bridal shower. I told her that I was trying to figure out ways to "Buy some happiness." (As I explained the issue, it began to dawn on me, dimly, that I might be becoming a happiness bore.) 45

She became quite indignant at my suggestion. "That's so wrong!" she said. "Money can't buy happiness!"

"You don't think so?"

"I'm the perfect example. I don't make much money. A few years back, I took my savings and bought a horse. My mother and everyone told me I was crazy. But that horse makes me incredibly happy—even though I end up spending all my extra money on him."

"But," I said, confused, "money *did* make you happy. It makes you so happy to have a horse!"

"But I don't have any money," she answered. "I spent it all." 50

"Right, because you used it to *buy a horse*."

She shook her head and gave up on me.

In some cases, though, when I tried to "Buy some happiness," it didn't work. I'd call this the "expensive-gym-membership effect," after the futile tendency to pay a lot for a gym membership with the thought, "Gosh, this costs so much, I'll feel like I have to go to the gym!"

I see the expensive-gym-membership effect when I pay money for something as a way to encourage myself to make time for something fun. For example, I went to three stores to hunt down the combination glue/sealer/finish Mod Podge, because I wanted to experiment with découpage. I really want to do it. But I bought that Mod Podge ages ago, and I've never used it. I want to take time for creative projects, but merely spending money on an art supply won't make it a priority. I have to decide to make time—and apparently I haven't. (Using Mod Podge can be another resolution for Happiness Project II.) Along the same lines, a workaholic friend of mine bought a fancy new tennis racquet because he wants to play more tennis, but he still hasn't used it. The tennis racquet is an expression of his desire to change something in his life, but just making a purchase won't accomplish that. He should have concentrated on fixing his calendar, not on finding the right racquet.

• • •

"Buy some happiness," of course, has its limits. I knew I'd better not overlook the effects of the hedonic treadmill, which quickly transforms delightful luxuries into dull necessities. Indulging in a modest splurge would give me a happiness jolt only if I did it rarely. Take room service. Until my honeymoon, I'd never had room service in my life—and it was a thrill. But if I traveled for business and got room service frequently, it wouldn't be a treat anymore.

"Because money permits a constant stream of luxuries and indulgences, it can take away their savor, and by permitting instant gratification, money shortcuts the happiness of anticipation."

Because money permits a constant stream of luxuries and indulgences, it can take away their savor, and by permitting instant gratification, money shortcuts the happiness of anticipation. Scrimping, saving, imagining, planning, hoping—these stages enlarge the happiness we feel.

Even a modest pleasure can be a luxury if it's scarce enough—ordering coffee at a restaurant, buying a book, or watching TV—which is why deprivation is one of the most effective, although unenjoyable, cures for the hedonic treadmill. A friend told me that when she lived in Russia in the 1990s, the hot water would periodically stop working for weeks at a time. She said that very few experiences in her life have matched the happiness she felt on the days when the hot water started working again. But now that she's back in the United States, where her hot water has never failed, she never thinks about it.

The hedonic treadmill means that spending often isn't a satisfying path to happiness, but nevertheless, money can help. My father still talks about the day he realized that he could afford to pay someone to mow the lawn. Some of the best things in life aren't free.

Another way to think about money's effect is in terms of the First Splendid Truth, as part of the "atmosphere of growth" that's so important to happiness. We need an atmosphere of *spiritual* growth, and as much as some people deny it, *material* growth is also very satisfying.

We're very sensitive to change. We measure our present against our past, and we're made happy when we see change for the better. In one study, people were asked whether they'd rather have a job that paid $30,000 in year one, $40,000 in year two, and $50,000 in year three or a job that paid $60,000, then $50,000 then $40,000. In general, people preferred the first option, with its raises—despite the fact that at the end of the three years, they would have earned only $120,000 instead of $150,000. Their decision might seem irrational, but in fact, the people who chose the first option understood the importance of *growth* to happiness. People are very sensitive to relative changes in their condition, for better or worse.

A sense of growth is so important to happiness that it's often preferable to be progressing to the summit rather than to be at the summit. Neither a scientist nor a philosopher but a novelist, Lisa Grunwald, came up with the most brilliant summation of this happiness principle: "Best is good, better is best."

One challenge of parenthood that I hadn't tackled in April, though perhaps I should have, was setting limits on buying treats for my children. For example, as a surprise, I bought Eliza a big book of optical illusions. As I expected, she loved the book—pored over it, looked at it with her friends, kept it out on her bedside table. I was so pleased with myself for choosing it for her. One day, not long after, I was in a drugstore that had a rack of cheap children's books. I spotted a book of optical illusions and almost bought it for Eliza; she'd enjoyed the other book so much. Then I stopped myself. She already had a book with three hundred illusions; this book probably didn't have much new. But even beyond that, I wondered if having two books of optical illusions might, in fact, dim Eliza's pleasure in the first book. It wouldn't seem as magical and definitive.

The head of Eliza's school told a story about a four-year-old who had a blue toy car he loved. He took it everywhere, played with it constantly. Then when his grandmother came to visit, she bought him ten toy cars, and he stopped playing with the cars altogether. "Why don't you play with your cars?" she asked. "You loved your blue car so much." "I can't love lots of cars," he answered.

It's easy to make the mistake of thinking that if you have something you love or there's something you want, you'll be happier with more.

Buy Needful Things

65 When I began to pay attention to people's relationship to money, I recognized two different approaches to buying: "underbuying" and "overbuying." I'm an underbuyer.

As an underbuyer, I delay making purchases or buy as little as possible. I buy saline solution, which I use twice a day, one little bottle at a time. I scramble to buy items like a winter coat or a bathing suit after the point at which I need them. I'm suspicious of buying things with very specific uses—suit bags, hand cream, hair conditioner, rain boots, Kleenex (why not just use toilet paper to blow your nose?). I often consider buying an item, then decide, "I'll get this some other time" or "Maybe we don't really need this." As an underbuyer, I often feel stressed because I don't have the things I need. I make a lot of late-night runs to the drugstore. I'm surrounded with things that are shabby, don't really work, or aren't exactly suitable.

I gaze in wonder at the antics of my overbuyer friends. Overbuyers often lay in huge supplies of slow-use items like shampoo or cough medicine. They buy things like tools or high-tech gadgets with the thought "This will probably come in handy someday." They make a lot of purchases before they go on a trip or celebrate a holiday. They throw things away—milk, medicine, even cans of soup—because they've hit their expiration date. They buy items with the thought "This will make a great gift!" without having a recipient in mind. Like me, overbuyers feel stressed. They're oppressed by the number of errands they feel obliged to do and by the clutter and waste often created by their overbuying. . . .

I knew that I'd be happier if I made a mindful effort to thwart my underbuying impulse and instead worked to buy what I needed. For instance, I ended my just-in-time policy for restocking toilet paper. One of my Secrets of Adulthood is "Keep a roll of toilet paper tucked away someplace," so we never actually ran out, but we teetered on the dreary brink.

I mentioned this problem to Jamie. "We're like Walmart," he said. "We keep all our capital working for us instead of sitting on a lot of inventory."

70 "Well," I said, "now we're going to invest in some redundant supply." Moderation is pleasant to the wise, but toilet paper was something I wanted to keep on hand. This kind of little annoyance puts a surprisingly

big drag on happiness. As Samuel Johnson° remarked, "To live in perpetual want of little things is a state, not indeed of torture, but of constant vexation."

Another thing that I really needed was white T-shirts, because I wear them practically every day. I enjoy shopping only when I'm with my mother, so I waited to buy my T-shirts until my mother was visiting from Kansas City. I wanted T-shirts that were soft, stretchy, not too thin, V-necked, and long-sleeved, and to me, tracking down and buying such shirts seemed like an overwhelming challenge. My mother was undaunted. "We'll go to Bloomingdale's," she decided.

Though I felt dazed the minute I entered the store, my mother walked purposefully from one area to the next. As she began her systematic inspection, I trailed along behind her and carried the shirts she'd pulled out. After she'd considered every white shirt on the floor, I tried on—conservative estimate—twenty shirts. I bought eight.

My mother had joined with zeal my quest for the perfect white T-shirt, but when she saw the stack of monochrome cotton at the cash register, she asked, "Are you sure you don't want any other colors or styles? This is a lot of white shirts."

"Well . . ." I hesitated. Did I really want this many white shirts? Then I remembered a study showing that people think they like variety more than they do. When asked to pick a menu of snacks for the upcoming weeks, they picked a variety, but if they chose week to week what to eat, they picked their favorite snack over and over.

75 In the store, it seemed like a good idea to have a variety of colors. But I knew from experience that when I stood in front of my closet, I always wanted to pull out the same things: white V-neck T-shirt; black yoga pants or jeans; and running shoes.

Buy needful things. "Yes, I just want white," I said firmly.

Inspired by my shirt success, I replaced our leaky blender. I bought a personalized return-address stamp. I'd realized that the paradoxical consequence of being an underbuyer was that I had to shop *more often*, while buying extras meant fewer trips to the cash register. I bought batteries, Band-Aids, lightbulbs, diapers—things I knew we would need eventually. I finally ordered business cards, which I'd been putting off for years. I was inspired when, at a meeting, someone handed me the best-looking business card I'd ever seen. I got all the information so I could order a copycat version for myself.

Samuel Johnson (1709–1784): English poet, essayist, and lexicographer, known as Dr. Johnson. His *A Dictionary of the English Language* (1755) was authoritative for more than a century.

My decision-making process for ordering a business card showed me that not only was I an "underbuyer," I was also a "satisficer"—as opposed to a "maximizer." *Satisficers* (yes, satisficers) are those who make a decision or take action once their criteria are met. That doesn't mean they'll settle for mediocrity; their criteria can be very high, but as soon as they find the hotel, the pasta sauce, or the business card that has the qualities they want, they're satisfied. *Maximizers* want to make the optimal decision. Even if they see a bicycle or a backpack that meets their requirements, they can't make a decision until after they've examined every option, so they can make the best possible choice.

Studies suggest that satisficers tend to be happier than maximizers. Maximizers spend a lot more time and energy to reach a decision, and they're often anxious about whether they did in fact make the best choice. As a shopper, my mother is a good example of what I'd call a "happy limited maximizer." In certain distinct categories, she's a maximizer, and she loves the very process of investigating every possibility. Now that Eliza and Eleanor were going to be flower girls in my sister's wedding, I knew my mother would love nothing more than to examine every possible dress, just for the fun of it. But too often maximizers find the research process exhausting yet can't let themselves settle for anything but the best. The difference between the two approaches may be one reason some people find a big city like New York disheartening. If you're a maximizer in New York City, you could spend months surveying your options for bedroom furniture or even wooden hangers. In Kansas City, even the most zealous maximizer can size up the available options pretty quickly.

Most people are a mix of both. In almost every category, I was a satisficer, and in fact, I often felt guilty about not doing more research before making decisions. In law school, one friend interviewed with fifty law firms before she decided where she wanted to go as a summer associate; I think I interviewed with six. We ended up at the same firm. Once I learned to call myself a "satisficer," I felt more satisfied with my approach to decision making; instead of feeling lazy and unconscientious, I could call myself prudent. A great example of reframing. 80

Spend Out

I tend to cling to things—to stuff, to ideas. I reuse razor blades until they're dull, I keep my toothbrushes until they're yellowed and frayed. There is a preppy wabi-sabi° to soft, faded khakis and cotton shirts, but

wabi-sabi: a Japanese aesthetic that emphasizes the beauty of imperfection.

it's not nice to be surrounded by things that are worn out or stained or used up. I often found myself saving things, even when it made no sense. Like those white T-shirts I bought. I'd surmounted the challenge of buying them; then came the challenge of *wearing* them. When I took them out of the shopping bag and laid them on my shelf—perfectly folded by the salesclerk as I've never learned to do—I could feel myself wanting to "save" them in their pristine glory. But not wearing clothes is as wasteful as throwing them away.

As part of my happiness project I wanted to stop hoarding, to trust in abundance, so that I could use things up, give things away, throw things away. Not only that—I wanted to stop worrying so much about keeping score and profit and loss. I wanted to *spend out.*

A few years ago, my sister gave me a box of beautiful stationery for my birthday. I loved it, but I'd never used it. When I was mailing some photos to the grandparents, I hesitated to use the new stationery because I was "saving" it; but to what better use could it be put? Of course I should use those notes. Spend out.

I looked through my apartment for ways to spend out. The toughest choices I made concerned things that sort of worked: the camera that had lost its zoom function, the label maker that didn't print properly. I hate waste, but it would probably have cost me as much money (and far more time) to repair these items as to replace them—and using them in their crippled states weighed me down. I replaced them.

My goal wasn't limited to my treatment of my possessions; it also involved my ideas. For example, when I thought of a great subject for a blog post, I often found myself thinking "That's a good idea, save it for another day." Why? Why delay? I needed to trust that there would be more, that I would have great ideas in the future and so should use my best stuff *now.* Pouring out ideas is better for creativity than doling them out by the teaspoon.

"Spending out" also meant not being rigidly efficient. The other night, Jamie and I rented *Junebug*—an extraordinary movie, all about the nature of love and happiness. I was tempted to watch a few of my favorite scenes again after we saw it the first time, but I decided that would be a "waste" of time. Then I remembered my resolution, which included spending out my time. After all, I know that sometimes the things I do when I'm wasting time turn out to be quite worthwhile. I went to "Scene Selection" to rewatch the scene at the church social.

The most important meaning of "Spend out," however, is not to be a scorekeeper, not to stint on love and generosity. This was related to my February resolution, "Don't expect praise or appreciation." I wanted to stop constantly demanding praise or insisting on getting paid back.

Saint Thérèse of Lisieux° wrote, "When one loves, one does not calculate." I'm a big calculator, always looking for a return, especially with Jamie.

"I gave Eleanor a bath last night, so you . . ."

"I let you take a nap, so you . . ."

"I had to make the plane reservations, so you . . ." 90

No! Spend out. Don't think about the return. "It is by spending oneself," the actress Sarah Bernhardt remarked, "that one becomes rich." What's more, one intriguing study showed that Sarah Bernhardt's pronouncement is *literally* true: people who give money to charity end up wealthier than those who don't give to charity. After doing complex number crunching to control for different variables, a researcher concluded that charitable giving isn't just correlated with higher income; it actually *causes* higher income. Some explanations for this surprising effect include the brain stimulation caused by charitable activity and also the fact that those who are seen behaving charitably are likely to be elevated to leadership positions.

It's certainly true in my household that spending out creates a wealth of love and tenderness, while calculation and scorekeeping build resentment.

To keep this important yet elusive resolution uppermost in my mind, I maintained a relic. In one of my last visits to my grandmother before she died, I picked up the My Sin perfume that had been sitting on her bureau for as long as I could remember. The bottle was still in its box, and when I opened it, I saw that it was still full to the top. I didn't ask her about it, but I'm sure someone, many years ago, gave her that bottle of perfume and she was "saving it." For what? After she died, I took the box home with me, and I keep it in my office to remind me to "Spend out."

Saint Thérèse of Lisieux (1873–1897): French nun, canonized in 1925, who died of tuberculosis at age 24. After her death, her spiritual autobiography *The Autobiography of Sister Thérèse of Lisieux: The Story of a Soul* was widely influential.

Understanding the Text

1. How might Rubin's material circumstances contribute to or affect her particular attitude toward money and its relationship to happiness?
2. In what ways is Rubin's attitude toward money informed by research, and in what ways is it informed by her own personality and tastes?
3. Make a list of Rubin's sources in the order that they are cited in her study. Which do you find most credible and why? Which do you question? Why?

Reflection and Response

4. What paragraph in the text produces the strongest response from you? Why? Write a paragraph in which you both summarize what Rubin says there and respond to it.
5. Rubin discusses the "hedonic treadmill" as an example of what she tries to avoid in her journey toward a happier life (par. 55). Make a list of everything you do in a 24-hour period. Thinking carefully about the word "hedonic," analyze your list. Does it support or refute Rubin's argument?

Making Connections

6. Write an essay in which you consider Rubin's argument from the vantage point of one of the authors in Chapter 4, "Do We Deserve to Be Happy?" How would the author you chose respond to Rubin's goals and advice?
7. Rubin develops a vocabulary — for example, "hedonic treadmill," "needful things," and "spend out" — to explore money and happiness in this essay. List Rubin's terms and then use them to analyze a recent article in a magazine or blog of your choice.
8. Compare Rubin's views to those of Aristotle ("Nicomachean Ethics," p. 82). What part do wisdom and philosophy play in Rubin's ideas about enhancing personal happiness? What part does money play in Aristotle's views? Write an imaginary dialogue, in which Rubin and Aristotle discuss or debate, or both, the best path to greater happiness.

Living with Less. A Lot Less.

Graham Hill

Graham Hill is a Canadian journalist, entrepreneur, and designer — as well as the founder of TreeHugger (treehugger.com), a Web site devoted to sustainability. He holds a degree in architecture from Carleton University in Ottawa, Canada, and studied industrial design at the Emily Carr University of Art and Design in Vancouver, Canada. He has founded and managed a number of enterprises. In 2010, he founded LifeEdited, a company that develops minimalist design strategies for living better "with less stuff, space and energy." The following article appeared in the *New York Times* in March 2013. Despite his remarkable success during the Internet boom of the 2000s, Hill argues that less really might be more.

I live in a 420-square-foot studio. I sleep in a bed that folds down from the wall. I have six dress shirts. I have 10 shallow bowls that I use for salads and main dishes. When people come over for dinner, I pull out my extendable dining room table. I don't have a single CD or DVD and I have 10 percent of the books I once did.

I have come a long way from the life I had in the late '90s, when, flush with cash from an Internet start-up sale, I had a giant house crammed with stuff—electronics and cars and appliances and gadgets.

Somehow this stuff ended up running my life, or a lot of it; the things I consumed ended up consuming me. My circumstances are unusual (not everyone gets an Internet windfall before turning 30), but my relationship with material things isn't.

We live in a world of surfeit stuff, of big-box stores and 24-hour online shopping opportunities. Members of every socioeconomic bracket can and do deluge themselves with products.

There isn't any indication that any of these things makes anyone any happier; in fact it seems the reverse may be true. 5

For me, it took 15 years, a great love and a lot of travel to get rid of all the inessential things I had collected and live a bigger, better, richer life with less.

It started in 1998 in Seattle, when my partner and I sold our Internet consultancy company, Sitewerks, for more money than I thought I'd earn in a lifetime.

To celebrate, I bought a four-story, 3,600-square-foot, turn-of-the-century house in Seattle's happening Capitol Hill neighborhood and, in a frenzy of consumption, bought a brand-new sectional couch (my first ever), a pair of $300 sunglasses, a ton of gadgets, like an Audible.com MobilePlayer (one of the first portable digital music players) and an audiophile-worthy five-disc CD player. And, of course, a black turbo-charged Volvo. With a remote starter!

I was working hard for Sitewerks' new parent company, Bowne, and didn't have the time to finish getting everything I needed for my house. So I hired a guy named Seven, who said he had been Courtney Love's assistant, to be my personal shopper. He went to furniture, appliance and electronics stores and took Polaroids of things he thought I might like to fill the house; I'd shuffle through the pictures and proceed on a virtual shopping spree.

10 My success and the things it bought quickly changed from novel to normal. Soon I was numb to it all. The new Nokia phone didn't excite me or satisfy me. It didn't take long before I started to wonder why my theoretically upgraded life didn't feel any better and why I felt more anxious than before.

"It took 15 years, a great love and a lot of travel to get rid of all the inessential things I had collected and live a bigger, better, richer life with less."

My life was unnecessarily complicated. There were lawns to mow, gutters to clear, floors to vacuum, roommates to manage (it seemed nuts to have such a big, empty house), a car to insure, wash, refuel, repair and register and tech to set up and keep working. To top it all off, I had to keep Seven busy. And really, a personal shopper? Who had I become? My house and my things were my new employers for a job I had never applied for.

It got worse. Soon after we sold our company, I moved east to work in Bowne's office in New York, where I rented a 1,900-square-foot SoHo loft that befit my station as a tech entrepreneur. The new pad needed furniture, housewares, electronics, etc.—which took more time and energy to manage.

• • •

And because the place was so big, I felt obliged to get roommates—who required more time, more energy, to manage. I still had the Seattle house, so I found myself worrying about two homes. When I decided to stay in New York, it cost a fortune and took months of cross-country trips—and big headaches—to close on the Seattle house and get rid of all of the things inside.

I'm lucky, obviously; not everyone gets a windfall from a tech start-up sale. But I'm not the only one whose life is cluttered with excess belongings.

In a study published last year titled "Life at Home in the Twenty-First Century," researchers at U.C.L.A. observed 32 middle-class Los Angeles families and found that all of the mothers' stress hormones spiked during the time they spent dealing with their belongings. Seventy-five percent of the families involved in the study couldn't park their cars in their garages because they were too jammed with things. 15

Our fondness for stuff affects almost every aspect of our lives. Housing size, for example, has ballooned in the last 60 years. The average size of a new American home in 1950 was 983 square feet; by 2011, the average new home was 2,480 square feet. And those figures don't provide a full picture. In 1950, an average of 3.37 people lived in each American home; in 2011, that number had shrunk to 2.6 people. This means that we take up more than three times the amount of space per capita than we did 60 years ago.

Apparently our supersize homes don't provide space enough for all our possessions, as is evidenced by our country's $22 billion personal storage industry.

What exactly are we storing away in the boxes we cart from place to place? Much of what Americans consume doesn't even find its way into boxes or storage spaces, but winds up in the garbage.

The Natural Resources Defense Council reports, for example, that 40 percent of the food Americans buy finds its way into the trash.

Enormous consumption has global, environmental and social consequences. For at least 335 consecutive months, the average temperature of the globe has exceeded the average for the 20th century. As a recent report for Congress explained, this temperature increase, as well as acidifying oceans, melting glaciers and Arctic Sea ice, are "primarily driven by human activity." Many experts believe consumerism and all that it entails—from the extraction of resources to manufacturing to waste disposal—plays a big part in pushing our planet to the brink. And as we saw with Foxconn and the recent Beijing smog scare,° many of the affordable products we buy depend on cheap, often exploitive overseas labor and lax environmental regulations. 20

Foxconn and the recent Beijing smog scare: Foxconn Technology is a large Taiwanese electronics manufacturer that assembles smartphones and other devices for Apple, Amazon, and other technology companies. Its labor practices, especially at the huge Foxconn City plant in mainland China, have been the subject of controversy. The "recent Beijing smog scare" refers to a widely publicized rise in air pollution levels around Beijing, China, in January 2013. The Air Quality Index maintained by the U.S. Embassy in Beijing considers pollution levels above 300 to be "hazardous." In January 2013, it recorded pollution levels above 500, or "Beyond Index," for 16 hours in a row.

Does all this endless consumption result in measurably increased happiness?

In a recent study, the Northwestern University psychologist Galen V. Bodenhausen linked consumption with aberrant, antisocial behavior. Professor Bodenhausen found that "irrespective of personality, in situations that activate a consumer mind-set, people show the same sorts of problematic patterns in well-being, including negative affect and social disengagement." Though American consumer activity has increased substantially since the 1950s, happiness levels have flatlined.

• • •

I don't know that the gadgets I was collecting in my loft were part of an aberrant or antisocial behavior plan during the first months I lived in SoHo. But I was just going along, starting some start-ups that never quite started up when I met Olga, an Andorran beauty, and fell hard. My relationship with stuff quickly came apart.

I followed her to Barcelona when her visa expired and we lived in a tiny flat, totally content and in love before we realized that nothing was holding us in Spain. We packed a few clothes, some toiletries and a couple of laptops and hit the road. We lived in Bangkok, Buenos Aires and Toronto with many stops in between.

A compulsive entrepreneur, I worked all the time and started new companies from an office that fit in my solar backpack. I created some do-gooder companies like We Are Happy to Serve You, which makes a reusable, ceramic version of the iconic New York City Anthora coffee cup, and TreeHugger.com, an environmental design blog that I later sold to Discovery Communications. My life was full of love and adventure and work I cared about. I felt free and I didn't miss the car and gadgets and house; instead I felt as if I had quit a dead-end job. 25

The relationship with Olga eventually ended, but my life never looked the same. I live smaller and travel lighter. I have more time and money. Aside from my travel habit—which I try to keep in check by minimizing trips, combining trips and purchasing carbon offsets—I feel better that my carbon footprint is significantly smaller than in my previous supersized life.

Intuitively, we know that the best stuff in life isn't stuff at all, and that relationships, experiences and meaningful work are the staples of a happy life.

I like material things as much as anyone. I studied product design in school. I'm into gadgets, clothing and all kinds of things. But my

Graham Hill is freed by the stark simplicity of his new life.

Feeling Great (oil on canvas), © Scott, Pat/Private Collection/Bridgeman Images

experiences show that after a certain point, material objects have a tendency to crowd out the emotional needs they are meant to support.

I wouldn't trade a second spent wandering the streets of Bangkok with Olga for anything I've owned. Often, material objects take up mental as well as physical space.

30 I'm still a serial entrepreneur, and my latest venture is to design thoughtfully constructed small homes that support our lives, not the other way around. Like the 420-square-foot space I live in, the houses I design contain less stuff and make it easier for owners to live within their means and to limit their environmental footprint. My apartment sleeps four people comfortably; I frequently have dinner parties for 12. My space is well-built, affordable and as functional as living spaces twice the size. As the guy who started TreeHugger.com, I sleep better knowing I'm not using more resources than I need. I have less—and enjoy more.

My space is small. My life is big.

Understanding the Text

1. Hill describes his previous life as "complicated" (par. 11). What was so complicated about it? What did he do to change that?
2. What is the relationship between space and consumption in Hill's argument? Are these two parts of the same problem?
3. The big life in a small space is central to Hill's essay. Do you find his style "big" or "small"? What is the relationship between content and form in this essay?

Reflection and Response

4. Hill mentions that he created a blog called TreeHugger (treehugger.com). Visit the blog and choose three entries to study. Write an essay in which you develop a theory of the way that treehugger.com invents a world for its viewers.
5. Once you've read Hill's article, you might feel tempted to try living with a lot less yourself. What would you do to downsize? What would you expect to gain from your efforts?

Making Connections

6. Would you consider "The Sermon on the Mount" (from the "Gospel of Matthew," p. 59) and "Freedom through Renunciation" (from the *Bhagavad Gita*, p. 67) as commentaries on Hill's main point? Write an essay in which you discuss whether Hill's essay constitutes a modern take on these ancient texts.
7. Write an ode to living with less, a lot less, in John Keats's style ("Ode on Melancholy," p. 264) but using Hill's ideas as the framework for your content. Be sure to figure out how odes are structured before writing yours.
8. Would Hill consider Noelle Oxenhandler's essay "Ah, But the Breezes . . ." (p. 314) an exercise in living with less (if not materially less, perhaps emotionally or spiritually less)? Why or why not? Write an essay in which you consider Hill, Oxenhandler, and Gretchen Rubin ("July: Buy Some Happiness," p. 291) as modern happiness theorists. What are their positions on this important issue?

Ah, But the Breezes . . .

Noelle Oxenhandler

Noelle Oxenhandler is a teacher and writer who has practiced Buddhism for 32 years. She has published three nonfiction books: *A Grief Out of Season: When Your Parents Divorce in Your Adult Years* (with psychologist Nancy Hillard, and published under her married name, Noelle Fintushel, 1991), *The Eros of Parenthood: Explorations of Light and Dark* (2001), and *The Wishing Year: A House, A Man, My Soul* (2008). This last chronicles a year during which she "undertook an experiment to make three wishes come true" — for a house of her own, a new romantic partner, and spiritual healing. All three in fact did come true. Oxenhandler is associate professor of English at Sonoma State University in Rohnert Park, California. She holds two master's degrees, one in philosophy from the University of Toronto and one in creative writing from the State University of New York at Brockport. Her essays have appeared in a wide range of periodicals, including the *New Yorker*, *Vogue*, *Tricycle*, and *Oprah* magazine, and have been selected for *The Best Spiritual Essays* and listed in *The Best Essays of the Year.* The following essay, which first appeared in *Tricycle* in 2002, explores an ancient problem — the relationship between happiness and suffering — but does so in practical and intimately personal terms, though informed by long reflection on philosophical insight and spiritual teaching.

Often a spiritual quest begins with the word *but.*

I have everything I need to make me happy, but I am not happy. . . .

For my neighbor, Sally, the quest began many years ago in a villa in southern France. It was a beautiful villa, covered with bougainvillea and facing the Mediterranean, and she was in the company of loving friends. "But I just couldn't be happy," she remembers. One restless, fitful night, she came across a book left behind by a previous guest. It was *The Autobiography of a Yogi,* and it led her to the practice that she has followed ever since.

As for Prince Siddhartha:° his parents made sure that he had everything on earth to make him happy. He lived in a beautiful palace and

Prince Siddhartha: Siddhartha Gautama (c. 563–c. 460 BCE), known as the Buddha, was born a prince but renounced his family and their wealth to become an ascetic. Eventually, he achieved enlightenment. See "The Dhammapada," p. 16.

roamed through lush gardens and enjoyed the company of loving friends and bountiful food and. . . .

Notice the *and*s? They were not enough to keep the *but* from his life. The *but* of an old man, a sick man, a corpse. . . . 5

One day these sights pierced through the shield of *and*s that the King and Queen had made for their son. The minarets and the marble, the jasmine and honeysuckle, the silks and sweets, the laughter, music, and dancing: all these could not shield the prince from the *but* of suffering that he discovered outside the palace gate.

Outside: the word *but* derives from the Latin *ob*, meaning "out." Suffering is what we want to keep out, but somehow it always gets into our lives.

It doesn't always come in a strong dose. Sometimes it's subtle, homeopathic.

When I was fifteen, I fell in love with a boy I met when I twisted my ankle and my ski went flying over a cliff in the Haute-Savoie mountains in France. A handsome, dark-haired boy took off over the cliff and, nearly an hour later, handed me the ski that had plunged into a deep ravine. His name was Michel. 10

He attended a Jesuit boarding school° in the nearby village, where he'd been sent for being unruly. When I visited him there, in his cell-like room, he read me the poems of his favorite poet, Rimbaud,° the "enfant terrible."° Then he showed me the secret stash of candy and cigarettes that he kept in a hollowed-out Bible. We went to the Mardi Gras celebration at his school that night, and he went as Lazarus,° wrapped in a white sheet. That was Michel, always defying something: a sheer cliff, a school's rules, the idea of death. . . .

We met several times again that year when Michel was visiting his parents in Paris, which was where my family was spending the year. Shortly before our return to California, Michel's parents invited me to spend the following summer with them in their chalet in the High French Alps.

Jesuit boarding school: a school run by the Society of Jesus, an order of Roman Catholic priests founded in 1534.
Rimbaud: Arthur Rimbaud (1854–1891) is a French symbolist poet and author of *Une Saison en enfer (A Season in Hell,* 1873) among other works.
"enfant terrible": French expression (literally "terrible child") meaning a young person whose behavior provokes shock or outrage.
Lazarus: The story of Lazarus of Bethany is told in the Gospel of John. Informed that Lazarus was ill, Jesus traveled to Bethany only to find that Lazarus had died four days earlier. But Jesus called him out of his tomb, raising him from the dead.

Now, between our handful of vivid moments from the past and the summer's wide open future, Michel and I had just enough raw matter to spin a dense web of fantasy. Back in California, I set my alarm clock an hour early on school nights so I'd have time to wake up and read his letters and to imagine, again and again, the scene of our reunion. *After a long journey, my train pulls up to the village station. Through the window I see a stone clock-tower, surrounded by white mountain peaks. And there he is. Waiting for me on the platform: handsome, dark-haired Michel. I step off the train, and we rush into each other's arms.*

At last the long school year came to an end, and I flew to Paris by myself and took the night-train that winds through the heart of France, from Paris all the way to Provence. Too excited to sleep on my narrow berth, I lay there in the dark, wrapped in my web of revery. At dawn's light, I looked out and saw meadows of wildflowers flying by, villages built of dark wood and stone, and brilliant white peaks in the distance. . . .

By late morning, the train arrived at the tiny village called Puy-St. Vincent. I stepped off the train and there he was, waiting for me: handsome, dark-haired Michel. We rushed toward each other, just as I had imagined. But in the moment of embracing him, I looked over his shoulder and saw a small pink plastic lobster, lying on the ground. Even in the bliss of being in his arms, I felt the shock of the alien thing, the thing that—in all those hours of daydreaming—I'd never once imagined. 15

It is thirty-four years since I stepped off the train in Puy-St. Vincent, and Michel died long ago in an avalanche on Mt. Everest. Yet there's a way that the moment of seeing the small pink lobster over his shoulder has happened again and again.

It's the moment of the *but*. The moment when something outside the pale of our own dreams, desires, expectations, intrudes. "But this wasn't in my plans! This is not what I had in mind!" Indeed, that summer in the Alps bore no resemblance to the summer I'd set my clock to dream of, morning after morning, in California. Unable to live up to the months of fantasy, my relationship with Michel quickly unraveled—and there I was, far from home, stuck for weeks in a house with a sullen boy who barely spoke to me. Looking back, it would be easy to see the lobster as a sinister omen. Yet from the first moment, I sensed it was a different kind of messenger. I didn't have words for it then, but somehow I knew that this was a small monster

"Can you include the outside, alien thing *in* the embrace? To truly answer this question is to come up against the very edge of the human psyche."

calling to me with life's big question. Can you include the outside, alien thing *in* the embrace?

To truly answer this question is to come up against the very edge of the human psyche. For from the very beginning, what we desire is *and*. The very opposite of *but*, the word *and* is linked to "in," and our life begins *in utero*. For the human infant, bliss is the *and* that comes as close as possible to that primal *in*: I am here *and* you are here *and* when I open my mouth your milk is *in* me *and* I am *in* your arms.

Alas, from the very beginning the *but* intrudes. Even the most attentive mother cannot fail to fail her infant at times: a hungry stomach aches, a wet diaper chafes, the bath water is too hot or too cold. . . . In the mouth of even the luckiest baby, sharp teeth soon intrude in the soft site of pleasure.

Yet our whole lives long, we go on wanting a version of the primal *and*. We fall in love, and we think we've found it again. My first two weeks in Puy-St. Vincent were blissful. Michel and I swam in deep, blue mountain lakes and hiked to where the world seemed nothing but glacier, rock, and clouds. Following the sound of a hundred small bells, we found the trail that led to the village shepherd: Bernard, a young man who spent his life alone with a hundred sheep. Back in the village, we had long, communal meals with his family and neighbors; we played volleyball in the evenings as the snowy mountains turned a flamboyant pink; we joined with other teenagers to help restore the crumbling Roman chapel, polishing old paintings with raw potato-halves and hearing each other's mock-confessions in the carved wooden booth. As a gift to Michel's family, I'd brought a beautiful white Mexican wedding hammock. Michel hung it up between two pine trees and we loved to lie in it, swinging out over the blue valley, murmuring to each other as we'd longed to during all those months of ink on paper. Whatever the words, in English or French, their import was this: You are here *and* I am here *and* you are *in* my arms *and* I am *in* your arms *and* this moment will go on *and* on *and* on. 20

In spite of my efforts to stay neutral, I got drawn into an escalating drama between Michel and his mother. She was terrified of his growing passion for scaling mountains, always higher and more inaccessible mountains. Deep down, she must have known where it would lead. I sympathized with her—and for this, Michel cut me off.

But this isn't what I wanted! This isn't how I thought it would be. . . .

Inevitably, we fall out of the hammock of bliss, the Garden of Eden. In some form or another, whether subtle or huge, the *but* arrives to thwart our desire.

Is this the end of the story?
No. 25

For there is another *but*, a *but* within the *but* of sorrow and disappointment. The poet Rilke° asks us to fear neither suffering nor sadness:

> The mountains are heavy, heavy the oceans,
> Ah, but the breezes, ah, but the spaces—

Breezes . . . spaces . . . what is this *but* that can blow through our lives, softening the hard mountain of suffering, opening us to something beyond the contraction of sorrow?

One night in the village of Puy-St. Vincent, a painful dream jolted me out of sleep with the words, "I can't take this anymore!" Michel's iciness was unyielding, and I felt overcome with hurt and homesickness. I got out of bed and threw open the heavy wooden shutters. The black sky swirled with stars over the luminous white mountains. The scale of everything out there was so vast, and as I leaned into it, I felt something happening inside me. It was something very soft—like a breeze—yet forceful, and inside the walls of my chest, it pressed against something that wanted to shut down.

The feeling was painful, as though I might burst, yet it brought an exquisite relief. It helped me to discover a buoyancy in the heart of the heaviness, and I was able to stay through the summer. Michel remained sullen, but I made other friends, grew close to his family, and made my own bond with the mountains. When, on my last night, I stood outside his door and said, "*Bonsoir*, Michel," he threw open the door and asked me to forgive him.

Two years later, when I met a monk from Thailand who taught me how 30 to meditate, I knew I'd found a link to that sustaining buoyancy. Though I was sitting in the basement of a college dormitory in Ohio, when I followed my breath I was opening those heavy wooden shutters again, inviting the breeze to come in, in. . . .

In Buddhism, the *but* of suffering—the old man, the sick man, the corpse—is met by the *but* of the path. "Existence is suffering," said the

Rilke: Rainer Maria Rilke (1875–1926) was an Austrian poet and author of the *Duino Elegies* (1923) and *Sonnets to Orpheus* (1923).

Buddha Gautama, "but there is a path to liberation." When we sit quietly in meditation, *but* after *but* presents itself. "But I don't want to feel this pain in my knees . . . this drowsiness . . . this restlessness . . . this anger . . . this grief . . . I can't bear to sit here anymore. I want *out*!"

Yet something remarkable happens when we go on sitting through all the *but*s, through all the thoughts, sensations, and emotions that we would so like to oust. Gradually they begin to feel less alien, less like *ob*-stacles in the way, rocks in the path. Our deepening awareness becomes a kind of dew, falling on everything equally, allowing everything to sparkle. Once, in the midst of a meditation retreat, a friend went for a walk in the woods and found to her amazement that the litter was beautiful. Rusty cans, a beer bottle lying on pine needles: everything was shining like a jewel. Once, after three months in a Zen° monastery, I was taking a night flight home across the country when I became aware of a constriction in my chest: my fear of dying in a plane crash. With difficulty, I brought my attention to the fear, and then something began to happen, something that had the same huge energy as the airplane, plowing so forcefully into the night. The fear of flying disappeared and—like the lens of a kaleidoscope narrowing, then opening out again into a different configuration—a new fear appeared, then another, and another. Cancer, fire, the death of loved ones. . . . Then fear turned to grief: the heartbreak of Michel, my parents' divorce, lost friends. . . . Each fear, each grief arose in a vivid display of color and shape that, amazingly, had its own perfection, like one shimmering firework after another. Faced with the sheer power of this display, there was no room for fear or grief—only awe, and a sense of immense relief as each fear, each grief melted away.

This magnificent melting was not an experience that could be sustained in its intensity: the plane came back down to ground on the other side of the continent, and I too had to come back to ground. But the experience radically altered my sense of horizon, my understanding of what the human mind can encompass.

Notice the *but* there? It's a *but* with a double edge. At times, when confidence deserts us, when we contract with pain or fear or doubt, the past experience of that infinitely expanding horizon sustains us, encouraging us to rediscover it anew. "I can't quite see it now, but I know it's there." At other times, the past experience seems to indict us, to accuse us of having

Zen: a Japanese school of Buddhism founded in the sixth century. It emphasizes the achievement of enlightenment through the practice of seated meditation (zazen).

let the hard-won jewel slip through our fingers. "I had such a powerful experience of release, but now I'm bound again." This *but* can be the hardest passage of all. It's as though, having once belted out "Amazing Grace," we now have to sing it backwards: "For I was found, but now I'm lost; could see, but now I'm blind. . . ."

This is the *but* that the medieval mystic, Julien of Norwich,° acknowledges in her description of the "rising" and "falling" of the spiritual life. "If there be anywhere on earth a lover of God who is always kept safe, I know nothing of it, for it was not shown to me. But this was shown: that in falling and rising again we are always kept in that same precious love." 35

And who was Julien of Norwich? The Queen of *and*. Her famous words, "all shall be well and all shall be well and all manner of thing shall be well," are spoken to those who have passed through the *but*—again and again and again. As Julien tells us, it's *and* that has the last word, ringing out like a bell in waves that encompass every sorrow. Yet without the *but*, we couldn't fully hear this sound. We'd be like those poor beautiful people in the deva realm who, having never experienced the least *ob*-struction, can never experience the joy of release. So it is that I propose the humble word *but* as our own seed-syllable, sacred mantra, secret of human happiness, breeze through the heart of suffering, conduit to the inexhaustible well of *and*.

Julien of Norwich (c. 1342–c. 1413, often spelled "Julian"): English Christian mystic and theologian and author of *Revelations of Divine Love* (c. 1395), possibly the first book in English by a woman.

Understanding the Text

1. The usually overlooked words "and" and "but" are central to this essay. As you read, pay close attention to the meanings that Oxenhandler finds in these words. In particular, note the *different* meanings that each of the words bears as the essay proceeds. How is the "but" of "Ah, but the breezes . . ." (in the poem, par. 26) different from the uses of "but" that Oxenhandler describes initially? In a notebook, list the principal meanings of "and" and "but" in the essay. Why does "but" become, in the end, the "secret of human happiness" (par. 36)? And what is the relationship, in the end, between "and" and "but" for Oxenhandler?
2. How would you describe the significance of the "small pink plastic lobster" (par. 15) for the essay? How does the final section of the essay help explain its meaning?

Reflection and Response

3. This essay is about an exploration or quest, but it is important to distinguish between the quest itself and the *story* of the quest. What are the

principal events in the story? What are the central questions that keep it moving forward? Where do you find major turning points and breakthroughs? How has Oxenhandler managed to *shape* a prolonged interior process into a short and readable essay?

4. At the center of Oxenhandler's essay is a story from her past, one that illustrates first "and" and later "but." Most of us have had an experience of this kind — not necessarily one that seemed dramatic or momentous at the time but one that involves, in some form, the experience of both "and" and "but." Write a brief essay that begins with a narrative of such an experience. Then write a section that explains and explores the element of "and" and "but" in the essay. Investigate the meaning of your experience as fully and faithfully as you can.

Making Connections

5. What is the central problem or question of this essay? Using your own words, formulate this central question as precisely as you can. Then write an essay that explores this question in relation to the central question of Matthieu Ricard's "The Alchemy of Suffering" (p. 34). Are the two authors' projects similar? How do they differ?
6. Compare Oxenhandler's views to those of Aristotle ("Nicomachean Ethics," p. 82). What part do ideas about "the good life" play in Oxenhandler's essay?

Sunflowers

Vincent van Gogh

Vincent van Gogh (1853–1890) produced several paintings of sunflowers, but this one, *Sunflowers*, in the National Gallery in London, England, is perhaps the most loved. Van Gogh painted it shortly after leaving Paris in 1888 for Arles in the south of France, where he hoped to start an art colony. It was one of several works intended to decorate a room in the house he rented, the "Yellow House," to be occupied by his friend Paul Gauguin (1848–1903). Grateful and impressed, Gauguin, in turn, would paint *Vincent van Gogh Painting Sunflowers* (1888). Van Gogh and Gauguin

Sunflowers, 1888 (oil on canvas), Gogh, Vincent van (1853–90)/*Neue Pinakothek, Munich, Germany/Bridgeman* Images

worked happily together at the Yellow House for about four months, until van Gogh had a nervous breakdown, cut off part of his ear, and entered an asylum. On the canvas measuring about 36" x 29", van Gogh used thick brushstrokes (impasto) to render the texture of the seeds and the fading leaves. Van Gogh had originally intended a more extensive series of sunflower paintings, writing to his brother Theo of plans for "a dozen panels . . . a symphony in blue and yellow." Eventually, *Sunflowers* formed part of a triptych, with two paintings of sunflowers flanking his portrait *La Berceuse*.

Understanding the Text

1. Although a painting does not say a word, many of us interpret van Gogh as having a message in his image. What does this image say to you? What details in the painting convey this concept or feeling? How do the brushstrokes or the special configuration or the colors contribute to your interpretation of the painting's meaning for you?
2. Find a critical interpretation of van Gogh's *Sunflowers* and copy it. Then, using details of the painting as your evidence, write 500 words in which you agree or disagree with this interpretation.

Reflection and Response

3. In an 1888 letter to his sister Willemien, van Gogh writes that "the uglier, older, meaner, iller, poorer I get the more I wish to take my revenge by doing brilliant color, well-arranged, resplendent" (Vincent van Gogh, Arles, September 9 and 14, 1888, to Willemien van Gogh). Would you say that the *Sunflowers* painting enacts van Gogh's "revenge"? If so, where do you see this? And if not, what do you see instead?
4. Consider van Gogh's choice of subject in this painting. You might want to learn a bit about the sunflower and its place in the part of Provence where van Gogh painted it. How does the flower lend itself to representations of "happy" or "unhappy"?

Making Connections

5. Would you argue that either van Gogh's or Pierre-Auguste Renoir's painting *Luncheon of the Boating Party* (p. 200) represents happiness? Make an argument about the two paintings in relation to the concept of "happiness." Ground your argument in definitions of happiness you've gleaned from working with at least two other essays in this book.
6. We might say that Jennifer Michael Hecht's "Remember Death" (p. 233) argues a point opposite to what van Gogh represents in *Sunflowers*. Do you agree? Why or why not? Summarize how each of these creative individuals represents ideas of "life" or "death," or both, in their work. Consider this an opportunity to explore the complexities of the crafts of writing and painting as well as the concepts you see embodied in their works.

Getting Off the Hedonic Treadmill, One Step at a Time

Daniel Mochon, Michael I. Norton, and Dan Ariely

Daniel Mochon, Michael I. Norton, and Dan Ariely are professors of business and marketing. Ariely is professor of psychology and behavioral economics at Duke University. He is a founding member of the Center for Advanced Hindsight. He has written three books: *Predictably Irrational: The Hidden Forces That Shape Our Decisions*, *The Upside of Irrationality: The Unexpected Benefits of Defying Logic at Work and at Home*, and *The (Honest) Truth about Dishonesty: How We Lie to Everyone — Especially Ourselves*. Norton is an associate professor of business administration at the Harvard Business School. With Elizabeth Dunn, Norton authored a book titled *Happy Money: The New Science of Smarter Spending*, in which he discusses research on the science of spending money. Mochon is an assistant professor in the A. B. Freeman School of Business at Tulane University. His research involves the study of consumer behavior and the ways consumers make decisions regarding spending money. In the following article from the *Journal of Economic Psychology*, the authors report on two studies that examine the long-term effect of "small but frequent boosts" to well-being, in the form of religious practice and exercise.

Abstract

Many studies have shown that few events in life have a lasting impact on subjective well-being because of people's tendency to adapt quickly; worse, those events that do have a lasting impact tend to be negative. We suggest that while major events may not provide lasting increases in well-being, certain seemingly minor events—such as attending religious services or exercising—may do so by providing small but frequent boosts: if people engage in such behaviors with sufficient frequency, they may cumulatively experience enough boosts to attain higher well-being. In Study 1, we surveyed places of worship for 12 religions and found that people did receive positive boosts for attending service, and that these boosts appeared to be cumulative: the more they reported attending, the happier they were. In Study 2, we generalized these effects to other regular activities, demonstrating that people received boosts for exercise and yoga, and that these boosts too had a cumulative positive impact on well-being. We suggest that shifting focus from the impact of major life changes on well-being to the impact of seemingly minor repeated behaviors is crucial for understanding how best to improve well-being.

Introduction

Understanding the determinants of subjective well-being has important implications for economics. At the micro level, well-being has been shown to affect the behavior of individuals. For example, some studies have found that there is a positive relation between workers' stable happiness and their work performance (Wright & Staw, 1999). People in positive moods have also been shown to be more creative problem solvers, more likely to attain a mutually favorable outcome while bargaining, and more willing to seek variety among positive choices (Isen, 2000).

At the macro level, policymakers must often decide among various programs that differ in the advantages they provide to the public. Understanding what factors truly improve well-being can guide such decisions, and help avoid choosing programs that bring expensive and nonlasting benefits. In contrast to models in which utility is inferred from people's choices, recent economic conceptualizations of utility include people's subjective feelings of utility—their reports of their subjective well-being—as an important input in determining overall utility. These reports of subjective well-being are increasingly a factor in determining the overall utility of some public policy decisions (e.g., Di Tella & MacCulloch, 2006; Kahneman, Krueger, Schkade, Schwarz, & Stone, 2004b). As a result, the scientific study of subjective well-being has received increased attention from economists (see Frey & Stutzer, 2002; Kahneman, Krueger, Schkade, Schwarz, & Stone, 2004a).

The literature on subjective well-being offers a paradox, however, that must be resolved before the construct can be fruitfully applied to improve people's lives: most studies have shown that people's overall level of happiness seems stubbornly impervious to change. While people accumulate experiences that most predict would affect their well-being, subjective well-being appears to be surprisingly stable. Indeed, if major life events such as winning a lottery fail to have a substantial lasting impact on well-being (Brickman, Coates, & Janoff-Bulman, 1978), it is hard to imagine that any single event could accomplish the feat. Therefore, it would seem that any policy geared towards maximizing subjective well-being would be doomed to fail from the outset. We believe, however, that it is possible to make lasting changes in subjective well-being if one focuses on the right types of behaviors. In this paper, we shift from a focus on the impact of single major life events toward a focus on the impact of seemingly minor behaviors such as exercising or attending religious services on well-being. We suggest that while single major events may be unlikely to have a lasting impact, smaller minor behaviors provide small boosts to well-being that can lead to real changes in overall well-being, especially if they are repeated with sufficient frequency over time: one cannot win the lottery every day, but one can exercise or attend religious services regularly, and these repeated behaviors may be enough to increase well-being over time.

Adaptation and the Stability of Well-Being

Brickman and Campbell (1971) coined the term "hedonic treadmill" to describe the now widely accepted notion that though people continue to accrue experiences and objects that make them happy—or unhappy—their overall level of well-being tends to remain fairly static. The logic behind this argument stems from adaptation level theory (Helson, 1964), which argues that people perceive objects not in any absolute sense, but rather relative to a level established by previous experiences. Therefore, when people experience a positive event, two effects take place: in the short run, well-being increases; in the long run, however, people habituate to their new circumstances, which diminishes the positive effect of that event. In the most famous demonstration of this course of events, Brickman et al. (1978) interviewed a sample of lottery winners, as well as a sample of accident victims who had become paralyzed. The sample was chosen such that the major life event had happened to them within the previous year and a half, but at least a month before the interview, to allow for adaptation to occur. Their results showed that the lottery winners did not rate themselves as happier than the control group, and while the accident victims rated themselves as less happy than the other groups, they still rated themselves above the midpoint of the scale. Similarly, Suh, Diener, and Fujita (1996) showed that while major life events that had occurred within the previous 3 months predicted well-being, those occurring further back in time did not. Other studies have shown that there is no difference in well-being between people who had recently experienced a romantic breakup versus those who had not, between assistant professors who had been denied tenure and those who had attained it, or between those whose preferred gubernatorial candidates had won or lost (Gilbert, Pinel, Wilson, Blumberg, & Wheatley, 1998). Taken together, these results suggest that most events have no lasting impact on our well-being (see Diener, Lucas, & Scollon, 2006; Frederick & Loewenstein, 1999; Frey & Stutzer, 2002).

Worse still, of those investigations that have demonstrated a lasting impact of major events on well-being, most have been in negative domains. Dijkers (1997) conducted a meta-analysis of 22 studies that looked at the relationship between spinal cord injury and quality of life, and found that degree of disability had a negative effect on quality of life. Lucas, Clark, Georgellis, and Diener (2003) examined the effects of marital status over time with a large representative sample. Although marriage had a strong initial positive effect, this effect disappeared after just one year. People who had been widowed, on the other hand, never fully adapted and remained less happy than their baseline before the event occurred. 5

What then does account for people's positive levels of well-being, if not major life events? Many studies have shown that there are strong effects of both genetic predisposition and stable personality traits on well-being. Lykken and Tellegen (1996) found that half of the variance associated with well-being was associated with genetic variation, and that this accounted for 80% of the stable component of the subjective well-being measure (see also Suh et al., 1996). Indeed, Headey and Wearing (1989) suggested that rather than life events causing changes in well-being, life events are to some degree endogenously caused by personality. Personality models of well-being thus suggest that though there may be short-lived effects of external shocks on well-being, people return to their baseline in the long run, a baseline which is determined primarily by their personalities and the events that those personalities cause them to pursue.

Can Well-Being Be Improved?

All of the previously cited research paints a rather discouraging picture about people's ability to increase their own well-being. Although some major negative events seem to be able to create lasting changes (Dijkers, 1997; Lucas, 2005; Lucas, Clark, Georgellis, & Diener, 2004), there seems to be little people can do to improve their well-being. At most, people may hope for temporary lifts from major life events (such as marriage, or winning the lottery) which quickly fade as they return to their usual baseline predetermined by genes and personality—requiring them to ever peruse the hedonic treadmill in the hope of finding some temporary increase in happiness. Given the frequency of winning the lottery or getting married (which for most people is a few times at most), the odds of improving well-being seem low. Of course, this is not as tragic as it sounds, since most people's equilibrium state is somewhat happy (Diener & Diener, 1996). Nonetheless, it seems as though people generally should not even bother to pursue goals that make them happy (and not try as hard to avoid many of the activities that they expect to cause them unhappiness), as achieving them will not have any lasting impact. It also appears as though any economic policy aimed at improving people's welfare is just a waste of time and money, since it will have no long-term effect. But is there truly nothing that people can do to improve their well-being?

We suggest that shifting from a focus on the impact of major life events to a focus on *minor* life events—the kinds of small activities people partake in every day—offers insight into how people might increase their well-being. Indeed, in contrast to the research reviewed above, some studies have shown that particular behaviors (such as religion and exercise) are related to higher levels of well-being. Importantly, these kinds of behaviors are *repeated* behaviors, rather than single-shot life events. We suggest that the cumulative impact of repeating minor but positive life events in the short-term—such as choosing to attend religious services each week or to work out several days a week—may be sufficient to increase well-being in the long-term.

We chose religious practice and exercise as our initial behaviors because both have been linked to well-being, and are precisely the kinds of minor repeated behaviors we propose may improve well-being. Indeed, religiosity and religious involvement have overwhelmingly been found to correlate with many measures of well-being. Myers (2000) reports data from a national sample showing that those who are most involved with their religion are almost twice as likely to report being "very happy" than those with the least involvement (see also Ferris, 2002). In a large cross-sectional national sample, Ellison (1991) found that religious variables accounted for 5–7% of the variance in life satisfaction (see also Witter, Stock, Okun, & Haring, 1985). Religious involvement has also been found to be positively related to more objective measures of well-being such as mental and physical health (e.g., Hackney & Sanders, 2003; Larson et al., 1992; Seybold & Hill, 2001). While not as widely studied, physical exercise is known to generate endorphins that improve mood (Thoren, Floras, Hoffmann, & Seals, 1990), regular engagement in exercise has been shown to have a positive impact on well-being (Biddle, 2000), and of course countless studies demonstrate the benefits of exercise for physical well-being (see Penedo & Dahn, 2005; Ross & Hayes, 1988).

How Might Repeated Minor Events Lead to Increased Well-Being?

How is it that religious involvement and exercise improve subjective well-being when most other factors—including events that seem to dwarf these in significance—seem to matter little? Why don't people adapt to religion and exercise, behaviors that most people have been engaged in their entire life, as they do to most other things? We suggest that these behaviors have a causal effect on well-being because they give regular and reliable, albeit small, boosts to well-being each time a member participates in one of these activities. Though each boost is not large and fades over time, both religion and exercise encourage regular participation, which might cause these small boosts to aggregate over time, leading to increased well-being.

Some evidence for the impact of small repeated events comes from the finding that commuting, a regular daily activity, is rated as a highly negative experience (Kahneman et al., 2004a), and commuting time correlates negatively with subjective well-being (Stutzer & Frey, 2004). In addition, Lyubomirsky, Sheldon, and Schkade (2005) suggest that intentional activities, discrete actions in which people choose to engage, can lead to higher levels of well-being because they draw attention to positive events, thus preventing them from fading into the background. However none of these studies have documented whether these activities cause small boosts in well-being every time they are performed, as we propose.

Overview

In order to test whether people in fact do get small boosts from engaging in religious activity, we measured the subjective well-being of people as they entered and exited religious services (Study 1), and as they entered and exited the gym and yoga (Study 2). We expected to observe increases in well-being from before to after such behaviors. In both studies, we also assessed people's reported frequency of such behaviors, to investigate whether increased frequency of engaging in these behaviors (and thus more frequent small boosts) was related to overall higher well-being.

Study 1

Method

Participants. Teams of undergraduate research assistants surveyed places of worship for 12 religions in the Boston/Cambridge area (see Table 5.1 for religions represented, number of places of worship surveyed, and number of members of each religion who participated). In total, 2,095 people participated (1,032 male, 1,063 female), with a mean age of 36.7.

Procedure. Participants were approached either before services or after services. We were concerned that approaching the same participants both pre- and post-service would create strong demand effects, with participants being motivated to report increased mood in order to justify their attendance. Therefore, we ensured that surveyors did not question

Table 5.1 **Number of Participants and Places of Worship Surveyed for 12 Religions (Study 1)**

Religion	Number of Places of Worship Surveyed	Number of Participants
Baha'i	1	39
Baptist	8	499
Catholic	4	120
Christian	6	161
Congregational	3	263
Episcopalian	5	438
Greek Orthodox	1	99
Lutheran	2	109
Methodist	3	208
Mormon	1	57
Quaker	2	42
Unitarian	1	60

the same participant twice, making this a true between-subjects design and minimizing these demand effects.

Participants were asked to rate, on a scale from 1 (very bad) to 100 (very good), "How do you feel right now?" "How satisfied are you with your life in general?" and "How satisfied are you with your spiritual and religious life?" While the limitations of doing field research limited us to just these three questions, previous research has suggested that even single item measures of well-being correlate well with more intensive surveys (e.g., Sandvik, Diener, & Seidlitz, 1993). Participants also reported how many times they had attended services in the last month and their age; surveyors recorded their gender. 15

Results

Since our three measures of well-being were highly correlated, we averaged them to create a composite measure of well-being (Cronbach's α° = 0.80). The average well-being reported in our sample was 81.2 (SD° = 13.0); in line with previous research, people in our sample tended to be happy (Diener & Diener, 1996).

Cronbach's α: a statistical formula for calculating the reliability or internal consistency of a test that contains multiple items with varying scores.
SD: abbreviation for "standard deviation."

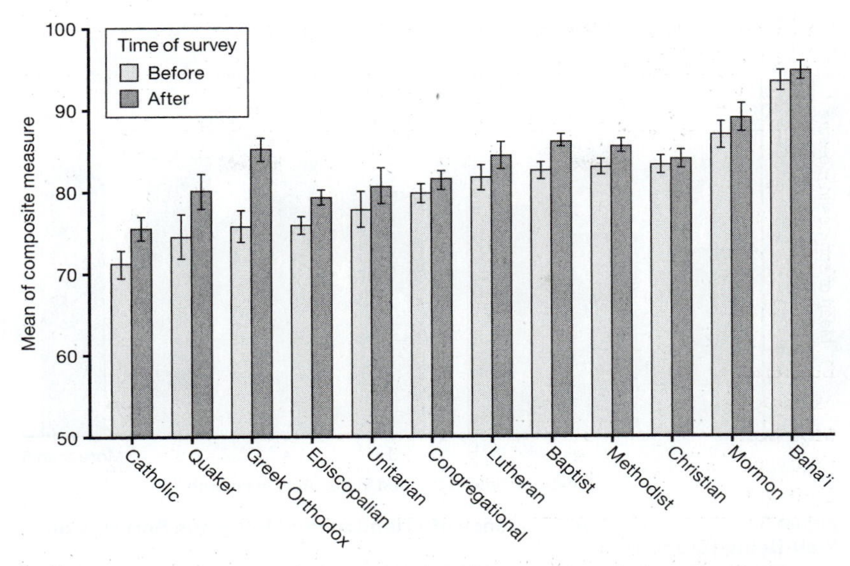

Figure 5.1 **Well-Being of 12 Religions before and after Religious Services (Study 1)**

Note: Error bars indicate standard error.

We next looked at the effect of attending a religious service on well-being by comparing the composite measure of participants surveyed before services and the different set of participants who were surveyed after services. As Fig. 5.1 shows, attending a religious service provided a small and positive boost to reported well-being, and this was true across all of the surveyed religions. Collapsing across all religions, those surveyed after their religious service ($M°$ = 82.8, SD = 12.0) reported a significantly higher level of well-being than those surveyed before (M = 79.6, SD = 13.8), $t(2{,}093) = 5.67$, $p < .001$.

Our first result showed that people tend to get a small positive boost in well-being from attending a specific religious service. We suggest that it is the aggregation of these small boosts over time that contributes to the positive relationship between religiosity and well-being. If this is the case, we would expect people who had attended more services in the previous month to report a higher level of well-being at baseline (before they had received a positive boost from attending the service). We therefore explored the relationship of our composite measure of well-being to

M: an abbreviation for "mean."

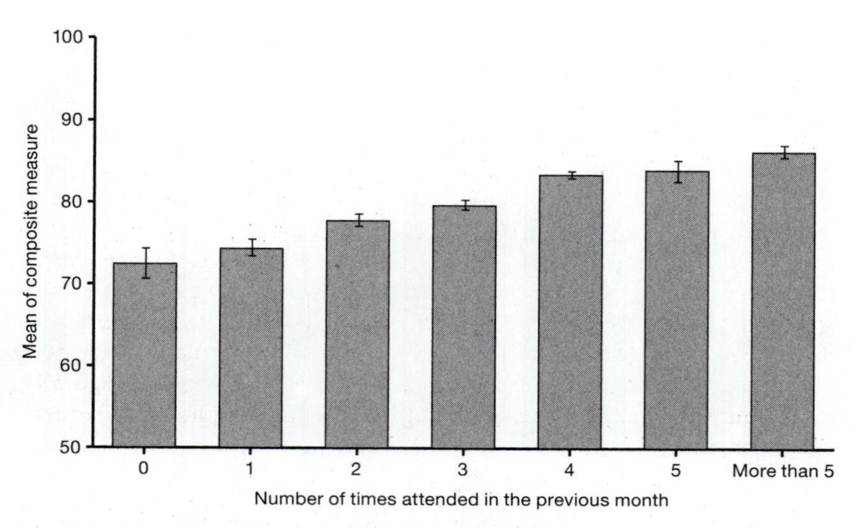

Figure 5.2 **The Impact of Frequency of Attendance of Religious Services on Well-Being (Study 1)**

Note: Error bars indicate standard error.

the number of times participants reported attending services in the previous month. On average, participants indicated that they had attended services 4.0 (SD = 3.7) times in the previous month, and as expected, the frequency of attendance was positively related to well-being, $\beta = 0.75$, $t(2{,}048) = 9.97$, $p < .001$: for every extra time a person had attended a religious service in the previous month, their baseline well-being was 0.75 points higher. As can be seen in Fig. 5.2, this effect is close to linear—the more people attend, the happier they are.

Discussion

These data offer an account for the relationship between religion and well-being, and help to explain why it is that religious people tend to be happier than non-religious people. While previous studies have shown that religious involvement is correlated with well-being, that correlation could have been caused by happier people being more religious, or some third factor. In Study 1, participants were randomly surveyed either before or after services, thus allowing us to conclude that religious adherents in fact report a higher level of well-being after participating in a religious service than before. Those actively involved in religion get small boosts to their well-being every time they attend a religious service, and when people attend religious services frequently enough, these boosts seem to lead to overall higher levels of well-being.[1] While this second result is purely correlational, there is good reason to believe that attending services frequently causes higher levels of well-being, rather than the other way around. As we have shown, people get boosts from attending religious services, showing that attending a service can cause a single-shot improvement to well-being. If people choose activities in order to maximize their well-being, one would expect the least happy people to attend the most often, since they would benefit most from these boosts, leading to a negative correlation rather than the positive one we found. In addition, Litwin (2007) found that after controlling for covariates such as social involvement and physical health, religious involvement only improved mortality risk for those who attended services regularly, consistent with our theory that lasting change only occurs with frequent involvement.

Study 2

Study 1 showed that religion is a behavior in which people can engage in to get off the hedonic treadmill. Every time people attend a service they get small boosts, which over time seem to lead to a permanent change in their baseline level of well-being. While the relationship of religion and well-being is among the most-studied, there is no reason to think that the regular practice of religion is privileged in its positive impact. In Study 2, we investigate another set of behaviors which involve frequent discrete events: physical activity, which has also been found to provide long-term benefits for well-being. We explore whether two activities—going to the gym and practicing yoga—provide small boosts to well-being with each iteration, and whether the frequency of engaging in these activities (and thus of getting these boosts) predicts baseline well-being.

20

Method

Participants. Teams of undergraduate research assistants surveyed a gym and two yoga classes in the Boston/Cambridge area. In total, 224 people participated (122 male, 102 female), with a mean age of 39.1. 164 were surveyed outside of the gym, while 60 were surveyed outside of a yoga class.

[1]An alternative explanation for our results (which may resonate with non-religious readers who were forced to attend religious services as children) is that rather than benefiting from attending religious services, the upward change merely reflects relief that they are over. This is unlikely, however, because participants reported very high levels of well-being before services had begun.

Procedure. As in Study 1, participants were approached as they were either entering or exiting their gym or yoga classes, and surveyors again did not question the same participant twice. Participants completed the same survey as in Study 1, which included the three measures of well-being, as well as the frequency with which they had attended their gym or yoga class in the previous month.

Results and Discussion

As in Study 1, we computed a composite measure by averaging the three well-being scales (Cronbach's $\alpha = 0.74$). The mean reported level of well-being in our sample was of 76.2 (SD = 13.8), indicating that overall most of the people in our sample were happy.

Was there an effect of engaging in physical activity similar to the one we observed with religious participation? As can be seen in Fig. 5.3, engaging in physical activity also provided a positive boost to well-being. Averaging across both groups, people who were surveyed after they engaged in physical activity reported significantly higher levels of well-being ($M = 79.2$, SD = 13.4) than those surveyed before they engaged in physical activity ($M = 72.7$, SD = 13.4), $t(222) = 3.65$, $p < .001$. As with people who attended religious services, we found that people who engaged in physical activity received a small positive boost to their well-being.

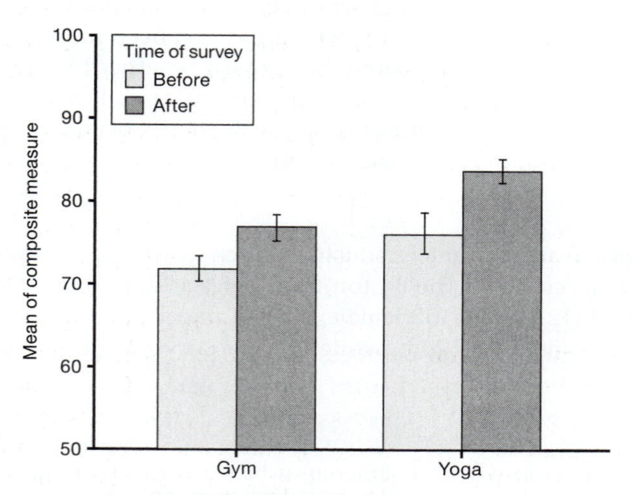

Figure 5.3 **Well-Being before and after Attending the Gym or Yoga Class (Study 2)**

Note: Error bars indicate standard error.

We next examined whether the frequency with which people had engaged in these activities in the previous month predicted their baseline well-being. On average, our participants indicated that they had attended the gym or a yoga class 12.0 (SD = 10.3) times in the previous month. We again found a positive relation between our composite measure of well-being and frequency of attendance, $\beta = 0.33$, $t(99) = 2.25$, $p < .05$: for each extra time they had attended their gym or yoga class in the previous month, participants experienced an increase in their well-being of about a third of a point. As in Study 1, there seems to be a cumulative effect of the small boosts of engaging in these behaviors, such that greater frequency was associated with greater well-being.

General Discussion

The data reported here address a seeming paradox: despite the many studies showing that very few events can have a lasting impact on subjective well-being because people adapt to their circumstances, some research suggests that certain behaviors are positively related to well-being. We posited that the reason that behaviors such as religious involvement and physical activity have a lasting effect on well-being is that these involve frequent small boosts to well-being, with a non-activity period preceding each activity, and are quite different from the infrequent large changes provided by major life events. We further suggested that while the effect of each one of these boosts might be small, people who engage in these activities often enough will end up with higher well-being. Using a paradigm in which we surveyed some participants before they attended religious services or exercised and others as they left these activities, Study 1 showed that people reported higher well-being after religious services, while Study 2 showed a similar effect for attending the gym or a yoga class. Equally important, frequency of engaging in these activities was a positive predictor of people's baseline well-being, suggesting that these small boosts have a cumulative positive effect on well-being.

Our findings imply that, in contrast to the notion of an inescapable hedonic treadmill, it is not pointless for people to seek to improve their well-being. However, improvement may not come from major events such as winning the lottery, despite the seemingly life-changing nature of such examples. Rather, it seems like the key for long lasting changes to well-being is to engage in activities that provide small and frequent boosts, which in the long run will lead to improved well-being, one small step at a time. In light of our results, we think it not coincidental that Karl Marx called religion the "opium of the masses," while athletes frequently refer to the "runner's high" that comes with strenuous exercise. In some sense, both attending religious services and exercising work like a drug in their impact on well-being; while the benefits of the former may be more psychological and the latter more physiological in nature, the two seem to have similar positive effects. If people are engaged in a rational pursuit of higher well-being, it is not surprising that people pursue these activities more and more to continue to receive the cumulative benefits. While it is possible that not everyone would benefit from these two activities, we suggest that everyone can and should find an activity with similar characteristics in order to create lasting improvements in their well-being.

"In contrast to the notion of an inescapable hedonic treadmill, it is not pointless for people to seek to improve their well-being. However, improvement may not come from major events such as winning the lottery."

Our findings also suggest that policies aimed at improving welfare are not a pointless endeavor, as the hedonic treadmill suggests. However, one must be careful when choosing these policies. Single-shot events such as a one time tax refund will probably have little lasting impact on the well-being of the country, while policies that lead to small but repeated gains are likely to succeed. Future research should explore what are the best policies for achieving lasting change.

References

Biddle, S. J. H. (2000). Emotion, mood and physical activity. In S. J. H. Biddle, K. R. Fox, & S. H. Boutcher (Eds.), *Physical activity and psychological well-being* (pp. 63–87). London: Routledge.

Brickman, P., & Campbell, D. T. (1971). Hedonic relativism and planning the good society. In M. H. Appley (Ed.), *Adaptation-level theory: A symposium* (pp. 287–302). New York: Academic Press.

Brickman, P., Coates, D., & Janoff-Bulman, R. (1978). Lottery winners and accident victims: Is happiness relative? *Journal of Personality and Social Psychology, 36*(8), 917–927.

Diener, E., & Diener, C. (1996). Most people are happy. *Psychological Science, 7*(3), 181–185.

Diener, E., Lucas, R. E., & Scollon, C. N. (2006). Beyond the hedonic treadmill. *American Psychologist, 61*(4), 305–314.

Dijkers, M. (1997). Quality of life after spinal cord injury: A meta analysis of the effects of disablement component. *Spinal Cord, 35*, 829–840.

Di Tella, R., & MacCulloch, R. (2006). Some uses of happiness data in economics. *Journal of Economic Perspectives, 20*(1), 25–46.

Ellison, C. G. (1991). Religious involvement and subjective well-being. *Journal of Health and Social Behavior, 32*(1), 80–99.

Ferris, A. L. (2002). Religion and the quality of life. *Journal of Happiness Studies, 3,* 199–215.

Frederick, S., & Loewenstein, G. (1999). Hedonic adaptation. In D. Kahneman, E. Diener, & N. Schwarz (Eds.), *Well-being: The foundations of a hedonic psychology* (pp. 302–329). New York: Russell Sage Foundation.

Frey, B. S., & Stutzer, A. (2002). What can economists learn from happiness research? *Journal of Economic Literature, 40*(June) 402–435.

Gilbert, D. T., Pinel, E. C., Wilson, T. D., Blumberg, S. J., & Wheatley, T. P. (1998). Immune neglect: A source of durability bias in affective forecasting. *Journal of Personality and Social Psychology, 75*(3), 617–638.

Hackney, C. H., & Sanders, G. S. (2003). Religiosity and mental health: A meta-analysis of recent studies. *Journal for the Scientific Study of Religion, 42,* 43–55.

Headey, B., & Wearing, A. (1989). Personality, life events, and subjective well-being: Toward a dynamic equilibrium model. *Journal of Personality and Social Psychology, 57*(4), 731–739.

Helson, H. (1964). *Adaptation-level theory: An experimental and systematic approach to behavior.* New York: Harper and Row.

Isen, A. (2000). Positive affect and decision making. In M. Lewis & J. M. Haviland-Jones (Eds.), *Handbook of Emotion* (pp. 417–435). New York: Guilford.

Kahneman, D., Krueger, A. B., Schkade, D., Schwarz, N., & Stone, A. (2004a). A survey method for characterizing daily life experience: The day reconstruction method. *Science, 306,* 1776–1780.

Kahneman, D., Krueger, A. B., Schkade, D., Schwarz, N., & Stone, A. (2004b). Toward national well-being accounts. *The American Economic Review, 94*(2), 429–434.

Larson, D. B., Sherrill, K. A., Lyons, J. S., Craigie, F. C., Thielman, S. B., Greenwold, M. A., & Larson, S. S. (1992). Associations between dimensions of religious commitment and mental health reported in the American Journal of Psychiatry and Archives of General Psychiatry: 1978–1989. *The American Journal of Psychiatry, 149*(4), 557–559.

Litwin, H. (2007). What really matters in the social network-mortality association? A multivariate examination among older Jewish–Israelis. *European Journal of Ageing, 4,* 71–82.

Lucas, R. E. (2005). Time does not heal all wounds. A longitudinal study of reaction and adaptation to divorce. *Psychological Science, 16*(12), 945–950.

Lucas, R. E., Clark, A. E., Georgellis, Y., & Diener, E. (2004). Unemployment alters the set point for life satisfaction. *Psychological Science, 15*(1), 8–13.

Lucas, R. E., Clark, A. E., Georgellis, Y., & Diener, E. (2003). Reexamining adaptation and the set point model of happiness: Reactions to changes in marital status. *Journal of Personality and Social Psychology 84*(3), 527–539.

Lykken, D., & Tellegen, A. (1996). Happiness is a stochastic phenomenon. *Psychological Science 7*(3), 186–189.

Lyubomirsky, S., Sheldon, K. M., & Schkade, D. A. (2005). Pursuing happiness: The architecture of sustainable change. *Review of General Psychology, 9*(2), 111–131.

Myers, D. G. (2000). The funds, friends, and faith of happy people. *American Psychologist, 55*(1), 56–67.

Penedo, F. J., & Dahn, J. R. (2005). Exercise and well-being: A review of mental and physical health benefits associated with physical activity. *Current Opinion in Psychiatry, 18,* 189–193.

Ross, C. E., & Hayes, D. (1988). Exercise and psychologic well-being in the community. *American Journal of Epidemiology, 127,* 762–771.

Sandvik, E., Diener, E., & Seidlitz, L. (1993). Subjective well-being: The convergence and stability of self-report and non-self-report measures. *Journal of Personality, 61*(3), 317–342.

Seybold, K. S., & Hill, P. C. (2001). The role of religion and spirituality in mental and physical health. *Current Directions in Psychological Science, 10*(1), 21–24.

Stutzer, A., & Frey, B. S. (2004). *Stress that doesn't pay: The commuting paradox.* IZA Discussion Papers, 1278. Bonn: Institute for the Study of Labor.

Suh, E., Diener, E., & Fujita, F. (1996). Events and subjective well-being: Only recent events matter. *Journal of Personality and Social Psychology, 70*(5), 1091–1102.

Thoren, P., Floras, J. S., Hoffmann, P., & Seals, D. R. (1990). Endorphins and exercise: Physiological mechanisms and clinical implications. *Medicine and Science in Sports and Exercise, 22*(4), 417–428.

Witter, R. A., Stock, W. A., Okun, M. A., & Haring, M. J. (1985). Religion and subjective well-being: A quantitative synthesis. *Review of Religious Research, 26*(4), 332–342.

Wright, T. A., & Staw, B. M. (1999). Affect and favorable work outcomes: Two longitudinal tests of the happy-productive worker thesis. *Journal of Organizational Behavior, 20,* 1–23.

Understanding the Text

1. What is the stubborn paradox that this essay seeks to explain?
2. Why did the authors choose the long-term effects of exercise and religion as their research topic?
3. What is the hedonic treadmill? Have you experienced anything like this in your own life?

Reflection and Response

4. Write an essay in which you consider this argument as the basis for a political speech. Drawing from its main points, make your own case about one of today's most pressing problems and solutions.
5. Find a few articles in the *New York Times* in which the issue of raising or lowering taxes figures prominently. Compare these arguments with what is

argued in the final pages of this piece. Write an essay in which you take a position on these arguments; which do you find more persuasive?

Making Connections

6. Gretchen Rubin ("July: Buy Some Happiness," p. 291) and Mochon, Norton, and Ariely advocate doing more with less, but do they argue this along similar principles? Analyze the place of possessions, objects, and desires in each piece.
7. Consider a few entries from these popular blogs: Zen Habits, Tiny House Blog, Apartment Therapy, Design Sponge. Choose two of the blogs and write an essay from the position of Mochon et al. and the Dalai Lama ("The Sources of Happiness," p. 21) in which you discuss these entries as examples of a particular cultural phenomenon you have observed.
8. Would Jennifer Michael Hecht's description of the power of the festival ("Remember Death," p. 233) qualify as another kind of happiness drug that Mochon et al. advocate?

Acknowledgments *(continued from page iv)*

Michael Argyle and Peter Hills. "The Oxford Happiness Questionnaire: A Compact Scale for the Measurement of Psychological Well-Being" from *Personality and Individual Differences*, November 2002. Vol. 33, Issue 7, pp. 1073–82. Copyright © 2002, with permission from Elsevier.

Aristotle. Excerpt from "Nicomachean Ethics," Book 1, Chapter 7, pp. 370–73, from *A New Aristotle Reader*, edited by J. L. Ackrill. Copyright © J. L. Ackrill 1987. Reprinted by permission of Princeton University Press via Copyright Clearance Center.

David Brooks. "What Suffering Does" from *The New York Times*, April 7, 2014. Copyright © 2014 The New York Times. All rights reserved. Used by permission and protected by the Copyright Laws of the United States. The printing, copying, redistribution, or retransmission of this Content without express written permission is prohibited.

Buddha. Excerpt from *The Dhammapada: The Buddha's Path of Wisdom*, translated from the Pali by Acharya Buddharakkhita with an Introduction by Bhikkhu Bodhi (Kandy: Buddhist Publication Society, 1985). Copyright © 1985 Buddhist Publication Society.

Mihaly Csikszentmihalyi. "If We Are So Rich, Why Aren't We Happy?" Copyright © 1999 by the American Psychological Association. Reproduced with permission. *American Psychologist*, 54(10), 821–27, October, 1999.

Dalai Lama and Howard C. Cutler. Excerpt from *The Art of Happiness: A Handbook for the Living* by Dalai Lama and Howard C. Cutler, copyright © 1998 by His Holiness the Dalai Lama and Howard C. Cutler, M.D. Used by permission of Riverhead, an imprint of Penguin Publishing Group, a division of Penguin Random House LLC.

Ed Diener and Robert Biswas-Diener. Excerpt ("Can Money Buy Happiness?") from *Happiness: Unlocking the Mysteries of Psychological Wealth*, by Ed Diener and Robert Biswas-Diener. Copyright © 2008 by Ed Diener and Robert Biswas-Diener. Reproduced with permission of Blackwell Publishing via Copyright Clearance Center.

Ed Diener and Martin E. P. Seligman. "Very Happy People" from *Psychological Science*, Volume 13, No. 1, January, 2002. Copyright © 2002 American Psychological Society. Reprinted by permission of Blackwell Publishing via Copyright Clearance Center.

Epictetus. Excerpt from *The Handbook of Epictetus*, translated by Nicholas P. White. Copyright © 1983 by Nicholas P. White. Reprinted by permission of Hackett Publishing Company, Inc. All rights reserved.

Giles Fraser. "Taking Pills for Unhappiness Reinforces the Idea That Being Sad Is Not Human." *The Guardian*, August 9, 2013. Copyright Guardian News & Media Ltd 2013. Reprinted by permission.

"Freedom through Renunciation." Excerpt from *Bhagavad Gita: A New Translation* by Stephen Mitchell, copyright © 2000 by Stephen Mitchell. Used by permission of Harmony Books, an imprint of the Crown Publishing Group, a division of Penguin Random House LLC. All rights reserved.

Daniel Gilbert. "Figure 16," "Figure 17," and "Figure 18" by Mapping Specialists, Ltd.; and excerpts from *Stumbling on Happiness* by Daniel Gilbert, copyright © 2006 by Daniel Gilbert. Used by permission of Alfred A. Knopf, an imprint of the Knopf Doubleday Publishing Group, a division of Penguin Random House LLC. All rights reserved.

Daniel M. Haybron. "Happiness and Its Discontents" from *The New York Times*, April 13, 2014. Copyright © 2014 The New York Times. All rights reserved. Used by permission and protected by the Copyright Laws of the United States. The printing, copying, redistribution, or retransmission of this Content without express written permission is prohibited.

Jennifer Michael Hecht. "Remembering Death" from *The Happiness Myth: The Historical Antidote to What Isn't Working Today* by Jennifer Michael Hecht. Copyright © 2007 by Jennifer Michael Hecht. Reprinted by permission of HarperCollins Publishers.

Graham Hill. "Living with Less. A Lot Less" from *The New York Times*, March 9, 2013. Copyright © 2013 The New York Times. All rights reserved. Used by permission and protected by the Copyright Laws of the United States. The printing, copying, redistribution, or retransmission of this Content without express written permission is prohibited.

Mohsen Joshanloo and Dan Weijers. Excerpt from "Aversion to Happiness across Cultures: A Review of Where and Why People Are Averse to Happiness" from *Journal of Happiness Studies* (2014) 15: 717–35; published online December 15, 2013. Copyright © Springer Science+Business Media Dordrecht 2013. *Journal of Happiness Studies* by International Society for Quality of Life Studies. Reproduced with permission of Kluwer Academic Publishers Group in the formal Book via Copyright Clearance Center.

Stefan Klein. *The Science of Happiness: How Our Brains Make Us Happy—and What We Can Do to Get Happier,* translated by Stephen Lehmann. Copyright © 2002 by Stefan Klein, Translation copyright © 2006 by Avalon Publishing Group, Inc. Reprinted by permission of Marlowe, a member of the Perseus Books Group.

Laozi. Excerpts (6, 8, 9, 13, 20, 33, 44, 67) from *Tao Te Ching by Lao Tzu, a New English Version, With Foreword and Notes by Stephen Mitchell.* Translation copyright © 1988 by Stephen Mitchell. Reprinted by permission of HarperCollins Publishers.

C. S. Lewis. Extract from *God in the Dock* by C. S. Lewis, copyright © C. S. Lewis Pte. Ltd. 1970. Extract reprinted by permission.

Sonja Lyubomirsky. Excerpt from *The How of Happiness: A Scientific Approach to Getting the Life You Want* by Sonja Lyubomirsky, copyright © 2007 by Sonja Lyubomirsky. Used by permission of Penguin Press, an imprint of Penguin Publishing Group, a division of Penguin Random House LLC.

Jordan McKenzie and Stu Horsfield. "The Sociology of Happiness and Contentment: An Interview with Dr. Jordan McKenzie" by Stu Horsfield (*Nucleus*, March 12, 2014). Reprinted by permission of *Nucleus* and Jordan McKenzie.

Daniel Mochon, Michael I. Norton, and Dan Ariely. "Getting Off the Hedonic Treadmill, One Step at a Time: The Impact of Regular Religious Practice and Exercise on Well-Being" reprinted from *Journal of Economic Psychology*, 29, pages 632–42, Copyright 2007 Elsevier B.V. Reprinted by permission of Elsevier.

Martha C. Nussbaum. Excerpt from "Who Is the Happy Warrior? Philosophy Poses Questions to Psychology" from *The Journal of Legal Studies* 37:2 (2008). Copyright © 2008. Reprinted by permission of the author and the University of Chicago Press.

Noelle Oxenhandler. "Ah, But the Breezes . . ." from *Tricycle*. Reprinted by permission of the author.

Matthieu Ricard. Excerpt from *Happiness: A Guide to Developing Life's Most Important Skill* by Matthieu Ricard, translated by Jesse Browner. Copyright © 2003 by Nil Editions. Translation copyright © Jesse Browner. Used by permission of Little, Brown and Company.

Gretchen Rubin. Excerpts from Chapter 7, *The Happiness Project* by Gretchen Rubin, copyright © 2009 by Gretchen Rubin. Reprinted by permission of HarperCollins Publishers.

Rumi. Excerpt from *Look! This Is Love: Poems of Rumi* by Annemarie Schimmel, © 1991 by Annemarie Schimmel. Reprinted by arrangement with The Permissions Company, Inc. on behalf of Shambhala Publications Inc., Boston, Massachusetts. www.shambhala.com.

Eric G. Wilson. Excerpt from "Terrible Beauty" from *Against Happiness: In Praise of Melancholy* by Eric G. Wilson. Copyright © 2008 by Eric G. Wilson. Reprinted by permission of Farrar, Straus and Giroux, LLC.

Index of Authors and Titles